P9-BJW-551

KAPLAN

Other Kaplan Books on Graduate School Admissions

Get into Graduate School: A Strategic Approach
GRE Biology
GRE Psychology
GRE Verbal Workbook
GRE/GMAT Math Workbook

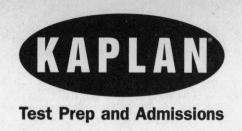

Test Prep and Admissions

GRE® Exam
2005

By the Staff of Kaplan Test Prep and Admissions

Simon & Schuster

NEW YORK · LONDON · SYDNEY · TORONTO

GRE® is a registered trademark of the Educational Testing Service, which is not affiliated with this product.

Kaplan Publishing
Published by Simon & Schuster
1230 Avenue of the Americas
New York, NY 10020

Kaplan® is a registered trademark of Kaplan, Inc.
GRE® is a registered trademark of the Educational Testing Service, which is not affiliated with this book.

Chapter 6, Test Mentality, is adapted from The Kaplan Advantage™ Stress Management System by Dr. Ed Newman and Bob Verini, © 1996 Kaplan Educational Centers.

"American Radical Historians on Their Heritage," by Aileen S. Kraditor, *Past and Present*, No. 56, August 1972. Reprinted by permission of *Past and Present*.

"Art and Experience in Classical Greece," by J. J. Pollitt, © 1972, Cambridge University Press. Reproduced with the permission of Cambridge University Press.

"A Unified Theory of Elementary Particles and Forces," by Howard Georgi, © *Scientific American*, April 1991. Reprinted with permission from *Technology Review*, V. 244.4.

Contributing Editors: Chip Hurlburt and Justin Serrano
Project Editor: Eileen Mager
Cover Design: Cheung Tai
Production Manager: Michael Shevlin
Managing Editor: Déa Alessandro
Executive Editor: Jennifer Farthing

Special thanks to: Ingrid Multhopp, Martha Torres, and Hugh Haggerty

Manufactured in the United States of America
Published simultaneously in Canada

July 2004

10 9 8 7 6 5 4 3 2 1

ISBN: 0-7432-5169-5

Contents

Dear Student:

For more than 65 years, Kaplan has been helping students meet their academic and admissions goals. More than three million students have passed through our doors, and as their evaluations of our courses have repeatedly shown, one thing stands out that sets Kaplan apart from the rest: our teachers.

We have long known that our outstanding teaching staff is Kaplan's most important asset. Throughout the years we have committed ourselves to finding expert, enthusiastic, and engaging teachers for every Kaplan course. That's why we interview only those candidates who scored high on the test they are to teach and from this pool select only the most promising candidates: individuals who are enthusiastic about helping students reach their goals. All prospective teachers complete an intensive Kaplan training, and from ongoing observations, evaluations, and reviews of student feedback, they get even better as they teach.

The knowledge and experience that our teachers have acquired from working with students like you—about standardized tests, study habits, test panic, and more—is something we'd like to share outside of the classroom. We're pleased to incorporate the wisdom, tips, and inspiration of Kaplan's teachers in this test-prep guide so that you may benefit from the best we have to offer. I hope you find their expertise useful in your quest for academic success. If you decide you'd also like to work with our first-rate instructors in person, give us a call at (800) KAP-TEST.

Sincerely,

Jonathan Grayer
CEO, Kaplan, Inc.

kaptest.com/booksonlline

Want more help preparing for the GRE? Log on to **kaptest.com/booksonline** to access a wide selection of additional practice questions. Prepare for all parts of the GRE online, or focus on those sections where you feel weakest.

Access to this selection of Kaplan's online GRE practice questions is free of charge to purchasers of this book. When you log on, you'll be asked to input the ISBN number of the book you purchased (see the bar code on the back cover). And you'll be asked for a specific password derived from a passage in this book, so have your book handy when you log on.

kaptest.com/publishing

The material in this book is up-to-date at the time of publication. However, the Educational Testing Service (ETS) may have instituted changes in the test or test registration process after this book was published. Be sure to carefully read the materials you receive when you register for the test.

If there are any important late-breaking developments—or any changes or corrections to the Kaplan test preparation materials in this book—we will post that information online at **kaptest.com/publishing**. Check to see if there is any information posted there for readers of this book.

kaplansurveys.com/books

What did you think of this book? We'd love to hear your comments and suggestions. We invite you to fill out our online survey form at **kaplansurveys.com/books**. Your feedback is extremely helpful as we continue to develop high-quality resources to meet your needs.

About the Authors

Eric Goodman has been teaching the Kaplan GRE, GMAT, and LSAT courses for over a decade and also works for Kaplan as a product consultant. When not teaching or writing for Kaplan, Eric works as a composer and musician in New York City.

Ray Ojserkis is Manager of GRE and GMAT Curriculum for Kaplan. During his tenure at Kaplan, he has researched the GRE extensively, and trained many students seeking entrance to graduate programs in classes and one-to-one sessions. He has a B.S. in Economics from Lehigh University, and a Masters and a Doctorate in International History from the London School of Economics and Political Science. He lives in New York City.

Bob Verini is currently Director of Academic Excellence for the western United States and a national training associate for Kaplan Educational Centers. Since joining Kaplan in 1980, Bob has taught thousands of students how to ace the GRE. He also trains new Kaplan instructors nationally, works in course development, and serves as academic counselor in Kaplan's one-on-one Admissions Consulting program. He holds a B.A. from SUNY/Albany and an M.F.A. from Indiana University. In his spare time, Bob is a writer, actor, and director, with several films and extensive stage experience to his credit. He is also one of the biggest money winners in the history of the game show *Jeopardy*™ and was a winner of the 1987 Tournament of Champions.

Readers' Comments

Here's what some of our readers have to say about previous editions of Kaplan's *GRE Exam*:

"I loved this book. It raised two of my scores up approximately 200 points after studying from it. Thanks, Kaplan. I knew just what to expect from the test on test day."
—*Marla Ross, Dieppe, New Brunswick, Canada*

"This study guide has been extremely useful in studying for the GRE. I have tried Barron's® study guide for the GRE, but it is not nearly as helpful as Kaplan's study guide."
—*Thana Hines, Houston, Texas*

"The Verbal section has always been hard for me. After reading this, I know I can do it. This book surpasses The Princeton Review® 1,000 times! Thanks!"
—*Kara Vick, Milledgeville, Georgia*

"This book helped to raise my score over 200 points from my first practice test to the actual test day. Thank you!"
—*Carolyn Stead, Schenectady, New York*

"I got an even better score than I had hoped for, and this book helped achieve this. I scored 200 points higher than my goal!"
—*Julia Durbin, Richmond, Kentucky*

"Kaplan's material is very detailed and was very well worth the time. I used two Kaplan resources—the *GRE Exam* and the *GRE Verbal Workbook*. The exam preparation paid off… I have been admitted to the one and only program where my GRE scores were sent: Michigan State University's Ph.D. program in Agricultural Economics."
—*Taylor Moore, Glen Ellyn, Illinois*

"All explanations were incredibly easy to understand, and the relaxed language of the book actually made it an enjoyable read. Thank you!"
—*Kim D'Ardenne, Roswell, Georgia*

"After my 2-week preparation, I realized that without Kaplan, I would have BOMBED the GRE! I also realized how well-prepared I was—thanks to you guys! Keep up the good work!"
—*James Ryan, Milton, Massachusetts*

"This book was very interesting to read—it wasn't your traditional text-book. And I felt completely prepared for the test."
—*Brandi Procell, Hattiesburg, Mississippi*

"I'm very thankful to this book, which helped me to prepare in such a short time."
—*Munoj Shah, India*

"This was a fantastic tool—my score improved from the 1200–1300 range to over 1900! Plus the cost was $20 compared to $100–$200 for a class—a total blessing!"
—*Etta Dahlquist, Como, Colorado*

"I felt completely prepared for the test. My computer scores were much higher than I had anticipated. I felt confident—when I am usually a nervous test taker! Thank you!"
—*Andrea L. Walton, Somers Point, New Jersey*

"I thought the book was concise—I was able to study for the GRE and read this whole book in a month—and I got a good score on the real test."
—*Natasha Silich, Champaign, Illinois*

"This book is effective and certainly more helpful than Princeton [Review]."
—*Dante Bellizzi, Coos Bay, Oregon*

"I have already recommended it to several of my friends!"
—*Katheryn Everts, Comstock Park, Michigan*

"I found this book to be the best study guide I've ever purchased. I felt very confident on exam day and scored VERY well."
—*Bhavi Kapadia, Garland, Texas*

"The math portion is wonderful because it explains how to do every problem at the end. It focuses on everything you need to pass the exam successfully."
—*Marlene L. Ramirez, Miami, Florida*

How to Use This Book

The Classic Plan

Ideally, you should take a couple of months to work through this book. Below you'll find some suggestions as to how you can most effectively use Kaplan's *GRE Exam* in your GRE preparation.

1. Read the Introduction and the "Test Mechanics" and "Test Mentality" chapters to set the stage for your training and testing success. In these chapters, we'll introduce you to the mysteries of the GRE and show you how to take control of the test-taking experience.

2. Read chapters 2, 3, and 4 completely, learning from the example problems and trying the practice sets at the end of each chapter. Spend sufficient time reviewing the questions you get wrong by reading carefully through the explanations to the practice set questions.

3. Study the appendixes at the back of the book for help with vocabulary and important math concepts. In Appendix B, the math concepts are grouped by level of difficulty; review any Level 1 or Level 2 math concepts you don't know before moving on to the more difficult Level 3 concepts.

4. Take the Practice Test under strictly timed conditions.

5. Score your Practice Test. Try not to confine yourself to the explanations of the questions you've answered incorrectly. Instead, read all of the explanations—to reinforce good habits and to sharpen your skills so that you can get the right answer even faster and more reliably next time.

6. Find out where you need help and then review the appropriate chapters and/or appendixes.

7. For additional GRE-like practice questions (free of charge only to purchasers of this book), log on to **www.kaptest.com/booksonline**. When you log on, you'll be asked to input the ISBN number of the book you purchased (see the bar code on the back cover). And you'll be asked for a specific password derived from a passage in this book, so you'll need to have this book handy when you go online.

8. Reread the "Test Mentality" and "Test Mechanics" chapters to make sure you're in top shape for the test. Then give yourself a day of rest right before the real exam.

The Emergency Plan

Maybe you have only two or three weeks—or even less time than that. Don't panic! Kaplan's *GRE Exam* has been designed to work for students in your situation, too. If you go through a chapter or two every day, you can finish this book in less than a week. If you have limited time to prepare for the GRE (fewer than six weeks), we suggest you do the following:

1. Take a slow, deep breath. Read the Introduction and the "Test Mechanics" and "Test Mentality" chapters to set the stage for your training and testing success.

2. Skim through chapters 2, 3, and 4, and complete as many of the practice sets as you can.

3. Take the Practice Test.

4. Review your results, paying special attention to the questions you missed.

5. Based on your performance on the Practice Test and the requirements of the graduate programs to which you are applying, review only those content areas you want the most help with.

6. Give yourself a night of rest right before the exam.

To help keep you on track, we've placed a Highlights box containing the most important test concepts at the beginning of each Test Content chapter. You'll also find important points regarding the GRE and invaluable Kaplan teacher advice in easy-to-read sidebars throughout the book.

A Special Note for International Students

About a quarter million international students pursue advanced academic degrees at the master's or Ph.D. level at U.S. universities each year. This trend of pursuing higher education in the United States, particularly at the graduate level, is expected to continue. Business, management, engineering, and the physical and life sciences are popular areas of study for students coming to the United States from other countries. Along with these academic options, international students are also taking advantage of opportunities for research grants, teaching assistantships, and practical training or work experience in U.S. graduate departments.

If you are not from the United States, but are considering attending a graduate program at a university in the United States, here is what you'll need to get started.

- If English is not your first language, start there. You will probably need to take the Test of English as a Foreign Language (TOEFL) or show some other evidence that you're proficient in English prior to gaining admission to a graduate program. Graduate programs will vary on what is an acceptable TOEFL score. For degrees in business, journalism, management, or the humanities, a minimum TOEFL score of 600 (250 on the computer-based TOEFL) or better is expected. For the hard sciences and computer technology, a TOEFL score of 550 (213 on the computer-based TOEFL) is a common minimum requirement.

- You may also need to take the GRE® (Graduate Record Exam).

- Since admission to many graduate programs is quite competitive, you may want to select three or four programs you would like to attend and complete applications for each program.

- Selecting the correct graduate school is very different from selecting a suitable undergraduate institution. You should research the qualifications and interests of faculty members teaching and doing research in your chosen field. Look for professors who share your specialty.

- You need to begin the application process at least a year in advance. Be aware that many programs offer only August or September start dates. Find out application deadlines and plan accordingly.

- Finally, you will need to obtain an 1-20 Certificate of Eligibility in order to obtain an F-1 Student Visa to study in the United States.

Kaplan English Programs*

If you need more help with the complex process of graduate school admissions, or assistance preparing for the TOEFL or GRE, you may be interested in Kaplan's programs for international students.

Kaplan's English Programs were designed to help students and professionals from outside the United States meet their educational and career goals. At locations throughout the United States, international students take advantage of Kaplan's programs to help them improve their academic and conversational English skills, raise their scores on the TOEFL, GRE, and other standardized exams, and gain admission to the schools of their choice. Our staff and instructors give international students the individualized instruction they need to succeed. Here is a brief description of some of Kaplan's programs for international students:

General Intensive English

Kaplan's General Intensive English classes are designed to help you improve your skills in all areas of English and to increase your fluency in spoken and written English. Classes are available for beginning to advanced students, and the average class size is 12 students.

General English Structured-Study

For students needing a flexible schedule, this course helps improve general fluency skills. Kaplan's General English Self-Study course employs the communicative approach and focuses on vocabulary building, reading and writing. You will receive books, audio and video materials as well as three hours of instructor contact per week.

TOEFL and Academic English

This course provides you with the skills you need to improve your TOEFL score and succeed in an American university or graduate program. It includes advanced reading, writing, listening, grammar and conversational English. You will also receive training for the TOEFL using Kaplan's exclusive computer-based practice materials.

TOEFL Test Preparation Course

Kaplan's TOEFL course can help you learn test taking skills and strategies to raise your TOEFL score. This course is for intermediate to advanced English learners with a TOEFL score of at least 517 (187 computer).

GRE for International Students

The Graduate Record Exam (GRE) is required for admission to many graduate programs in the United States. Nearly one-half million people take the GRE each year. A high score can help you stand out from other test takers. This course, designed especially for non-native English speakers, includes the skills you need to succeed on each section of the GRE, as well as access to Kaplan's exclusive computer-based practice materials and extra verbal practice.

Other Kaplan Programs

Since 1938, more than 3 million students have come to Kaplan to advance their studies, prepare for entry to American universities, and further their careers. In addition to the above programs, Kaplan offers courses to prepare for the SAT, GMAT, LSAT, MCAT, DAT, USMLE, NCLEX, and other standardized exams at locations throughout the United States.

Applying to Kaplan English Programs

To get more information, or to apply for admission to any of Kaplan's programs for international students and professionals, contact us at:

Kaplan English Programs
700 South Flower, Suite 2900
Los Angeles, CA 90017, USA
Phone (if calling from within the United States): 800-818-9128
Phone (if calling from outside the United States): 213-452-5800
Fax: 213-892-1364
Website: www.kaplanenglish.com
Email: world@kaplan.com

* Kaplan is authorized under federal law to enroll nonimmigrant alien students.
Kaplan is accredited by ACCET (Accrediting Council for Continuing Education and Training).

Getting a Higher Score on the GRE

CHAPTER ONE

An Introduction to the GRE

HIGHLIGHTS

- Understand how the GRE is constructed
- Get acquainted with the Kaplan Three-Level Master Plan

This book will explain more than just a few basic strategies. It will cover practically everything that's ever on the GRE.

No kidding.

We can do this because we don't explain questions in isolation or focus on particular problems. Instead, we explain the underlying principles behind *all* of the questions on the GRE. We give you the big picture.

Understanding the GRE CAT

One of the keys to getting the big picture is knowing how the test is constructed. Why should you care how the GRE is constructed? Because if you understand the difficulties that the people at ETS have when they make this test, you'll understand what it is you have to do to overcome it. As someone famous once said, "Know thine enemy." And you need to know firsthand the way this test is put together if you want to take it apart.

Kaplan Tip

You can't cram for the GRE, but you can prepare for it by learning to think the GRE way.

Note

About half a million people take the GRE each year. By reading the following chapters, you'll learn the underlying principles of GRE questions and acquire test strategies that will help increase your score.

 3

Before you begin, though, remember that the test makers sometimes change the content, administration, and scheduling of the GRE too quickly for a published guide to keep up with. For the latest, up-to-the-minute news about the GRE, visit Kaplan's website at *kaptest.com*, or use AOL keyword: *Kaplan*.

The Secret Code

There is a sort of unwritten formula at the heart of the GRE. First, there's psychometrics, a peculiar kind of science used to write standardized tests. Also, ETS bases its questions on a certain body of knowledge, which doesn't change. ETS tests the same concepts in every GRE. The useful thinking skills and shortcuts that succeed on one exam—the exam that you're signing up to take, for instance—have already succeeded and will continue to succeed, time and time again.

Play the Game

There are a great many people who think of these exams as cruel exercises in futility, as the oppressive instruments of a faceless societal machine. People who think this way usually don't do very well on these tests.

The key discovery that people who ace standardized tests have made, though, is that fighting the machine doesn't hurt it. If that's what you choose to do, you will just waste your energy. So, instead, they choose to think of the test as a game. Not an instrument of punishment, but an opportunity for reward. And like any game, if you play it enough times, you get really good at it.

Acquire the Skills

You may think that the GRE isn't fair or decent, but that attitude won't help you get into graduate school.

None of the GRE experts who work at Kaplan were *born* acing the GRE. No one is. That's because these tests do not measure innate skills; they measure *acquired* skills. People who are good at standardized tests are, quite simply, people who've already acquired the necessary skills. Maybe they acquired them in math class, or by reading a lot, or by studying logic in college, or perhaps the easiest way—in one of Kaplan's GRE classes. But they have, perhaps without realizing it, acquired the skills that bring success on tests like the GRE. And if *you* haven't, you have nothing whatsoever to feel bad about. You simply must acquire them now.

Same Problems—but Different

We know it sounds incredible, but it's true: The test makers use the same problems on every GRE. Only the words and the numbers change. They test the same principles over and over.

Kaplan Tip

Think of the GRE as a game—one that you can improve at the more times you play.

Kaplan Tip

Standardized tests measure acquired skills. The people who succeed on them are those who have acquired the skills that the test measures.

Here's an example: This is a type of math problem known as a Quantitative Comparison. (Look familiar? These are also on the SAT.) Your job is to pick (A) if the term in Column A is bigger, (B) if the term in Column B is bigger, (C) if they're equal, or (D) if there is not enough information given to solve the problem.

Column A | Column B

$$2x^2 = 32$$

x | 4

Most people answer (C), that they're equal. They divide both sides of the equation by 2 and then take the square root of both sides.

Wrong. The answer isn't (C), because x doesn't have to be 4. It could be 4 *or* –4. Both work. If you just solve for 4 you'll get this problem—and every one like it—wrong. ETS figures that if you get burned here, you'll get burned again next time. Only next time it won't be $2x^2 = 32$; it will be $y^2 = 36$ or $s^4 = 81$.

The concepts that are tested on any particular GRE—Pythagorean triangles, simple logic, word relationships, and so forth—are the underlying concepts at the heart of *every* GRE.

ETS makes changes only after testing them exhaustively. This process is called *norming,* which means taking a normal test and a changed test and administering them to a random group of students. As long as the group is large enough for the purposes of statistical validity and the students get consistent scores from one test to the next, then the revised test is just as valid and consistent as any other GRE.

That may sound technical, but norming is actually quite an easy process. We do it at Kaplan all the time—for the tests that we write for our students. The test at the back of this book, for instance, is a normed exam. While the interactive, computer-based test experience of the GRE is impossible to reproduce on paper, the paper-based test in our book is a normed exam that will produce an equivalent score.

How the GRE is Organized

The Graduate Record Examination (GRE) is administered on computer and is between two and three-quarters and three and a quarter hours long. The exam consists of three scored sections, with different amounts of time allotted for you to complete each section.

VERBAL	
Time	30 minutes
Length	30 multiple-choice questions
Format	Analogies, sentence completion, antonyms, and reading comprehension
Content	Tests vocabulary, verbal reasoning skills, and the ability to read with understanding and insight

QUANTITATIVE	
Time	45 minutes
Length	28 multiple-choice questions
Format	Problem solving, quantitative comparison, and graph problems
Content	Tests basic mathematical skills, ability to understand mathematical concepts, and quantitative reasoning skills

ANALYTICAL WRITING	
Time	75 minutes
Length	2 essay questions
Format	Perspective on an Issue essay and Analyze an Argument essay
Content	Tests ability to understand and analyze arguments and to understand and draw logical conclusions

Kaplan Tip

Don't try to figure out which section of your test is experimental. If you guess wrong, you could torpedo your score. Just do your best on each section.

You may also see two more sections: an Experimental section and a Research section. The Experimental section is unscored. That means that if you could identify the Experimental section, you could doodle for half an hour, guess in a random pattern, or daydream and still get exactly the same score on the GRE. However, the Experimental section is disguised to look like a real section—there is no way to identify it. All you will really know on the day of the test is that one of the subject areas will have two sections instead of one. Naturally, many people try to figure out which section is Experimental. But because ETS really wants you to try hard on it, they do their best to keep you guessing. If you guess wrong, you could blow the whole test, so we urge you to treat all sections as scored unless you are told otherwise.

The Research section is also unscored, and is not always included in the GRE. If you see a Research section on Test Day, ETS will be kind enough to tell you when it appears. So there is no reason whatsoever for you to complete it, unless you feel like doing ETS a favor, or unless they offer you some reward (which they have been known to do).

What's a CAT?

A CAT, or *computer-adaptive test*, is a computer-based test that you take at a special test center, by yourself, at a time you schedule. A CAT "adapts" to your performance. Each test taker is given a different mix of questions depending on how well he or she is doing on the test. This means the questions get harder or easier depending on whether you answer them correctly. Your score is not directly determined by how many questions you get right, but by how hard the questions you get right are.

When you start a section, the computer:
- assumes you have an average score.
- gives you a medium-difficulty question. About half the people who take the test would get this question right, and half would get it wrong.

What happens next depends on whether you answer the question correctly.

If you answer the question correctly:
- your score goes up.
- you are given a slightly harder question.

If you answer the question incorrectly:
- your score goes down.
- you are given a slightly easier question.

This continues for the rest of the test. Every time you get the question right, the computer raises your score, then gives you a slightly harder question. Every time you get a question wrong, the computer lowers your score, then gives you a slightly easier question. In this way, the computer is able to "hone in" on your score.

Why are we explaining all of this technical stuff, you ask? Because both the Verbal and Quantitative sections of the GRE are CATs. Don't panic:

Note

The Verbal and Quantitative sections of the GRE are computer-adaptive. The questions in those sections will get harder or easier depending on whether you answered the previous question correctly.

The process really isn't as confusing as it sounds! To learn more about the CAT, including CAT-specific test-taking strategies that will help maximize your score, be sure to read chapter 5 of this book, "Test Mechanics."

Scoring

The Analytical Writing section is scored on a scale of 0–6 in half-point increments. (See chapter 4 for more information on this scoring process.) The Verbal and Quantitative sections each yield a scaled score within a range of 200 to 800. These scaled scores are like the scores that you received if you took the SAT. You cannot score higher than 800 on any one section, no matter how hard you try. Similarly, it's impossible (again, no matter how hard you try) to have a score lower than 200 on either section.

But you don't receive *only* scaled scores. You will also receive a percentile rank, which will place your performance relative to those of a large sample population of other GRE takers. Percentile scores tell graduate schools just what your scaled scores are worth. For instance, even if everyone got very high scaled scores, universities would still be able to differentiate candidates by their percentile score.

Percentile ranks match with scaled scores differently, depending on the measure. Let's imagine that our founder, Stanley H. Kaplan, were to take the GRE this year. He would (no doubt) get a perfect 800 on each measure type, but that would translate into different percentile ranks. In Verbal, he'd be scoring above 99 percent of the population, so that would be his percentile rank. But in the Quantitative section, many other people will score very high as well. Difficult as this section may seem, so many people score so well on it that high scaled scores are no big deal. Mr. Kaplan's percentile rank for Quantitative, even if he doesn't miss a single question, would be in only the 96th percentile. So many other people are scoring that high in Quantitative that no one can score above the 96th percentile!

What this means is that it's pretty easy to get good scaled scores on the GRE and much harder to get good percentile ranks. A Quantitative score of 600, for example, might be okay if you're applying to a humanities program; but if you're applying to science or engineering programs, it would be a handicap at most schools. Even a score of 700 in Quantitative is relatively low for many very selective programs in the sciences or engineering—after all, it's only the 79th or 80th percentile.

The relative frequency of high scaled scores means that universities pay great attention to percentile rank. What you need to realize is that scores that seemed good to you when you took the SAT might not be all that good on the GRE. It's important that you do some real research into the programs you're thinking about. Many schools have cut-off scores below which they don't even consider applicants. But be careful! If a school tells you they look for applicants scoring 600 average per section, that doesn't mean they think those are good scores. That 600 may be the baseline. You owe it to yourself to find out what kinds of scores *impress* the schools you're interested in and work hard until you get those scores. You can definitely get there if you want to and if you work hard enough. We see it every day.

A final note about percentile rank: The sample population that you are compared against in order to determine your percentile is not everyone else who takes the test the same day as you do. ETS doesn't want to penalize an unlucky candidate who takes the GRE on a date when everyone else happens to be a rocket scientist. So they compare your performance with those of a random three-year population of recent GRE test takers. Your score will not in any way be affected by the other people who take the exam on the same day as you. We often tell our students, "Your only competition in this classroom is yourself."

Canceling Your Scores

At the end of the exam, you'll be asked if you want to see and keep your score or not. If you answer "yes," you are given your score right then and there on the computer screen and it is entered into your ETS record. If you answer "no," you are not given your score and no score is entered. However, the fact that you took the test on that date and canceled the scores will still be listed in your ETS record.

Requested score reports are sent to schools within 10–15 days after the exam. All GRE testing administrations will be listed (and usable) in your ETS record for 5 years.

Test Registration

The GRE is offered the first three weeks of every month. To register for and schedule your GRE, use one of the options below. (If you live outside the United States, Canada, American Samoa, Guam, the U.S. Virgin Islands, or Puerto Rico, visit *www.gre.org* for instructions on how to register.)

You should first obtain a copy of the *GRE Registration Bulletin*. This booklet contains information on scheduling, pricing, repeat testing, cancellation policies, and more. You can receive the booklet by calling the Educational Testing Service at (609) 771-7670, or by downloading it from *www.gre.org*.

Definition

The **percentile figure** tells you how many other test takers scored at or below your level. In other words, a percentile figure of 80 means than 80 percent did as well or worse than you did and that only 20 percent did better.

Register by Phone
Call 1-800-GRE-CALL or 1-800-529-3590 (TTY). A confirmation number, reporting time, and test center location will be given to you when you call. Though you can register by phone up to two days before the exam, registering earlier is strongly recommended since spaces often fill quickly. Payments can be made with a Visa, MasterCard, or American Express card.

Register by Mail
Complete the Authorization Voucher Request Form found in the *GRE Registration Bulletin*. Mail the fee and voucher request form in the CBT envelope to the address printed on the voucher.

ETS advises that you allow two to four weeks for processing before you receive your voucher in the mail. When you receive your voucher, call to schedule an appointment. Vouchers are valid for one year from the date of issue.

The Kaplan Three-Level Master Plan

To give your best performance on the GRE, you'll need to have the right kind of approach for the entire test as a whole. We've developed a plan to help you, which we call (cleverly enough) "The Kaplan Three-Level Master Plan for the GRE." You should use this plan as your guide to preparing for and taking the GRE. The three levels of the plan are: test content, test mechanics, and test mentality.

Level 1: Test Content
In the first part of the book, we'll teach you how to deal with individual short verbal questions, reading passages, math problems, and analytical essays. For success on the GRE, you'll need to understand how to work through each of these question types. What's the difference between antonym and analogy questions? What are the best ways of handling each? What's a sentence completion and how do I approach it? How should I read a reading comprehension passage and what should I focus on? What's the best way to approach quantitative comparisons? Our instruction in Level 1 will provide you with all of the information, strategies, and techniques you'll need to answer these questions and more.

Kaplan Rules

The three levels of the Kaplan Master Plan are:

1. Test content
2. Test mechanics
3. Test mentality

Level 2: Test Mechanics

Next, we'll move up the ladder from individual question types to a discussion of how to handle the GRE's unique computer-adaptive testing format. We'll reveal the test mechanics that will help you to use the strategies you learned in Level 1 to maximum effect.

Level 3: Test Mentality

On this final level, we'll help you pull everything you've learned together. By combining the question strategies and test mechanics, you'll be in control of the entire test experience. With a good test mentality, you can have everything at your fingertips—from building good bridges to gridding techniques, from writing good outlines to pacing methods. We'll also outline all of the subtle attitudinal factors that will help you perform your absolute best on the day of the test.

Understanding the three levels, and how they interrelate, is the first step in taking control of the GRE. We'll start, in the next chapter, with the first level: test content.

> ### Teacher Tip
>
> "Learn the process of question creation. Always ask, 'why did the test maker do it this way?' when going over explanations. And don't forget that the test is only a part (albeit an important part) of the overall application experience."
> —Chris Skinner
> Santa Barbara, California

CHAPTER TWO

Test Content: Verbal

- Study the Kaplan Word Families and the 52 Most Common GRE Words

- Learn the Basic Principles and the Kaplan Method for answering Sentence Completions, Analogies, Antonyms, and Reading Comp questions

- Focus on the different types of Reading Comp questions and targeted strategies for answering each type

- Complete the Verbal Practice Set

In this chapter and the two chapters that follow, we'll give you the nuts and bolts of GRE preparation—the strategies and techniques for each of the individual question types on the test. For each of the multiple-choice sections—Verbal and Quantitative—we'll present you with the following:

Kaplan Tip

The Verbal section tests your vocabulary and your ability to read passages quickly and efficiently.

- **Directions and General Information**
  The specific directions for each section will introduce you to the question types. We'll also give you some ground rules for each question type.

- **Basic Principles**
  These are the general rules-of-thumb that you need to follow to succeed on this section.

- **Common Question Types**
  Certain types of questions appear repeatedly on each section. We'll show you what these question types are and how best to deal with each one.

• **The Kaplan Method**

This is a step-by-step way of organizing your work on every question in the section. The Kaplan Method will allow you to orchestrate all of the individual strategies and techniques into a flexible, powerful modus operandi.

At a Glance

There are four types of verbal questions:

• Sentence completions
• Analogies
• Antonyms
• Reading comprehension

Now let's begin with an important part of the GRE, the Verbal Section. You'll have 30 minutes to complete 30 questions, which are broken down into four types: sentence completion, analogies, reading comprehension, and antonyms. The chart below shows roughly how many questions correspond to each question type and how much time you should spend on each question type.

	SENTENCE COMPLETION	ANALOGIES	READING COMPREHENSION	ANTONYMS
Number of Questions	about 6	about 7	about 8	about 9
Time per Question	20–45 seconds	30–45 seconds	> 1 minute	30 seconds

The computer determines the sequence and difficulty of the questions, so you will not be able to tell what sort of question you will get next, or how hard it will be.

There are two basic things that the Verbal section tests: your vocabulary and your ability to read a particular kind of passage quickly and efficiently. You may have wondered how the material we covered earlier about test construction is going to help you in the GRE Verbal sections. Well, just like the math questions, which are the same from test to test (just with different numbers), the verbal questions are the same (just with different words).

Vocabulary—the Most Basic Principle for Verbal Success

Have you ever heard the expression, "That's an SAT word"? It's a commonly used phrase among high school students, and it refers to any member of a very particular class of prefixed and suffixed words derived from Latin or Greek. For instance, *profligate* is a great SAT word. It's also a great GRE word. Many of the same kinds of words that would commonly show up on the SAT are likely candidates for the GRE as well, though GRE words tend to be harder.

The GRE tests the same kinds of words over and over again. (Remember, for ETS, consistency is key.) We'll call these words "GRE words," and we're going to make a point of including them in the rest of this chapter. That way, you can get a feel for what they look and sound like, and you can see them used in context. The GRE words used in context in this vocabulary section will appear in **boldface**. So if you see a word in this book that's unfamiliar, take a moment to look it up in the dictionary and reread the sentence with the word's definition in mind.

Word Families Are Key

The GRE does not test whether you know *exactly* what a particular word means. If you have only an idea what the word means, you will get just as many points for that question as you will if you know the precise dictionary definition of the word. That's because ETS isn't interested in finding out whether you're a walking dictionary. They want to see if you have a broad and diverse (but, of course, classically based) vocabulary.

The words in the list below all mean nearly the same thing. They all have something to do with the concept of criticism, a concept often tested on the GRE. The GRE that you take could well test you on one of these words or one of the other synonyms for *criticize*. A great way to prepare for GRE Verbal, then, is to learn which word concepts are tested most frequently and learn all those words.

CRITICIZE/CRITICISM

calumny
castigate
chastise
deride/derisive
derogate
diatribe
harangue
lambaste
oppugn
pillory
rebuke
remonstrate

On the test, for instance, you might see an antonym question like this:

REMONSTRATE:

(A) show
(B) atone
(C) vouchsafe
(D) laud
(E) undo

Kaplan Tip

The same kinds of vocabulary words that you saw on the SAT may well appear on your GRE.

Kaplan Rules

The best way to prepare for GRE Verbal questions is to learn the word concepts that are tested most frequently on the GRE.

Kaplan Tip

You don't have to know the exact meaning of a word to get the right answer on a GRE question.

Or an analogy question that looks something like this:

VITUPERATE : DISPARAGE ::

- (A) profligate : bilk
- (B) equivocate : reduce
- (C) parody : excuse
- (D) lie : prevaricate
- (E) brave : succeed

There are many such families of word synonyms whose members appear frequently on the GRE. We'll run across more as we proceed.

$20\% \times 500 > 100\% \times 50$

This simply means that it's better to know 20 percent of the definition of 500 words than it is to know the exact definition of 50 words. Or, more generally put, it's better to know a little bit about a lot of words than to know a lot about just a few. In fact, it's a lot better. And it's a lot easier.

Thesaurus > Dictionary

The *criticize* family is not the only family of synonyms whose members appear frequently on the GRE. There are plenty of others. And lists of synonyms are much easier to learn than many words in isolation. So don't learn words with a dictionary; learn them with a thesaurus. Make synonym index cards based on the common families of GRE words and **peruse** those lists periodically. It's like weight-lifting for vocabulary. Pretty soon you will start to see results.

If you think this might be **fallacious,** then check this out. The words in the list below all have something to do with the concept of falsehood. Their precise meanings vary: *erroneous* means "incorrect," whereas *mendacious* means "lying." But the majority of test questions won't require you to know the exact meanings of these words. You will most likely get the question right if you simply know that these words have something to do with the concept of falsehood.

FALSE

apocryphal	guile
dissemble	mendacious
duplicity	mendacity
equivocate	prevaricate
equivocation	prevarication
erroneous	specious
ersatz	spurious
fallacious	

The way that you should use a list like this is to look it over once or twice a week for 30 seconds every week until the test. If you don't have much time until the exam date, look over your lists more frequently. Then, by the day of the test, you should have a rough idea of what most of the words on your lists mean. If you get an antonym question such as:

HONESTY:

- (A) displeasure
- (B) mendacity
- (C) disrepute
- (D) resolution
- (E) failure

You might not know exactly what *mendacity* means, but you'll know that it's "one of those *false* words," which will be enough to get the question right. Your subconscious mind has done most of the work for you!

It might be **vexatious** to learn word meanings the slow way, but you'll be amazed how easy and **facile** vocabulary building can be when you do it this way. Here are some more word families:

ANNOY	BEGINNER	FOUL
aggravate	acolyte	festering
irk	neophyte	fetid
irritate	novice	fulsome
perturb	proselyte	invidious
vex	tyro	noisome

You may not know exactly what *invidious* means, but if you study the last list, pretty soon you will know that it refers to something foul.

Kaplan Word Families

We're now going to give you a lot of common GRE words grouped together by meaning. This isn't high-stress learning. All you have to do is make flash cards from these lists and look over your cards a few times a week from now until the day of the test. You'll find that your subconscious mind does much of the work for you.

Note: The categories in which these words are listed are *general* and should *not* be interpreted as the exact definitions of the words.

DIFFICULT TO UNDERSTAND
abstruse
arcane
enigmatic
esoteric
inscrutable
obscure
opaque
rarefied
recondite
turbid

DEBAUCHERY
bacchanalian
carousal
depraved
dissipated
iniquity
libertine
libidinous
licentious
reprobate
ribald
salacious
sordid
turpitude

SMART/LEARNED
astute
canny
erudite
perspicacious

CHANGING QUICKLY
capricious
mercurial
volatile

CRITICIZE
aspersion
belittle
berate
calumny
castigate
decry
defamation
deride/derisive
diatribe
disparage
excoriate
gainsay
harangue
impugn
inveigh
lambaste
obloquy
objurgate
opprobrium
pillory
rebuke
remonstrate
reprehend
reprove
revile
vituperate

PRAISE
accolade
aggrandize
encomium
eulogize
extol
laud/laudatory
venerate/veneration

POOR
destitute
esurient
indigent
impecunious

Kaplan Tip

Lists of synonyms are easier to learn than long lists of unrelated words.

WITHDRAWAL/RETREAT
abeyance
abjure
abnegation
abortive
abrogate
decamp
demur
recant
recidivism
remission
renege
rescind
retrograde

TRUTH
candor/candid
fealty
frankness
indisputable
indubitable
legitimate
probity
sincere
veracious/verity

BITING (as in wit/temperament)
acerbic
acidulous
acrimonious
asperity
caustic
mordant
mordacious
trenchant

WEAKEN
adulterate
enervate
inhibit
obviate
stultify
undermine
vitiate

HARMFUL
baleful
baneful
deleterious
inimical
injurious
insidious
minatory
perfidious
pernicious

TIMID
craven
diffident
pusillanimous
recreant
timorous
trepidation

STUBBORN
implacable
inexorable
intractable
intransigent
obdurate
obstinate
pertinacious
recalcitrant
refractory
renitent
untoward

BEGINNING/YOUNG
burgeoning
callow
engender
inchoate
incipient
nascent

Kaplan Tip

Make flash cards from these lists and look over your cards a few times a week from now until the day of the test.

OVERBLOWN/WORDY
bombastic
circumlocution
garrulous
grandiloquent
loquacious
periphrastic
prolix
turgid
verbose

HOSTILE
antithetic
churlish
curmudgeon
irascible
malevolent
misanthropic
truculent
vindictive

BORING
banal
clichéd
fatuous
hackneyed
insipid
mundane
pedestrian
platitude
prosaic
quotidian
trite

TERSE
compendious
curt
laconic
pithy
succinct
taciturn

INEXPERIENCED
credulous
gullible
naive
ingenuous
novitiate
tyro

ASSIST
abet
advocate
ancillary
bolster
corroborate
countenance
espouse
mainstay
munificent
proponent
stalwart
sustenance

GREEDY
avaricious
covetous
mercenary
miserly
penurious
venal

SATISFY
ameliorate
appease
assuage
defer
mitigate
mollify
pacify
placate
propitiate
satiate
slake

Know Your Roots

You knew that this dreaded word from grade school was going to come up sooner or later. Because GRE words are so heavily drawn from Latin and Greek, roots can be extremely useful, both in deciphering words with obscure meanings and in guessing intelligently.

You'll learn more words in less time if you learn them in groups. Once you know, for example, that the root PLAC means "to please," you have a hook for remembering the meanings of several words: *placate, implacable, placid, placebo,* and *complacent.*

Sometimes you can use roots to figure out the meaning of an unfamiliar word. Suppose, for example, you come across the word circumnavigate and don't know what it means. If you know that the root CIRCUM means "around" and that the root NAV means "ship, sail," then you can guess that *circumnavigate* means "to sail around," as in "*circumnavigate* the globe."

But don't get too excited. Roots offer the common heritage of words thousands of years old—but things have changed a lot. Roots don't *always* point to the right way to go.

Example: *Affinity* is of the root FIN, meaning end. But *affinity* means a kinship, or attractive force.

Sometimes, the meaning is close, but the spelling has gone haywire.

Example: *Cogent* is actually of the root, ACT/AG (to do, to drive to lead). *Cogent* means "convincing" or "having the power to compel." These two are somewhat close in meaning, but you can see what we mean about the spelling.

There are other problems with using roots to pinpoint a definition. Looking at the etymology of a word is a great trick if you know Greek, Latin, or French. For example, DEM in Greek means "people." DEMocracy essentially means government of the people. Neat and tidy. Right? Sure, but look what you've got to get right first. It helps if you study and learn where there are exceptions.

Example: The word *venal.* The root VEN/VENT means "to come" or "to move toward." But *venal* means "corrupt or capable of being bought." *Adventure, convene, event, avenue, advent,* and *circumvent* clearly spring from the root meaning. *Venal* is a bit of a stretch.

Kaplan Tip

Pencil a check mark by each word you don't know. Quiz yourself on them, erasing check marks as you learn words.

Kaplan Tip

The more roots you know, the better you'll be at deciphering perplexing words on the GRE and at coming up with smart guesses.

Note

See Appendix A for hundreds of GRE words grouped by roots. See Appendix B for the top 200 GRE words used in context.

Example: The word *pediatrician* has PED for a root. PED has to do with the foot. But a *pediatrician* is a children's doctor. A *podiatrist* is a foot doctor.

As it turns out, the etymology of a word is merely a good trick. It can help you to figure out and remember the meaning of a word. But it won't work every time, and it certainly can't provide the basic definition of a word. It may even put you on the wrong track.

So why bother? Because if you don't have a clue what a word means, you have to start somewhere. Roots are an **efFICacious** place to begin (FIC: to do, to make).

Use the Kaplan Root List in the back of this book to pick up the most valuable GRE roots. Target these words in your vocabulary prep. Learn a few new roots a day, familiarizing yourself with the meaning.

Words in Context

Learning words in context is one of the best ways for the brain to retain their meanings. In Appendix B at the back of this book, we've not only listed the top 200 GRE words with their definitions, but we've also used all of these words *in context* to help you to remember them.

Reading is ultimately the best way to increase your vocabulary, although it also takes the most time. Of course, some types of reading material contain more GRE vocabulary words than others. You should get into the habit of reading high-level publications, such as *The Wall Street Journal* and *The New York Times*. And because you'll have to read from the computer screen on Test Day, we recommend that you start reading these publications online, if possible.

Vocabulary Wrap-Up

In review, the three best ways to improve your GRE vocabulary are:

* Learning families of words
* Deciphering words by their roots
* Learning words in context

Of course, some words appear on the GRE more frequently than others. The following words all turn up regularly on the test. You should start by learning these words and the groups of words that have similar meanings to them.

Kaplan Rules

Learning words in context is a good way to retain their meanings.

The top 12 words on the GRE are:

anomaly	assuage	enigma
equivocal	erudite	fervid
lucid	opaque	placate
precipitate	prodigal	zeal

The next 20 most popular words are:

abstain	adulterate	apathy
audacious	capricious	corroborate
homogenous	desiccate	engender
ephemeral	gullible	pedant
laconic	laudable	loquacious
mitigate	pragmatic	propriety
vacillate	volatile	

The next 20 most popular words after these are:

advocate	antipathy	bolster
cacophony	deride	dissonance
enervate	eulogy	garrulous
ingenuous	lethargic	malleable
misanthrope	obdurate	ostentation
paradox	philanthropic	prevaricate
venerate	waver	

Kaplan Tip

Start reading newspapers and other difficult materials online. You'll not only expand your vocabulary and lengthen your attention span, but you'll also get used to reading and scrolling through dense passages on the computer.

A broader vocabulary will serve you well on all four GRE Verbal question types (and will also be extremely helpful in the Analytical Writing section!). Now let's look at each of the four Verbal question types, starting with Sentence Completions.

Sentence Completions

The directions for this question type look like this:

The question includes a sentence that has either one or two blanks. The blanks indicate that a piece of the sentence is missing. Each sentence is followed by five answer choices that consist of words or phrases. Select the answer choice that completes the sentence <u>best</u>.

The difficulty of the sentence completions you will see on the CAT depends on how many questions you get right.

The Four Basic Principles of Sentence Completion

1. Every Clue Is Right in Front of You
Each sentence contains a few crucial clues that determine the answer. In order for a sentence to be used on the GRE, the answer must already be in the sentence. Clues *in the sentence* limit the possible answers, and finding these clues will guide you to the correct answer.

For example, could the following sentence be on the GRE?

The student thought the test was quite _____ .

(A) long
(B) unpleasant
(C) predictable
(D) ridiculous
(E) indelible

No. Because nothing in the sentence hints at which word to choose, it would be a terrible test question. You would *never* see a question like this on the GRE. Now let's change the sentence to get a question that *could* be answered:

Since the student knew the form and content of the questions in advance, the test was quite _____ for her.

(A) long
(B) unpleasant
(C) predictable
(D) ridiculous
(E) indelible

What are the important clues in this question? Well, the word *since* is a great structural clue. It indicates that the missing word follows logically from part of the sentence. Specifically, the missing word must follow from "knew the form and content . . . in advance." That means the test was predictable.

2. Look for What's Directly Implied and Expect Clichés
We're not dealing with poetry here. These sentences aren't excerpted from the works of Toni Morrison or William Faulkner. The correct answer is the one most directly implied by the meanings of the words in the sentence.

3. Don't Imagine Strange Scenarios
Read the sentence literally, not imaginatively. Pay attention to the meaning of the words, not associations or feelings that you have.

4. Look for Structural Roadsigns
Structural roadsigns, such as *since,* are keywords that will point you to the right answer. The missing words in sentence completions will usually have a relationship similar or opposite to other words in the sentence. Keywords, such as *and* or *but,* will tell you which it is.

On the GRE, a semicolon by itself always connects two closely related clauses. If a semicolon is followed by another roadsign, then that roadsign determines the direction. Just like on the highway, there are roadsigns on the GRE that tell you to go ahead and that tell you to take a detour.

"Straight ahead" signs are used to make one part of the sentence support or elaborate another part. They continue the sentence in the same direction. The positive or negative charge of what follows is not changed by these clues. Straight-ahead clues include: *and, similarly, in addition, since, also, thus, because, ; (semicolon),* and *likewise.*

"Detour" signs change the direction of the sentence. They make one part of the sentence contradict or qualify another part. The positive or negative charge of an answer is changed by these clues. Detour signs include: *but, despite, yet, however, unless, rather, although, while, unfortunately,* and *nonetheless.*

In the following examples, test your knowledge of sentence completion roadsigns by finding the right answers (in the parentheses):

1. The winning argument was _____ *and* persuasive. (cogent, flawed)

2. The winning argument was _____ *but* persuasive. (cogent, flawed)

3. The play's script lacked depth and maturity; *likewise,* the acting was altogether _____. (sublime, amateurish)

Kaplan Rules

When working through a sentence completion question:

- Look for clues in the sentence.
- Focus on what's directly implied.
- Pay attention to the meanings of the words.
- Keep an eye out for structural roadsigns.

Teacher Tip

"Students should recast their thinking to realize that they aren't picking the wrong choice. Rather, the test maker is making the noncredited response seem reasonable to them in some way. Their job is to find the patterns that will assist them in resisting the charms of the noncredited response."
—Chris Skinner
Santa Barbara, California

Definition

"Straight ahead" road-signs—such as *because*, *thus*, and *consequently*—continue the sentence in the same direction.

Definition

"Detour" signs—such as *but*, *however*, and *on the other hand*—change the direction of the sentence.

4. The populace _____ the introduction of the new taxes, *since* they had voted for them overwhelmingly. (applauded, despised)

5. *Despite* your impressive qualifications, I am _____ to offer you a position with our firm. (unable, willing)

6. Scientists have claimed that the dinosaurs became extinct in a single, dramatic event; *yet* new evidence suggests a _____ decline. (headlong, gradual)

7. The first wave of avant-gardists elicited _____ from the general population, *while* the second was completely ignored. (indifference, shock)

By concentrating on the roadsigns, wasn't it easy to find your way through the question and arrive at the right answer? (See the "Answers to the Roadsign Questions" sidebar on the next page.)

The Kaplan Four-Step Method for Sentence Completions

Now that you have the basics, here's how to combine skills.

1. Read the sentence strategically, looking for structural roadsigns and other clues to see where the sentence is heading.
2. In your own words, anticipate its answer.
3. Look for answers close in meaning to yours and eliminate tempting wrong answers using the clues.
4. Read your choice back into the sentence to make sure it fits.

Using the Kaplan Four-Step Method

Try the following sentence completion questions using the Kaplan Four-Step Method. These are more difficult, but you should be able to do them. Time yourself: you only have 30–45 seconds to do each question.

1. The yearly financial statement of a large corporation may seem _____ at first, but the persistent reader soon finds its pages of facts and figures easy to decipher.

    (A) bewildering
    (B) surprising
    (C) inviting
    (D) misguided
    (E) uncoordinated

2. Usually the press secretary's replies are terse, if not downright
    _____, but this afternoon his responses to our questions were
    remarkably comprehensive, almost _____.

    - (A) rude . . . concise
    - (B) curt . . . verbose
    - (C) long-winded . . . effusive
    - (D) enigmatic . . . taciturn
    - (E) lucid . . . helpful

3. Organic farming is more labor intensive and thus initially more
    _____, but its long-term costs may be less than those of con-
    ventional farming.

    - (A) uncommon
    - (B) stylish
    - (B) restrained
    - (D) expensive
    - (E) difficult

4. Unfortunately, there are some among us who equate tolerance
    with immorality; they feel that the _____ of moral values in a
    permissive society is not only likely, but _____.

    - (A) decline . . . possible
    - (B) upsurge . . . predictable
    - (C) disappearance . . . desirable
    - (D) improvement . . . commendable
    - (E) deterioration . . . inevitable

Think about how you solved these sentence completion questions. You
should use the same method when you encounter sentence completion
questions on the GRE.

Now let's move to the next question type: Analogies.

Review

Answers to the roadsign
questions:

1. cogent
2. flawed
3. amateurish
4. applauded
5. unable
6. gradual
7. shock

Kaplan Rules

The Kaplan Sentence
Completion Method:

- Focus on where the sen-
  tence is heading.
- Anticipate the answer in
  your own words.
- Look for answers that are
  similar to yours.
- Plug your choice into the
  sentence to see if it fits.

Review

Answers to the sentence completion questions:

1. A
2. B
3. D
4. E

Analogies

The directions for this question type look like this:

> **This question consists of a pair of words or phrases that are separated by a colon and followed by five answer choices. Choose the pair of words or phrases in the answer choices that best expresses a relationship similar to that expressed in the original pair.**

On the GRE, the more questions you get right, the harder the analogies you will see.

The Four Basic Principles of Analogies

1. Every Analogy Question Consists of Two Words, Called the Stem Pair, that Are Separated by a Colon
Below the stem pair are five answer choices. That means analogy questions look like this:

MAP : ATLAS ::

- (A) key : lock
- (B) street : sign
- (C) ingredient : cookbook
- (D) word : dictionary
- (E) theory : hypothesis

2. There Will Always Be a Direct and Necessary Relationship Between the Words in the Stem Pair
You express this relationship by making a short sentence that we call a *bridge*. A bridge is whatever simple sentence you come up with to relate the two words. Your goals when you build your bridge should be to keep it as short and as clear as possible.

A weak bridge expresses a relationship that isn't necessary or direct. For the sample analogy question above, weak bridges include:

- Some maps are put in atlases.
- A map is usually smaller than an atlas.
- Maps and atlases have to do with geography.
- A page in an atlas is usually a map.

You know you have a weak bridge if it contains such words as *usually, can, might,* or *sometimes.*

A strong bridge expresses a direct and necessary relationship. For the analogy above, strong bridges include:

- Maps are what an atlas contains.
- Maps are the unit of reference in an atlas.
- An atlas collects and organizes maps.

Strong bridges express a definite relationship and can contain an unequivocal word, such as *always, never,* or *must.* The best bridge is a strong bridge that fits exactly one answer choice.

3. Always Try to Make a Bridge Before Looking at the Answer Choices
ETS uses certain kinds of bridges over and over on the GRE. Of these we have identified five classic bridges. Exposing yourself to them now will give you a feel for the sort of bridge that will get you the right answer. Try to answer these questions as you go through them.

1. The definition bridge (*is always* or *is never*)

    PLATITUDE : TRITE ::

    (A) riddle : unsolvable
    (B) axiom : geometric
    (C) omen : portentous
    (D) syllogism : wise
    (E) circumlocution : concise

2. The function/purpose bridge

    AIRPLANE : HANGAR ::

    (A) music : orchestra
    (B) money : vault
    (C) finger : hand
    (D) tree : farm
    (E) insect : ecosystem

3. The lack bridge

    LUCID : OBSCURITY ::

    (A) ambiguous : doubt
    (B) provident : planning
    (C) furtive : legality
    (D) economical : extravagance
    (E) secure : violence

Definition

Analogy questions consist of two words—the **stem pair**—that are separated by a colon. Stem pairs look like this:

PREPARATION : SUCCESS

Definition

A **bridge** is a short sentence that connects the two words in the stem pair. You should always make a bridge before you look at the answer choices.

4. The characteristic actions/items bridge

PIROUETTE : DANCER ::

- (A) sonnet : poet
- (B) music : orchestra
- (C) building : architect
- (D) parry : fencer
- (E) dress : seamstress

5. The degree (often going to an extreme) bridge

ATTENTIVE : RAPT ::

- (A) loyal : unscrupulous
- (B) critical : derisive
- (C) inventive : innovative
- (D) jealous : envious
- (E) kind : considerate

So there you have them, the five classic bridges. Keep them in mind as you practice for the GRE.

4. Don't Fall for "Both Are" Analogies
"Both Are" Analogies are pairs of words that are not related to each other but only to a third word.

For instance, it may seem as though there is a strong relationship in RING : NECKLACE; they're both types of jewelry. But this type of relationship will never be a correct answer choice on the GRE. If you see an answer choice like this—where the two words are not directly related to one another but only to a third word (like *jewelry*)—you can always eliminate it.

Now that you have a grasp of the Basic Principles of Analogies, let's take a look at the Kaplan method for solving analogy questions.

The Kaplan Four-Step Method for Analogies

1. Find a strong bridge between the stem words.
2. Plug the answer choices into the bridge. Be flexible: Sometimes it's easier to use the second word first.
3. Adjust the bridge as necessary. You want your bridge to be simple and somewhat general, but if more than one answer choice fits into your bridge, it was too general. Make it a little more specific and try those answer choices again.
4. If stuck, eliminate all answer choices with weak bridges. If two choices have the same bridge—for example, (A) TRUMPET : INSTRUMENT or (B) SCREWDRIVER : TOOL—eliminate them both. Try to work backwards from remaining choices to stem pair and make your best guess.

Using the Kaplan Four-Step Method
Let's try an example to learn how to use the four-step method.

AIMLESS : DIRECTION ::

- (A) enthusiastic : motivation
- (B) wary : trust
- (C) unhealthy : happiness
- (D) lazy : effort
- (E) silly : adventure

For this question, a good bridge is: "Someone *aimless* lacks *direction.*" Now plug that into the answer choices. Only choice (B) fits. If you were stuck, you should have eliminated choices (A), (C), and (E), because their bridges are weak. Remember: If an answer choice has a weak bridge it cannot be correct, because no stem pair that you'll find on the GRE will ever have a weak bridge. To be correct, an answer choice must have a strong, clear relationship.

If you can't build a good bridge because you don't know the definition of one or both stem words, all is not lost. Even when you can't figure out the bridge for the words in the stem pair, you can guess intelligently by eliminating answer choices. In the following questions, there are no stem words. How are you supposed to do them, you ask? Well, do you remember the scene in *Star Wars* when Obi Wan Kenobi is teaching Luke Skywalker about the Force? He put that helmet on Luke's head so that Luke couldn't see when the little robot tried to zap him. This entire scene was actually just a clever (if subtle) metaphor for what it's like to do an analogy when you don't know what the stem words mean.

Review

Answers to the five classic bridges drill:

1. C
2. B
3. D
4. D
5. B

Kaplan Rules

To solve an analogy:

1. Build a bridge between the stem words.
2. Plug in the answer choices.
3. Build a stronger bridge, if necessary.
4. If all else fails, eliminate answer choices with weak bridges.

Kaplan Tip

Don't waste valuable time reading the directions on test day. Learn them now.

Take a look at the following sets of answer choices and eliminate all choices that have a weak bridge. Also, if two choices in the same problem have the same bridge, you can eliminate them both (because if one of them were correct the other would have to be also).

1. _ _ _ _ : _ _ _ _ ::

   (A) pliant : yield
   (B) sinister : doubt
   (C) trivial : defend
   (D) irksome : annoy
   (E) noble : admire

2. _ _ _ _ : _ _ _ _ ::

   (A) enlist : draft
   (B) hire : promote
   (C) resign : quit
   (D) pacify : mollify
   (E) endanger : enlighten

3. _ _ _ _ : _ _ _ _ ::

   (A) congratulate : success
   (B) amputate : crime
   (C) annotate : consultation
   (D) deface : falsehood
   (E) cogitate : habit

4. _ _ _ _ : _ _ _ _ ::

   (A) tepid : hot
   (B) lackluster : catatonic
   (C) unusual : rare
   (D) pedantic : didactic
   (E) unique : popular

Now let's turn to the third Verbal question type that you'll be dealing with: Antonyms.

Antonyms

The directions for this question type will look like this:

> **This question consists of a single word in capital letters followed by five answer choices. Select the answer choice that has the meaning most <u>opposite</u> to the word in capital letters.**

On the GRE, the more questions you get right, the harder the antonym questions you'll see.

The Seven Basic Principles of Antonyms

1. Think of a Context in Which You've Heard the Word Before
For example, you might be able to figure out the meaning of the italicized words in the following phrases from their context: "*travesty* of justice," "crimes and *misdemeanors*," "*mitigating* circumstances," and "*abject* poverty."

2. Look at Word Roots, Stems, and Suffixes
Even if you don't know what *benediction* means, its prefix (*bene*, which means good) tells you that its opposite is likely to be something bad. Perhaps the answer will begin with *mal*, as in *malefaction*.

3. Use Your Knowledge of a Romance Language
For example, you might guess at the meaning of *credulous* from the Italian, *credere; moratorium* from the French, *morte;* and *lachrimose* from the Spanish, *lagrima*.

4. Use the Positive or Negative Charges of the Words to Help You
Use your scratch paper to make little + signs for words with positive connotations, − signs for those with negative connotations, and = signs for neutral words. This strategy can work wonders. For instance:

$$
\overset{-}{\text{PERDITION}} : \overset{-}{(A)}\ \text{deterrent} \quad \overset{=}{(B)}\ \text{rearrangement}
$$

$$
\overset{=}{(C)}\ \text{reflection} \quad \overset{+}{(D)}\ \text{salvation} \quad \overset{-}{(E)}\ \text{rejection}
$$

Teacher Tip

"Some students give up too easily on short verbal questions, especially the analogies and antonyms, because they have no idea what a word means. The Kaplan methods help you eliminate wrong answers even when you don't know definitions."
—Derek Veazey
Fort Worth, Texas

Kaplan Rules

Strategy for antonyms:

1. Define the root word.
2. Reverse it.
3. Find a similar opposite in the answer choices.
4. If all else fails, eliminate answer choices and guess.

Review

Answers to the answer choice elimination drill:

1. Eliminate A and D because they have the same bridge. Eliminate B and C because they have weak bridges.
2. Eliminate B, D, and E because they have weak bridges.
3. Eliminate B, C, D, and E because they have weak bridges.
4. Eliminate B and C because they have the same bridge. Eliminate E because it has a weak bridge.

5. Eliminate Any Answer Choices That Do Not Have a Clear Opposite
For instance, in the sample problem above, neither choice (B) nor choice (C) has a clear and obvious opposite. They are unlikely to be correct.

6. On Hard Antonym Questions, Watch out for Trick Choices and Eliminate Them
For instance, if you come across:

CEDE :

- (A) make sense of
- (B) fail
- (C) get ahead of
- (D) flow out of
- (E) retain

you should eliminate B, C, and D. Why? Because *cede* will remind some people of *succeed,* they will pick B. It will remind others of *recede,* as in *receding hairline* or *receding tide,* so they will pick C or D. ETS never rewards people for goofing up. No one ever "lucks" into the right answer on the GRE by making a mistake.

7. Choose Answers Strategically
When in doubt, try to eliminate incorrect answer choices and then guess.

Now that you have a grasp of the basic principles of antonyms, let's look at the Kaplan method for solving antonym questions.

The Kaplan Four-Step Method for Antonyms
1. Define the root word.
2. Reverse it by thinking about the word's opposite.
3. Now go to the answer choices and find the opposite—that is, the choice that matches your preconceived notion of the choice.
4. If stuck, eliminate any choices you can and guess among those remaining.

Using the Kaplan Four-Step Method

Now let's put this method to the test. Suppose you encounter *loiter* in an antonym question:

Step One: Ask yourself what *loiter* means. Write a definition below:

_____

_____

Step Two: Think about *loiter*'s opposite.

The opposite of *loiter* is _____ .

Step Three: Choose the answers that best matches your reversal of the original word.

LOITER:

- (A) change direction
- (B) move purposefully
- (C) inch forward
- (D) clean up
- (E) amble

What's the *opposite* of the choice you picked? Does that match the meaning of the original word?

The opposite of *move purposefully* is *stand around,* or *loiter.*

Step Four: If you get stuck, eliminate choices and guess. (A) change direction, and (D) clean up, seem to be unlikely choices and can be eliminated.

Teacher Tip

"Knowing what makes an answer wrong is just as important as knowing what makes an answer right. They're two sides of the same coin."
—Marilyn Engle
Encino, California

Reading Comprehension

Reading comprehension is the only question type that appears on all major standardized tests, and the reason isn't too surprising. No matter what academic area you pursue, you'll have to make sense of some dense, unfamiliar material. The topics for GRE reading comp passages are taken from three areas: social sciences, natural sciences, and humanities.

These passages tend to be wordy and dull, and you may find yourself wondering where the test makers get them (probably from the same source as computer installation manuals). Well, actually, the test makers go out and collect the most boring and confusing essays available, then chop them up beyond all recognition or coherence. The people behind the GRE know that you'll have to read passages like these in graduate school, so they choose test material accordingly. In a way, reading comp is the most realistic of all the question types on the test. And right now is a good time to start shoring up your critical reading skills, both for the test and for future study in your field.

Format and Directions

The directions for this question type look like this:

> **The questions in this group are based on the content of the passage. After reading the passage, choose the best answer to each question. Answer each question based upon what's <u>stated</u> or <u>implied</u> in the passage.**

On the CAT you will see two to four reading comp passages, each with two to four questions. You will have to tackle the passage and questions as they are given to you.

The Seven Basic Principles of Reading Comprehension

To improve your reading comp skills, you'll need a lot of practice—and patience. You may not see dramatic improvement after only one drill. But with ongoing practice, the seven basic principles will help to increase your skill and confidence on this section by the day of the test. After reviewing the following principles, you'll find your first opportunity to apply them by working on a sample passage. And later, on the practice test, you'll have an opportunity to master these skills.

1. Pay Special Attention to the First Third of the Passage
The first third of a reading comp passage usually introduces its topic and scope, the author's main idea or primary purpose, and the author's tone. It almost always hints at the structure that the passage will follow. Let's take a closer look at these important elements of a reading comp passage.

Topic and Scope. *Topic* and *scope* are both objective terms. That means they include no specific reference to the author's point of view. The difference between them is that the topic is broader; the scope narrows the topic. Scope is particularly important because the answer choices (often many) that depart from it will always be wrong. The broad topic of "The Battle of Gettysburg," for example, would be a lot to cover in 450 words. So if you encountered this passage, you should ask yourself, "What aspect of the battle does the author take up?" Because of length limitations, it's likely to be a pretty small chunk. Whatever that chunk is—the prebattle scouting, how the battle was fought—that will be the passage's scope. Answer choices that deal with anything outside of this narrowly defined chunk will be wrong.

Author's Purpose. The distinction between topic and scope ties into another important issue: the author's purpose. In writing the passage, the author has deliberately chosen to narrow the scope by including certain aspects of the broader topic and excluding others. Why the author makes those choices gives us an important clue as to why the passage is being written in the first place. From the objective and broadly stated topic (for instance, a passage's topic might be *solving world hunger*) you zoom in on the objective but narrower scope (*a new technology for solving world hunger*), and the scope quickly leads you to the author's subjective purpose (*the author is writing in order to describe a new technology and its promising uses*). The author's purpose is what turns into the author's main idea, which will be discussed at greater length in the next principle.

So don't just "read" the passage; instead, try to do the following three things:

1. Identify the topic.
2. Narrow it down to the precise scope that the author includes.
3. Make a hypothesis about why the author is writing and where he or she is going with it.

Structure and Tone. In their efforts to understand what the author says, test takers often ignore the less glamorous but important structural side of the passage—namely, how the author says it. One of the keys to success on this section is to understand not only the passage's purpose but also the structure of each passage. Why? Simply because the questions at the end of the passage ask both what the author says *and* how he or she says it. Here's a list of the classic GRE passage structures:

- Passages arguing a position (often a social sciences passage)
- Passages discussing something specific within a field of study (for instance, a passage about Shakespearean sonnets in literature)
- Passages explaining some significant new findings or research (often a science passage)

Most passages that you'll encounter will feature one of these classic structures, or a variation thereof. You've most likely seen these structures at work in passages before, even if unconsciously. Your job is to actively seek them out as you begin to read a passage. Usually, the structure is announced within the first third of the passage. Let these classic structures act as a jump start in your search for the passage's "big picture" and purpose.

As for how the author makes his or her point, try to note the author's position within these structures, usually indicated by the author's tone. For example, in passages that explain some significant new findings or research structure, the author is likely to be clinical in description. In passages that argue a position, the opinion could be the author's, in which case the author's tone may be opinionated or argumentative. On the other hand, the author could simply be describing the strongly held opinions of someone else. In the latter case the author's writing style would be more descriptive, factual, even-handed. His or her method may involve mere storytelling or the simple relaying of information, which is altogether different from the former case.

Notice the difference in tone between the two types of authors (argumentative versus descriptive). Correct answer choices for a question about the main idea would, in the former case, use such verbs as *argue for, propose,* or *demonstrate,* whereas correct choices for the same type of question in the latter case would use such verbs as *describe* or *discuss.* Correct answers are always consistent with the author's tone, so noting the author's tone is a good way to understand the passage.

2. Focus on the Main Idea

Every passage boils down to one big idea. Your job is to cut through the fancy wording and focus on this big idea. Very often, the main idea will be presented in the first third of the passage, but occasionally the author will build up to it gradually, in which case you may not have a firm idea of it.

In any case, the main idea always appears somewhere in the passage, and when it does, you must take note of it. For one thing, the purpose of everything else in the passage will be to support this idea. Furthermore, many of the questions—not only "main idea" questions but all kinds of questions—are easier to handle when you have the main idea in the forefront of your mind. Always look for choices that sound consistent with the main idea. Wrong choices often sound inconsistent with it.

3. Get the Gist of Each Paragraph

It will come as no surprise to you that the paragraph is the main structural unit of any passage. After you've read the first third of the passage carefully, you need to find the gist, or general purpose, of each paragraph and then try to relate each paragraph back to the passage as a whole. To find the gist of each paragraph, ask yourself:

- Why did the author include this paragraph?
- What shift did the author have in mind when moving on to this paragraph?
- What bearing does this paragraph have on the author's main idea?

4. Don't Obsess over Details

There are differences between the reading skills required in an academic environment and those that are useful on standardized tests. In school, you probably read to memorize information for an exam. But this isn't the type of reading that's good for racking up points on the GRE reading comprehension section. On the test, you'll need to read for short-term retention. When you finish the questions on a certain passage, that passage is over, gone, done with. Go ahead, forget everything about it!

What's more, there's no need to waste your time memorizing details. The passage will always be right there in front of you. You always have the option to find any details if a particular question requires you to do so. If you have a good sense of a passage's structure and paragraph topics, then you should have no problem navigating back through the text.

5. Attack the Passages, Don't Just Read Them

Remember when you took the SAT? Like some of us, did you celebrate when you finally finished the passage and then treat the questions as afterthoughts? If so, we suggest that you readjust your thinking. Remember: you get no points for just getting through the passage.

When we read most materials, a newspaper, for example, we start with the first sentence and read the article straight through.

The words wash over us and are the only things we hear in our minds. This is typical of a passive approach to reading, and this approach won't cut it on the GRE.

To do well on this test you'll need to do more than just read the words on the page. You'll need to read actively. Active reading involves keeping your mind working at all times, while trying to anticipate where the author's points are leading. It means thinking about what you're reading as you read it. It means paraphrasing the complicated-sounding ideas and jargon. It means asking yourself questions as you read:

Kaplan Tip

You don't have to memorize or understand every little thing as you read the passage. Remember, you can always refer back to the passage to clarify the meaning of any specific detail.

Kaplan Tip

Read the newspaper daily, either just in the weeks before the test or as part of your permanent routine. You'll have practice overcoming the hurdle of reading unfamiliar or difficult material, and as a bonus you'll sound intelligent and connected during interviews.

• What's the author's main point here?
• What's the purpose of this paragraph? Of this sentence?

While reading actively you keep a running commentary in your mind. You may want to jot down notes in the margin or underline. When you read actively, you don't absorb the passage, you attack it!

6. Beware of Classic Wrong Answer Choices

Knowing the most common wrong answer types can help you to eliminate wrong choices quickly, which can save you a lot of time. Of course, ideally, you want to have prephrased an answer choice in your mind before looking at the choices. When that technique doesn't work, you'll have to go to the choices and eliminate the bad ones to find the correct one. If this happens, you should always be on the lookout for choices that:

• Contradict the facts or the main idea
• Distort or twist the facts or the main idea
• Mention true points not relevant to the question (often from the wrong paragraph)
• Raise a topic that's never mentioned in the passage
• Are too strongly worded
• Sound off the wall or have the wrong tone

Being sensitive to these classic wrong choices will make it that much easier to zero in on the correct choice quickly and efficiently.

7. Use Outside Knowledge Carefully

You can answer all the questions correctly even if you don't know anything about the topics covered in the passages. Everything you'll need to answer every question is included in the passages themselves. However, as always, you have to be able to make basic inferences and extract relevant details from the texts.

Using outside knowledge that you may have about a particular topic can be beneficial to your cause, but watch out! Outside knowledge can also mess up your thinking. If you use your knowledge of a topic to help you understand the author's points, then you're taking advantage of your knowledge in a useful way. However, if you use your own knowledge to answer the questions, then you may run into trouble because the questions test your understanding of the author's points, not your previous understanding or personal point of view on the topic.

So the best approach is to use your own knowledge and experience to help you to comprehend the passages, but be careful not to let it interfere with answering the questions correctly.

Reading Comprehension Test Run

Here's a chance to familiarize yourself with a short reading comp passage and questions. You'll have more opportunities to practice later, under timed conditions. For now, we want you to take the time to read actively, to give the seven principles a test run.

The questions in this group are based on the content of the passage. After reading the passage, choose the best answer to each question. Answer each question based upon what's <u>stated</u> or <u>implied</u> in the passage.

Migration of animal populations from one region to another is called faunal interchange. Concentrations of species across regional boundaries vary, however, prompting zoologists to classify routes along which
(5) penetrations of new regions occur.

A corridor, like the vast stretch of land from Alaska to the southeastern United States, is equivalent to a path of least resistance. Relative ease of migration often results in the presence of related species along the entire length of
(10) a corridor; bear populations, unknown in South America, occur throughout the North American corridor. A desert or other barrier creates a filter route, allowing only a segment of a faunal group to pass. A sweepstakes route presents so formidable a barrier that penetration is
(15) unlikely. It differs from other routes, which may be crossed by species with sufficient adaptive capability. As the name suggests, negotiation of a sweepstakes route depends almost exclusively on chance, rather than on physical attributes and adaptability.

1. It can be inferred from the passage that studies of faunal interchange would probably

   (A) fail to explain how similar species can inhabit widely separated areas

   (B) be unreliable because of the difficulty of observing long-range migrations

   (C) focus most directly on the seasonal movements of a species within a specific geographic region

   (D) concentrate on correlating the migratory patterns of species that are biologically dissimilar

   (E) help to explain how present-day distributions of animal populations might have arisen

Kaplan Rules

The seven basic principles of reading comprehension:

1. Read the first third of the passage very carefully.
2. Focus on the main idea.
3. Get the gist of each paragraph.
4. Don't obsess over details.
5. Attack the passages, don't just read them.
6. Beware of classic wrong answer choices.
7. Use outside knowledge carefully.

2. The author's primary purpose is to show that the classification of migratory routes

   Ⓐ is based on the probability that migration will occur along a given route
   Ⓑ reflects the important role played by chance in the distribution of most species
   Ⓒ is unreliable because further study is needed
   Ⓓ is too arbitrary, because the regional boundaries cited by zoologists frequently change
   Ⓔ is based primarily on geographic and climactic differences between adjoining regions

3. The author's description of the distribution of bear populations (lines 10–11) suggests which of the following conclusions?

   I. The distribution patterns of most other North American faunal species populations are probably identical to those of bears.
   II. There are relatively few barriers to faunal interchange in North America.
   III. The geographic area that links North America to South America would probably be classified as either a filter or a sweepstakes route.

   Ⓐ I only
   Ⓑ II only
   Ⓒ III only
   Ⓓ I and II only
   Ⓔ II and III only

4. According to the passage, in order to negotiate a sweepstakes route an animal species

   Ⓐ has to spend at least part of the year in a desert environment
   Ⓑ is obliged to move long distances in short periods of time
   Ⓒ must sacrifice many of its young to wandering pastures
   Ⓓ must have the capacity to adapt to a very wide variety of climates
   Ⓔ does not need to possess any special physical capabilities

How Did You Do?

Were you able to zoom in from the broad topic (migration) to the scope (classification of migration routes)? Did the author's tone and purpose become clear, then, as explanatory rather than argumentative? And were you able to focus on the correct answers and not get distracted by outside knowledge or misleading details? You'll be able to assess your performance and skills as you review the next section, where we'll explore the strategies for dealing with the three question types and how these strategies apply to the above questions.

The Three Common Reading Comp Question Types

We find it useful to break the reading comp section down into the three main question types that accompany each passage: global, explicit detail, and inference. Most test takers find explicit detail questions to be the easiest type in the reading comp section, because they're the most concrete. Unlike inferences, which hide somewhere between the lines, explicit details sit out in the open—in the lines themselves. That's good news for you, because when you see an explicit detail question you'll know that the correct answer requires only recall, and not analysis. Let's look at each of these question types more closely, using the sample questions you just dealt with for illustration.

1. Global Questions

Description. A global question will ask you to sum up the author's overall intentions, ideas, or passage structure. It's basically a question whose scope is the entire passage. Global questions account for 25 to 30 percent of all reading comp questions. Question 2 in the preceding sample is a global question because it asks you to identify the author's primary purpose.

Strategy. In general, any global question choice that grabs onto a small detail—or zeroes in on the content of only one paragraph—will be wrong. Often, scanning the verbs in the global question choices is a good way to take a first cut at the question. The verbs must agree with the author's tone and the way in which he or she structures the passage, so scanning the verbs and adjectives can narrow down the options quickly. The correct answer must be consistent with the overall tone and structure of the passage, whereas common wrong-answer choices associated with this type of question are those that are too broad or narrow in scope and those that are inconsistent with the author's tone. You'll often find global questions at the beginning of question sets, and often one of the wrong choices will play on some side issue discussed at the tail end of the passage.

Answers to reading comp questions:

1. E
2. A
3. E
4. E

At a Glance

Global questions:

- Represent 25 to 30 percent of reading comp questions
- Sum up author's overall intentions or passage structure
- Nouns and verbs must be consistent with the author's tone and the passage's scope
- Main idea and primary purpose, title, structure, and tone questions are related

Kaplan Tip

Key phrases in the global question stem include:

- Which of the following best expresses the main idea . . .
- The author's primary purpose is . . .
- Which of the following best describes the content as a whole . . .
- Which of the following best describes the organization . . .
- The author's tone can best be described as . . .

Strategy Applied. Take a closer look at the global question, number 2 in the sample. You've already articulated the passage's topic (migration), scope (the classification of migration routes), and tone (explanatory). The author mentions three different classifications of migration routes—corridors, filter routes, and sweepstakes routes. And what distinguishes one kind of route from another? The likelihood of migration, from the most likely (corridors, with no barriers to migration) to least likely (sweepstakes routes, with barriers that species can cross only by chance). So the author's primary purpose here is to show how the classifications are defined according to how likely migration is along each type of route. That should have led you directly to choice (A).

A scan of verbs and adjectives is enough to eliminate choices (C) and (D); both imply that the author is making judgments about the classification, but the tone of the passage is objective and explanatory. Meanwhile, (B) focuses too much on one part of the passage—the explanation of sweepstakes routes—where the role of chance is mentioned only in relation to that one classification. And (E) is a distortion, because the author nowhere mentions climatic and geographic differences between adjoining regions.

Main Idea and Primary Purpose Questions. The two main types of global questions are main idea and primary purpose questions. We discussed these types a little earlier, noting that main idea and purpose are inextricably linked, because the author's purpose is to convey his or her main idea. The formats for these question types are pretty self-evident:

Which one of the following best expresses the main idea of the passage?

or

The author's primary purpose is to . . .

Title Questions. A very similar form of global question is one that's looking for a title that best fits the passage. A title, in effect, is the main idea summed up in a brief, catchy way. This question may look like this:

Which of the following titles best describes the content of the passage as a whole?

Be sure not to go with a choice that aptly describes only the latter half of the passage. A valid title, much like a main idea and primary purpose, must cover the entire passage.

Structure Questions. Another type of global question is one that asks you to recognize a passage's overall structure. Here's what this type of question might sound like:

> Which of the following best describes the organization
> of the passage?

Answer choices to this kind of global question are usually worded very generally; they force you to recognize the broad layout of the passage as opposed to the specific content. For example, here are a few possible ways that a passage could be organized:

> A hypothesis is stated and then analyzed.
> A proposal is evaluated and alternatives are explored.
> A viewpoint is set forth and then subsequently defended.

When picking among these choices, literally ask yourself, "Was there a hypothesis here? Was there an evaluation of a proposal or a defense of a viewpoint?" These terms may all sound similar but, in fact, they're very different things. Learn to recognize the difference between a proposal, a viewpoint, and so on. Try to keep a constant eye on what the author is doing as well as what the author is saying, and you'll have an easier time with this type of question.

Tone Questions. Finally, one last type of global question is the tone question, which asks you to evaluate the style of the writing or how the author sounds. Is the author passionate, fiery, neutral, angry, hostile, opinionated, low-key? Here's an example:

> The author's tone in the passage can best be
> characterized as . . .

Make sure not to confuse the nature of the content with the tone in which the author presents the ideas: a social science passage based on trends in this century's grisliest murders may be presented in a cool, detached, strictly informative way. Once again, it's up to you to separate what the author says from how he or she says it.

2. Explicit Detail Questions

Description. The second major category of reading comprehension questions is the explicit detail question. As the name implies, an explicit detail question is one whose answer can be directly pinpointed and found in the text. This type makes up roughly 20 to 30 percent of the reading comp questions. Question 4 in the sample above is an explicit detail question because it asks you to go back to the passage and examine the description of a sweepstakes route.

Strategy. Often, these questions provide very direct clues as to where an answer may be found, such as a line reference or some text that links up with the passage structure. (Just be careful with line references; they'll bring you to the right area, but usually the actual answer will be found in the lines immediately before or after the referenced line.) Detail questions are usually related to the main idea, and correct choices tend to be related to major points.

Now, you may recall that we advised you to skim over details in reading comp passages in favor of focusing on the big idea, topic, and scope. But now here's a question type that's specifically concerned with details, so what's the deal? The fact is, most of the details that appear in a typical passage aren't tested in the questions. Of the few that are, you'll either:

- Remember them from your reading
- Be given a line reference to bring you right to them
- Simply have to find them on your own in order to track down the answer

In the third case, if your understanding of the purpose of each paragraph is in the forefront of your mind, it shouldn't take long at all to locate the details in question and then choose an answer. And if even that fails, as a last resort you have the option of putting that question aside and returning to it if and when you have the time later to search through the passage. The point is, even with the existence of this question type, the winning strategy is still to note the purpose of details in each paragraph's argument but not to attempt to memorize the details themselves.

Strategy Applied. Take a closer look at the explicit detail question in the sample, Question 4. When an explicit detail question directs you to a specific place in the passage, as Question 4 does to the discussion of sweepstakes routes, your first job is to go right to that spot in the passage and reread it. And if you do that here, you read that negotiation of a sweepstakes route depends "almost entirely on chance, rather than on physical attributes and adaptability." The discounting of physical attributes here should have led you directly to choice (E).

Choice (A)'s mention of a desert environment sinks that choice, because the desert was mentioned by the author in the discussion of filter routes. As for the other choices, "short periods of time," "wandering pastures," and "a wide variety of climates" aren't mentioned in the passage with regard to sweepstakes routes.

At a Glance

Explicit detail questions:

- Represent 20 to 30 percent of reading comp questions
- Answers can be found in the text
- Sometimes includes line references to help you locate the relevant material
- Are concrete and, therefore, the easiest reading comp question type for most people

Kaplan Tip

Key phrases in the explicit detail question stem include:

- According to the passage/author . . .
- The author states that . . .
- The author mentions which one of the following as . . .

3. Inference Questions

Description. An inference is something that is almost certainly true, based on the passage. Inferences require you to "read between the lines." Questions 1 and 3 in the preceding sample are Inference questions. Question 1 specifically asks you what can be "inferred from the passage" and Question 3 asks you to glean possible conclusions based on what is presented.

Strategy. The answer to an inference question is something that the author strongly implies or hints at but does not state directly. Furthermore, the right answer, if denied, will contradict or significantly weaken the passage.

Extracting valid inferences from reading comp passages requires the ability to recognize that information in the passage can be expressed in different ways. The ability to bridge the gap between the way information is presented in the passage and the way it's presented in the correct answer choice is vital. In fact, inference questions often boil down to an exercise in translation.

Strategy Applied. Take a closer look at the sample inference questions, numbers 1 and 3. Question 1 asks you to select a possible application of the migration study, based only on what you know from the passage. Because the different concentrations of animals prompted the zoologists to classify the migration routes in the first place (line 5), it would make sense that the migration study would help explain how these different concentrations, or distributions, would have arisen. So choice (E) is correct.

Choice (A) contradicts the purpose of the passage, which we discussed for question 2, and unless we're told in the passage that the study was a failure (which we are not), we can't guess that it would be one. Choice (B) is outside of the passage's scope because the passage never touches on the reliability of the study or on any difficulties in observing long-range migrations. The answer must be based on the passage. Choices (C) and (D) are misleading distortions. The study does focus on movements of species, but there's no mention of a seasonal influence, and the study does focus on route comparisons but not on species comparisons.

Question 3 asks you to look back to the passage for the example of the bears and decide what conclusion(s) could be drawn based on this example. We read that bear populations occur throughout North America because North America is a "path of least resistance," meaning there are relatively few barriers. The bears did not continue to migrate further south, however, because they're "unknown in South America." This suggests that South America is either a filter or a sweepstakes route. Nowhere are the bears compared with other species, because the focus isn't the bears but the routes. So option I can be eliminated, and options II and III are accurate. This should have led you, then, to choice (E).

The Kaplan Four-Step Method for Reading Comprehension

Now that you've got the basics of GRE reading comp under your belt, you'll want to learn our four-step method that allows you to put it all together into a single aggressive and energetic *modus operandi*.

1. Attack the first third of the passage.
As outlined in the basic principles section, read the first third of the passage with care, thinking about what you're reading, paraphrasing the complicated parts, and identifying the main idea and author's purpose in writing the passage. Two caveats, however: First, in some passages, the author's main idea won't become clear until the end of the passage. Second, some passages don't contain a main idea, being purely descriptive, with an even-handed tone and no strong opinions. Bottom line: Don't panic if you can't immediately pin down the author's main idea and purpose. Read on.

2. Create a mental roadmap.
As you quickly read through the rest of the passage, take note of each paragraph, reading for the gist and not the details. Try to get a sense of what's covered in each paragraph and how it fits into the overall structure of the passage. This will help you get a fix on the passage as a whole, and will help you locate specific details later on.

3. Stop to sum up.
Before answering the questions, take a few seconds to summarize your mental road map and re-phrase the main idea of the passage in your own words.

4. Attack the questions.
Answer the questions based upon your mental roadmap. As necessary, go back into the passage to locate answers to specific questions. Eliminate wrong answers aggressively, and select the choice that best paraphrases the answer you've found.

Using the Kaplan Four-Step Method

Now let's apply the Four-Step Method to an actual GRE-strength reading comp passage.

The questions in this group are based on the content of the passage. After reading the passage, choose the best answer to each question. Answer each question based upon what's <u>stated</u> or <u>implied</u> in the passage.

The search for an explanation of the frequency, as well as the weakness, of U.S. third party movements is illuminated by examining the conditions that have favored the growth of a strong two-party system. Different interests and voting blocs
(5) predominate in different regions, so that the electorate is geographically fragmented. This heterogeneity is complemented by a federal political structure that forces the major parties to find voter support at state and local levels in separate regions. Historically, for example, the Democratic Party drew support
(10) simultaneously from northern Black urban voters and segregationists. Such pressures encourage the major parties to avoid political programs that are too narrowly or sharply defined. Instead, they seek broad appeal, supported by sometimes competing promises made to sectional interests. The non-doctrinal
(15) character of U.S. politics means that important new issues and voting blocs tend to be initially ignored by the major parties. Such issues—opposition to immigration and the abolition of slavery are two historic examples—tend to gain political prominence through third parties.
(20) Ironically, the same factors that lead to the emergence of third parties contribute to the explanation of their failure to gain national political power. Parties based on narrow or ephemeral issues remain isolated or fade rapidly. At the same time, those that raise increasingly urgent social issues also face
(25) inherent limits to growth. Long before a third party can begin to substantially broaden its base of voter support, the major parties are able to move to attract the minority of voters that it represents. The Democratic Party, for instance, appropriated the agrarian platform of the Populist Party in 1896, and
(30) enacted Socialist welfare proposals in the 1930s, in both cases winning much of the popular bases of these parties. Except for the Republican Party, which gained national prominence as the Whigs were declining in the 1850s, no third party has ever

achieved national major party status. Only at state and local
(35) levels have a handful of third parties been sustained by a stable voting bloc that remains unrepresented by a major party.

1. The main concern of the author of this passage is to

    (A) examine the appeal of U.S. third parties at state and local levels
    (B) trace the historical rise and decline of third party movements in the U.S.
    (C) explain why most U.S. third party movements have failed to gain major party status
    (D) demonstrate the non-ideological character of U.S. politics
    (E) suggest a model to explain why certain U.S. third party movements have succeeded while others have failed

2. According to the author, the major factor responsible for the rise of third parties in the U.S. has been the

    (A) domination of major parties by powerful economic interests
    (B) inability of major parties to bring about broad consensus among a variety of voters and interest groups
    (C) slow response of major parties to new issues and voting groups
    (D) exclusion of immigrants and minorities from the mainstream of U.S. politics
    (E) variety of motivations held by voting blocs in different regions

3. It can be inferred that which of the following contributed to the "nondoctrinal character of U.S. politics" (lines 14–15)

    I.   The regional diversity of the country
    II. The national political structure
    III. The avoidance of divisive ideological programs by the major parties

    (A) I only
    (B) III only
    (C) I and II only
    (D) II and III only
    (E) I, II, and III

4. Which of the following does the author suggest was an important factor in the establishment of the Republican Party as a major national party?

    (A) the polarization of national opinion at the time of a major social crisis

    (B) the unique appeal of its program to significant sectional interests

    (C) the acceptance of its program by a large bloc of voters unrepresented by a major party

    (D) the simultaneous decline of an established major party

    (E) the inability of the major parties of the era to appeal to all sectional interests

Here's how the Kaplan method works with this passage.

1. Attack the first third of the passage.
The very first sentence introduces the topic—third-party movements—as well as the scope and author's purpose—understanding the factors hindering their success and favoring the two-party system. The author then quickly proceeds to enumerate these factors. So just from reading this first part of the passage closely, you have a strong sense of its overall structure and purpose.

2. Create a road map.
Notice how paragraph two also opens with a topic sentence that neatly announces what will be covered therein. Make note of the author's point-by-point examination, but don't try to memorize details. You can always refer to the passage to answer questions.

3. Stop to sum up.
Now it's time to sum up your road map—from the paragraph gists you should be able to quickly paraphrase the main idea of the entire passage. After that, it's time to dance. As long as you have a sense of where the various details can be found, you should be able to find them when you need them.

You might have paraphrased the main idea like this: "Factors that lead to the emergence of third parties also lead to their eventual downfall, at least on the national level."

Armed with this recap, you should be able to move confidently through the questions. You may not be able to answer every question on sight, but you'll know where to locate the details for those questions, which means quick, correct answers.

Teacher Tip

"If you don't have a method that breaks the passage down and reveals its structure, then the passage is just 'oatmeal'—a big, undifferentiated, boring mess."
—Kurt Keefner
Bethesda, Maryland and Washington, DC

4. Attack the questions.

Work the questions as they appear. Most of the questions should be easy to crack after checking the details, an easy matter with your roadmap.

Answers and Explanations

1. **(C)** is the only choice that fits the topic (third-party movements), scope (how they fare on the national level) and the author's purpose (explaining why they have failed to gain national power). Choices (A) and (D) clearly misrepresent all of these, and (E) is out because no model is suggested, particularly one explaining why some third-party movements have succeeded. (B) might seem tempting at first, but beware of verbs such as *trace*, which are too ambitious for a GRE-length passage—there's certainly no attempt made to *trace* these movements throughout U.S. history.

2. **(C)** This detail question asks for a factor responsible for the *rise* of third parties, so you'll probably want to research the passage for the answer. You'll find the relevant discussion at the end of paragraph one, which is neatly paraphrased in choice (C).

3. **(E)** Again, you'll probably want to research the relevant part of the passage, a task which in this case is facilitated by the line reference, although here you'll need to read most of paragraph one for the answer. You'll find that item I is confirmed on line 6, item II on line 8, and item III on line 15. The lesson to be learned here is that even on so-called "inference" questions, the answers are very often paraphrases of information found in the passage.

4. **(D)** Once again, this detail question seems to ask for an inference, but if you look for the relevant discussion of the Republican Party (which is easily found by scanning for the word *Republican*), you'll find (on lines 31–33) that choice (D) directly paraphrases what you find there.

Review Exercises

Because reading comp primarily tests your ability to read actively, paraphrasing as you go and paying attention to purpose and structure, let's spend some time practicing those critical reading skills.

Big Ideas and Details

It's important that you're able to pull out the main idea and supporting details quickly and easily on the day of the test. Covering up the sidebars, read the following three minipassages, jotting down their big ideas in the margin and underlining details. Then compare your answers with ours.

Few historians would contest the idea that Gutenberg's invention of the printing press revolutionized the production of literature. Before the press became widely available in the late 1400s, every book published had to be individually copied by a scribe working from a master manuscript. With Gutenberg's system of moveable type, however, books could be reproduced in almost limitless quantities once the laborious process of typesetting was complete. . . .

Big Idea: Gutenberg revolutionized book publishing.

Details: late 1400s, moveable type, limitless quantities, typesetting

Plate tectonics, the study of the interaction of the earth's plates, is generally accepted as the best framework for understanding how the continents formed. New research suggests, however, that the eruption of mantle plumes from beneath the plate layer may be responsible for the formation of specific phenomena in areas distant from plate boundaries. A model of mantle plumes appears to explain a wide range of observations relating to both ocean island chains and flood basalt provinces, for example. . . .

Big Idea: Mantle plume eruptions, not plate tectonics, may explain certain phenomena.

Details: ocean island chains, flood basalt provinces

Most of the developed countries are now agreed on the need to take international measures to reduce the emission of carbons into the atmosphere. Despite this consensus, a wide disagreement among economists as to how much emission reduction will actually cost continues to forestall policy making. Analysts who believe the energy market is efficient predict that countries that reduce carbon emission by as little as 20 percent will experience a significant depreciation in their national product. Those that hold that the market is inefficient, however, estimate much greater long-term savings in conservation and arrive at lower costs for reducing emissions. . . .

Big Idea: Economists disagree on the cost of emission reduction.

Details: international measures, carbon emission, greater savings, conservation

Paraphrasing: The Key Skill in Reading Comp

Many people have a hard time paraphrasing passages. Taking dense, academic prose and turning it into everyday English isn't easy under the pressure of time constraints. Yet, this is the most important skill in reading comp. If you are having trouble with paraphrasing, spend some time with the following exercise.

> For centuries, the Roman Empire ruled large parts of Europe, Asia, and Africa. Rome had two assets that made continued domination possible. First, its highly trained army was superior to those of its potential adversaries. Second, and more important, Rome built a sophisticated transportation network linking together all of the provinces of its far flung empire. When necessary, it could deploy powerful military forces to any part of the empire with unmatched speed.

Summarize these lines in your own words:

Roman Army large 2 factors for strength.

highly train army   2nd good transport

to deploy asap

Now find the best paraphrase:

A. Rome's army defeated its opponents because it could move quickly along the empire's excellent transportation network.

B. Rome had a big empire, a powerful army, and a good transportation system.

C. Rome was able to maintain a large empire because it had an excellent transportation system that allowed its efficient army to move quickly from place to place.

D. Rome ruled large parts of Europe, Asia, and Africa for centuries because its army was always better than those of its adversaries.

E. Because it built a sophisticated transportation system, Rome was able to build a big empire in parts of Europe, Asia, and Africa.

Teacher Tip

"Ordinary reading is too slow to find things and too fast to analyze text. Good test takers scan quickly to find what they need and then analyze intensely. Structural keywords and references from the stem are crucial. Looking for a conclusion? Scan for keywords and for words with heavy emotional content. If the stem asks for an assumption made by a researcher, scan for the word 'research' or 'researcher.' Then read up and down from that spot."
—Eirik Johnson
Chicago, Illinois

Despite overwhelming evidence to the contrary, many people think that flying is more dangerous than driving. Different standards of media coverage account for this erroneous belief. Although extremely rare, aircraft accidents receive a lot of media attention because they are very destructive. Hundreds of people have been killed in extreme cases. Automobile accidents, on the other hand, occur with alarming frequency, but attract little media coverage because few, if any, people are killed or seriously injured in any particular mishap.

Summarize these lines in your own words:

media attention given to aircraft t automobile acide

Now find the best paraphrase:

(A) Compared to rare but destructive aircraft accidents, car accidents are frequent but relatively minor.

(B) Because aircraft accidents get a lot of media attention, while car accidents get much less, many people wrongly believe that flying is more dangerous than driving.

(C) Driving is more dangerous than flying because different standards of media coverage have forced airlines to improve their safety standards.

(D) Many people believe that flying is more dangerous than driving, even though overwhelming evidence points to the opposite conclusion.

(E) Media coverage is responsible for the belief that flying is more dangerous than driving, even though every year more people are killed on the roads than in the air.

Keywords

Remember these? Kaplan keywords are words in reading comprehension passages that link the text together structurally and thematically. Paying attention to keywords will help you understand the passage better, and will also help you get some easy points. Here are some keywords that you should look for when reading a passage:

CONTRADICTION:
However
But
Yet
On the other hand
Rather
Instead

SUPPORT:
For example
One reason that
In addition
Also
Moreover
Consequently

EMPHASIS:
Of primary importance
Especially important
Of particular interest
Crucial
Critical
Remarkable

Take a moment and circle the structural signal words in this short reading comprehension passage:

> Gettysburg is considered by most historians to be a turning point in the American Civil War. Before Gettysburg, Confederate forces under General Robert E. Lee had defeated their Union counterparts—sometimes by
> (5) considerable margins—in a string of major battles. In this engagement, however, the Confederate army was defeated and driven back. Even more important than their material losses, though, was the Confederacy's loss of momentum. Union forces took the initiative, finally

Review

Paraphrase answers:

Roman Empire: (C)
Flying: (B)

KAPLAN

(10) defeating the Confederacy less than two years later. By invading Union territory, the Confederate leadership had sought to shatter the Union's will to continue the war and to convince European nations to recognize the Confederacy as an independent nation. Instead, the Union's
(15) willingness to fight was strengthened and the Confederacy squandered its last chance for foreign support.

Words of emphasis, though rare, are the most important category of Kaplan keywords. Why? Because if you see an emphasis keyword in a sentence, you will always get a question about that sentence. Think about it—if the author thinks something is "of primary importance," it would be pretty silly for the test maker not to ask you about it.

In the Gettysburg passage, did you circle *even more important* (line 7)? You should have. You were bound to get a question about it.

You can also get the gist of this paragraph by paying close attention to the contrast words, beginning on line 6: "In the engagement, *however*, the Confederate army was defeated and driven back." Ah, so they weren't doing so well anymore. Contrast words signal a change in direction, and for this reason they often introduce thematically important information. In fact, if a paragraph contains a contrast word, the topic sentence will almost always be that sentence or the next. And the next sentence, which is indeed the topic sentence, contains another contrast word: "Even more important than their material losses, *though*, was the Confederacy's loss of momentum." Finally, the last sentence contains one more contrast word and introduces one more important idea: "*Instead*, the Union's willingness to fight was strengthened and the Confederacy squandered its last chance of foreign support."

The moral of this story is that by paying attention to keywords, you can be sure that you won't lose sight of the most important information that the author is trying to convey.

By using all of the techniques discussed above, you will be able to tackle the most difficult reading comprehension questions. And now that you have the tools to handle the Verbal sections of the GRE, take a swing at the set of practice questions that follow. Then we'll move on and take a look at the Quantitative sections of the test.

Verbal Practice Set

Question 1

Victorien Sardou's play *La Tosca* was originally written as a _____ for Sarah Bernhardt and later _____ into the famous Puccini opera.

- (A) role . . . reincarnated
- (B) biography . . . changed
- (C) metaphor . . . edited
- (D) present . . . fictionalized
- (E) vehicle . . . adapted

Question 2

Because the law and custom require that a definite determination be made, the judge is forced to behave as if the verdict is _____, when in fact the evidence may not be _____.

- (A) negotiable . . . persuasive
- (B) justified . . . accessible
- (C) unassailable . . . insubstantial
- (D) incontrovertible . . . admissible
- (E) self-evident . . . conclusive

Question 3

The author presumably believes that all businessmen are _____, for her main characters, whatever qualities they may lack, are virtual paragons of _____.

- (A) clever . . . ingenuity
- (B) covetous . . . greed
- (C) virtuous . . . deceit
- (D) successful . . . ambition
- (E) cautious . . . achievement

Question 4

Satire is a marvelous reflection of the spirit of an age; the subtle _____ of Swift's epistles mirrored the eighteenth century delight in elegant _____.

- (A) profundity . . . ditties
- (B) poignancy . . . pejoratives
- (C) contempt . . . anachronisms
- (D) provinciality . . . rusticity
- (E) vitriol . . . disparagement

Questions 5

Ginnie expects her every submission to be published or selected for performance, and this time her _____ is likely to be _____.

- (A) candor . . . dispelled
- (B) anticipation . . . piqued
- (C) enthusiasm . . . dampened
- (D) optimism . . . vindicated
- (E) awareness . . . clouded

Question 6

His opponent found it extremely frustrating that the governor's solid support from the voting public was not eroded by his _____ of significant issues.

- (A) exaggeration
- (B) misapprehension
- (C) discussion
- (D) selection
- (E) acknowledgment

Question 7

VEGETATE : ACTIVE ::

- (A) resist : beaten
- (B) mope : gloomy
- (C) grow : small
- (D) hassle : obnoxious
- (E) accept : questioning

Question 8

PROPONENT : THEORY ::

- (A) nonbeliever : sin
- (B) traitor : country
- (C) adherent : belief
- (D) attorney : law
- (E) scientist : hypothesis

Question 9

SPECIES : ORGANISM ::

- (A) specialty : physician
- (B) origin : idea
- (C) language : foreigner
- (D) genre : literature
- (E) family : ancestry

Question 10

DISCHARGED : SOLDIER ::

- (A) fired : cannon
- (B) graduated : student
- (C) appointed : judge
- (D) transferred : employee
- (E) docked : salary

Question 11

CUT : LACERATION ::

- (A) park : place
- (B) slit : gap
- (C) knife : separation
- (D) hole : puncture
- (E) boil : blister

Question 12

OUTFOX : STRATEGY ::

- (A) outdo : trickery
- (B) defeat : stamina
- (C) outlast : force
- (D) victimize : terror
- (E) outrun : speed

Question 13

COAX : BLANDISHMENTS ::

- (A) amuse : platitudes
- (B) compel : threats
- (C) deter : tidings
- (D) batter : insults
- (E) exercise : antics

Question 14

TITLED : NOBLE ::

- (A) elected : candidate
- (B) acclaimed : artist
- (C) commissioned : officer
- (D) deposed : ruler
- (E) initiated : argument

Questions 15–17:

The four Galilean satellites of Jupiter probably experienced early, intense bombardment. Thus, the very ancient surface of Callisto remains scarred by impact craters. The younger, more varied surface of Ganymede reveals distinct light and dark areas, the light areas featuring networks of intersecting grooves and ridges, probably resulting from later iceflows. The impact sites of Europa have been almost completely erased, apparently by water outflowing from the interior and instantly forming vast, low, frozen seas. Satellite photographs of Io, the closest of the four to Jupiter, were revelatory. They showed a landscape dominated by volcanos, many erupting, making Io the most tectonically active object in the solar system. Since a body as small as Io cannot supply the energy for such activity, the accepted explanation has been that, forced into a highly eccentric orbit, Io is engulfed by tides stemming from a titanic contest between the other three Galilean moons and Jupiter.

Question 15

According to the passage, which of the following is probably NOT true of the surface of Io?

- (A) It is characterized by intense tectonic activity.
- (B) Its volcanos have resulted from powerful tides.
- (C) It is younger than the surface of Callisto.
- (D) It is distinguished by many impact craters.
- (E) It has apparently not been shaped by internal force.

Question 16

It can be inferred that the geologic features found in the light areas of Ganymede were probably formed

- (A) subsequent to the features found in the dark areas
- (B) in an earlier period than those in the dark areas
- (C) at roughly the same time as the features found in the dark areas
- (D) primarily by early bombardment
- (E) by the satellite's volcanic activity

Question 17

It can be inferred that the author regards current knowledge about the satellites of Jupiter as

- (A) insignificant and disappointing
- (B) grossly outdated
- (C) complete and satisfactory
- (D) ambiguous and contradictory
- (E) persuasive though incomplete

Question 18

ZEAL:

- (A) dissatisfaction
- (B) coarseness
- (C) apathy
- (D) wrath
- (E) impudence

Question 19

ERRONEOUS:

- (A) careful
- (B) vigorous
- (C) accurate
- (D) convincing
- (E) thoughtful

Question 20

COGNIZANT:

- (A) obsequious
- (B) oblivious
- (C) vigilant
- (D) intangible
- (E) unwise

Question 21

TENTATIVE:

- (A) permanent
- (B) finite
- (C) definite
- (D) adjacent
- (E) amiable

Question 22

BAWDY:

- (A) prudish
- (B) superfluous
- (C) gaunt
- (D) ethereal
- (E) legitimate

Question 23

ABET:

- (A) exaggerate
- (B) arrange
- (C) refuse
- (D) deter
- (E) confuse

Question 24

DISPASSIONATE:

- (A) sentient
- (B) conspicuous
- (C) compassionate
- (D) partisan
- (E) heedless

Question 25

PANEGYRIC:

- (A) defamatory essay
- (B) formal monologue
- (C) binding contract
- (D) witty aside
- (E) closing remark

Question 26

PROLIX:

- (A) recalcitrant
- (B) unimportant
- (C) obstinate
- (D) diverse
- (E) pithy

Questions 27–30:

A pioneering figure in modern sociology, French social theorist Emile Durkheim examined the role of societal cohesion on emotional well-being. Believing that scientific methods should be applied to the study of society, Durkheim studied the level of integration of various social formations and the impact that such cohesion had on individuals within the group. He postulated that social groups with high levels of integration serve to buffer their members from frustrations and tragedies that could otherwise lead to desperation and self-destruction. Integration, in Durkheim's view, generally arises through shared activities and values.

Durkheim distinguished between *mechanical solidarity* and *organic solidarity* in classifying integrated groups. *Mechanical solidarity* dominates in groups in which individual differences are minimized and group devotion to a common aim is high. Durkheim identified *mechanical solidarity* among groups with little division of labor and high rates of cultural similarity, such as among more traditional and geographically isolated groups. *Organic solidarity*, in contrast, prevails in groups with high levels of individual differences, such as those with a highly specialized division of labor. In such groups, individual differences are a powerful source of connection, rather than of division. Because people engage in highly differentiated ways of life, they are by necessity interdependent. In these societies, there is greater freedom from some external controls, but such freedom occurs in concert with the interdependence of individuals, not in conflict with it.

Durkheim realized that societies may take many forms and consequently that group allegiance can manifest itself in a variety of ways. In both types of societies outlined above, however, Durkheim stressed that adherence to a common set of assumptions about the world was a necessary prerequisite for maintaining group integrity and avoiding social decay.

Question 27

The author is primarily concerned with

(A) supporting a specific approach to the study of the integration of social groups

(B) comparing different ways that group dynamics maintain allegiance among group members

(C) illustrating how a highly specialized division of labor can protect individuals from depression

(D) determining what type of society will best suit an individual's emotional needs

(E) contrasting a traditional view of a social phenomenon with a more recent one

Question 28

The passage contrasts *mechanical solidarity* with *organic solidarity* along which of the following parameters?

(A) the degree to which each relies on objective measures of group coherence

(B) the manner and degree to which members are linked to the central group

(C) the means by which each allows members to rebel against the group norm

(D) the length of time that each has been used to describe the structure of societies

(E) the effectiveness of each in serving the interests of its members

KAPLAN

Question 29

It can be inferred from the passage that

(A) as societies develop, they progress from *organic solidarity* to *mechanical solidarity*

(B) group integration enables societies to mask internal differences to the external world

(C) Durkheim preferred *organic solidarity* to *mechanical solidarity*

(D) individuals from societies with high degrees of *organic solidarity* would be unable to communicate effectively with individuals from societies that rest on *mechanical solidarity*

(E) the presence of some type of group integration is more important for group perpetuation than the specific form in which it is manifest

Question 30

The passage states that *organic solidarity* predominates in societies with relatively high levels of intragroup dissimilarity because

(A) it enables individual differences to be minimized

(B) it causes societies to become more highly specialized, thus aiding industrialization

(C) individuals who engage in highly specialized activities must rely on others to ensure that their basic needs are met

(D) these societies are at greater risk of being affected by social stressors

(E) these societies are more likely to engage in shared activities and values

Answer Key

1. E	9. D	17. E	25. A
2. E	10. B	18. C	26. E
3. A	11. B	19. C	27. B
4. E	12. E	20. B	28. B
5. D	13. B	21. C	29. E
6. B	14. C	22. A	30. C
7. E	15. D	23. D	
8. C	16. A	24. D	

Explanations

Question 1

Taking a creative work like a play and moving it into another medium is an act of adaptation, so having seen *adapted* among the choices you might have been drawn right away to correct choice (E). And *vehicle* should not have been problematic for you—the sentence refers to *vehicle* not as a means of conveyance but as a means of display or expression. We can infer that *La Tosca* was Bernhardt's vehicle in the sense that it was created for her, to display her particular talents. (The purpose of any "star vehicle" is to showcase that star.)

It is incorrect to say that a play is written as a "role" (A)—written "to provide a role" would be more acceptable grammatically—and a work is not "reincarnated" from one medium into another, that verb being best reserved for the reembodiment or rebirth of living entities. The idea of *La Tosca*'s being a "biography" (B) for Bernhardt doesn't make sense (if the play were about her life, *biography of* would work), so this choice is out even though *changed* isn't bad in the second blank. A *metaphor* (C) is a poetic or figurative representation of something, and though we might call a play a metaphor for some event or idea we would not be likely to do so for a human being; *edited* provides a further complication, in that the process of editing requires pruning and revision, whereas changing a play into a musical drama requires a great deal more firsthand creativity. And while M. Sardou might well have offered *La Tosca* as a "present" to Mme. Bernhardt (D), *fictionalized* won't do; a real-life event can be fictionalized—into a play or an opera—but that verb cannot apply to something that is already fiction.

Question 2

If the requirement is that the verdict be a "definite determination," then a judge is pressured to consider a verdict to be definitely determined even when there is some room for doubt. (This analysis is supported by the author's use of the phrases *as if,* meaning something hypothetical, and *when in fact,* meaning that which is actually true.) Thus, if the evidence in a case is not "conclusive" (E), if there is room for doubt as to the guilt of the accused, a verdict based upon it probably will not be "self-evident" but will have to be treated as such by a judge (in the face of law and custom, that is).

Certainly if the evidence in a case is not "persuasive" (A), if the conclusion stemming from the evidence is debatable, it surely does suggest there's room for doubt. But pressure for a definite determination would hardly force a judge to view a verdict as "negotiable," that is, open for debate among the interested parties and possibly subject to revision. On the contrary, the more "negotiable" the verdict, the less "definitely determined" it's likely to be. *Justified* (B) works well—the judge might have to consider this verdict warranted even if the evidence didn't support it—but *accessible* in none of its meanings (easily approached; obtainable; open to influence) fits the context. Similarly the first words of (C) and (D), *unassailable* and *incontrovertible* respectively, give us what we need—a verdict that must be seen as a "definite determination"—but their respective second words shoot the choices down. Evidence that's not "insubstantial" is substantial, and there's no contradiction between an "unassailable" verdict and one based on substantial evidence. *Admissible* plays on your associations with real-life law, but the issue of whether or not something may properly be brought into evidence is far removed from the author's central point.

Question 3

The author mentioned in this sentence believes that businessmen are models of some quality; *whatever qualities they may lack* implies that whatever bad points they possess, there's this one particular good thing about them. All of this should lead you to (A)—if an author's main characters are businessmen, and if they're all paragons of "ingenuity" (meaning inventively talented), one could easily be led to the presumption that the author thinks all businessmen are "clever."

Several of the wrong answers play off your possible biases about people in the business world, (B) being the most blatant in that regard. That choice is tempting only because an author's use of many "greedy" businessman characters might suggest that that author thinks all businessmen are "covetous." But labeling businessmen as greedy contradicts the sense of "whatever qualities they may lack"—as we noted, we need a positive quality. (Also, *paragons of greed* is awkward.) One who is morally upright or "virtuous" (C) would hardly be a paragon of "deceit" (lying, falseness). Characters possessing great "ambition" (D) wouldn't necessarily make one presume that the author believes all such people are "successful," since ambition and success in a field don't always go hand in hand; and there's even less connection between businessman characters who demonstrate great "achievement" (E) and a conclusion that, in the creator's opinion, all businessmen are "cautious."

Question 4

The idea being communicated is that satire reflects the spirit of the age in which it's written, and the semicolon suggests that what's coming up is an example. So Swift must be a satirist, and something "subtle" about his work parallels something "elegant" about his work, which in turn parallels something "elegant" about his era. No outside knowledge of the eighteenth century is needed, because the only

choice that works is (E). *Vitriol* is sulfuric acid in chemistry but sarcastic criticism in literature; literary vitriol, especially the "subtle" kind, would certainly mirror the spirit of an age that took delight in suave put-downs, or elegant "disparagement."

(A) presents a grave contradiction: An age fond of "ditties," brief and insubstantial songs or poems, would hardly be mirrored by "profound" (weight or deep) literary achievement. Two problems with (B): Not only is *poignancy*—the quality of affecting the emotions in a heartfelt way—not a characteristic usually found in any kind of satire, but poignancy would not "mirror the spirit" of elegant "pejoratives," that is, disparaging remarks. Good, wicked satire might very well display scorn or "contempt" (C), but that would have nothing to do with elegant "anachronisms," obsolete or archaic people or devices. (D) is the only choice providing two words that do, in a sense, mirror each other. *Provinciality* is rough-hewn unsophistication associated with those living in provinces, or a limited point of view—also called *parochial*. And *rusticity*, which is a country lifestyle, can also be boorishness and a lack of couth. But the two words aren't associated with the rest of the sentence, in which references to subtlety and (especially) elegance suggest something quite different from rusticity.

Question 5

The "submissions" described must be manuscripts: Apparently Ginnie is an author who believes she'll strike gold every time she sends in a story or play. The structural signal *and* suggests that her expectations are going to be taken a step further. Now her "optimism" will be "vindicated" (D) and she'll be published. That structural signal, by the way, is what keeps (C) from being correct: If the signal were *but*, then we'd need a contrast, and Ginnie's "dampened enthusiasm" would contrast strongly with her typical expectations of success. Since Ginnie always figures that her stuff will be accepted, there's no reason for the sentence to point to her "anticipation" being " piqued" (B) on this particular occasion: her anticipation is always piqued (aroused, excited). Nothing in the sentence refers to or even hints at Ginnie's habit of speaking frankly, so it would be improper to conclude with a reference to her "candor" (A), "dispelled" or not. Similarly, Ginnie's perennial optimism about her chances at publication really has nothing to do with her "awareness" (E), but even if you justify it as a reference to "awareness of her chances to be published," a "clouded" awareness would suggest she's going to get shot down this time, and would require a contrast signal like *but* rather than *and*.

Question 6

No candidate would be pleased at his or her opponent's "solid support from the voting public," but any candidate would become mighty frustrated if such support continued despite overwhelming reasons why it should cease. In this instance, we can infer that the popular governor remains popular despite the fact that he either doesn't understand "significant issues" or has made foolish choices as to what the "significant issues" are. In line with that analysis only (B) works: if the governor "misapprehended," or misunderstood, the issues, how frustrating it would be to his opponent when the public seemed not to care!

You might have been tempted by (C) or (D), and both are wrong for pretty much the same reason— each is too neutral in tone. The other choices are a good deal worse. It's not clear how a candidate would "exaggerate" (A) significant issues, nor why public support would be expected to erode as result of such overstatement; and a candidate's "acknowledgment" (E) of the key issues—recognition of their existence, perhaps even of their significance—would probably have an effect opposite to the erosion of voter support.

Question 7

One who *vegetates* is inert or not *active*. If this gave you trouble, think of vegetables, which are markedly inactive living things, or perhaps the expression "veg out" meaning to stagnate, not think or do anything.

Similarly, one who *accepts* (E) takes things as they are without doubting, doesn't call things into question; he or she is therefore not *questioning*.

Notice that the stimulus conveys a sense of definition—a vegetator by definition is not active; such a sense is missing from (A), since one who *resists* may or may not be *beaten*, now or at some future time. When one *mopes* (B), it's usually because one feels *gloomy*—a gloomy person is characterized by moping, not a lack thereof. If a plant *grows* (C) from a height of 2 feet and 9 inches to a whopping 3 feet, it has indeed grown but remains *small*. As for (D), someone who *hassles* you is probably *obnoxious*, or at least can't be said to show a lack of obnoxiousness.

Question 8

A *proponent* is someone who argues in favor of or supports some idea or practice. Someone who supports the civil-rights movement can be said to be a proponent of that cause. So we could say that one who supports a particular *theory* is a *proponent* of that *theory*, just as one who support or argues in favor of a particular *belief* (C) can be called an *adherent* of that *belief*. If *adherent* gave you trouble, think of *adhere* (to sick to) or *adhesive* (something that makes things stick together).

While a *nonbeliever* (A) might be likely to commit a sin in the eyes of others, the term *nonbeliever* is rarely applied to a person who supports a particular *sin*. A *traitor* (B) doesn't support his particular *country*, he betrays it; in betraying one country he may be supporting another, but in that sense he becomes a patriot, not a traitor, so this still doesn't work out. Now an *attorney* (D) does deal with the *law*, and must (or should, anyway) support the law. But we really can't say that an attorney is someone who supports a particular law—attorneys deal with all sorts of laws, and are honor-bound to respect them all, whereas adherents or proponents are so-called because of their devotion to one particular idea. And a *scientist* (E) is just as likely to condemn a given *hypothesis* as support it—and at any rate, his position on hypotheses is not what defines him as a scientist.

Question 9

Species is a category of living things, and living things are known as *organisms*. *Species* refers to the particular type of organism in question, just as *genre* (D) is a term used to classify or categorize types of *literature*. Human beings are the species known as *Homo sapiens,* so that's how we're classified among all organisms. The novels of Agatha Christie are classified as mysteries: *mystery* is the classification of them among books.

Physicians (A) are, to an extent, categorized by their *specialty*—the obstetricians are different from the pediatricians, etcetera. But *species* and *genre* are both formal means of classification of their respective worlds, and they specifically break down the various groups for purposes of study. The specialty of a physician, on the other hand, isn't so definitive—it's just the branch of medicine the doctor happens to be most involved with. And no one breaks down the group *physicists* into specialties for the purposes of study. The *origin* (B) of an *idea* is not the idea's category—it's where the idea comes from. And the *language* (C) of a *foreigner* is not a category. Finally, *family* (E) is used in several figurative senses to classify things (for example, the tiger is a member of the cat family), but as it relates to *ancestry* it really carries no meaning other than that of a synonym (your ancestry, or the line of your ancestors, is your family).

Question 10

Discharged is what a *soldier* is said to be when his or her tour of duty is up and he or she is released from commitment to the armed forces, just as *graduated* (B) is what a *student* is said to be when he or she has completed a particular stage of schooling, and is released. *Fired* (A) can be applied to a *cannon* that has made a shot, but it's the cannonball in this case that's released, not the cannon. In states in which *judges* (C) are not elected, they are *appointed* to the bench—that is, an important official such as the governor or the president appoints the judge to a job. But that begins his or her commitment rather than ends it. An *employee* (D) who has been *transferred* has not been released, but had his responsibilities shifted or been relocated. And *docked* (E), as it pertains to *salary,* refers to money withheld from an employee, usually as punishment for poor work. *Docked* does not refer to a salary that has finished its responsibility.

Question 11

A *laceration* is a large *cut,* especially as it pertains to a wound. Or you could say a cut is an especially small or minor laceration. (A laceration might require stitches—a cut generally requires a Band-Aid.) Similarly, a *slit* (B) is a tiny crack, cut, or separation in something, and can be called a small *gap.*

The precise relationship between *park* (A) and *place* isn't entirely clear—perhaps "the park is a place" or "I can't find a place to park"? (And in Monopoly, there's always Park Place.) At any rate, this isn't what we're after. By cutting, a *knife* (C) can separate, but a knife isn't a small *separation* itself. A *hole* (D) and a *puncture* are really the same thing, and you can't say that the former is a smaller version of the latter. And as for (E), not only are *boils* and *blisters* very different from each other, medically speaking, but even if they were more alike, blisters are often smaller sores than boils.

Question 12

To *outfox* someone is to defeat or win out over him by means of superior *strategy*, just as to *outrun* (E) someone is to beat him by means of superior *speed*. This is one of those items in which the vocabulary is simple, and you may therefore be prone to overconfidence and careless mistakes. The choices have to be examined carefully here. The most tempting wrong answer was perhaps (A), since it is true that one can *outdo* another by means of *trickery*. But *outfoxing, outrunning*, and *outlasting* are all specific kinds of outdoing that have to do with specific method, whereas *outdoing* is very general, and could apply to strategy and speed just as easily as it applies to trickery—there are unlimited ways to outdo someone. The same is true of *defeat* (B)—it's simply too general, and there are many means of defeating someone other than having greater *stamina*. To *outlast* someone (C) is, of course, to defeat him by means of superior endurance, or superior patience, not specifically by means of superior *force*. And *victimizing* someone (D) may indeed require *terror*, but victimizing has nothing to do with winning, and there are means other than terror by which people are victimized.

Question 13

The stimulus and correct answer are really flip sides of each other, but the actions they describe share a common purpose—to get someone to do what you want him to do. In fact, if the stimulus failed—if you couldn't *coax* (or persuade) someone through a series of flattering and cajoling actions and speeches known as *blandishments*, you might take the next step and attempt to *compel* (B) him by making *threats*.

Platitudes (A) are trite, dull remarks, usually trotted out as if they were fresh and new but not usually trotted out for the purpose of *amusing* someone. If your aim was to *deter* (C) someone from a particular course, there are many more effective tools than *tidings*, which are news, information, or data. You might *batter* someone (D) with *insults*—in a figurative sense, at least—but you would not use them to batter someone into doing something. And to *exercise* (E) often amounts to engaging in *antics*, but you don't use antics to exercise someone into doing something—not even in the alternative meaning of the verb *exercise*, that is, to annoy or make uneasy.

Question 14

Here's one that's easier to work with if we phrase the relationship from right to left. A person is called a *noble* (noun) because he or she is *titled*—that is, he or she has been bestowed with a title, such as Sir, Lord, or Squire. Similarly, an *officer* (C), especially one of the military,

is an officer because he or she's been *commissioned*.

A *candidate* (A) may or may not be *elected*—the first word describes an ambition rather than an existing status. An especially good *artist* may be *acclaimed* (B), or highly praised, but that doesn't make him or her an artist. A *deposed* (D) *ruler* is one who has been kicked out. What initiates an argument cannot be made analogous to the stimulus.

Question 15

GRE science passages often focus on one big contrast—and the questions will focus on the same contrast, again and again. Thus even detail questions like this one are really "main idea" questions in disguise. In this passage, the big contrast is between moons that have remained unchanged since their "early, intense bombardment" (sentence 1), and those whose surfaces have been altered in more recent epochs. Io is mentioned in the last three sentences. These sentences stress recent, indeed ongoing, changes in the satellite's surface. By inference, most impact craters from the long-ago bombardments have probably been obliterated (D). Continuing tectonic activity (A) is mentioned explicitly; tides (B) are mentioned in the final sentence as the probable cause of the tectonic activity, and hence the active volcanos. Inferably Io's surface is younger than the "very ancient" surface of Callisto, (C). (E) is the only tricky choice. The phrase *tectonically active* may automatically conjure up the idea of internal forces, since these cause tectonic activity on the earth. But it's explicitly stated (last sentence) that Io is too small to supply its own energy for such activity, so (E) is true.

Question 16

Again, keep your eye on the big contrast. The bombardments, and the craters that record them, were laid down long ago; thus a surface marked by impact craters (the dark areas of Ganymede) is older than one not so marked (the lighter areas). In addition, it's mentioned that some features of the light areas probably result from later iceflows. Thus, (A) is correct, ruling out (B) and (C). The light areas feature grooves and ridges probably resulting from these iceflows, not from early bombardment (D). Volcanic activity, (E), is not mentioned in relation to Ganymede.

Question 17

The passage conveys a great deal of information, which the author implicitly accepts, ruling out (A). (The word used for the photographs of Io—*revelatory*—is enough by itself to eliminate this choice.) The fact that information about Io comes from satellite photographs rules out (B). No contradictions are mentioned, and though areas of uncertainty remain, (D)'s *ambiguous and contradictory* will not work as a general characterization. On the other hand, (C) is out because of the cautious language used throughout: *probably* (twice), *apparently*, and *the accepted explanation*. Hence the knowledge is persuasive though incomplete, as specified in (E).

Question 18

Zeal means enthusiasm or fanaticism, so if you predict its opposite you should come up with something like *indifference*, or the actual correct response, (C) *apathy*.

Question 19

Erroneous means incorrect, so a good prediction for its opposite would be *correct*. Of the answer choices, the closest match is (C), *accurate*.

Question 20

To be *cognizant* is to be aware. Look for a word that means *unaware*. (B), *oblivious*, is a nice match. (A), *obsequious*, means overly flattering or servile. If you get stuck, try making opposites of the answer choices and comparing the opposites with the stem word. This should help you eliminate close seconds such as (E), *unwise*.

Question 21

Tentative means provisional or unsettled, as in "a tentative plan"—one that may or may not be carried out. So its best opposite would be (C), *definite*. If you were familiar with the phrase "a tentative plan" you could have also used this phrase to eliminate answer choices. If you can describe a plan as *tentative*, you should also be able to use the opposite of *tentative* to describe a plan. But a *permanent* plan, a *finite* plan, an *adjacent* plan, and an *amiable* plan all sound a bit funny. Only a *definite* plan makes sense.

Question 22

Bawdy means racy or lewd. A good opposite would be *straitlaced* or *proper*. (A), *prudish*, fits perfectly. Of the wrong answers, *superfluous* means unnecessary, *gaunt* means thin, *ethereal* means heavenly or immaterial, and *legitimate* means legal or authentic.

Question 23

To *abet* means to aid or assist. The phrase "aiding and abetting" is actually a redundancy, much like the phrase "to cease and desist." A good opposite for abet, therefore, would be *hinder*. Choice (D), *deter*, is a good match.

Question 24

Someone who's *dispassionate* is unbiased or objective. A good prediction for its opposite would be *biased* or *unfair*. Choice (D), *partisan*, meaning biased in favor of one side, matches beautifully. Of the wrong answer choices, *sentient* means conscious or aware; *stoic* means expressionless or impassive.

Question 25

A *panegyric* is a tough GRE-friendly word meaning formal or elaborate praise in writing or oration. Therefore the best opposite would be (A), *defamatory essay*. On tough Antonyms, particularly ones with phrases in the answer choices, you can always go to answer choices and try to make opposites of them; not all words or phrases have good opposites, and these can be eliminated. For instance, what's a good opposite for (D), *witty aside*? Likewise, (B), *formal monologue*, and (C), *binding contract*, don't lead to clear-cut opposites. The best rule of thumb when you're dealing with unfamiliar Antonym stems is to make opposites of the answer choices, eliminating any choice that takes you more than five seconds to come up with an opposite, make your best guess, and when stuck between two good guesses, go for the one that's more extreme.

Question 26

Once again you're given a tough GRE-friendly stem word, *prolix*, so if you knew that *prolix* means wordy you could come up with the correct answer, (E), *pithy*, meaning to the point. Otherwise, once again you'd have to work with the answer choices. For instance, if you had a sense that *prolix* has a somewhat negative word charge, you eliminate choices that have negative word charges, (A), (B), and (C). You could also make opposites of the answer choices; for instance, the opposite of (D), *diverse*, would be similar. If you don't think that *prolix* means similar, you can eliminate that answer choice. A final word about Antonyms: Sometimes you simply won't know the stem word— staring at it for a couple of minutes is not going to get you closer to the correct answer. Using word charge, word roots, and word associations, and making opposites of the answer choices can all help you, but at some point, you just have to make your best guess and move on.

Question 27

The topic of this passage is Emile Durkheim's study of social cohesion in society and the author's purpose might be summed up as describing two different ways that societies can maintain social integration among their members. A road map of the paragraph structure might look like this: paragraph 1 introduces Durkheim and his study of social groups; paragraph 2 discusses two ways societies can maintain social integration; paragraph 3 offers a broader context for interpreting the evidence in paragraph 2.

The final paragraph gives you the key to answering this global question. The author is describing different ways that societies can function without choosing a side or advocating a specific position. You can rule out (A) immediately for its strong stand. (C) distorts a detail beyond its acceptable scope. While the passage does discuss how social cohesion can function in societies with high degrees of labor specialization, this is not the author's main goal. (D) takes a prescriptive stance, and the author never tells us how to live our lives. Finally, (E) makes a comparison that is not there. Both of the mechanisms for maintaining social solidarity were developed by Durkheim at the same time and are part of the same worldview, namely, his. The comparison between a traditional and a recent view is inapplicable here.

Question 28

What is the crucial difference between *mechanical solidarity* and *organic solidarity*? The level of homogeneity in the group in which each functions. Neither one relies on any measure, objective or otherwise, of group coherence. Rather, they describe the way societies function naturally, ruling out (A). (C) introduces the notion of rebellion, a concept that is not mentioned in the passage and hence, cannot be correct. (D) is wrong because the two types of solidarity were developed at the same time by Durkheim; we do not have a traditional view and a more recent view of the same phenomenon, but rather two different ways that societies can function within the same worldview. (E) brings into question the effectiveness of each, and the last paragraph makes it clear that either one can serve its members needs equally well.

Question 29

In this inference question, you will need to think about the author's opinion as you approach the answer choices. (A) is wrong because the author never discusses the two forms of *solidarity* as being related to each other, nor does he discuss the transformation of societies over time. (B) is outside the scope, as the relationship of individual societies to the world-at-large is not an issue that concerns the author. (C) makes a subjective statement about Durkheim that is never suggested by the passage. (D) makes a comparison between the two types of social groups that is not supported by the passage. (E), however, is basically a close paraphrase of the final paragraph of the passage. The particular type of integration that exists within a given society is less important than that it is present in some form.

Question 30

In this detail question, you should research the second paragraph, where *organic solidarity* is discussed. There you'll find Durkheim's reasoning for why it exists in societies with high levels of heterogeneity. *Organic solidarity* prevails in societies with fewer similarities among members because when a society is highly specialized its members rely on each other out of necessity—as a way to ensure that everyone's needs are met. Reading through the answers, (C) should jump out at you as conveying this sentiment.

(A) is the opposite of what we want. In societies in which *organic solidarity* dominates, individual differences are relatively high. (B) implies a causal relationship between *organic solidarity* and the way a society is organized, but *organic solidarity* is simply a term to describe the way a society *is* functioning; it is not an active agent of anything. (D) uses information that was never mentioned in the passage—namely, that some societies are more likely to be affected by social stressors. Finally, (E) misappropriates information from the section on societies in which *mechanical solidarity* dominates. Societies that operate by *organic solidarity*, by contrast, tend not to be comprised of members who lead highly similar lives.

CHAPTER THREE

Test Content: Quantitative

- Learn the Basic Principles and the Kaplan Method for answering QCs, Problem Solving, and Graph questions

- Review the key concepts of percentages, simultaneous equations, symbolism, special triangles, multiple and oddball figures, the three Ms, range, and probability

- Complete the Quantitative Practice Set

You'll have 45 minutes to complete 28 questions in the Quantitative section. The GRE tests the same sort of mathematical concepts that the SAT does: arithmetic, algebra, and geometry. There is no trigonometry or calculus tested on the GRE. However, the test does contain some mathematical concepts that you didn't see on the SAT: median, mode, range, standard deviation, and simple probability.

There are three formats of GRE math questions: problem solving, which have five answer choices each; graph questions, which have five answer choices each and which are based on one or more graphs; and quantitative comparisons (QCs), which have only four answer choices each. Because about half of the questions on each math section are QCs, let's look at these first.

Kaplan Rules

To score high on QCs, learn what the answer choices stand for, and know these cold.

Quantitative Comparisons

In QCs, instead of solving for a particular value, you need to compare two quantities. At first, QCs may appear really difficult because of their unfamiliar format. However, once you become used to them, they can be quicker and easier than the other types of math questions.

The Questions

The difficulty of the QCs will depend on how well you are doing in the section. In each question, you'll see two mathematical expressions. One is in Column A, the other in Column B. Your job is to compare them. Some questions include additional information about one or both quantities. This information is centered, and is essential to making the comparison.

The Answer Choices and Directions

QCs are the only questions type on the GRE with four instead of five answer choices. The answer choices to QCs never change and here's what they look like:

- Ⓐ **The quantity in Column A is greater**
- Ⓑ **The quantity in Column B is greater**
- Ⓒ **The two quantities are equal**
- Ⓓ **The relationship cannot be determined from the information given**

Because the answer choices to QCs never change, from here on in we will omit the answer choices from the QC examples in this book. The directions to QCs look something like this:

> **This question consists of two quantities, one in Column A and another in Column B. You are to compare the two quantities and decide whether**
>
> > **the quantity in Column A is greater;**
> >
> > **the quantity in Column B is greater;**
> >
> > **the two quantities are equal;**
> >
> > **the relationship cannot be determined from the information given**
>
> <u>Common information:</u> **In a question, information concerning one or both of the quantities to be compared is centered above the two columns. A symbol that appears in both columns represents the same thing in Column A as it does in Column B.**

Basic Principles of Quantitative Comparisons

Choices (A), (B), and (C) all represent definite relationships between the quantities in Column A and Column B. But choice (D) represents a relationship that cannot be determined. Here are two things to remember about choice (D) that will help you decide when to pick it:

- **Choice (D) is never correct if both columns contain only numbers.** The relationship between numbers is unchanging, but choice (D) means more than one relationship is possible.
- **Choice (D) is correct if you can demonstrate two different relationships between the columns.**

Suppose you ran across the following QC:

Column A	Column B
$2x$	$3x$

If x is a positive number, Column B is greater than Column A. If $x = 0$, the columns are equal. If x equals any negative number, Column B is less than Column A. Because more than one relationship is possible, the answer is (D). In fact, as soon as you find a second possibility, stop work and pick choice (D).

The Kaplan Method for Quantitative Comparisons

Here are six Kaplan strategies that will enable you to make quick comparisons. In the rest of this chapter you'll learn how they work and you'll try them on practice problems.

1. *Compare piece by piece.*
   This works on QCs that compare two sums or two products.

2. *Make one column look like the other.*
   This is a great approach when the columns look so different that you can't compare them directly.

3. *Do the same thing to both columns.*
   Change both columns by adding, subtracting, multiplying, or dividing by the same amount on both sides in order to make the comparison more apparent.

4. *Pick numbers.*
   Use this to get a handle on abstract algebra QCs.

5. *Redraw the diagram.*
   Redrawing a diagram can clarify the relationships between measurements.

6. *Avoid QC traps.*
   Stay alert for questions designed to fool you by leading you to the obvious, wrong answer.

Note

No calculators are allowed during the GRE. The test center will provide you with scratch paper on which you can work out your calculations.

Now let's look at how these strategies work.

1. Compare Piece by Piece

<table>
<tr><td>Column A</td><td>Column B</td></tr>
</table>

$$w > x > 0 > y > z$$

Column A	Column B
$w + y$	$x + z$

In this problem, there are four variables—w, x, y, and z. Compare the value of each "piece" in each column. If every "piece" in one column is greater than a corresponding "piece" in the other column and the only operation involved is addition, the column with the greater individual values will have the greater total value.

From the given information we know that $w > x$ and $y > z$. Therefore, the first term in Column A, w, is greater than the first term in Column B, x. Similarly, the second term in Column A, y, is greater than the second term in Column B, z. Because each piece in Column A is greater than the corresponding piece in Column B, Column A must be greater; the answer is (A).

2. Make One Column Look Like the Other
When the quantities in Columns A and B are expressed differently, you can often make the comparison easier by changing one column to look like the other. For example, if one column is a percent, and the other a fraction, try converting the percent to a fraction.

Column A	Column B
$x(x - 1)$	$x^2 - x$

Here Column A has parentheses, and Column B doesn't. So make Column A look more like Column B: get rid of those parentheses. You then end up with $x^2 - x$ in both columns, which means they are equal and the answer is (C).

Try another example, this time involving geometry.

Column A	Column B

The diameter of circle O is d and the area is a.

Column A	Column B
$\dfrac{\pi d^2}{2}$	a

Make Column B look more like Column A by rewriting a, the area of the circle, in terms of the diameter, d. The area of any circle equals πr^2, where r is the radius.

Since the radius is half the diameter, we can plug in $\frac{d}{2}$ for r in the area formula to get $\pi\left(\frac{d}{2}\right)^2$ in Column B. Simplifying we get $\frac{\pi d^2}{4}$. Since both columns contain π, we can simply compare $\frac{d^2}{2}$ with $\frac{d^2}{4}$. $\frac{d^2}{4}$ is half as much as $\frac{d^2}{2}$, and since d^2 must be positive, Column A is greater and choice (A) is correct.

3. Do the Same Thing to Both Columns

Some QC questions become much clearer if you change not just the appearances but also the values of both columns. Treat them like two sides of an inequality, with the sign temporarily hidden.

You can add or subtract the same amount from both columns, and multiply or divide by the same positive amount without altering the relationship. You can also square both columns if you're sure they're both positive. But watch out: Multiplying or dividing an inequality by a negative number reverses the direction of the inequality sign. Since it alters the relationship between the columns, avoid multiplying or dividing by a negative number.

In the QC below, what could you do to both columns?

Column A	Column B

$$4a + 3 = 7b$$

Column A	Column B
$20a + 10$	$35b - 5$

All the terms in the two columns are multiples of 5, so divide both columns by 5 to simplify. You're left with $4a + 2$ in Column A and $7b - 1$ in Column B. This resembles the equation given in the centered information. In fact, if you add 1 to both columns, you have $4a + 3$ in Column A and $7b$ in Column B. The centered equation tells us they are equal. Thus choice (C) is correct.

Kaplan Tip

Don't multiply or divide both QC columns by a negative number.

In the next QC, what could you do to both columns?

Column A	Column B

$$y > 0$$

$$1 + \frac{y}{1+y} \qquad\qquad\qquad 1 + \frac{1}{1+y}$$

Solution: First subtract 1 from both sides. That gives you $\frac{y}{1+y}$ in Column A, and $\frac{1}{1+y}$ in Column B. Then multiply both sides by $1 + y$, which must be positive since y is positive. You're left comparing y with 1.

You know y is greater than 0, but it could be a fraction less than 1, so it could be greater or less than 1. Since you can't say for sure which column is greater, the answer is (D).

4. Pick Numbers

If a QC involves variables, try picking numbers to make the relationship clearer. Here's what you do:

- Pick numbers that are easy to work with.
- Plug in the numbers and calculate the values. Note the relationship between the columns.
- Pick another number for each variable and calculate the values again.

Column A	Column B

$$r > s > t > w > 0$$

$$\frac{r}{t} \qquad\qquad\qquad \frac{s}{w}$$

Try $r = 4$, $s = 3$, $t = 2$, and $w = 1$. Then Column A $= \frac{r}{t} = \frac{4}{2} = 2$. And Column B $= \frac{s}{w} = \frac{3}{1} = 3$. So in this case Column B is greater than Column A.

Always Pick More Than One Number and Calculate Again. In the example above, we first found Column B was bigger. But that doesn't mean Column B is always bigger and that the answer is (B). It does mean the answer is not (A) or (C). But the answer could still be (D)—not enough information to decide.

If time is short, guess between (B) and (D). But whenever you can, pick another set of numbers and calculate again.

As best you can, make a special effort to find a second set of numbers that will alter the relationship. Here for example, try making r a lot larger. Pick $r = 30$ and keep the other variables as they were. Now Column A $= \frac{30}{2} = 15$. This time, Column A is greater than Column B, so answer choice (D) is correct.

Pick Different Kinds of Numbers. Don't assume all variables represent positive integers. Unless you're told otherwise, variables can represent zero, negative numbers, or fractions. Since different kinds of numbers behave differently, always pick a different kind of number the second time around. In the example above, we plugged in a small positive number the first time and a larger number the second.

In the next three examples, we pick different numbers and get different results. Since we can't find constant relationships between Columns A and B, in all these cases the answer is (D).

Column A	Column B
w	$-w$

If $w = 5$, Column A = 5 and Column B = –5, so Column A is greater.
If $w = -5$, Column A = –5 and Column B = 5, so Column B is greater.

Column A	Column B
	$x \neq 0$
x	$\frac{1}{x}$

If $x = 3$, Column A = 3 and Column B = $\frac{1}{3}$, so Column A is greater.

If $x = \frac{1}{3}$, Column A = $\frac{1}{3}$ and Column B = $\frac{1}{\frac{1}{3}} = 3$, so Column B is greater.

Kaplan Tip

If the relationship between Columns A and B changes when you pick other numbers, (D) must be the answer.

Column A	Column B
x	x^2

If $x = \frac{1}{2}$, Column A $= \frac{1}{2}$ and Column B $= \frac{1}{4}$, so Column A is greater.

If $x = 2$, Column A $= 2$ and Column B $= 4$, so Column B is greater.

5. Redraw the Diagram
- Redraw a diagram if the one that's given confuses you.
- Redraw scale diagrams to exaggerate crucial differences.

Some geometry diagrams may be misleading. Two angles or lengths may look equal as drawn in the diagram, but the given information tells you that there is a slight difference in their measures. The best strategy is to redraw the diagram so that their relationship can be clearly seen.

Column A	Column B

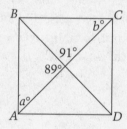

ABCD is a rectangle.

a	b

Redraw this diagram to exaggerate the difference between the 89° degree angle and the 91° angle. In other words, make the larger angle much larger, and the smaller angle much smaller. The new rectangle that results is much wider than it is tall.

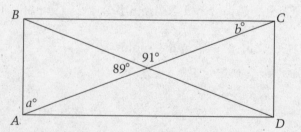

In the new diagram, where the crucial difference jumps out, a is clearly greater than b.

6. Avoid QC Traps
To avoid QC traps, always be alert. Don't assume anything. Be especially cautious near the end of the question set.

Don't Be Tricked by Misleading Information.

Column A	Column B
	John is taller than Bob.	
John's weight in pounds	Bob's weight in pounds

The test makers hope you think, "If John is taller, he must weigh more." But there's no guaranteed relationship between height and weight, so you don't have enough information. The answer is (D). Fortunately, problems like this are easy to spot if you stay alert.

Don't Assume. A common QC mistake is to assume that variables represent positive integers. As we saw in using the picking numbers strategy, fractions or negative numbers often show another relationship between the columns.

Column A	Column B
When 1 is added to the square of x the result is 37.	
x	6

It is easy to assume that x must be 6, since the square of x is 36. That would make choice (C) correct. However, it is possible that $x = -6$. Since x could be either 6 or -6, the answer is (D).

Don't Forget to Consider Other Possibilities.

Column A	Column B

$$\begin{array}{r} R \\ S \\ +T \\ \hline 1\,W \end{array}$$

In the addition problem above, R, S, and T are different digits that are multiples of 3, and W is a digit.

Column A	Column B
W	8

Kaplan Tip

Be aware of negative numbers!

Because you're told that R, S, and T are digits and different multiples of 3, most people will think of 3, 6, and 9, which add up to 18. That makes W equal to 8, and Columns A and B equal. But that's too obvious for a QC at the end of the section.

There's another possibility. 0 is also a multiple of 3. So the three digits could be 0, 3, and 9, or 0, 6, and 9, which give totals of 12 and 15, respectively. That means W could be 8, 2, or 5. Since the columns could be equal, or Column B could be greater, answer choice (D) must be correct.

Don't Fall for Look-Alikes.

Column A	Column B
$\sqrt{5} + \sqrt{5}$	$\sqrt{10}$

At first glance, forgetting the rules of radicals, you might think these quantities are equal and that the answer is (C). But use some common sense to see this isn't the case. Each $\sqrt{5}$ in Column A is bigger than $\sqrt{4}$, so Column A is more than 4. The $\sqrt{10}$ in Column B is less than another familiar number, $\sqrt{16}$, so Column B is less than 4. The answer is (A).

Now use Kaplan's six strategies to solve nine typical QC questions. Then check your work against our solutions.

Practice Problems

	Column A	Column B
1.	$x^2 + 2x - 2$	$x^2 + 2x - 1$

$$x = 2y$$
$$y > 0$$
y is a positive integer.

	Column A	Column B
2.	4^{2y}	2^x

$$\frac{x}{y} = \frac{z}{4}$$

x, y, and z are positive.

	Column A	Column B
3.	$6x$	$2yz$

Column A	Column B

q, r, and s are positive integers.

$$qrs > 12$$

4. $\dfrac{qr}{5}$ $\qquad\qquad\qquad\qquad$ $\dfrac{3}{s}$

$$x > 1$$
$$y > 0$$

5. y^x $\qquad\qquad\qquad\qquad$ $y^{(x+1)}$

$$7p + 3 = r$$
$$3p + 7 = s$$

6. r $\qquad\qquad\qquad\qquad$ s

In triangle XYZ, the measure of angle X equals the measure of angle Y.

7. The degree measure of angle Z $\qquad$ The degree measure of angle X plus the degree measure of angle Y

$$h > 1$$

8. The number of minutes in h hours $\qquad$ $\dfrac{60}{h}$

Square A   Square B

9. $\dfrac{\text{Perimeter of square } A}{\text{Perimeter of square } B}$ $\qquad$ $\dfrac{\text{Length of } WY}{\text{Length of } PR}$

Answer Key

1. (B) Comparing the respective pieces of the two columns, the only difference is the third piece: -2 in Column A and -1 in Column B. We don't know the value of x, but whatever it is, x^2 in Column A must have the same value as x^2 in Column B, and $2x$ in Column A must have the same value as $2x$ in Column B. Since any quantity minus 2 must be less than that quantity minus 1, Column B is greater than Column A.

2. (A) Replacing the exponent x in Column B with the equivalent value given in the problem, we're comparing 4^{2y} with 2^{2y}. Since y is a positive integer, raising 4 to the exponent $2y$ will result in a greater value than raising 2 to the exponent $2y$.

3. (B) Do the same thing to both columns until they resemble the centered information. When we divide both columns by $6y$ we get $\frac{6x}{6y}$ or $\frac{x}{y}$ in Column A, and $\frac{2yz}{6y}$, or $\frac{z}{3}$ in Column B. Since $\frac{x}{y} = \frac{z}{4}$, and $\frac{z}{3} > \frac{z}{4}$ (because z is positive), $\frac{z}{3} > \frac{x}{y}$.

4. (D) Do the same thing to both columns to make them look like the centered information. When we multiply both columns by $5s$ we get qrs in Column A and 15 in Column B. Since qrs could be any integer greater than 12, it could be greater than, equal to, or less than 15.

5. (D) Try $x = y = 2$. Then Column A $= y^x = 2^2 = 4$. Column B $= y^{x+1} = 2^3 = 8$, making Column B greater. But if $x = 2$ and $y = \frac{1}{2}$, Column A $= \left(\frac{1}{2}\right)^2 = \frac{1}{4}$ and Column B $= \left(\frac{1}{2}\right)^3 = \frac{1}{8}$. In this case, Column A is greater than Column B, so the answer is (D).

6. (D) Pick a value for p, and see what effect this has on r and s. If $p = 1$, $r = (7 \times 1) + 3 = 10$, and $s = (3 \times 1) + 7 = 10$, and the two columns are equal. But if $p = 0$, $r = (7 \times 0) + 3 = 3$, and $s = (3 \times 0) + 7 = 7$, and Column A is smaller than Column B. Since there are at least two different possible relationships, the answer is choice (D).

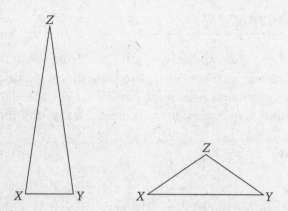

7. (D) Since angle X = angle Y, this is an isosceles triangle. We can draw two diagrams with X and Y as the base angles of an isosceles triangle. In one diagram, make the triangle tall and narrow, so that angle X and angle Y are very large, and angle Z is very small. In this case, column B is greater. In the second diagram, make the triangle short and wide, so that angle Z is much larger than angle X and angle Y. In this case, Column A is greater. Since more than one relationship between the columns is possible, the correct answer is choice (D).

8. (A) The "obvious" answer here is choice (C), because there are 60 minutes in an hour, and 60 appears in Column B. But the number of minutes in h hours would equal 60 times h, not 60 divided by h. Since h is greater than 1, the number in Column B will be less than the actual number of minutes in h hours, so Column A is greater. (A) is correct.

9. (C) We don't know the exact relationship between Square A and Square B, but it doesn't matter. The problem is actually just comparing the ratios of corresponding parts of two squares. Whatever the relationship between them is for one specific length in both squares, the same relationship will exist between them for any other corresponding length. If a side of one square is twice the length of a side of the second square, the diagonal will also be twice as long. The ratio of the perimeters of the two squares is the same as the ratio of the diagonals. Therefore, the columns are equal. (C) is correct.

Kaplan Tip

You will save time on Test Day if you can translate common percents into their fraction and decimal equivalents.

$\frac{1}{5} = 20\% = .20$

$\frac{1}{4} = 25\% = .25$

$\frac{1}{3} = 33\frac{1}{3}\% = .\overline{3}$

$\frac{1}{2} = 50\% = .5$

$\frac{2}{3} = 66\frac{2}{3}\% = .\overline{6}$

$\frac{3}{4} = 75\% = .75$

Problem Solving

In problem solving, you will have to solve problems that test a variety of mathematical concepts. Problem solving questions typically deal with percentages, simultaneous equations, symbolism, special triangles, multiple and oddball figures, mean, median, mode, range, and probability.

The Format

The Questions

You can expect about 10 problem solving questions. As with other question types, the more questions you get right, the harder the problem solving questions you will see.

The Directions

The directions that you'll see will look something like this:

Each of Questions 16–20 has five answer choices. For each of these questions, select the best answer choice given.

The Kaplan Approach to Percentages

Last year Julie's annual salary was $20,000. This year's raise brings her to an annual salary of $25,000. If she gets the same percent raise every year, what will her salary be next year?

(A) $27,500

(B) $30,000

(C) $31,250

(D) $32,500

(E) $35,000

In percent problems, you're usually given two pieces of information and asked to find the third. When you see a percent problem, remember:

• If you are solving for a percent:

$$\text{Percent} = \frac{\text{Part}}{\text{Whole}}$$

• If you need to solve for a part:

$$\text{Percent} \times \text{Whole} = \text{Part}$$

This problem asks for Julie's projected salary for next year—that is, her current salary plus her next raise.

You know last year's salary ($20,000), and you know this year's salary ($25,000), so you can find the difference between the two salaries:

$$\$25,000 - \$20,000 = \$5,000 = \text{her raise}$$

Now find the percent of her raise, by using the formula

$$\text{Percent} = \frac{\text{Part}}{\text{Whole}}$$

Since Julie's raise was calculated on last year's salary, divide by $20,000.

$$\text{Percent raise} = \frac{\$5,000}{\$20,000} = \frac{1}{4} = 25\%$$

You know she will get the same percent raise next year, so solve for the part. Use the formula: Percent × Whole = Part. Her raise next year will be $25\% \times \$25,000 = \frac{1}{4} \times 25,000 = \$6,250$. Add that amount to this year's salary and you have her projected salary:

$$\$25,000 + \$6,250 = \$31,250 \text{ or answer choice (C).}$$

Make sure that you change the percent to either a fraction or a decimal before beginning calculations.

Practice Problems

Column A	Column B
1. 5% of 3% of 45	6.75

2. If a sweater sells for $48 after a 25 percent markdown, what was its original price?

A $56
B $60
C $64
D $68
E $72

Kaplan Tip

Be sure you know which whole to plug in. Here you're looking for a percent of $20,000, not $25,000.

Review

x percent of $y = y$ percent of x

20% of 50 = 50% of 20

$\frac{1}{5} \times 50 = \frac{1}{2} \times 20$

10 = 10

Solutions

1. (B) Percent × Whole = Part. 5% of (3% of 45) = .05 × (.03 × 45) = .05 × 1.35= .0675, which is less than 6.75 in Column B.

2. (C) We want to solve for the original price, the Whole. The percent markdown is 25%, so $48 is 75% of the whole: Percent × Whole = Part.

$$75\% \times \text{Original Price} = \$48$$
$$\text{Original Price} = \frac{\$48}{0.75} = \$64$$

The Kaplan Approach to Simultaneous Equations

If $p + 2q = 14$ and $3p + q = 12$, then $p =$

- (A) −2
- (B) −1
- (C) 1
- (D) 2
- (E) 3

Kaplan Tip

Combine the equations—by adding or subtracting them—to cancel out all but one of the variables.

In order to get a numerical value for each variable, you need as many different equations as there are variables to solve for. So, if you have two variables, you need two independent equations.

You could tackle this problem by solving for one variable in terms of the other, and then plugging this expression into the other equation. But the simultaneous equations that appear on the GRE can usually be handled in an easier way.

You can't eliminate p or q by adding or subtracting the equations in their present form. But look what happens if you multiply both sides of the second equation by 2:

$$2(3p + q) = 2(12)$$
$$6p + 2q = 24$$

Now when you subtract the first equation from the second, the qs will cancel out so you can solve for p:

$$6p + 2q = 24$$
$$-[p + 2q = 14]$$
$$\overline{5p + 0 = 10}$$

If $5p = 10$, $p = 2$.

Practice Problems

1. If $x + y = 8$ and $y - x = -2$, then $y =$

   (A) -2
   (B) 3
   (C) 5
   (D) 8
   (E) 10

2. If $m - n = 5$ and $2m + 3n = 15$, then $m + n =$

   (A) 1
   (B) 6
   (C) 7
   (D) 10
   (E) 15

Solutions

1. (B) When you add the two equations, the x's cancel out and you find that $2y = 6$, so $y = 3$.

2. (C) Multiply the first equation by 2, then subtract the first equation from the second to eliminate the m's and find that $5n = 5$, or $n = 1$. Plugging this value for n into the first equation shows that $m = 6$, so $m + n = 7$, choice (C).

$$2m + 3n = 15 \qquad m - n = 5 \qquad m + n = 6 + 1 = 7$$
$$-2m + 2n = -10 \qquad m - 1 = 5$$
$$5n = 5 \qquad\qquad m = 6$$
$$n = 1$$

The Kaplan Approach to Symbolism

If $a \star b = \sqrt{a + b}$ for all nonnegative numbers, what is the value of $10 \star 6$?

(A) 0
(B) 2
(C) 4
(D) 8
(E) 16

Kaplan Tip

When a symbolism problem includes parentheses, do the operations inside the parentheses first.

You should be quite familiar with the arithmetic symbols $+$, $-$, $\times$, $\div$, and %. Finding the value of $10 + 2$, $18 - 4$, 4×9, or $96 \div 16$ is easy.

However, on the GRE, you may come across bizarre symbols. You may even be asked to find the value of $10 \star 2$, $5 \divideontimes 7$, $10 \divideontimes 6$, or $65 \heartsuit 2$.

The GRE test makers put strange symbols in questions to confuse or unnerve you. Don't let them. The question stem always tells you what the strange symbol means. Although this type of question may look difficult, it is really an exercise in plugging in.

To solve, just plug in 10 for a and 6 for b into the expression $\sqrt{a + b}$. That equals $\sqrt{10 + 6}$ or $\sqrt{16}$ or 4, choice (C).

How about a more involved symbolism question?

Kaplan Tip

When two questions include the same symbol, expect the second question to be more difficult and be extra careful.

If $a \blacktriangle$ means to multiply a by 3 and $a \divideontimes$ means to divide a by -2, what is the value of $((8 \divideontimes) \blacktriangle) \divideontimes$?

(A) -6
(B) 0
(C) 2
(D) 3
(E) 6

First find $8 \divideontimes$. This means to divide 8 by -2, which is -4. Working out to the next set of parentheses, we have $(-4) \blacktriangle$, which means to multiply -4 by 3, which is -12. Lastly, we find $(-12) \divideontimes$, which means to divide -12 by -2, which is 6, choice (E).

Practice Problems

Column A   Column B

If $x \neq 0$, let $\spadesuit \, x$ be defined by $\spadesuit \, x = x - \dfrac{1}{x}$

1. -3 $\spadesuit \, (-3)$

---

2. If $r \heartsuit s = r(r - s)$ for all integers r and s, then $4 \heartsuit (3 \heartsuit 5)$ equals

   (A) -8

   (B) -2

   (C) 2

   (D) 20

   (E) 40

Questions 3–4 refer to the following definition:

$$c \bigstar d = \frac{c - d}{c}, \text{ where } c \neq 0$$

3. $12 \bigstar 3 =$

   (A) -3

   (B) $\dfrac{1}{4}$

   (C) $\dfrac{2}{3}$

   (D) $\dfrac{3}{4}$

   (E) 3

4. If $9 \bigstar 4 = 15 \bigstar k$, then $k =$

   (A) 3

   (B) 6

   (C) $\dfrac{20}{3}$

   (D) $\dfrac{25}{3}$

   (E) 9

Solutions

1. (B) Plug in -3 for x: $\spadesuit x = -3 - \frac{1}{-3} = -3 + \frac{1}{3} = -2\frac{2}{3}$, which is greater than -3 in Column A.

2. (E) Start in the parentheses and work out: $(3 \heartsuit 5) = 3(3-5) = 3(-2) = -6$; $4 \heartsuit (-6) = 4[4 - (-6)] = 4(10) = 40$.

3. (D) Plug in 12 for c and 3 for d: $12 \star 3 = \frac{12-3}{12} = \frac{9}{12} = \frac{3}{4}$.

4. (C) Plug in on both sides of the equation:

$$\frac{9-4}{9} = \frac{15-k}{15}$$

$$\frac{5}{9} = \frac{15-k}{15}$$

Cross-multiply and solve for k:

$$75 = 135 - 9k$$

$$-60 = -9k$$

$$\frac{-60}{-9} = k$$

$$\frac{20}{3} = k$$

The Kaplan Approach to Special Triangles

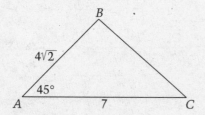

In the triangle above, what is the length of side *BC* ?

- (A) 4
- (B) 5
- (C) 4 √2
- (D) 6
- (E) 5 √2

   Special triangles contain a lot of information. For instance, if you know the length of one side of a 30-60-90 triangle, you can easily work out the lengths of the others. Special triangles allow you to transfer one piece of information around the whole figure.

   The following are the special triangles you should look for on the GRE.

Equilateral Triangles
All interior angles are 60° and all sides are of the same length.

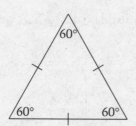

Isosceles Triangles
Two sides are of the same length and the angles facing these sides are equal.

Right Triangles
Contain a 90° angle. The sides are related by the Pythagorean theorem. $a^2 + b^2 = c^2$ where a and b are the legs and c is the hypotenuse.

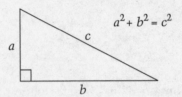

The "Special" Right Triangles
Many triangle problems contain "special" right triangles, whose side lengths always come in predictable ratios. If you recognize them, you won't have to use the Pythagorean theorem to find the value of a missing side length.

The 3-4-5 Right Triangle
(Be on the lookout for multiples of 3-4-5 as well.)

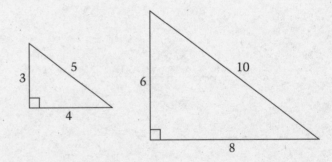

KAPLAN

The Isosceles Right Triangle
(Note the side ratio: 1 to 1 to $\sqrt{2}$.)

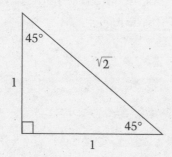

The 30-60-90 Right Triangle
(Note the side ratio: 1 to $\sqrt{3}$ to 2, and which side is opposite which angle.)

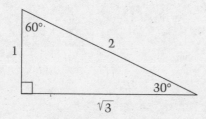

Getting back to our example, you can drop a vertical line from *B* to line *AC*. This divides the triangle into two right triangles.

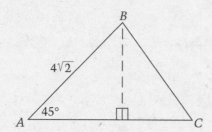

That means you know two of the angles in the triangle on the left: 90° and 45°. So this is an isosceles right triangle, with sides in the ratio of 1 to 1 to $\sqrt{2}$. The hypotenuse here is $4\sqrt{2}$, so both legs have length 4. Filling this in, you have:

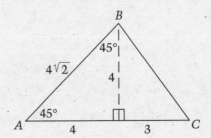

Now you can see that the legs of the smaller triangle on the right must be 4 and 3, making this a 3-4-5 right triangle, and the length of hypotenuse *BC* is 5.

Practice Problems

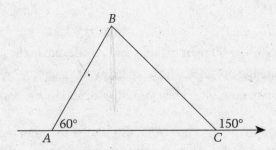

1. In triangle *ABC*, if *AB* = 4, then *AC* =

A 10

B 9

C 8

D 7

E 6

Column A   Column B

In the coordinate plane, point *R* has coordinates (0,0) and point *S* has coordinates (9,12).

2. The distance from *R* to *S*   16

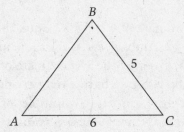

3. If the perimeter of triangle *ABC* above is 16, what is its area?

A 8

B 9

C 10

D 12

E 15

Solutions

1. (C) Angle *BCA* is supplementary to the angle marked 150°, so angle *BCA* = 180° − 150° = 30°. Since the interior angles of a triangle sum to 180°, angle *A* + angle *B* + angle *BCA* = 180°, so angle *B* = 180° − 60° − 30° = 90°. So triangle *ABC* is a 30-60-90 right triangle, and its sides are in the ratio 1: $\sqrt{3}$: 2. The side opposite the 30°, *AB*, which we know has length 4, must be half the length of the hypotenuse, *AC*. Therefore *AC* = 8, and that's answer choice (C).

2. (B) Draw a diagram. Since *RS* isn't parallel to either axis, the way to compute its length is to create a right triangle with legs that are parallel to the axes, so their lengths are easy to find. We can then use the Pythagorean theorem to find the length of *RS*.

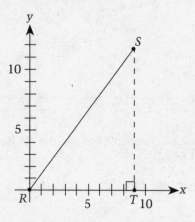

Since *S* has a *y*-coordinate of 12, it's 12 units above the *x*-axis, so the length of *ST* must be 12. And since *T* is the same number of units to the right of the *y*-axis as *S*, given by the *x*-coordinate of 9, the distance from the origin to *T* must be 9. So we have a right triangle with legs of 9 and 12. You should recognize this as a multiple of the 3-4-5 triangle. 9 = 3 × 3; 12 = 3 × 4; so the hypotenuse *RS* must be 3 × 5, or 15. That's the value of Column A, so Column B is greater.

3. (D) To find the area you need to know the base and height. If the perimeter is 16, then *AB* + *BC* + *AC* = 16; that is, *AB* = 16 − 5 − 6 = 5. Since *AB* = *BC*, this is an isosceles triangle. If you drop a line from vertex *B* perpendicular to *AC*, it will divide the base in half. This divides the triangle up into two smaller right triangles:

KAPLAN

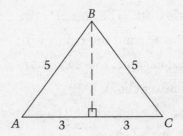

These right triangles each have one leg of 3 and a hypotenuse of 5; therefore they are 3-4-5 right triangles. So the missing leg (which is also the height of triangle *ABC*) must have length 4. We now know that the base of *ABC* is 6 and the height is 4, so the area is $\frac{1}{2} \times 6 \times 4$, or 12, answer choice (D).

The Kaplan Approach to Multiple and Oddball Figures

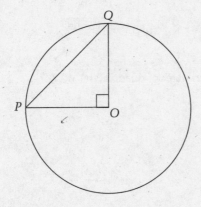

Kaplan Tip

Look for pieces the figures have in common.

In the figure above, if the area of the circle with center *O* is 9π, what is the area of triangle *POQ*?

    Ⓐ 4.5

    Ⓑ 6

    Ⓒ 3.5π

    Ⓓ 4.5π

    Ⓔ 9

In a problem that combines figures, you have to look for the relationship between the figures. For instance, if two figures share a side, information about that side will probably be the key.

In this case the figures don't share a side, but the triangle's legs are important features of the circle—they are radii. You can see that $OP = OQ$ = the radius of circle *O*.

The area of the circle is 9π. The area of a circle is πr^2, where r is the radius. So $9\pi = \pi r^2$, $9 = r^2$, and the radius r is 3. The area of a triangle is $\frac{1}{2}$ base times height. Therefore, the area of ΔPOQ is $\frac{1}{2}$ (leg$_1$ $\times$ leg$_2$) = $\frac{1}{2}$ (3 $\times$ 3) = $\frac{9}{2}$ = 4.5, answer choice (A).

But what if, instead of a number of familiar shapes, you are given something like this?

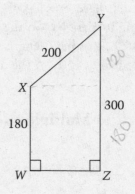

What is the perimeter of quadrilateral *WXYZ*?

    (A)   680

    (B)   760

    (C)   840

    (D)   920

    (E)   1,000

Try breaking the unfamiliar shape into familiar ones. Once this is done, you can use the same techniques that you would for multiple figures. Perimeter is the sum of the lengths of the sides of a figure, so you need to find the length of *WZ*. Drawing a perpendicular line from point *X* to side *YZ* will divide the figure into a right triangle and a rectangle. Call the point of intersection *A*.

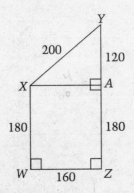

Opposite sides of a rectangle have equal length, so $WZ = XA$ and $WX = ZA$. WX is labeled as 180, so $ZA = 180$. Since YZ measures 300, AY is $300 - 180 = 120$. In right triangle XYA, hypotenuse $XY = 200$ and leg $AY = 120$; you should recognize this as a multiple of a 3-4-5 right triangle. The hypotenuse is 5×40, one leg is 3×40, so XA must be 4×40 or 160. (If you didn't recognize this special right triangle you could have used the Pythagorean theorem to find the length of XA.) Since $WZ = XA = 160$, the perimeter of the figure is $180 + 200 + 300 + 160 = 840$, answer choice (C).

Practice Problems

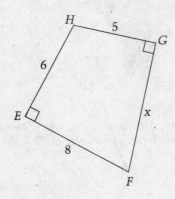

1. What is the value of x in the figure above?

    Ⓐ 4
    Ⓑ $3\sqrt{3}$
    Ⓒ $3\sqrt{5}$
    Ⓓ $5\sqrt{3}$
    Ⓔ 9

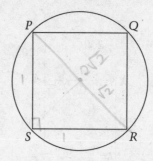

2. In the figure above, square *PQRS* is inscribed in a circle. If the area of square *PQRS* is 4, what is the radius of the circle?

   (A) 1

   (B) $\sqrt{2}$

   (C) 2

   (D) $2\sqrt{2}$

   (E) $4\sqrt{2}$

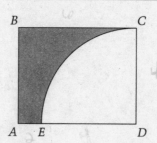

3. In the figure above, the quarter circle with center *D* has a radius of 4 and rectangle *ABCD* has a perimeter of 20. What is the perimeter of the shaded region?

   (A) $20 - 8\pi$

   (B) $10 + 2\pi$

   (C) $12 + 2\pi$

   (D) $12 + 4\pi$

   (E) $4 + 8\pi$

Solutions

1. (D) Draw a straight line from point *H* to point *F*, to divide the figure into two right triangles.

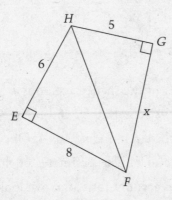

ΔEFH is a 3-4-5 right triangle with a hypotenuse of length 10. Use the Pythagorean theorem in ΔFGH to find *x*:

$$x^2 + 5^2 = 10^2$$
$$x^2 + 5^2 = 100$$
$$x^2 = 75$$
$$x = \sqrt{75}$$
$$x = \sqrt{25}\sqrt{3}$$
$$x = 5\sqrt{3}$$

2. (B) Draw in diagonal *QS* and you will notice that it is also a diameter of the circle. Since the area of the square is 4 its sides must each be 2. The diagonal of a square is always the length of a side times $\sqrt{2}$.

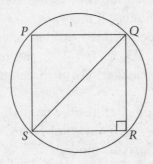

Think of the diagonal as dividing the square into two isosceles right triangles. Therefore, the diagonal = $2\sqrt{2}$ = the diameter; the radius is half this amount or $\sqrt{2}$.

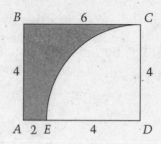

3. (C) The perimeter of the shaded region is $BC + AB + AE +$ arc EC. The quarter circle has its center at D, and point C lies on the circle, so side DC is a radius of the circle and equals 4. Opposite sides of a rectangle are equal so AB is also 4. The perimeter of the rectangle is 20, and since the two short sides account for 8, the two longer sides must account for 12, making BC and AD each 6. To find AE, subtract the length of ED, another radius of length 4, from the length of AD, which is 6; $AE = 2$. Since arc EC is a quarter circle, the length of the arc EC is $\frac{1}{4}$ of the circumference of a whole circle with radius 4: $\frac{1}{4} \times 2\pi r = \frac{1}{4} \times 8\pi = 2\pi$. So the perimeter of the shaded region is $6 + 4 + 2 + 2\pi = 12 + 2\pi$.

Mean, Median, Mode, and Range

The GRE has always tested the concept of a mean, which is also called the arithmetic mean, for no good reason. The mean of several numbers is simply their average. Whenever you see *arithmetic mean* on the GRE, it's not a trick—it just means *average*.

The median of several terms is the number that evenly divides the terms into two groups; half of the terms are larger than the median and half of the terms are smaller than the median. If there is an odd number of terms, the median will be the same as the middle number (not necessarily the average or the mode). If there are an even number of terms, the median will be halfway between the two terms closest to the middle.

For the set {4, 5, 7, 23, 5, 67, 10}, the median is 7, since this divides the set into two smaller sets of three terms each, {4, 5, 5} and {10, 23, 67}.

The mode is even simpler. It's just the term with the most occurrences in a set of numbers. If two or more numbers are tied for the most occurrences, then each is considered a mode.

For the set {4, 5, 7, 23, 5, 67, 10}, the mode is 5, because it occurs the greatest number of times of any of the terms.

Definition

Mean is the average of a set of numbers.

Median is the "middle" value in a set of numbers that have been arranged from smallest to greatest. In an odd-numbered set, it's simply the middle term; in an even-numbered set, it's the value halfway between the two terms closest to the middle.

Mode is the term that occurs the most in a set of numbers.

The range is the simplest of these four concepts. It's just the difference between the largest term and the smallest term in a set of numbers. Just subtract the smallest from the biggest and you will have the range.

For the set {4, 5, 7, 23, 5, 67, 10}, the range is 63, because the greatest number, 67, minus the smallest, 4, equals 63.

Practice Problems

Column A	Column B
1. The median of the integers from 1 through 31, inclusive.	16

2. 2^6	The range of the series {8, 9, 9, 15, 71}

3. The only test scores for the students in a certain class are 44, 30, 42, 30, x, 44, and 30. If x equals one of the other scores and is a multiple of 5, what is the mode for the class?

(A) 5
(B) 6
(C) 15
(D) 30
(E) 44

4. If half the range of the increasing series {11, A, 23, B, C, 68, 73} is equal to its median, what is the median of the series?

(A) 23
(B) 31
(C) 33
(D) 41
(E) 62

Solutions

1. (C) *Inclusive* just means you should include the numbers on the ends—in this case, 1 and 31. The number right in the middle of this series is 16. There are 15 numbers smaller than it and 15 numbers greater than it.

2. (A) 2^6 equals 64. The range of the series in Column B equals $71 - 8$, which equals 63.

3. (D) Since x equals one of the other scores, it must equal either 30, 42, or 44. And since it must also be a multiple of 5, we can conclude that x equals 30. That means that four of the students—more than earned any other score—earned a score of 30, which makes 30 the mode.

4. (B) Don't get confused by all the variables; just concentrate on what you know. The range must be the difference of the smallest term and the largest term. Since this is an increasing series, the smallest term must be 11 and the largest must be 73. The difference between them is 62, so that's the range. Half of the range, then, is 31, so 31 must equal the median of the series.

Probability

A probability is the fractional likelihood of an event occurring. It can be represented by a fraction ("the probability of it raining today is $\frac{1}{2}$"), a ratio ("the odds of it raining today are 50:50"), or a percent ("the probability of rain today is 50 percent"). You can translate probabilities easily into everyday language: $\frac{1}{100}$ = "one chance in a hundred" or "the odds are one in a hundred."

To find probabilities, count the number of desired outcomes and divide by the number of possible outcomes.

Probability = (Number of Desired Outcomes/Number of Possible Outcomes)

For example, what is the probability of throwing a 5 on a six-sided die? There is one desired outcome—throwing a 5. There are six possible outcomes—one for each side of the die. So the probability = $\frac{1}{6}$.

Definition

A **probability** is the fractional likelihood that a given event will occur. To get a probability, divide the number of desired events by the number of possible events.

All probabilities are between 0 and 1 inclusive. A 0 probability means there is zero chance of an event occurring (i.e., it can't happen). A 1 probability means that an event has a 100 percent chance of occurring (i.e., it must occur). The higher the probability, the greater chance that an event will occur. You can often eliminate answer choices by having some idea where the probability of an event occurring falls within this range.

The odds of throwing a 5 on a die are $\frac{1}{6}$, so the odds of not throwing a 5 are $\frac{5}{6}$. Therefore, you have a much greater probability of not throwing a 5 on a die than of throwing a 5.

Practice Problems

<u>Column A</u>   <u>Column B</u>

The probability of rain on Thursday is 50 percent. The probability that it will not rain on Friday is $\frac{1}{4}$.

1. The probability of rain on Thursday   The probability of rain on Friday

---

A hat contains an equal number of red, blue, and green marbles.

2. The probability of picking a red marble out of the hat   The probability of picking a green marble out of the hat

---

3. If there are 14 women and 10 men employed in a certain office, what is the probability that one employee picked at random will be a woman?

(A) $\frac{1}{6}$

(B) $\frac{1}{14}$

(C) $\frac{7}{12}$

(D) 1

(E) $\frac{7}{5}$

4. If Tom flips a fair coin twice, what is the probability that at least one head will be thrown?

(A) $\frac{1}{4}$

(B) $\frac{1}{3}$

(C) $\frac{1}{2}$

(D) $\frac{2}{3}$

(E) $\frac{3}{4}$

Solutions

1. (B) The probability of rain on Thursday is $\frac{1}{2}$ and the probability of rain on Friday is $\frac{3}{4}$.

2. (C) The number of desired outcomes is the same in each case, since there are an equal number of red and green marbles. The number of possible outcomes in each case is also the same, since the marbles are all being pulled from the same hat. Therefore the probabilities are the same.

3. (C) Probability = (Number of Desired Outcomes/Number of Possible Outcomes) = (Number of Women/Number of People) = $\frac{14}{24} = \frac{7}{12}$.

4. (E) Desired outcomes = HH or HT or TH. Possible outcomes = HH or HT or TH or TT. Probability = $\frac{3}{4}$.

Graphs

In the GRE math section, you are likely to get four questions that will be based on one or more graphs. Exactly what ETS is trying to test with these questions we have never been able to determine, unless you need to sharpen your clerical skills before you pursue that Ph.D. in electrical engineering.

The Basic Principles of Graphs

Some Will Be Fairly Basic
You will have to do something like find a value from the graph(s) or compare values in the graph(s). They will take only a few steps.

Others Will Be Fairly Difficult
They always require more than just a few steps. They may fool you into thinking that they're easy, but there will be a trick involved. Never, ever pick the obvious answer without checking it first.

The Kaplan Method for Graphs
We recommend the following method for graph problems:

1. Familiarize Yourself with the Graph(s)
Graphs often come in pairs, so get to know the graphs before you tackle the questions.

- Read the title(s).
- Check the scales to see how the information is measured.
- Read any accompanying notes.
- If there are multiple bars or lines on the graph, make sure to refer to the key that explains the distinctions between them.

2. Answer the Questions That Follow
Graph questions require a strong understanding of fractions and percents and good attention to detail, but little else.

Graph questions come in sets consisting of one or more graphs accompanied by several questions. You are likely to see either two sets, each accompanied by two questions, or one such set accompanied by four questions. In either case, it's helpful to realize that late questions tend to be trickier than early questions. For instance, when the set contains two graphs, the first question is likely to refer to just one graph, whereas a late question will require you to take data from both graphs and combine this information to answer the question. If you haven't used both graphs for this late question, you're almost certain to get it wrong.

Kaplan Rules

The Kaplan method for graph problems:

1. Familiarize yourself with the graph(s).
2. Answer the questions that follow.
3. Approximate wherever possible.

Kaplan Tip

The most common trick in graph questions is to confuse you with the difference between an actual value (a fixed number) and a relative value (a fraction or percent). Make sure you always know which one you're working with.

3. Approximate Wherever Possible

No matter how hard they may appear at first glance, graph questions can usually be made easier if you take advantage of the large spread that is typically found among the quantities in the answer choices—by approximating rather than calculating wherever possible. Since graph questions generally take more time to solve than other GRE math questions, if you are not gunning for a super high quantitative score you may want to consider, if you are running into time trouble, guessing and moving on when you encounter a hard graph question.

Practice Problems

Questions 1–5 are based on the following graphs.

MEGACORP, INC.
REVENUE AND PROFIT DISTRIBUTION FOR FOOD- AND NONFOOD-RELATED OPERATIONS, 1984–1989

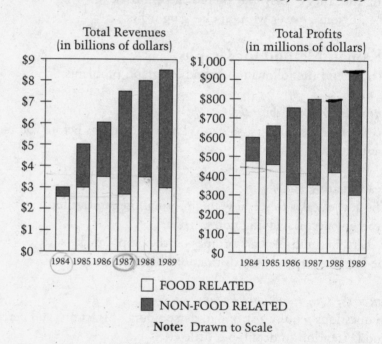

Note: Drawn to Scale

PERCENT OF REVENUES FROM FOOD-RELATED OPERATIONS IN 1989 BY CATEGORY

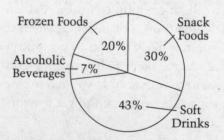

KAPLAN

1. Approximately how much did total revenues increase from 1984 to 1987?

   (A) $0.5 billion
   (B) $1.5 billion
   (C) $4.0 billion
   (D) $4.5 billion
   (E) $5.0 billion

2. For the year in which profits from food-related operations increased over the previous year, *total revenues* were approximately

   (A) $3.5 billion
   (B) $4.5 billion
   (C) $5.7 billion
   (D) $6.0 billion
   (E) $8.0 billion

3. In 1988, total profits represented approximately what percent of Megacorp's total revenues?

   (A) 50%
   (B) 20%
   (C) 10%
   (D) 5%
   (E) 1%

4. For the first year in which revenues from nonfood-related operations surpassed $4.5 billion, total profits were approximately

   (A) $250 million
   (B) $450 million
   (C) $550 million
   (D) $650 million
   (E) $800 million

5. In 1989, approximately how many millions of dollars were revenues from frozen food operations?

   (A) 1,700
   (B) 1,100
   (C) 900
   (D) 600
   (E) 450

Solutions

   1. (D) This question asks about total revenues, so you should refer to the left bar graph. The trickiest part is making sure you correctly extract information from the appropriate bars, in this case for 1984 and 1987. Total revenues for 1984 appear to be $3 million and for 1987 they appear to be about $7.5 million (if you're ever having trouble getting a fix on a quantity on a bar graph, place the edge of a piece of paper along the top of the bar to read the scale better). So the increase is roughly $7.5 billion – $3 million = $4.5 billion.

2. (E) The wording is somewhat tricky here, and you have to refer to both bar graphs. First you have to refer to the right bar graph to find the lone year in which food-related profits increased over the previous year—the only year in which the unshaded portion of the bar goes up is 1988. Now that you've zeroed in on the year, you must refer to the left bar graph to determine the total *revenues* for that year, which appear to be about $8.0 billion.

3. (C) This is percent question, so first you have to extract the information from the bar graphs. From the right bar graph, the total profits for 1988 appear to be $800 million; from the left bar graph, total revenues for that year appear to be $8.0 billion (i.e., $8,000 million). Now you just have to convert the part/whole into a percent: $\frac{800 \text{ million}}{8,000 \text{ million}} = \frac{1}{10} = 10\%$.

4. (E) First you have to find the year for which revenues from nonfood-related operations surpassed $4.5 billion, so refer to the left bar graph. Finding the correct bar is made more difficult by the fact that you have to deal with the shaded portion, which is not grounded at $0. So you may want to make a ruler from a sheet of paper, using the scale to mark off the length represented by $4.5 billion, and using this to locate the appropriate bar. You should then be able to see that 1987 is the year in question. The question asks for total *profits*, so once again refer to the right bar graph and you'll see the profits for that year are around $800 million.

5. (D) Finally you have a question that refers to the pie chart. You are asked about revenues from frozen food operations, and the pie chart informs you that frozen foods represent 20 percent of all food-related revenues for 1989. To convert this into an amount you need to locate the amount of food-related revenues for 1989, so once again refer to the left bar graph where you'll find the food-related revenues in 1989 were about $3 billion, or $3,000 million. 20 percent of $3,000 million is $600 million.

By using all of the techniques discussed above, you will be able to tackle the most difficult Quantitative questions. (You can brush up on all of your math by referring to the Math Reference Appendix in the back of this book.) And now that you have the tools to handle the Quantitative section of the GRE, try the following set of practice questions. After that, we'll move on and take a look at the Analytical section of the test.

Quantitative Practice Set

Numbers

All numbers are real numbers.

Figures

The position of points, lines, angles, etcetera, may be assumed to be in the order shown; all lengths and angle measures may be assumed to be positive.

Lines shown as straight may be assumed to be straight.

Figures lie in the plane of the paper unless otherwise stated.

Figures that accompany questions are intended to provide useful information. However, unless a note states that a figure has been drawn to scale, you should solve the problems by using your knowledge of mathematics, and not by estimation or measurement.

Directions

Each of the Questions 1–17 below consists of two quantities, one in Column A and another in Column B. You are to compare the two quantities and answer

- Ⓐ if the quantity in Column A is greater
- Ⓑ if the quantity in Column B is greater
- Ⓒ if the two quantities are equal
- Ⓓ if the relationship cannot be determined from the information given

Common Information

In a question, information concerning one or both of the quantities to be compared is centered above the two columns. A symbol that appears in both columns represents the same thing in Column A as it does in Column B. (Answers and explanations can be found at the end of the set of questions.)

	Column A	Column B
1.	$\frac{1}{3} + \frac{1}{3}$	$\frac{1}{3} \times \frac{1}{3}$

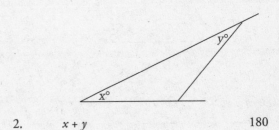

	Column A	Column B
2.	$x + y$	180
3.	16 percent of 30	15 percent of 31

$$x^5 = -32$$

	Column A	Column B
4.	x^3	$2x^2$

$$x < y < z$$
$$0 < z$$

	Column A	Column B
5.	x	0

$$6(10)^n > 60{,}006$$

	Column A	Column B
6.	n	6

In a three-digit positive integer y, the hundreds' digit is three times the units' digit.

	Column A	Column B
7.	The units' digit of y	4
8.	The perimeter of a square with side 4	The circumference of a circle with diameter 5

Column A	Column B	Column A	Column B

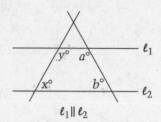

$\ell_1 \parallel \ell_2$

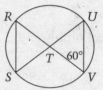

The circle has center T. The measure of angle TVU is 60°.

9. $2(x + y)$ $x + a + y + b$

15. RT RS

$$\frac{2x}{3} = \frac{2y}{5} = \frac{2z}{7}$$

z is positive.

After five adults leave a party, there are three times as many children as adults. After a further 25 children leave the party, there are twice as many adults as children.

10. $x + y$ z

16. The original number   14
of adults

The product of two integers is 10.

11. The average (arithmetic   3
mean) of the two integers

There are at least 200 apples in a grocery store. The ratio of the number of oranges to the number of apples is 9 to 10.

17. The number of oranges   200
in the store

$n > 0$.
The remainder when n is divided by 3 is 1, and the remainder when $n + 1$ is divided by 2 is 1.

12. The remainder when $n - 1$ 3
is divided by 6

The average (arithmetic mean) bowling score of n bowlers is 160. The average of these n scores together with a score of 170 is 161.

13. n 10

14. $7^5 + 7^6$ 8×7^5

18. How many odd integers are between $\frac{10}{3}$ and $\frac{62}{3}$?

Ⓐ 19
Ⓑ 18
Ⓒ 10
Ⓓ 9
Ⓔ 8

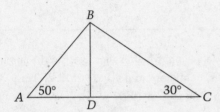

19. In the figure above, if BD bisects $\angle ABC$, then the measure of $\angle BDC$ is

Ⓐ 50°
Ⓑ 90°
Ⓒ 100°
Ⓓ 110°
Ⓔ 120°

20. If $d = \frac{c-b}{a-b}$, then $b =$

Ⓐ $\frac{c-d}{a-d}$
Ⓑ $\frac{c+d}{a+d}$
Ⓒ $\frac{ca-d}{ca+d}$
Ⓓ $\frac{c-ad}{1-d}$
Ⓔ $\frac{c+ad}{d-1}$

21. If $x > 0$, then $(4^x)(8^x) =$

Ⓐ 2^{9x}
Ⓑ 2^{8x}
Ⓒ 2^{6x}
Ⓓ 2^{5x}
Ⓔ 2^{4x}

22. In one class in a school, 30 percent of the students are boys. In a second class that is half the size of the first, 40 percent of the students are boys. What percent of both classes are boys?

Ⓐ 20%
Ⓑ 25%
Ⓒ 28%
Ⓓ 30%
Ⓔ $33\frac{1}{3}$%

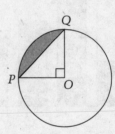

23. In a circle O above, if $\triangle POQ$ is a right triangle and radius OP is 2, what is the area of the shaded region?

Ⓐ $4\pi - 2$
Ⓑ $4\pi - 4$
Ⓒ $2\pi - 2$
Ⓓ $2\pi - 4$
Ⓔ $\pi - 2$

24. If $n = 14 \times 22 \times 39$, which of the following is NOT an integer?

    Ⓐ $\dfrac{n}{21}$

    Ⓑ $\dfrac{n}{24}$

    Ⓒ $\dfrac{n}{26}$

    Ⓓ $\dfrac{n}{42}$

    Ⓔ $\dfrac{n}{77}$

Question 25–28 refer to the following graphs:

Team Revenues for 1997

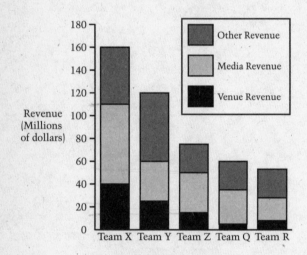

Percentages of Venue Revenues for Team X, 1997

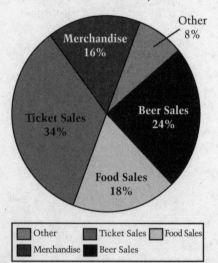

25. For the team with the median amount of venue revenue for 1997, media revenue represented approximately what percent of that team's total revenue for that year?

    Ⓐ 25%

    Ⓑ 30%

    Ⓒ 40%

    Ⓓ 55%

    Ⓔ 60%

26. Of the following, which is the closest to the amount of revenues, in millions of dollars, earned by Team X through food sales in 1997?

    Ⓐ 7

    Ⓑ 10

    Ⓒ 14

    Ⓓ 18

    Ⓔ 22

27. Ticket sales represented approximately what percent of total revenue for Team X in 1997?

    Ⓐ   4%

    Ⓑ   8%

    Ⓒ 13%

    Ⓓ 34%

    Ⓔ 54%

28. If Team Y earned a total revenue of $150 million in 1998, Team Y's total revenue increased by approximately what percent from 1997 to 1998?

    Ⓐ 20%

    Ⓑ 25%

    Ⓒ 30%

    Ⓓ 35%

    Ⓔ 40%

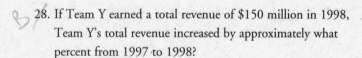

Answer Key

1. A	8. A	15. C	22. E
2. B	9. C	16. A	23. E
3. A	10. A	17. D	24. B
4. B	11. D	18. E	25. C
5. D	12. C	19. C	26. A
6. D	13. B	20. D	27. B
7. B	14. C	21. D	28. B

Explanations

Question 1

$\frac{1}{3} + \frac{1}{3}$ is $\frac{2}{3}$. $\frac{1}{3} \times \frac{1}{3} = \frac{1}{9}$. Since $\frac{2}{3} > \frac{1}{9}$, column A is larger.

Question 2

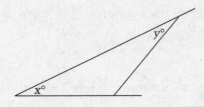

The sum of the three interior angles of a triangle is 180°. Since x and y are only two of the angles, their sum must be less than 180 degrees. Column B is greater.

Question 3

Sixteen percent of 30 is $\frac{16}{100}(30)$ or $\frac{(16)(30)}{100}$. Similarly, 15 percent of 31 is $\frac{15}{100}(31)$ or $\frac{(15)(31)}{100}$. We can ignore the denominator of 100 in both columns, and just compare $(16)(30)$ in Column A to $(15)(31)$ in column B. Divide both columns by 15; we're left with 31 in Column B and $(16)(2)$ or 32 in column A. Since $32 > 31$, Column A is larger.

Question 4

Start by working with the sign of x, and hope that you won't have to go any further than that. If x^5 is negative, then what is the sign of x? It must be negative—if x were positive, then any power of x would also be positive. Since x is negative, Column A, x^3, which is a negative number raised to an odd exponent, must also be negative. But what about column B? Whatever x is, x^2 must be positive (or zero, but we know that x can't be zero); therefore, the quantity in Column B must be positive. We have a positive number in column B and a negative number is column A; Column B must be greater.

Question 5

We could pick numbers here, or else just use logic. We know that z is positive, and that x and y are less than z. But does that mean that x or y must be negative? Not at all—they could be, but they could also be positive. For instance, suppose $x = 1$, $y = 2$, and $z = 3$. Then Column A would be larger. However, if $x = -1$, $y = 0$, and $z = 1$, then Column B would be larger. We need more information to determine the relationship between the columns.

Question 6

Divide both sides of the inequality by 6. We're left with $(10)^n > 10{,}001$. $10{,}001$ can also be written at $10^4 + 1$, so we know that $(10)^n > 10^4 + 1$. Therefore, the quantity in Column A, n, must be 5 or greater. Column B is 6; since n could be less than, equal to, or greater than 6, we need more information.

Question 7

Try to set the columns equal. Could be units' digit of *y* be 4? If it is, and the hundreds' digit is three times the units' digit, then the hundreds' digit must be . . . 12? That can't be right. A digit must be one of the integers 0 through 9; 12 isn't a digit. Therefore, 4 is too big to be the units' digit of *y*. We don't know what the units' digit of *y* is (and we don't care either), but we know that it must be less than 4. Column B is greater than Column A.

Question 8

The perimeter of a square with side 4 is 4(4) or 16. The circumference of a circle is the product of π and the diameter, so the circumference in Column B is 5π. Since π is approximately 3.14, $5(\pi)$ is approximately 5(3.14) or 15.70, which is less than 16. Column A is greater.

Question 9

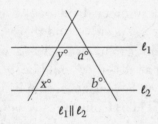

Column B is the sum of all the angles in the quadrilateral. The sum of the angles in any quadrilateral is 360 degrees. Column B is 360. In Column A, angle *x* and angle *y* are angles made when a transversal cuts a pair of parallel lines, in this case, ℓ_1 and ℓ_2. Such angles are either equal or supplementary. Angles *x* and *y* obviously aren't equal, so they must be supplementary, and their sum is 180. Then Column A is 2(*x* + *y*) = 2 × 180 or 360. The columns are equal.

Question 10

One way to work here is to pick numbers. Just make sure that anything you pick satisfies the requirements of the problem. How about picking *x* = 3, *y* = 5, and *z* = 7, since in the equation these numbers would cancel with their denominators, thus leaving us with the equation 2 = 2 = 2. Therefore, we know that these values satisfy the equation. In addition, if *z* = 7, then *z* is positive, so we have satisfied the other requirement as well. Then the sum of *x* and *y*, in Column A, is 3 + 5 or 8. This is larger than *z*, so in this case, Column A is larger. That's just one example though; we should really try another one. In fact, any other example we pick that fits the initial information will have Column A larger. To see why, we have to do a little messy work with the initial equations; on the test, you should just pick a couple of sample values, then go on to the next questions.

Start by dividing all of the equations through by 2, and multiply all of the terms through by 3 × 5 × 7, to eliminate all the fractions. This leaves us with:

$$35x = 21y = 15z$$

Now let's put everything in terms of *x*.

$$x = x \qquad y = \frac{35}{21}x = \frac{5}{3}x \qquad x = \frac{35}{15}x = \frac{7}{3}x$$

Then in Column A, the sum of *x* and *y* is $x + \frac{5}{3}x = \frac{8}{3}x$. In column B, the value of *z* is $\frac{7}{3}x$. Now since *z* is positive, *x* and *y* must also be positive. (If one of them is negative, that would make all of them negative.) Since *x* is positive, $\frac{8}{3}x > \frac{7}{3}x$. Column A is greater.

KAPLAN

The moral here is that proving that one column must be bigger can involve an awful lot of time on some GRE QC questions—more time than you can afford on the test. Try to come up with a good answer, but don't spend a lot of time proving it. Even if you end up showing that your original suspicion was wrong, it's not worth it if it took five minutes away from the rest of the problems.

Question 11

The best place to start here is with some pairs of integers that have a product of 10. The numbers 5 and 2 have a product of 10, as do 10 and 1, and the average of each of these pairs is greater than 3, so you may have thought that (A) was the correct answer. If so, you should have stopped yourself, saying, "That seems a little too easy for such a late QC question. They're usually trickier than that." In fact, this one was. There's nothing in the problem that limits the integers to positive numbers: they can just as easily be negative. The numbers –10 and –1 also have a product of 10, but their average is a negative number—in other words, less than Column B. We need more information here; the answer is (D).

Question 12

The best way to do this question is to pick numbers. First we have to figure out what kind of number we want. Since $n + 1$ leaves a remainder of 1 when it's divided by 2, we know that $n + 1$ must be an odd number. Then n itself is an even number. We're told that n leaves a remainder of 1 when it's divided by 3. Therefore, n must be 1 more than a multiple of 3, or $n - 1$ is a multiple of 3. So what are we looking for? We've figured out that n should be an even number, that's one more than a multiple of 3. So let's pick a number now. How about 10 ? That's even, and it's one more than a multiple of 3. Then what's the remainder when we divide $n - 1$, or $10 - 1 = 9$, by 6? We're left with a remainder of 3: 6 divides into 9 one time, with 3 left over. In this case, the columns are equal.

Now since this a QC question and there's always a possibility that we'll get a different result if we pick a different number, we should either pick another case, or else use logic to convince ourselves that the columns will always be equal. Let's do the latter here. Since n is even, $n - 1$ must be odd. We saw before that $n - 1$ is a multiple of 3, so we now know that it is an odd multiple of 3. Does this tell us anything about $n - 1$'s relation to 6? Yes, it does: $n - 1$ is 3 multiplied by an odd number m, which can be written as $2p + 1$ where p is an integer. So $n - 1 = 3(2p + 1) = 6p + 3$. $6p$ is a multiple of 6, so the remainder when $n - 1$ is divided by 6 must be 3. The answer is (C).

Question 13

A quick way to analyze a problem such as this one is to realize that the additional bowler with a score of 170 is raising everyone else's average by one point from 160 to 161. Her score is 161 + 9, so she has 9 extra points that she can distribute to the remaining bowlers by which to raise their scores. Therefore, she can raise the average score of exactly 9 other bowlers from 160 to 161, so $n = 9$ and Column B is greater.

Question 14

Remember, compare, don't calculate! But in order to compare, you need to put both columns into a similar form. Factoring 7^5 out of both terms in Column A will help you to do just that: $7^5 + 7^6 = 7^5(1 + 7) = 7^5 \times 8 = 8 \times 7^5$. So the two quantities are equal.

Question 15

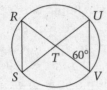

There are many steps involved with this problem, but none of them is too complicated. The circle has its center at point *T*. To start with the triangle at the right, its vertices are at *T* and two points on the circumference of the circle. This makes two of its sides radii of the circle. Since all radii must have equal length, this makes the triangle an isosceles triangle. In addition, we're told one of the base angles of this triangle has measure 60°. Then the other base angle must also have measure 60° (since the base angles in an isosceles triangle have equal measure). Then the sum of the two base angles is 120°, leaving 180 − 120 or 60° for the other angle, the one at point *T*.

Now, ∠*RTS* is opposite this 60° angle; therefore, its measure must also be 60°. △*RST* is another isosceles triangle; since ∠*RTS* has measure 60°, the other two angles in the triangle must also measure 60°. So what we have in the diagram is two equilateral triangles. *RT* and *RS* are two sides in one of these triangles; therefore, they must be of equal length, and the two columns are equal.

Question 16

Start by setting the columns equal. Suppose there were originally 14 adults at the party. Then after five of them leave, there are 14 − 5 or nine adults left. There are three times as many children as adults, so there are 3 × 9 or 27 children. Then 25 children leave the party, so there are 27 − 25 or two children left. So nine adults and two children remain at this party. Is that twice as many adults as children? No, it is more than four times as many, So this clearly indicates that the columns can't be equal—but does it mean that Column A is bigger or Column B is

bigger? Probably the simplest way to decide is to pick another number for the original number of adults, and see whether the ratio gets better or worse. Suppose we start with 13 adults. After five adults leave, there are 13 − 5 or eight adults. Multiplying 3 times 8 gives 24 children. Now if 25 children leave, we're left with 24 − 25 or −1 children. But that's no good; how can you have a negative number of children? This means we've gone the wrong way; our ratio has gotten worse instead of better. So 14 isn't right for the number of adults, and 13 is even worse, so the correct number must be something more than 14, and Column A is larger.

Question 17

We know that the ratio of oranges to apples is 9 to 10, and that there are "at least" 200 apples. The ratio tells us that there are more apples than oranges. How does that help us? Good question. It helps us because it tells us that there could be fewer than 200 oranges in the store. Could there be more than 200? Sure. If there were a lot more than 200 apples, say 600 apples, then there would be a lot more than 200 oranges. So we have one situation in which Column A is larger, and another case in which Column B is larger. We need more information to decide.

Question 18

Here we're asked for the odd integers between $\frac{10}{3}$ and $\frac{62}{3}$. First let's be clearer about this range. $\frac{10}{3}$ is the same as $3\frac{1}{3}$, and $\frac{62}{3}$ is the same as $20\frac{2}{3}$. So we need to count the odd integers between $3\frac{1}{3}$ and $20\frac{2}{3}$. We can't include 3, since 3 is less than $3\frac{1}{3}$. Similarly, we can't include 21, since it's larger than $20\frac{2}{3}$. So the odd integers in the appropriate range are 5, 7, 9, 11, 13, 15, 17, and 19. That's a total of 8.

Question 19

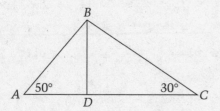

Notice that we're given the measures of two interior angles in $\triangle ABC$: $\angle BAC$ measures 50° and $\angle BCA$ measures 30°. Therefore, $\angle ABC$, the third interior angle in $\triangle ABC$, measures $180 - (50 + 30)$, or $180 - 80$, or 100°. Since BD bisects $\angle ABC$, BD splits up $\angle ABC$ into two smaller angles equal in measure, $\angle ABD$ and $\angle DBC$. Therefore, the measure of $\angle DBC$ is half the measure of $\angle ABC$, so $\angle DBC$ measures $\frac{1}{2}(100)$, or 50°. Now we can use this information along with the fact that $\angle BCD$ measures 30° to find $\angle BDC$. Since these three angles are interior angles of $\triangle BDC$, their measures sum to 180°. So $\angle BDC$ measures $180 - (50 + 30)$, or 100°.

Question 20

Solve for b in terms of a, c, and d.

$$d = \frac{c-b}{a-b}$$

Clear the denominator by
multiplying both sides by $a - b$. $\quad d(a - b) = c - b$
Multiply out parentheses. $\quad\quad\quad da - db = c - b$

Gather all bs on one side. $\quad\quad b - db = c - da$

Factor out the bs on the
left hand side. $\quad\quad\quad\quad b(1 - d) = c - da$

Divide both sides by $1 - d$ to isolate b. $\quad b = \frac{c - ad}{1 - d}$

Question 21

Remember the rules for operations with exponents. First you have to get both powers in terms of the same base so you can combine the exponents. Note that the answer choices all have base 2. Start by expressing 4 and 8 as powers of 2.

$$(4^x)(8^x) = (2^2)^x \times (2^3)^x$$

To raise a power to an exponent, multiply the exponents:

$$(2^2)^x = 2^{2x}$$
$$(2^3)^x = 2^{3x}$$

To multiply powers with the same base, add the exponents:

$$2^{2x} \times 2^{3x} = 2^{(2x + 3x)}$$
$$= 2^{5x}$$

Question 22

Pick a sample value for the size of one of the classes. The first class might have 100 students. That means there are 30 percent of 100 or 30 boys in the class. The second class is half the size of the first, so it has 50 students, of which 40 percent of $50 = 20$ are boys. This gives us $100 + 50 = 150$ students total, of whom

$30 + 20 = 50$ are boys. So $\frac{50}{150} = \frac{1}{3}$ of both classes are boys. Now convert $\frac{1}{3}$ to a percent. $\frac{1}{3} = \frac{1}{3} \times 100\% = 33\frac{1}{3}\%$.

Question 23

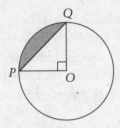

The area of the shaded region is the area of the quarter-circle (sector OPQ) minus the area of right triangle OPQ. The radius of circle O is 2, so the area of the quarter-circle is

$$\frac{1}{4}\pi r^2 = \frac{1}{4} \times \pi(2)^2 = \frac{1}{4} \times 4\pi = \pi$$

Each leg of the triangle is a radius of circle O, so the area of the triangle is

$$\frac{1}{2}bh = \frac{1}{2} \times 2 \times 2 = 2$$

Therefore, the area of the shaded region is $\pi - 2$.

Question 24

The easiest way to handle this type of question is to break n even further down into prime factors. Thus $n = 2 \times 7 \times 2 \times 11 \times 3 \times 13$. Now check out the answer choices:

(A) $\dfrac{n}{21} = \dfrac{2 \times 7 \times 2 \times 11 \times 3 \times 13}{3 \times 7} = 2 \times 2 \times 11 \times 13$

(B) $\dfrac{n}{24} = \dfrac{2 \times 7 \times 2 \times 11 \times 3 \times 13}{2 \times 2 \times 2 \times 3} = \dfrac{7 \times 11 \times 13}{2}$

(C) $\dfrac{n}{26} = \dfrac{2 \times 7 \times 2 \times 11 \times 3 \times 13}{2 \times 13} = 7 \times 2 \times 11 \times 3$

(D) $\dfrac{n}{42} = \dfrac{2 \times 7 \times 2 \times 11 \times 3 \times 13}{7 \times 3 \times 2} = 2 \times 11 \times 13$

(E) $\dfrac{n}{77} = \dfrac{2 \times 7 \times 2 \times 11 \times 3 \times 13}{7 \times 11} = 2 \times 2 \times 3 \times 13$

Only (B) is not an integer.

Question 25

Before you get started answering any graph question, begin by examining the graphs. Here you have two graphs, a segmented bar graph representing team revenue breakdowns for 5 teams, and a pie chart showing the distribution of venue revenues for Team X. You're now ready to attack the question, which asks you to find the team with the median revenue for 1997 and to determine what percent of that team's revenues are media revenue. This question must refer to the first graph, and the first part of question—finding the team with the "median" revenue—is a simple matter. "Median" refers to the number in the middle, and since here the bar graphs are arranged in ascending order, the question clearly refers to Team Z, the bar in the middle of the graph. The fastest approach to the answer here (and throughout graph questions generally) is to approximate. The downside to bar graphs is that it's often very hard to get a read on the values. The upside is that if you approximate, often you don't have to read the values. Here we need to determine what percent of the bar is represented by media revenue (the segment in the middle—always be especially careful to isolate the correct piece of data). By approximating, you should be able to see that the middle segment is more than a third and less than a half of the entire bar. Thus the correct answer has to be between 33% and 50%. The only answer that works is (C), 40%.

KAPLAN

Question 26

The trick to this question is that it involves *both* graphs. The question asks for the amount Team X earned through food sales, which takes us first to the pie chart, where we see that food sales accounted for 18% of the venue revenues for Team X. But to convert that to a dollar amount, we need a figure for the amount earned in venue revenues by Team X. According to the bar graph, this is somewhere around $40 million. Now we just have to take 18% of $40 million: $.18 \times 40 = 7.2$, so the closest answer is (A) 7.

Question 27

This question also involves both graphs, since you have to determine the percent of *total* team revenues represented by ticket sales. Beginning at the pie chart, you see that ticket sales represent 34% of the venue revenue for Team X. But venue revenue represents only one portion of the total team revenue, so (D), 34%, is out, as well as (E), since the answer must be less than 34%. Next, examine the bar graph. We've already seen that venue revenue is approximately $40 million, it looks like total team revenue is approximately $160 million, so venue revenue represents about one quarter of the total team revenue. The easiest approach to the answer is to approximate by dividing 34% by 4, since ticket sales represent around 34% of one-quarter of the total team revenue. One-fourth of 34% is 8.5%, so the closest answer choice is choice (B), 8%.

Question 28

Percent change problems are extremely popular graph questions, and as long as you know how to set them up they're generally no problem. This question asks for the approximate percent increase in Team Y's total revenue from 1997 to 1998, so we need to figure out (roughly) the amount of increase, place that over the original (or smaller) amount, and then convert the fraction into a percent. We are given the total revenue for 1998 as $150 million, so we just need to locate the total revenue for 1997 from the bar graph. It looks to be approximately $120 million, so the amount of increase is $30 million, and the original (or smaller) amount is $120 million. Now let's apply our formula:

$$\text{Percent increase} = \frac{\$30\,\text{million}}{\$120\,\text{million}} \times 100\% = \frac{1}{4} \times 100\% = 25\%$$

So (B) is the answer.

CHAPTER FOUR

Test Content: Analytical Writing

HIGHLIGHTS

- Learn the Four Basic Principles and the Kaplan Method for GRE Writing
- Learn and practice Kaplan's 22 Principles for Effective Writing
- Practice writing and evaluating Issue and Argument essays

The ability to write clearly about complex subjects is an important part of graduate school. In October 1999, ETS introduced a standardized way for schools to evaluate a student's academic writing ability: a separate test called the Analytical Writing Assessment (AWA). Because this element was so successful, ETS decided to incorporate it into the GRE General Test.

What to Expect

The Analytical Writing section consists of two timed essay sections. The first is what ETS calls *Present Your Perspective on an Issue* (we'll just call it *the Issue essay*): You'll be shown two essay topics—each a sentence or paragraph that expresses an opinion on an issue of general interest. You must choose one of the two topics. You'll then have 45 minutes to plan and write an essay that communicates your own view on the issue. Whether your agree or disagree with the opinion on the screen is irrelevant: What matters is that you support your view with relevant examples and statements.

The second of the two writing tasks is *Analyze an Argument* (or *the Argument essay*). This time, you'll be shown a paragraph that argues a certain point. You will then be given 30 minutes to assess that argument's logic. As with the Issue essay, it won't matter whether you agree with what

Note

The mandatory Analytical Writing section is identical to the old, stand-alone Analytical Writing Assessment: They contain the same tasks and are evaluated in the same way.

Note

ETS publishes a pool of potential topics for both the Issue essay and the Argument essay. To view this list online, visit www.gre.org/stuwrit.html.

you see on the screen. The test makers want you to critique the reasoning behind the argument, and not the argument itself.

How the Essays Are Administered

For the Analytical Writing section of the GRE General Test, the essay directions and prompts will be delivered on the computer and you'll have to word-process your essays. At the start of the section, you will be given a brief tutorial on how to use the word processor. Don't worry: Using the word processor for the Analytical Writing section is very simple, since the program was designed for people who might not be familiar with computers. The only functions you'll use are as follows: *insert text*, *delete text*, *cut and paste*, and *undo*. You'll be well acquainted with these commands by the time you start writing.

Holistic Scoring

Unlike the Verbal and Quantitative sections, the Analytical Writing section does not use computer scoring. Instead, the essays are read and scored by two trained readers who will have no knowledge of your identity. You'll receive your Analytical Writing score by mail within 10–15 days of the test administration.

Another difference: The Analytical Writing section is scored holistically. Holistic scoring uses a single letter or a number—on the GRE it's a number from 0 to 6—to provide an overall evaluation of an essay as a whole. A holistic score emphasizes the interrelation of different thinking and writing qualities in an essay (such as content, organization, or syntax) and tries to denote the unified effect that all of these elements combine to produce. Although the Analytical Writing section consists of two separate essays, a single score is reported, representing the average of your scores for the two essays.

While each of the two essay tasks requires a different type of response and so has a slightly different set of grading criteria, the following list will give you a general idea of the guidelines a GRE grader will have in mind when reading your essays.

Note

Because your essays need to be read and scored by real-live people, you will not receive your Analytical Writing score at the test center (though you'll still receive your unofficial Verbal and Quantitative scores at the test center). You will receive your Analytical Writing score by mail within 10–15 days of the test administration.

6: "Outstanding" Essay
- Insightfully presents and convincingly supports an opinion on the issue or a critique of the argument
- Ideas are very clear, well organized and logically connected
- Shows superior control of language: grammar, stylistic variety, and accepted conventions of writing; minor flaws may occur

5: **"Strong" Essay**
- Presents well-chosen examples and strongly supports an opinion on the issue or a critique of the argument
- Ideas are generally clear and well organized; connections are logical
- Shows solid control of language: grammar, stylistic variety, and accepted conventions of writing; minor flaws may occur

4: **"Adequate" Essay**
- Presents and adequately supports an opinion on the issue or a critique of the argument
- Ideas are fairly clear and adequately organized; logical connections are satisfactory
- Shows satisfactory control of language: grammar, stylistic variety, and accepted conventions of writing; some flaws may occur

3: **"Limited" Essay**
- Succeeds only partially in presenting and supporting an opinion on the issue or a critique of the argument
- Ideas may be unclear and poorly organized
- Shows less than satisfactory control of language: contains significant mistakes in grammar, usage, and sentence structure

2: **"Weak" Essay**
- Shows little success in presenting and supporting an opinion on the issue or a critique of the argument
- Ideas lack clarity and organization
- Meaning is impeded by many serious mistakes in grammar, usage, and sentence structure

1: **"Fundamentally Deficient" Essay**
- Fails to present a coherent opinion and/or evidence on the issue or a critique of the argument
- Ideas are seriously unclear and disorganized
- Lacks meaning due to widespread, severe mistakes in grammar, usage, and sentence structure

0: **"Unscorable" Essay**
- Completely ignores topic

Note

Your official Analytical Writing score represents the average of your two essay scores.

The Four Basic Principles of GRE Writing

GRE writing is a simple, two-stage process: First you decide what you want to say about a topic, and then you figure out how to say it. If your writing style isn't clear, your ideas won't come across, no matter how brilliant they are. Good GRE English is not only grammatical but also clear and concise, and by using some basic principles, you'll be able to express your ideas clearly and effectively in both of your essays.

1. Your Control of Language Is Important

Writing that is grammatical, concise, direct, and persuasive displays the "superior control of language" (as the test makers call it) that earns top GRE scores. To achieve effective GRE style in your essays, you should pay attention to the following points.

Grammar
Your writing must follow the rules of standard written English. If you're not confident of your mastery of grammar, brush up before the test.

Diction
Diction means word choice. For example, do you use the words *affect* and *effect* correctly? Be careful with such commonly confused words as *precede/proceed, principal/principle, whose/who's,* and *stationary/stationery.*

Syntax
Syntax refers to sentence structure. Do you construct your sentences so that your ideas are clear and understandable? Do you vary your sentence structure, sometimes using simple sentences and other times using sentences with clauses and phrases?

2. It's Better to Keep Things Simple

Perhaps the single most important thing to bear in mind when writing GRE essays is to keep everything simple. This rule applies to word choice, sentence structure, and organization. If you obsess about how to spell an unusual word, you can lose your flow of thought. The more complicated your sentences are, the more likely it is that they will be plagued by errors. The more complex your organization gets, the more likely it is that your argument will get bogged down in convoluted sentences that obscure your point. But keep in mind that simple does not mean simplistic. A clear, straightforward approach can still be sophisticated and convey perceptive insights.

3. Minor Grammatical Flaws Won't Torpedo Your Score

Many test takers mistakenly believe that they'll lose points because of a few mechanical errors such as misplaced commas, misspellings, or other

Kaplan Rules

The Basic Principles of GRE Writing:

1. Use language effectively.
2. Keep it simple.
3. Don't worry excessively about making minor errors.
4. Keep sight of your goal: to demonstrate that you can think logically and communicate clearly.

minor glitches. Occasional mistakes of this type will not dramatically affect your GRE essay score. In fact, the test makers' description of a top-scoring essay acknowledges that there may be minor grammatical flaws. The essay graders understand that you are writing first-draft essays. They will not be looking to take points off for minor errors, provided you don't make them consistently. However, if your essays are littered with mis-spellings and grammar mistakes, then the graders may conclude that you have a serious communication problem.

To write an effective essay, you must be concise, forceful, and correct. An effective essay wastes no words, makes its point in a clear, direct way, and conforms to the generally accepted rules of grammar and form.

4. Keep Sight of Your Goal

Remember, your goal isn't to become a prize-winning stylist; it's to write two solid essays that will convince admissions officers you can analyze and construct an argument and communicate your ideas to a reader. GRE essay graders don't expect rhetorical flourishes, but they do expect effective expression.

The Kaplan Five-Step Method for GRE Writing

Here's the deal: You have a limited amount of time to show the graduate school admissions people that you can think logically and express yourself in clearly written English. They don't care how many syllables you can cram into a sentence or how fancy your phrases are. They care that you're making sense. Whatever you do, don't try to hide beneath a lot of hefty words and abstractions. Just make sure that everything you say is clearly written and relevant to the topic. Get in there, state your main points, back them up, and get out.

1. **Take the Issue/Argument Apart**
    - Identify the topic (the broad subject), the scope (the specific aspect of the topic you'll be dealing with), and the conclusion (the main idea the author wanted to establish in the prompt).

    - Locate the evidence used to support the conclusion.

    - Look for assumptions (pieces of evidence that are not explicitly stated, but that must be true in order for the argument to hold water).

    - Note any terms that are ambiguous and need defining.

Kaplan Tip

The GRE graders will focus more on the analytical logic of your essays than on the spelling, grammar, or syntax. The mechanics of writing are weighed in their ratings only to the extent that these impede clarity of meaning.

2. **Select the Points You Will Make**
   - In the Issue essay, think of the arguments for both sides and make a decision as to which side you will support or the exact extent to which you agree with the stated position.
   - In the Argument essay, identify all the important gaps between the evidence and the conclusion. Think of remedies for the problems you discover.

3. **Organize Your Thoughts**
   - Outline what you want to say in.the introduction, in the middle paragraphs (one point per paragraph), and in your final paragraph.
   - Lead with your best arguments.
   - Think about how the essay as a whole will flow.

4. **Write Your Essay**
   - Start out and conclude with strong statements.
   - Be forceful.
   - Make transitions, link related ideas; it will help your writing flow.

5. **Proofread**
   - Save enough time to read through the entire essay.
   - Have a sense of the errors you are liable to make.

The Issue Essay

The Perspective on an Issue essay requires you to construct your own argument by making claims and providing evidence to support your position on a given issue.

The screen directions will ask you to take a position on the issue and instruct you to explain your position convincingly, using reasons or examples to back up your assertions.

The directions for the Issue essay will be similar to this:

Directions: You will have 45 minutes to plan and write an essay that communicates your perspective on a given topic. Choose one of the two topics provided. No other topics are admissible for this essay.

The topic is a short quotation that expresses an issue of general interest. Write an essay that agrees with, refutes, or qualifies the quotation, and support your opinion with relevant information drawn from your academic studies, reading, observation, or other experiences.

Teacher Tip

"Use your scratch paper to write a first draft of your opening sentence (starting strong is great!), and then outline the points you want to make in order. Good logical planning will impress every reader."
—Bob Verini
Los Angeles, California

KAPLAN

Feel free to consider the issue for a few minutes before you beginning your writing. Be certain that your ideas are fully developed and organized logically and make sure you have enough time left to review and revise what you've written.

The Issue Prompt

Expect a sentence or two that discuss a broad, general issue, sometimes presenting two competing points of view, sometimes only one. Either way, it will state an argument for which one or more counterarguments could be constructed. While the issue will be one upon which reasonable people could disagree, it will not bring up an emotionally charged religious or social issue.

In short, the topic will present a point of view. Your job is to form an opinion on the topic and make a case for that opinion.

The Issue topics you see may be similar to these:

The invention of gunpowder was the single most destructive achievement in history.

* * *

The main purpose of a college education should be to prepare oneself for a specific career.

* * *

The drawbacks to the use of nuclear power mean that it is not a long-term solution to the problem of meeting ever-increasing energy needs.

Applying the Kaplan Five-Step Method to the Issue Essay

Let's use the Kaplan Five-Step method on this sample Perspective on an Issue prompt:

The drawbacks to the use of nuclear power mean that it is not a long-term solution to the problem of meeting ever-increasing energy needs.

1. *Take the Issue Apart*
   Topic: Energy sources

   Scope: Whether or not nuclear power is a suitable replacement for other forms of energy

   Conclusion: Nuclear power is not a solution to the problem of meeting ever-increasing energy needs

   Evidence: Unnamed drawbacks

   Assumptions:
   - Nuclear power has the potential to meet long-term energy needs.
   - Nuclear power is not our only energy option.

At a Glance

The tasks in a Perspective on an Issue essay are to state your position on an issue and to defend your position with relevant support.

Kaplan Rules

The Kaplan Method for
Issue Essays:

1. Take the issue apart
2. Select a position
3. Organize your argument
4. Compose your essay
5. Proofread your work

2. Select the Points You Will Make

Your job, as stated in the directions, is to decide whether or not you agree and explain your decision. Some would argue that the use of nuclear power is too dangerous, while others would say that we can't afford not to use it. So which side do you take? Remember, this isn't about showing the admissions people what your deep-seated beliefs about the environment are—it's about showing that you can formulate an argument and write it down. Quickly think through the pros and cons of each side, and choose the side for which you have the most relevant things to say. For this topic, that process might go something like this:

Arguments for the use of nuclear power:
- Inexpensive compared to other forms of energy
- Fossil fuels will eventually be depleted
- Solar power still too problematic and expensive

Arguments against the use of nuclear power:
- Harmful to the environment
- Dangerous to mankind
- Safer alternatives already exist
- Better alternatives may lie undiscovered

Again, it doesn't matter which side you take. Let's say that in this case you decide to argue against nuclear power. Remember, the question is asking you to argue why the cons of nuclear power outweigh the pros—the inadequacy of this power source is the end you're arguing toward, so don't list it as a supporting argument.

3. Organize Your Argument

You've already begun to think out your arguments—that's why you picked the side you did in the first place. Now's the time to write them all out, including ones that weaken the opposing side.

Nuclear power is not a viable alternative to other sources of energy because:
- Radioactive, spent fuel has leaked from storage sites (too dangerous)
- Reactor accidents can be catastrophic—Three Mile Island, Chernobyl (too dangerous)
- More research into solar power will bring down its cost (weakens opposing argument)
- Solar-powered homes and cars already exist (alternatives proven viable)

- Renewable resources require money only for the materials needed to harvest them (alternatives are cheaper in the long run)
- Energy companies don't spend money on alternatives; no vested interest (better alternatives lie undiscovered)

4. Write Your Essay

Remember, open up with a general statement and then assert your position. From there, get down your main points.

Your essay for this assignment might look like one of the following sample essays. As a basis for comparison, we've included one outstanding essay that deserves a score of "6," and one adequate essay that deserves a score of "4." Think about the differences you find in these two essays, then read our own assessments.

Sample Issue Essay 1

Proponents of nuclear energy as "the power source for the future," have long touted its relative economy, "clean burning" technology, and virtually inexhaustible fuel supply. However, a close examination of the issue reveals that nuclear energy proves more problematic and dangerous than other forms of energy production and thus is not an acceptable solution to the problem of meeting ever-increasing energy needs.

First and foremost, nuclear power production presents the problem of radioactive waste storage. Fuel byproducts from nuclear fission remain toxic for thousands of years, and the spills and leaks from existing storage sites have been hazardous and costly to clean up. This remains true despite careful regulation and even under the best of circumstances. Even more appalling is the looming threat of accidents at the reactor itself: Incidents at the Three Mile Island and Chernobyl power plants and at other production sites have warned us that the consequences of a nuclear meltdown can be catastrophic and felt worldwide.

But beyond the enormous long-term environmental problems and short-term health risks, the bottom line issue for the production of energy is one of economics. Power production in our society is a business just like any other, and the large companies that produce this country's electricity and gas claim they are unable to make alternatives such as solar power affordable. Yet—largely due to incentives from the federal government—there already exist homes heated by solar power, and cars fueled by the sun. If the limited resources devoted to date to such energy alternatives have already produced working models, a more intensive, broadly based, and supported effort is likely to make those alternatives less expensive and problematic.

> ## Teacher Tip
>
> "When trial lawyers recognize a weakness in their case, they usually try to bring it up under favorable conditions during direct examination rather than allow their opponents to bring it up under cross examination. You can use this same concept in your Analysis of Issue essay: Forthrightly admit (but downplay the significance of) weaknesses in your case or strengths of the opposing side. In this way, you cannot be accused of having ignored something. Instead, you have considered it but found it to be relatively less important."
> —Vince LoCascio
> New Brunswick, New Jersey

Besides the benefits in terms of both of cost and safety, renewable resources such as solar and hydroelectric power represent far better options in the long run for development: They require money only for the materials needed to harvest them. While sunlight and water are free, the innovative technologies and industrial strategies devised to harness them have created a geometric progression of spin-offs affecting fields as diverse as agriculture, real estate, space exploration, and social policy. They have also repeatedly produced secondary economic and social benefits, such as the large recreational and irrigation reservoirs created in the American Southwest behind large hydro-electric dams like the Hoover and Grand Coullee.

While it may now be clear that the drawbacks to the use of nuclear power are too great, it should also be apparent that the long-term benefits of renewable resources would reward investment. If these alternatives are explored more seriously than they have been in the past, safer and less expensive sources of power will undoubtedly live up to their promise. With limited resources at our disposal and a burgeoning global population to consider, further investment in nuclear power would mark an unconscionable and unnecessary waste of time and money.

Sample Issue Essay 2

That there may be drawbacks in the production of nuclear power is undeniable but I believe that one cannot underestimate the need for and importance of this form of energy in addressing our long-term energy needs. The ever-increasing demand for energy is a good example of a problem that requires the development of many sources. If there were no nuclear energy there would be no reliable and readily available alternatives to imported oil for the majority of our energy needs.

There are some problems that must get solved in the long term for nuclear energy, but there are other problems that will certainly follow if we depend only on the alternatives. Fossil fuels will eventually be depleted, while solar power remains problematic and expensive. It will take years to be able to develop, never mind whether it will ever make sense in economical or even technological terms. Nuclear power is already inexpensive compared to these other forms, in a technology that exists today. And in the meantime long term problems such as nuclear fuel sources and waste storage might be solved by technological means such as the development of nuclear fusion.

I am currently working in the financial field where the need for cheap energy becomes obvious. Such recent crises as the California power crisis, OPEC quotas, the fight over ANWR and the collapse of Enron have contributed to a faltering economy. It would be unrealistic, not to mention unfair to the general public, to expect them to continue to endure these crises and threats and perhaps go to war when a viable virtually inexhaustible supply of energy lies at hand. The key is to not give up on this source while it holds long-term promise. My personal experience as a trader tells me that a long term commitment to nuclear power would help stabilize the energy sector, while not doing so means that the uncertainty of the status quo will remain. Whether it be an OPEC decision, a war or a coup, a nationalization of resources or any other crisis, the current energy supply is under constant threat. The list of scenarios can go on longer than one would think and it's just impossible for us to predict where the next shock will come from.

Although the need for safety and continuing research is apparant, it would be hard to survive in the present circumstances without the nuclear power option also. When our nation depends on others, we open ourselves up to potential blackmail. Nuclear power, a technology that we developed and at which we excel, is there to help add the long-term stability that may be lacking. The most important thing to remember with nuclear power is both its strengths and weaknesses and capitalize on the strengths to achieve the energy goal that is desired.

5. Proofread Your Work
Take that last couple of minutes to catch any glaring errors.

Assessment of Sample Issue Essay 1: Outstanding, Score of "6"
This essay is carefully constructed throughout, enabling the reader to move effortlessly from point to point as the writer examines the multifaceted implications of the issue. The writer begins by acknowledging arguments for the opposing side, and then uses his thesis statement ("a close examination of the issue reveals that nuclear energy proves more problematic and dangerous than other forms of energy production") to explain his own position on the issue. He proceeds to provide compelling reasons and examples to support the premise, and then takes the argument to an effective conclusion. The writing is clean, concise, and error-free. Sentence structure is varied, and diction and vocabulary are strong and expressive.

Assessment of Sample Issue Essay 2: Adequate, Score of "4"
This essay presents a generally competent argument on one side of the topic at hand. The writer points out the need for a "reliable and readily available" alternative to fossil fuel energy supplies and argues that both will be needed in the short run. But by the time we reach the third paragraph, the discussion wanders. The final paragraph adds little, and the last sentence in particular is ineffective. The writer displays only adequate control of syntax and usage throughout the essay, and the vocabulary, while up to the task, lacks precision.

Teacher Tip

"You want to know if others are doing well on an AWA question? Listen for the clicking of the keyboard. Others who will be taking this test will start typing the minute the test begins. By the time the 30 minutes are up, they will have written a wandering collection of words that sort of address the issue or argument. By following the Kaplan Five-Step Method, you will write a tight, cogent, and well-scored essay. Quantity counts for nothing on the AWA."
—Jason Anderson
Chicago, Illinois

The Argument Essay

The Analyze an Argument essay requires you to critique the construction of someone else's argument by assessing its claims and evaluating the evidence provided. You are not being asked to agree or disagree with the author's *position* or *conclusion*; instead, you must analyze the *line of reasoning* used in the argument.

The screen directions will instruct you to decide how convincing you find the argument. To make your case, first analyze the argument itself and evaluate its use of evidence; second, explain how a different approach or more information would make the argument itself better (or possibly worse).

The directions for the Argument essay will look something like this:

Directions: You will have 30 minutes to plan and write a critique of an argument presented in the form of a short passage. You will be asked to consider the logical soundness of the argument. No other topics are admissible for this essay.

Your essay will be evaluated in terms of the following:

- **Identifying and analyzing the argument's important points**
- **Organizing, developing, and expressing your ideas**
- **Supporting your ideas with relevant reasons and/or examples**
- **Demonstrating a knowledge of standard written English**

Feel free to consider the issue for a few minutes before planning your response and beginning your writing. Be certain that your ideas are fully developed and organized logically, and make sure you have enough time left to review and revise what you've written.

The Argument Prompt

This time you're given an expressed point of view—an "argument"—that contains a conclusion and supporting evidence. Here the writer tries to persuade you of something (her conclusion) by citing some evidence. You should read the "arguments" in the Analyze an Argument questions with a critical eye. Be on the lookout for *assumptions* in the way the writer moves from evidence to conclusion.

The topic you see in the Argument section may be similar to these:

The problem of poorly trained teachers that has plagued the state public school system is bound to become a good deal less serious in the future. The state has initiated comprehensive guidelines that oblige state teachers to complete a number of required credits in education and educational psychology at the graduate level before being certified.

KAPLAN

* * *

The commercial airline industry in the country of Freedonia has experienced impressive growth in the past three years. This trend will surely continue in the years to come, since the airline industry will benefit from recent changes in Freedonian society: Incomes are rising, most employees now receive more vacation time, and interest in travel is rising, as shown by an increase in media attention devoted to foreign cultures and tourist attractions.

* * *

The Kiddie Candy Company has instituted a new policy of paying factory employees for the number of candies each employee produces, rather than for the time they spend producing the candy. This policy will increase the number and raise the quality of the candies produced, allow the company to reduce their staff size, and enable their factories to operate for fewer hours. Ultimately, both the factory employees and the company will benefit from these changes, as the best workers will keep their jobs and the company will earn a profit in the coming year.

Applying the Kaplan Five-Step Method to an Argument Essay

Let's use the Kaplan Five-Step Method on this Analyze an Argument topic:

The following appeared in a memo from the secretary of the state's new teacher development committee:

The problem of poorly performing teachers that has plagued the state public school system is bound to become a good deal less serious in the future. The state has initiated comprehensive guidelines that oblige state teachers to complete a number of required credits in education and educational psychology at the graduate level before being certified.

Explain how logically persuasive you find this argument. In discussing your viewpoint, analyze the argument's line of reasoning and its use of evidence. Also explain what, if anything, would make the argument more valid and convincing or help you to better evaluate its conclusion.

1. *Take the Argument Apart*
   Topic: The state public school system
   Scope: How to solve the problem of poorly performing teachers
   Conclusion (the point the argument's trying to make): The problem of poorly performing teachers that has plagued the state public school system is bound to become a good deal less serious in the future.

> ### Kaplan Tip
>
> The author's conclusion need not appear at the end of the argument. The conclusion could be the first sentence with the evidence following; it could be the last sentence, preceded by evidence; or it could be any sentence in between.

Evidence (basis offered to support the conclusion): The state has initiated comprehensive guidelines that oblige state teachers to complete a number of required credits in education and educational psychology at the graduate level before being certified.

Assumptions (unspoken conditions or beliefs necessary for the conclusion to make sense in light of the evidence):

- Credits in education will improve teachers' classroom performance.
- Current bad teachers haven't already met this standard of training.
- Current bad teachers will not still be teaching in the future, or will have to be trained, too.

2. Select the Points You Will Make

Analyze the use of evidence in the argument. Determine whether there's anything relevant that's not discussed.

- Whether the training will actually address the cause of the problems
- What "poorly performing" means
- How to either improve or remove the bad teachers now teaching

Also determine what types of evidence would make the argument stronger or more logically sound. In this case, we need some new evidence supporting the assumptions.

- Evidence verifying that this training will make better teachers
- Evidence making it clear that current bad teachers haven't already had this training
- Evidence suggesting why all or many bad teachers won't still be teaching in the future (or why they'll be better trained)

3. Organize Your Essay

For an essay on this topic, your opening sentence might look like this:

The argument that improved academic training, ensured by requiring credits in education and psychology, will substantially alleviate the current problem of poorly trained teachers may seem logical at first glance.

Then use your notes as a working outline. You will primarily be addressing the ways in which the assumptions seem unsupported. You might also recommend new evidence you'd like to see and explain why. Remember to lead with your best arguments.

Kaplan Rules

In taking the argument apart, remember to:
- Jot down the conclusion
- Identify the evidence
- Find the assumptions

4. Write Your Essay

Begin writing your essay now. Your essay for this assignment might look like one of the following sample essays. As a basis for comparison, we've included one outstanding essay that deserves a score of "6," and one adequate essay that deserves a score of "4."

Sample Argument Essay 1

The argument that improved academic training, ensured by requiring credits in education and psychology, will substantially alleviate the current problem of poorly performing teachers may seem logical at first glance. However, the conclusion relies upon assumptions for which there is no clear evidence and upon terms which lack definition.

First, the writer assumes that the required courses will produce better teachers. In fact, the courses might be entirely irrelevant to the teachers' failings. Suppose, for example, the main problem lies in cultural and linguistic gaps between teacher and student; graduate-level courses that do not address these specific issues would be of little use in bridging these gaps and improving educational outcomes. The notion that the coursework will provide better teachers would be strengthened by a clear definition of "poor perfomance" in the classroom and by additional evidence that the training will address the relevant issues.

Furthermore, the writer assumes that poorly performing teachers currently in the schools have not already met this standard of training. In fact, the writer makes no useful distinction between excellent and inadequate classroom performance in the matter of training. The argument would be strengthened considerably if the writer provided evidence of a direct correlation between teachers' educational backgrounds and their level of effectiveness in the classroom.

Finally, the writer provides no evidence that poorly performing teachers currently working will either stop teaching in the near future or will undergo additional training. In its current form, the argument implies that only brand-new teachers—those not previously certified—will receive the specified training. If this is the case, the bright future that the writer envisions may be decades away. The conclusion requires the support of evidence demonstrating that all teachers in the system will receive the remedial training and will then change their teaching methods accordingly.

The writer would not be wrong to conclude that the state's comprehensive guidelines will potentially lead to some improvement in the educational environment in the public schools. After all, the additional training will certainly not adversely affect classroom performance in any way. But in order to support the current conclusion that the guidelines will, in effect, solve the state's problem, the writer must first define the scope of the problem more

> ### Teacher Tip
>
> "An assumption is that which an author takes for granted as true in proceeding to his conclusion. Assumptions are neither bad nor good. They're simply risky, as the author is depending on them on faith. If an assumption is proven to be false, then a wedge has been created between evidence and conclusion, and the argument has been weakened."
> —Bob Verini
> Los Angeles, California

clearly and demonstrate a more complete understanding of the need for and benefits of the new requirements.

Sample Argument Essay 2

Although the argument stated above discusses the likelihood that teacher training in the public school system will improve, the reasons given are vague and inconclusive. Simply because the state has imposed guidelines that require teachers to complete a number of graduate credits in education and educational psychology does not automatically improve their classroom performance. The term "poorly performing" may imply a great variety of shortcomings. The types of problems the state could face in achieving its goal are its assumptions that coursework in education will actually improve the teachers' classroom performance, that present bad teachers haven't already met this new standard of training, and that current poor teachers will not be teaching in the future or will get training too. Whether the training will actually address the cause of the problems remains to be seen. Not clear as well is how to either improve or remove the poor teachers now teaching. The writer needs to provide evidence verifying that this training will make better teachers, evidence proving that present bad teachers haven't already had this training, and evidence which suggests why all or many of these inadequate teachers won't still be teaching in the future. Only when such evidence is convincingly presented will the reader feel compelled to accept the argument. The prediction made in the above reasoning is lacking in proper evidence considering its assertions and therefore must be further examined and modified so that conclusion can be properly supported.

5. Proofread

Save a few minutes to go over your essay and catch any obvious errors.

Assessment of Sample Argument Essay 1: Outstanding, Score of "6"

An outstanding response demonstrates the writer's insightful analytical skills. The introduction notes the prompt's specious reasoning occasioned by unsupported assumptions and a lack of definition and evidence. The writer follows this up with a one-paragraph examination of each of the root flaws in the argument. Specifically, the author exposes these points undermining the argument:

- The assumption that the required courses will make better teachers
- The assumption that poorly performing teachers currently in the schools have not already had the proposed training
- The complete lack of evidence that ineffective teachers currently working will either stop teaching in the future or will successfully adapt the required training to their classroom work

Each point receives thorough and cogent development (given the time constraints) in a smooth and logically organized discourse. In succinct, economical, and error-free writing, sentences vary in length and complexity, while the diction and vocabulary stands out as both precise and expressive.

Assessment of Sample Argument Essay 2: Adequate, Score of "4"
This essay adequately targets the argument's vague and inadequate evidence. The essay identifies and critiques the illogical reasoning that results from misguided assumptions and poorly defined terms:

- That requiring educational course credits will address the root of the problem
- That "poorly performing" teachers will actually improve in the classroom
- That teachers currently performing at a below average level have not already met the requirements

The writer clearly grasps the argument's central weaknesses. But although the ideas are clear, the essay lacks transitional phrases and is not well-organized. While the writer demonstrates a better than adequate control of language and ably conforms to the conventions of written English, this "4" essay suffers from a lack of the more thorough development of a typical "5" response.

Kaplan's 22 Principles of Effective Writing

To write an effective analytical essay, there are three main goals you need to meet:

- **Be concise:** Waste no words.
- **Be forceful:** Make a point.
- **Be correct:** Conform to the generally accepted rules of grammar and form.

Let's break down the three broad objectives of conciseness, forcefulness, and correctness into 22 specific principles. (Don't panic! Many of the principles will already be familiar to you.) Each principle is illustrated by exercises so that you can immediately practice what you learn; the answers to these exercises are located at the end of this section. Do the exercises and then compare your answers to ours. Make sure you understand what the error was in each sentence. Then use what you learn in this section to help you write and proofread your practice essays.

Kaplan Tip

Write your essay in a clear, straightforward manner. Keep your word choice, sentence structure, and argument simple (but not simplistic).

Principle 1: Avoid Wordiness

Why use several words when one will do? Many people make the mistake of writing phrases such as *at the present time* or *at this point in time* instead of the simpler *now*, or *take into consideration* instead of simply *consider*, in an attempt to make their prose seem more scholarly or more formal. It won't work. Instead, their prose ends up seeming inflated and pretentious. Don't waste your words or your time.

WORDY: I am of the opinion that the aforementioned managers should be advised that they will be evaluated with regard to the utilization of responsive organizational software for the purpose of devising a responsive network of customers.

CONCISE: We should tell the managers that we will evaluate their use of flexible computerized databases to develop a customer network.

Exercise 1: Wordy Phrases
Improve the following sentences by omitting or replacing wordy phrases.

1. The agency is not prepared to undertake expansion at this point in time.

2. In spite of the fact that she only has a little bit of experience in photography right now, she will probably do well in the future because she has a great deal of motivation to succeed in her chosen profession.

3. Although not untactful, George is a man who says exactly what he believes.

4. Accuracy is a subject that has great importance to English teachers and company presidents alike.

5. Ms. Miller speaks with a high degree of intelligence with regard to many aspects of modern philosophy.

Principle 2: Don't Be Redundant

Redundancy means that the writer needlessly repeats an idea. It's redundant to speak of *a beginner lacking experience*. The word *beginner* implies lack of experience by itself. You can eliminate redundant words or phrases without changing the meaning of the sentence.

Here are some common redundancies:

REDUNDANT	CONCISE
refer back	refer
few in number	few
small-sized	small
grouped together	grouped
in my own personal opinion	in my opinion
end result	result
serious crisis	crisis
new initiatives	initiatives

Exercise 2: Redundancy
Repair the following sentences by crossing out redundant elements.

1. All of these problems have combined together to create a serious crisis.

   _____

2. A staff that large in size needs an effective supervisor who can get the job done.

   _____

3. He knows how to follow directions and he knows how to do what he is told.

   _____

4. The writer's technical skill and ability do not mask his poor plot line.

   _____

5. That monument continues to remain a significant tourist attraction.

   _____

6. The recently observed trend of spending on credit has created a middle class that is poorer and more impoverished than ever before.

   _____

7. Those who can follow directions are few in number.

   _____

Principle 3: Avoid Needless Qualification

Since the object of your essay is to convince your reader, you will want to adopt a reasonable tone. There will likely be no single, clear-cut "answer" to the essay topic, so don't overstate your case. Occasional use of such

Kaplan Tip

Watch out for words that add nothing to the sense of the sentence. Redundancy often results from carelessness, but you can easily eliminate redundant elements when proofreading your essay.

qualifiers as *fairly*, *rather*, *somewhat*, and *relatively*, and of such expressions as *seems to be*, *a little*, and *a certain amount of* will let the reader know you are reasonable, but overusing such modifiers weakens your argument. Excessive qualification makes you sound hesitant. Like wordy phrases, qualifiers can add bulk without adding substance.

WORDY: This rather serious breach of etiquette may possibly shake the very foundations of the corporate world.

CONCISE: This serious breach of etiquette may shake the foundations of the corporate world.

Just as bad is the overuse of the word *very*. Some writers use this intensifying adverb before almost every adjective in an attempt to be more forceful. If you need to add emphasis, look for a stronger adjective or adverb.

WEAK: Novak is a very good pianist.

STRONG: Novak is a virtuoso pianist.

OR Novak plays beautifully.

And don't try to qualify words that are already absolute.

WRONG	CORRECT
more unique	unique
the very worst	the worst
completely full	full

Exercise 3: Excessive Qualification
Although reasonable qualification benefits an essay, excessive qualification debilitates your argument. Practice achieving conciseness by eliminating needless qualification in the sentences below.

1. She is a fairly excellent teacher.

_____

2. Ferrara seems to be sort of a slow worker.

_____

3. It is rather important to pay attention to all the details of a murder trial as well as to the larger picture.

_____

4. You yourself are the very best person to decide what you should do for a living.

_____

Kaplan Tip

Qualifiers add bulk without adding substance. They can also make you sound unsure of yourself.

5. In Italy, I found about the best food I have ever eaten.

_____

6. Needless to say, children should be taught to cooperate at home and also in school.

_____

Principle 4: Do Not Write Sentences Just to Fill Up Space

This principle suggests several things:

- Don't write a sentence that gets you nowhere.
- Don't ask a question only to answer it.
- Don't merely copy the essay's directions.
- Don't write a whole sentence only to announce that you're changing the subject.

If you have something to say, say it without preamble. If you need to smooth over a change of subject, do so with a transitional word or phrase, rather than with a meaningless sentence.

WORDY: Which idea of the author's is more in line with what I believe? This is a very interesting question.

CONCISE: The author's beliefs are similar to mine.

The author of the wordy example above is just wasting words and time. Get to the point quickly and stay there. Simplicity and clarity win points.

Kaplan Tip

Simplicity and clarity win points in GRE writing. Get to the point quickly and stay there.

Exercise 4: Unnecessary Sentences
Rewrite each of these two-sentence statements as one concise sentence.

1. In the dawn of the twenty-first century, the Earth can be characterized as a small planet. Advanced technology has made it easy for people who live vast distances from each other to communicate.

_____

2. What's the purpose of getting rid of the chemical pollutants in water? People cannot safely consume water that contains chemical pollutants.

_____

3. Napoleon suffered defeat in Russia because most of his troops perished in the cold. Most of his men died because they had no winter clothing to protect them from the cold.

_____

4. Third, I do not believe those who argue that some of Shakespeare's plays were written by others. There is no evidence that other people had a hand in writing Shakespeare's plays.

_____

5. Frank Lloyd Wright was a famous architect. He was renowned for his ability to design buildings that blend into their surroundings.

_____

6. A lot of people find math a difficult subject to master. They have trouble with math because it requires very precise thinking skills.

_____

Principle 5: Avoid Needless Self-Reference

Avoid such unnecessary phrases as _I believe_, _I feel_, and _in my opinion_. There is no need to remind your reader that what you are writing is your opinion. Self-reference is another form of qualifying what you say—a very obvious form.

WEAK: I am of the opinion that air pollution is a more serious problem than most people realize.

FORCEFUL: Air pollution is a more serious problem than most people realize.

Exercise 5: Needless Self-Reference
Eliminate needless self-references in these sentences.

1. I feel we ought to pay teachers more than we pay actors.

_____

2. The author, in my personal opinion, is stuck in the past.

_____

3. I do not think this argument can be generalized to most business owners.

_____

4. Although I am no expert, I do not think privacy should be valued more than social concerns.

_____

5. I must emphasize that I am not saying the author does not have a point.

_____

6. If I were a college president, I would implement several specific reforms to combat apathy.

_____

7. It is my belief that either alternative would prove disastrous.

_____

Principle 6: Use the Active Voice

Using the passive voice is a way to avoid accountability. Put verbs in the active voice whenever possible. In the active voice, the subject performs the action (e.g., we write essays). In the passive voice, the subject is the receiver of the action and is often only implied (e.g., essays are written).

PASSIVE: The estimate of this year's tax revenues was prepared by the General Accounting Office.

ACTIVE: The General Accounting Office prepared the estimate of this year's tax revenues.

The passive voice creates weak sentences and is usually the product of writing before you think. Avoid this by prewriting. Take a few minutes to find out what you want to say before you say it. To change from the passive to the active voice, ask yourself WHO or WHAT is performing the action. In the sentence above, the General Accounting Office is performing the action. Therefore, the GAO should be the subject of the sentence.

You should avoid the passive voice EXCEPT in the following cases:
- When you do not know who performed the action: _The letter was opened before I received it._
- When you prefer not to refer directly to the person who performs the action: _An error has been made in computing this data._

Exercise 6: Undesirable Passives
Replace passive voice with active wherever possible.

1. The Spanish-American War was fought by brave but misguided men.

_____

2. The bill was passed in time, but it was not signed by the President until the time for action had passed.

_____

Kaplan Tip

To change from the passive voice to the active voice, ask yourself **who** or **what** is performing the action.

3. Advice is usually requested by those who need it least; it is not sought out by the truly lost and ignorant.

_____

4. That building should be relocated where it can be appreciated by the citizens.

_____

5. Garbage collectors should be generously rewarded for their difficult labors.

_____

6. The conditions of the contract agreement were ironed out minutes before the strike deadline.

_____

7. Test results were distributed with no concern for confidentiality.

_____

Principle 7: Avoid Weak Openings

Try not to begin a sentence with _there is_, _there are_, or _it is_. These roundabout expressions usually indicate that you are trying to distance yourself from the position you are taking. Again, weak openings usually result from writing before you think, hedging until you find out what you want to say.

Exercise 7: Weak Openings
Rewrite these sentences to eliminate weak openings.

1. It would be unwise for businesses to ignore the illiteracy problem.

_____

2. There are several reasons why this plane is obsolete.

_____

3. It would be of no use to fight a war on poverty without waging a battle against child labor.

_____

4. There are many strong points in the candidate's favor; intelligence, unfortunately, is not among them.

_____

Kaplan Tip

Avoid writing sentences that start with **there is**, **there are**, or **it is**. Weak openings result in weak sentences, which lead to weak arguments in a weak essay. Be strong!

5. It is difficult to justify building a more handsome prison.

_____

6. There seems to be little doubt that Americans like watching television better than conversing.

_____

7. It is obvious that intelligence is a product of environment and heredity.

_____

Principle 8: Avoid Needlessly Vague Language

Don't just ramble on when writing your GRE essays. Choose specific, descriptive words. Vague language weakens your writing because it forces the reader to guess what you mean instead of concentrating fully on your ideas and style. The essay topics you'll be given aren't going to be obscure. You will be able to come up with specific examples and concrete information about the topics. Your argument will be more forceful if you stick to this information.

WEAK:	Ms. Brown is highly educated.
FORCEFUL:	Ms. Brown has a master's degree in business administration.
WEAK:	She is a great communicator.
FORCEFUL:	She speaks persuasively.

Notice that sometimes, to be more specific and concrete, you will have to use more words than you might with vague language. This principle is not in conflict with the general objective of conciseness. Being concise may mean eliminating unnecessary words. Avoiding vagueness may mean adding necessary words.

Exercise 8: Needlessly Vague Language
Rewrite these sentences to replace vague language with specific, concrete language.

1. Water is transformed into steam when the former is heated up to 100° C.

_____

2. The diplomat was required to execute an agreement that stipulated that he would live in whatever country the federal government thought necessary.

_____

3. Arthur is a careless person.

_____

4. She told us that she was going to go to the store as soon as her mother came home.

_____

5. A radar unit is a highly specialized piece of equipment.

_____

6. Thousands of species of animals were destroyed when the last ice age occurred.

_____

7. The secretary was unable to complete the task that had been assigned.

_____

Principle 9: Avoid Clichés

Clichés are overused expressions, expressions that may once have seemed colorful and powerful but are now dull and worn out. Time pressure and anxiety may make you lose focus; that's when clichés may slip into your writing. A reliance on clichés will suggest you are a lazy thinker. Keep them out of your essay.

WEAK: Performance in a crisis is the acid test for a leader.

FORCEFUL: Performance in a crisis is the best indicator of a leader's abilities.

Putting a cliché in quotation marks in order to indicate your distance from the cliché does not strengthen the sentence. If anything, it just makes weak writing more noticeable. Notice whether or not you use clichés. If you do, ask yourself if you could substitute more specific language for the cliché.

Exercise 9: Clichés
Make the following sentences more forceful by replacing clichés with cliché-free formulations.

1. Beyond the shadow of a doubt, Jefferson was a great leader.

_____

2. I have a sneaking suspicion that families spend less time together than they did 15 years ago.

_____

3. The pizza delivery man arrived in the sequestered jury's hour of need.

_____

4. Trying to find the employee responsible for this embarrassing information leak is like trying to find a needle in a haystack.

_____

5. Both strategies would be expensive and completely ineffective, so it's six of one and half a dozen of the other.

_____

6. Older doctors should be required to update their techniques, but you can't teach an old dog new tricks.

_____

Principle 10: Avoid Jargon

Jargon includes two categories of words that you should avoid. First is the specialized vocabulary of a group, such as that used by doctors, lawyers, or baseball coaches. Second is the overly inflated and complex language that burdens many students' essays. You will not impress anyone with big words that do not fit the tone or context of your essay, especially if you misuse them.

If you are not certain of a word's meaning or appropriateness, leave it out. An appropriate word, even a simple one, will add impact to your argument. As you come across words you are unsure of, ask yourself, "Would a reader in a different field be able to understand exactly what I mean from the words I've chosen? Is there any way I can say the same thing more simply?"

WEAK: The international banks are cognizant of the new law's significance.

FORCEFUL: The international banks are aware of the new law's significance.

The following are commonly used jargon words:

prioritize	parameter	optimize	user-friendly
time frame	input/output	utilize	mutually beneficial
finalize	assistance	conceptualize	target
maximize	blindside	designate	downside
originate	ongoing	facilitate	bottom line

Kaplan Tip

Resist the temptation to use inflated language in your GRE essays. You won't impress anyone by using big words that don't fit the tone or context of your essays.

Exercise 10: Jargon
Replace the jargon in the following sentences with more appropriate language.

1. The research-oriented person should not be hired for a people-oriented position.

_____

2. Foreign diplomats should always interface with local leaders.

_____

3. Pursuant to your being claimed as a dependent on the returns of another taxpayer or resident wage earner, you may not consider yourself exempt if your current income exceeds five hundred dollars.

_____

4. There is considerable evidentiary support for the assertion that Vienna sausages are good for you.

_____

5. With reference to the poem, I submit that the second and third stanzas connote a certain despair.

_____

6. Allow me to elucidate my position: This horse is the epitome, the very quintessence of equine excellence.

_____

7. In the case of the recent railway disaster, it is clear that governmental regulatory agencies obfuscated in the preparation of materials for release to the public through both the electronic and print media.

_____

Principle 11: Pay Attention to Subject-Verb Agreement

A verb must agree with its subject in number regardless of intervening phrases. Do not let the words that come between the subject and the verb confuse you as to the number (singular or plural) of the subject. Usually one word can be pinpointed as the grammatical subject of the sentence. The verb, no matter how far removed, must agree with that subject in number.

INCORRECT: The joys of climbing mountains, especially if one is a novice climber without the proper equipment, escapes me.

CORRECT: The *joys* of climbing mountains, especially if one is a novice climber without the proper equipment, *escape* me.

Watch out for collective nouns like *group*, *audience*, *committee*, or *majority*. These take a singular noun unless the individuals forming the group are to be emphasized.

CORRECT: A *majority* of the committee *have signed* their names to the report. (The individual members of the committee are being emphasized.)

CORRECT: A *majority* of the jury *thinks* that the defendant is guilty. (The collective is being emphasized.)

A subject that consists of two or more nouns connected by the conjunction *and* takes the plural form of the verb.

CORRECT: *Karl*, an expert in cooking Hunan chicken, *and George*, an expert in preparing Hunan spicy duck, *have combined* their expertise to start a new restaurant.

However, when the subject consists of two or more nouns connected by *or* or *nor*, the verb agrees with the CLOSEST noun.

CORRECT: Either the senators or the *President is* misinformed.

CORRECT: Either the President or the *senators are* misinformed.

There are some connecting phrases that look as though they should make a group of words into a plural but actually do not. The only connecting word that can make a series of singular nouns into a plural subject is *and*. In particular, the following connecting words and phrases do NOT result in a plural subject:

along with	besides	together with
as well as	in addition to	

INCORRECT: The President, along with the Secretary of State and the Director of the CIA, are misinformed.

CORRECT: The *President*, along with the Secretary of State and the Director of the CIA, *is* misinformed.

If a sentence that is grammatically correct still sounds awkward, you should probably rephrase your thought.

Kaplan Tip

You can usually trust your ear to give you the correct verb form. However, subject-verb agreement can be tricky in the following instances:
• When the subject and verb are separated
• When the subject is an indefinite pronoun
• When the subject consists of more than one noun

Exercise 11: Subject-Verb Agreement
Fix or replace the incorrect verbs in the following sentences.

1. The logical structure of his complicated and rather tortuous arguments are always the same.

_____

2. The majority of the organization's members is over 60 years old.

_____

Kaplan Tip

If you write a sentence that is grammatically correct but awkward sounding, try to rephrase your thought.

3. A case of bananas have been sent to the local distributor in compensation for the fruit that was damaged in transit.

_____

4. A total of 50 editors read each article, a process that takes at least a week, sometimes six months.

_____

5. Neither the shipping clerk who packed the equipment nor the truckers who transported it admits responsibility for the dented circuit box.

_____

6. I can never decide whether to eat an orange or a Belgian chocolate; each of them have their wondrous qualities.

_____

7. Everyone in the United States, as well as the Canadians, expect the timber agreement to fall through.

_____

Principle 12: Pay Attention to Modification

Modifiers should be placed as close as possible to what they modify. In English, the position of the word within a sentence often establishes the word's relationship to other words in the sentence. If a modifier is placed too far from the word it modifies, the meaning may be lost or obscured. Notice, in the following sentences, the ambiguity that results when the modifying phrases are misplaced in the sentence.

UNCLEAR: Gary and Martha sat talking about the problem in the office.

UNCLEAR: They wondered how much the house was really worth when they bought it.

CLEAR: Gary and Martha sat in the office talking about the problem.

CLEAR: When they bought the house, they wondered how
            much it was really worth.

In addition to misplaced modifiers, watch for dangling modifiers: modifiers whose intended referents are not even present.

INCORRECT: Coming out of context, Peter was startled by Julia's
           perceptiveness.
CORRECT: Julia's remark, coming out of context, startled Peter
           with its perceptiveness.

Exercise 12: Faulty Modification
Rewrite these sentences to put modifiers closer to the words they modify.

1. Mr. Bentley advised him quickly to make up his mind.

   _____

2. The Governor's conference met to discuss student protest in the auditorium.

   _____

3. All of his friends were not able to come, but he decided that he preferred small parties anyway.

   _____

4. Madeleine remembered she had to place a telephone call when she got
   home.

   _____

5. George told Suzette he did not like to discuss politics as they walked
   through the museum.

   _____

6. Having worked in publishing for ten years, Spencer's resume shows
   that he is well qualified.

   _____

7. A politician would fail to serve her constituents without experience in
   community service.

   _____

Kaplan Tip

Avoid ambiguity by
placing modifiers as close
as possible to the words
they are intended to
modify.

Principle 13: Use Pronouns Carefully

A pronoun is a word that replaces a noun in a sentence. Every time you write a pronoun—*he, him, his, she, her, it, its, they, their, that,* or *which*—be sure there can be absolutely no doubt what its antecedent is. (An antecedent is the particular noun a pronoun refers to or stands for). Careless use of pronouns can obscure your intended meaning.

UNCLEAR: The teacher told the student he was lazy. (Does *he* refer to *teacher* or *student?*)

UNCLEAR: Sara knows more about history than Irina because she learned it from her father. (Does *she* refer to *Sara* or *Irina?*)

You can usually rearrange a sentence to avoid ambiguous pronoun references.

CLEAR: The student was lazy, and the teacher told him so.

CLEAR: The teacher considered himself lazy and told the student so.

CLEAR: Since Sara learned history from her father, she knows more than Irina does.

CLEAR: Because Irina learned history from her father, she knows less about it than Sara does.

If you are worried that a pronoun reference will be ambiguous, rewrite the sentence so that there is no doubt. Do not be afraid to repeat the antecedent if necessary:

UNCLEAR: I would rather settle in Phoenix than in Albuquerque, although it lacks wonderful restaurants.

CLEAR: I would rather settle in Phoenix than in Albuquerque, although Phoenix lacks wonderful restaurants.

A reader must be able to pinpoint the pronoun's antecedent. Even if you think the reader will know what you mean, do not use a pronoun without a clear and appropriate antecedent.

INCORRECT: When you are painting, be sure not to get it on the floor. (*It* could only refer to the noun *paint.* But do you see the noun *paint* anywhere in the sentence? Pronouns cannot refer to implied nouns.)

CORRECT: When you are painting, be sure not to get any paint on the floor.

Definition

A **pronoun** is a word that replaces a noun in a sentence. An **antecedent** is the particular noun the pronoun stands for. Make sure each pronoun in your essay refers clearly to one and only one antecedent.

Exercise 13: Faulty Pronoun Reference
Correct the pronoun references in the following sentences.

1. Clausen's dog won first place at the show because he was well bred.

   _____

2. The critic's review made the novel a commercial success. He is now a rich man.

   _____

3. The military advisor was more conventional than his commander, but he was a superior strategist.

   _____

4. Bertha telephoned her friends in California before going home for the night, which she had not done for weeks.

   _____

5. Although John hoped and prayed for the job, it did no good. When he called him the next morning, they had hired someone else.

   _____

6. You must pay attention when fishing—otherwise, you might lose it.

   _____

7. Zolsta Karmagi is the better musician, but he had more formal training.

   _____

Principle 14: Use Parallelism Correctly

It can be rhetorically effective to use a particular construction several times in succession, in order to provide emphasis. The technique is called parallel construction, and it is effective only when used sparingly.

> EXAMPLE: *As a* leader, Lincoln inspired a nation to throw off the chains of slavery; *as a* philosopher, he proclaimed the greatness of the little man; *as a* human being, he served as a timeless example of humility.

The repetition of the italicized construction provides a strong sense of rhythm and organization to the sentence and alerts the reader to yet another aspect of Lincoln's character.

Definition

Parallelism means that similar elements in a series should be in similar form.

Matching constructions must be expressed in parallel form. Writers often use a parallel structure incorrectly for dissimilar items.

> INCORRECT: They are sturdy, attractive, and cost only a dollar each. (The phrase *They are* makes sense preceding the adjectives *sturdy* and *attractive*, but cannot be understood before *cost only a dollar each*.)
>
> CORRECT: They are sturdy and attractive, and they cost only a dollar each.

Kaplan Tip

When proofreading your essay, be sure that each item in a series agrees with the word or phrase that begins the series.

Parallel constructions must be expressed in parallel grammatical form: all nouns, all infinitives, all gerunds, all prepositional phrases, or all clauses.

> INCORRECT: All business students should learn word processing, accounting, and how to program computers.
>
> CORRECT: All business students should learn word processing, accounting, and computer programming.

This principle applies to any words that might begin each item in a series: Either repeat the word before every element in a series or include it only before the first item. (In effect, your treatment of the second element of the series determines the form of all subsequent elements.)

> INCORRECT: He invested his money in stocks, in real estate, and a home for retired performers.
>
> CORRECT: He invested his money in stocks, in real estate, and in a home for retired performers.
>
> CORRECT: He invested his money in stocks, real estate, and a home for retired performers.

A number of constructions call for you to always express ideas in parallel form. These constructions include:

> X is as _____ as Y.
> X is more _____ than Y.
> X is less _____ than Y.
> Both X and Y ...
> Either X or Y ...
> Neither X nor Y ...
> Not only X but also Y ...

X and Y can stand for as little as one word or as much as a whole clause, but in any case the grammatical structure of X and Y must be identical.

> INCORRECT: The view from this apartment is as spectacular as from that mountain lodge.

CORRECT: The view from this apartment is as spectacular as the view from that mountain lodge.

Exercise 14: Parallelism
Correct the faulty parallelism in the following sentences.

1. The dancer taught her understudy how to move, how to dress, and how to work with choreographers and deal with professional competition.

_____

2. Merrill based his confidence on the futures market, the bond market, and on the strength of the president's popularity.

_____

3. The grocery baggers were ready, able, and were quite determined to do a great job.

_____

4. The requirements for a business degree are not as stringent as a law degree.

_____

Principle 15: Do Not Shift Narrative Voice

True, principle 5 advised you to avoid needless self-reference. But an occasional self-reference may be appropriate in your GRE essays. You may even call yourself *I* if you want, as long as you keep the number of first-person pronouns to a minimum. Less egocentric ways of referring to the narrator include *we* and *one*. If these more formal ways of writing seem stilted, stay with *I*.

- In my lifetime, I have seen many challenges to the principle of free speech.
- We can see …
- One must admit …

The method of self-reference you select is called the narrative voice of your essay. Any of the above narrative voices are acceptable. Nevertheless, whichever you choose, you must be careful not to shift narrative voice in your essay. If you use *I* in the first sentence, for example, do not use *we* in a later sentence.

INCORRECT: In my lifetime, *I* have seen many challenges to the principle of free speech. *We* can see how a free society can get too complacent when free speech is taken for granted.

It is likewise wrong to shift from *you* to *one*:

INCORRECT: Just by following the news, *you* can readily see how politicians have a vested interest in pleasing powerful interest groups. But *one* should not generalize about this tendency.

Kaplan Tip

Be sure to present a consistent point of view in your essay. If you refer to yourself as "I" in one paragraph, do not refer to yourself as "we" in the next paragraph.

Exercise 15: Shifting Narrative Voice
Rewrite these sentences to give each a consistent point of view.

1. I am disgusted with the waste we tolerate in this country. One cannot simply stand by without adding to such waste: Living here makes you wasteful.

   _____

2. You must take care not to take these grammar rules too seriously, since one can often become bogged down in details and forget why he is writing at all.

   _____

3. We all must take a stand against waste in this country; or how will one be able to look at oneself in the mirror?

   _____

Principle 16: Avoid Slang and Colloquialisms

Conversational speech is filled with slang and colloquial expressions. But you should avoid slang on the GRE. Slang terms and colloquialisms can be confusing to the reader, since these expressions are not universally understood. Even worse, such informal writing may give readers the impression that you are poorly educated or arrogant.

INAPPROPRIATE: He is really into gardening.
CORRECT: He enjoys gardening.
INAPPROPRIATE: She plays a wicked game of tennis.
CORRECT: She excels at tennis.
INAPPROPRIATE: Myra has got to go to Memphis for a week.
CORRECT: Myra must go to Memphis for a week.
INAPPROPRIATE: Joan's been doing science for eight years now.
CORRECT: Joan has been a scientist for eight years now.

Exercise 16: Slang and Colloquialisms
Replace the informal elements of the following sentences with more appropriate terms.

1. Cynthia Larson sure knows her stuff.

   _____

2. The crowd was really into watching the fire-eating juggler, but then the dancing horse grabbed their attention.

   _____

3. As soon as the personnel department checks out his resume, I'm sure we'll hear gales of laughter issuing from the office.

   _____

4. The chef has a nice way with salmon: His sauce was simple but the effect was sublime.

   _____

5. Normal human beings can't cope with repeated humiliation.

   _____

6. If you want a good cheesecake, you've got to make a top-notch crust.

   _____

7. The environmentalists aren't in it for the prestige; they really care about protecting the yellow-throated hornswoggler.

   _____

Principle 17: Watch Out for Sentence Fragments and Run-On Sentences

Every sentence in formal expository writing must have an independent clause: a clause that contains a subject and a predicate. A sentence fragment has no independent clause; a run-on sentence has two or more independent clauses that are improperly connected. As you edit your practice essays, check your sentence constructions, noting any tendency toward fragments or run-on sentences.

FRAGMENT: Global warming. That is what the scientists and journalists are worried about this month.

CORRECT: Global warming is the cause of concern for scientists and journalists this month.

FRAGMENT: Seattle is a wonderful place to live. Mountains, ocean, and forests, all within easy driving distance. If you can ignore the rain.

Kaplan Tip

By using informal language on the GRE, you run the risk of sounding ignorant or even arrogant. Stick to standard usage.

CORRECT: Seattle is a wonderful place to live, with mountains, ocean, and forests all within easy driving distance. However, it certainly does rain often.

FRAGMENT: Why do I think the author's position is preposterous? Because he makes generalizations that I know are untrue.

CORRECT: I think the author's position is preposterous because he makes generalizations that I know are untrue.

Beginning single-clause sentences with coordinate conjunctions—*and, but, or, nor,* and *for*—is acceptable in moderation (although some readers still object to beginning a sentence with *and*).

CORRECT: Most people would agree that indigent patients should receive wonderful health care. But every treatment has its price.

Time pressure may also cause you to write two or more sentences as one. When you proofread your essays, watch out for independent clauses that are not joined with any punctuation at all or are only joined with a comma.

RUN-ON: Current insurance practices are unfair they discriminate against the people who need insurance most.

You can repair run-on sentences in any one of three ways. First, you could use a period to make separate sentences of the independent clauses.

CORRECT: Current insurance practices are unfair. They discriminate against the people who need insurance most.

Second, you could use a semicolon. A semicolon is a weak period. It separates independent clauses but signals to the reader that the ideas in the clauses are related.

CORRECT: Current insurance practices are unfair; they discriminate against the people who need insurance most.

The third method of repairing a run-on sentence is usually the most effective. Use a conjunction to turn an independent clause into a dependent one and to make explicit how the clauses are related.

CORRECT: Current insurance practices are unfair, because they discriminate against the people who need insurance most.

A common cause of run-on sentences is the misuse of adverbs like *however*, *nevertheless*, *furthermore*, *likewise*, and *therefore*.

RUN-ON: Current insurance practices are discriminatory, furthermore they make insurance too expensive for the poor.

CORRECT: Current insurance practices are discriminatory. Furthermore, they make insurance too expensive for the poor.

Exercise 17: Sentence Fragments and Run-On Sentences
Repair the following by eliminating sentence fragments and run-on sentences.

1. The private academy has all the programs Angie will need. Except the sports program, which has been phased out.

   _____

2. Leadership ability. That is the elusive quality which our current government employees have yet to capture.

   _____

3. Antonio just joined the athletic club staff this year but Barry has been with us since 1975, therefore we would expect Barry to be more skilled with the weight-lifting equipment. What a surprise to find Barry pinned beneath a barbell on the weight-lifting bench with Antonio struggling to lift the three-hundred-pound weight from poor Barry's chest.

   _____

   _____

4. However much she tries to act like a Southern belle, she cannot hide her roots. The daughter of a Yankee fisherman, taciturn and always polite.

   _____

5. There is time to invest in property. After one has established oneself in the business world, however.

   _____

6. Sentence fragments are often used in casual conversation, however they should not be used in written English under normal circumstances.

   _____

Definition

An **independent clause** contains a subject and a predicate. Make sure that every sentence in your essay has at least one independent clause.

Principle 18: Use Commas Correctly

Use commas to separate items in a series. If more than two items are listed in a series, they should be separated by commas. The final comma—the one that precedes the word *and*—is optional (but be consistent throughout your essays!).

CORRECT: My recipe for buttermilk biscuits contains flour, baking soda, salt, shortening and buttermilk.

CORRECT: My recipe for buttermilk biscuits contains flour, baking soda, salt, shortening, and buttermilk.

Don't place commas before the first element of a series or after the last element.

INCORRECT: My investment advisor recommended that I construct a portfolio of, stocks, bonds, commodities futures, and precious metals.

INCORRECT: The elephants, tigers, and dancing bears, were the highlights of the circus.

Use commas to separate two or more adjectives before a noun, but don't use a comma after the last adjective in the series.

CORRECT: I can't believe you sat through that long, dull, uninspired movie three times.

INCORRECT: The manatee is a round, blubbery, bewhiskered, creature whose continued presence in American waters is endangered by careless boaters.

Use commas to set off parenthetical clauses and phrases. (A parenthetical expression is one that is not necessary to the main idea of the sentence.)

CORRECT: Gordon, who is a writer by profession, bakes an excellent cheesecake.

The main idea is that Gordon bakes an excellent cheesecake. The intervening clause merely serves to identify Gordon; thus, it should be set off with commas.

Use commas after introductory, participial, or prepositional phrases.

CORRECT: Having watered his petunias every day during the drought, Harold was very disappointed when his garden was destroyed by insects.

CORRECT: After the banquet, Harold and Martha went dancing.

At a Glance

Use commas to do the following:
- Separate items in a series
- Separate two or more adjectives before a noun
- Set off a parenthetical expression
- Set off an introductory, participial, or prepositional phrase
- Separate independent clauses connected by a coordinate conjunction

Use commas to separate independent clauses (clauses that could stand alone as complete sentences) connected by coordinate conjunctions such as *and*, *but*, *yet*, etc.

CORRECT: Susan's old car has been belching blue smoke from the tailpipe for two weeks, but it has not broken down yet.

CORRECT: Zachariah's pet frog eats fifty flies a day, yet it has never gotten indigestion.

INCORRECT: Susan's old car has been belching blue smoke from the tailpipe for two weeks, but has not broken down yet.

INCORRECT: Zachariah's pet frog eats fifty flies a day, and never gets indigestion.

Exercise 18: Commas
Correct the punctuation errors in the following sentences.

1. Peter wants me to bring records games candy and soda to his party.

   _____

2. I need, lumber, nails, a hammer and a saw to build the shelf.

   _____

3. It takes a friendly energetic person to be a successful salesman.

   _____

4. I was shocked to discover that a large, modern, glass-sheathed, office building had replaced my old school.

   _____

5. The country club, a cluster of ivy-covered whitewashed buildings was the site of the president's first speech.

   _____

6. Pushing through the panicked crowd the security guards frantically searched for the suspect.

   _____

7. Despite careful analysis of the advantages and disadvantages of each proposal Harry found it hard to reach a decision.

   _____

Principle 19: Use Semicolons Correctly

Use a semicolon instead of a coordinate conjunction such as *and*, *or*, or *but* to link two closely related independent clauses.

INCORRECT: Whooping cranes are an endangered species; and they are unlikely to survive if we continue to pollute.

CORRECT: Whooping cranes are an endangered species; there are only fifty whooping cranes in New Jersey today.

CORRECT: Whooping cranes are an endangered species, and they are unlikely to survive if we continue to pollute.

Use a semicolon between independent clauses connected by words like *therefore*, *nevertheless*, and *moreover*.

CORRECT: The staff meeting has been postponed until next Thursday; therefore, I will be unable to get approval for my project until then.

CORRECT: Farm prices have been falling rapidly for two years; nevertheless, the traditional American farm is not in danger of disappearing.

Exercise 19: Semicolons
Correct the punctuation errors in the following sentences.

1. Morgan has five years' experience in karate; but Tyler has even more.

2. Very few students wanted to take the class in physics, only the professor's kindness kept it from being canceled.

3. You should always be prepared when you go on a camping trip, however you must avoid carrying unnecessary weight.

Principle 20: Use Colons Correctly

In formal writing, the colon is used only as a means of signaling that what follows is a list, definition, explanation, or concise summary of what has gone before. The colon usually follows an independent clause, and it will frequently be accompanied by a reinforcing expression like *the following*, *as follows*, or *namely*, or by an explicit demonstrative like *this*.

Definition

A **semicolon** is a weak period; it separates independent clauses but signals to the reader that the ideas in the clauses are related.

CORRECT: Your instructions are as follows: Read the passage care-
             fully, answer the questions on the last page, and turn
             over your answer sheet.

CORRECT: This is what I found in the refrigerator: a moldy lime,
             half a bottle of stale soda, and a jar of peanut butter.

Be careful not to put a colon between a verb and its direct object.

INCORRECT: I want: a slice of pizza and a small green salad.

CORRECT: This is what I want: a slice of pizza and a small green
             salad. (The colon serves to announce that a list is
             forthcoming.)

CORRECT: I don't want much for lunch: just a slice of pizza and a
             small green salad. (Here what follows the colon defines
             what *don't want much* means.)

Context will occasionally make clear that a second independent clause is
closely linked to its predecessor, even without an explicit expression like
those used above. Here, too, a colon is appropriate, although a period will
always be correct too.

CORRECT: We were aghast: The "charming country inn" that had
             been advertised in such glowing terms proved to be a
             leaking cabin full of mosquitoes.

Exercise 20: Colons
Edit these sentences so they use colons correctly.

1. I am sick and tired of: your whining, your complaining, your nagging,
   your teasing, and, most of all, your barbed comments.

   _____

2. The chef has created a masterpiece, the pasta is delicate yet firm, the
   mustard greens are fresh, and the medallions of veal are melting in my
   mouth.

   _____

3. In order to write a good essay, you must: practice, get plenty of sleep,
   and eat a good breakfast.

   _____

Definition

A **colon** signals that what
follows is a list, definition,
explanation, or summary
of the clause preceding it.

Principle 21: Use Hyphens and Dashes Correctly

Use a hyphen with the compound numbers twenty-one through ninety-nine, and with fractions used as adjectives.

CORRECT: Sixty-five students constituted a majority.

CORRECT: A two-thirds vote was necessary to carry the measure.

Use a hyphen with the prefixes *ex*, *all*, and *self* and with the suffix *elect*.

CORRECT: The constitution protects against self-incrimination.

CORRECT: The president-elect was invited to chair the meeting.

Use a hyphen with a compound adjective when it comes before the word it modifies but not when it comes after the word it modifies.

CORRECT: The no-holds-barred argument continued into the night.

CORRECT: The argument continued with no holds barred.

Use a hyphen with any prefix used before a proper noun or adjective.

CORRECT: His pro-African sentiments were heartily applauded.

CORRECT: They believed that his accent was un-Australian.

Use a hyphen to separate component parts of a word in order to avoid confusion with other words or to avoid the use of a double vowel.

CORRECT: The sculptor was able to re-form the clay after the dog knocked over the bust.

CORRECT: The family re-entered their house after the fire marshal departed.

Use a dash to indicate an abrupt change of thought.

CORRECT: The inheritance must cover the entire cost of the proposal—Gail has no other money to invest.

CORRECT: To get a high score—and who doesn't want to get a high score?—you need to devote yourself to prolonged and concentrated study.

Exercise 21: Hyphens and Dashes

Edit these sentences so they use hyphens and dashes correctly.

1. The child was able to count from one to ninety nine.

Kaplan Tip

A dash (—) can indicate an abrupt change of thought. However, on the GRE, try to avoid such abrupt changes by planning what you want to say in advance.

2. The adults only movie was banned from commercial TV.

_____

3. It was the first time she had seen a movie that was for adults-only.

_____

4. John and his ex wife remained on friendly terms.

_____

5. A two thirds majority would be needed to pass the budget reforms.

_____

6. The house, and it was the most dilapidated house that I had ever seen was a bargain because the land was so valuable.

_____

Principle 22: Use the Apostrophe Correctly

Use an apostrophe in a contraction to indicate that one or more letters have been eliminated. But try to avoid using contractions altogether on the GRE: Using the full form of a verb is more appropriate in formal writing.

CONTRACTED: We'd intended to address the question of equal rights, but it's too late to begin the discussion now.

FULL FORM: We had intended to address the question of equal rights, but it is too late to begin the discussion now.

One of the most common errors involving use of the apostrophe is using it in the contraction *you're* or *it's* to indicate the possessive form of *you* or *it*. When you write *you're*, ask yourself whether you mean *you are*. If not, the correct word is *your*. Similarly, are you sure you mean *it is*? If not, use the possessive form *its*.

INCORRECT: You're chest of drawers is ugly.
INCORRECT: The dog hurt it's paw.
CORRECT: Your chest of drawers is ugly.
CORRECT: The dog hurt its paw.

Kaplan Tip

Try to avoid using contractions on the GRE (i.e., write "you are" instead of "you're"). Contractions are too casual and are often the cause of thoughtless spelling errors.

Use the apostrophe to indicate the possessive form of a noun.

NOUN	POSSESSIVE
the boy	the boy's
Harry	Harry's
the children	the children's
the boys	the boys'

NOTE: The word *boy's* could have one of three meanings:
- The boy's an expert at chess. (contraction: The boy is …)
- The boy's left for the day. (contraction: The boy has …)
- The boy's face was covered with pie. (possessive: The face of the boy)

The word *boys'* can have only one meaning: a plural possessive (the___ of the boys).

CORRECT: Ms. Fox's office is on the first floor. (One person possesses the office.)

CORRECT: The Foxes' apartment has a wonderful view. (There are several people named Fox living in the same apartment. First you must form the plural, then add the apostrophe to indicate possession.)

Possessive pronouns do not use an apostrophe (with the exception of the neutral *one*, which forms its possessive by adding *'s*).

INCORRECT: The tiny cabin had been our's for many years.

CORRECT: The tiny cabin had been ours for many years.

Exercises for Principle 22: Apostrophes
Edit these sentences so they use apostrophes correctly.

1. The Presidents limousine had a flat tire.

   _____

2. You're tickets for the show will be at the box office.

   _____

3. The opportunity to change ones lifestyle does not come often.

   _____

4. The desks' surface was immaculate, but it's drawers were messy.

   _____

5. The cat on the bed is hers'.

   _____

Answers to 22 Principles Exercises

Answers to Exercise 1: Wordy Phrases

1. The agency is not prepared to expand now.

2. Although she is inexperienced in photography, she will probably succeed because she is motivated.

3. Although tactful, George says exactly what he believes.

4. Accuracy is important to English teachers and company presidents alike.

5. Ms. Miller speaks intelligently about many aspects of modern philosophy.

Answers to Exercise 2: Redundancy

1. All of these problems have combined to create a crisis.

2. A staff that large needs an effective supervisor.

3. He knows how to follow directions.

4. The writer's technical skill does not mask his poor plot line.

5. That monument remains a significant tourist attraction.

6. The recent trend of spending on credit has created a more impoverished middle class.

7. Few people can follow directions.

Answers to Exercise 3: Excessive Qualification

1. She is an effective teacher.

2. Ferrara is a slow worker.

3. In a murder trial, it is important to pay attention to the details as well as to the "larger picture.'"

4. You are the best person to decide what you should do for a living.

5. In Italy, I found the best food I have ever eaten.

6. Children should be taught to cooperate at home and in school.

Kaplan Tip

Our answers to these exercises probably won't be identical to the answers you came up with. That's okay. Just make sure you understand how these answers address the errors and weaknesses found in the original sentences.

Answers to Exercise 4: Unnecessary Sentences
1. Advanced technology has made it easy for people who live vast distances from each other to communicate.

2. People cannot safely consume water that contains chemical pollutants.

3. Napoleon suffered defeat in Russia because most of his troops perished in the cold.

4. No present evidence suggests that Shakespeare's plays were written by others.

5. The architect Frank Lloyd Wright was famous for his ability to design buildings that blend into their surroundings.

6. Many people find math a difficult subject because it requires very precise thinking skills.

Answers to Exercise 5: Needless Self-Reference
1. We ought to pay teachers more than we pay actors.

2. The author is stuck in the past.

3. This argument cannot be generalized to most business owners.

4. Privacy should not be valued more than social concerns.

5. The author has a point.

6. College presidents should implement several specific reforms to combat apathy.

7. Either alternative would prove disastrous.

Answers to Exercise 6: Undesirable Passives
1. Brave but misguided men fought the Spanish-American War.

2. Congress passed the bill in time, but the President did not sign it until the time for action had passed.

3. Those who need advice least usually request it; the truly lost and ignorant do not seek it.

4. We should relocate that building where citizens can appreciate it.

5. City government should generously reward garbage collectors for their difficult labors.

6. Negotiators ironed out the conditions of the contract agreement minutes before the strike deadline.

7. The teacher distributed test results with no concern for confidentiality.

Answers to Exercise 7: Weak Openings
1. Businesses ignore the illiteracy problem at their own peril.

2. This plane is obsolete for several reasons.

3. The government cannot fight a war on poverty effectively without waging a battle against child labor.

4. The candidate has many strong points; intelligence, unfortunately, is not among them.

5. The city cannot justify building a more handsome prison.

6. Americans must like watching television better than conversing.

7. Intelligence is a product of environment and heredity.

Answers to Exercise 8: Vague Language
1. When water is heated to 100° C, it turns into steam.

2. The diplomat had to agree to live wherever the government sent him.

3. Arthur often forgets to do his chores.

4. She told us that she would go to the store when her mother came home.

5. A radar unit registers the distance to an aircraft.

6. Thousands of animal species were destroyed in the last ice age.

7. The secretary was unable to type the document.

Answers to Exercise 9: Clichés
1. Jefferson was certainly a great leader.

2. Families probably spend less time together than they did fifteen years ago.

Kaplan Tip

Some of the most effective writing is simple and straightforward.

3. The pizza delivery man arrived just when the sequestered jury most needed him.

4. Trying to find the employee responsible for this embarrassing information leak may be impossible.

5. Both strategies would be expensive and completely ineffective: They have an equal chance of failing.

6. Older doctors should be required to update their techniques, but many seem resistant to changes in technology.

Answers to Exercise 10: Jargon

1. A person who likes research should not be hired for a position that requires someone to interact with customers all day.

2. Foreign diplomats should always talk to local leaders.

3. If someone claims you as a dependent on a tax return, you may still have to pay taxes on your income in excess of five hundred dollars.

4. Recent studies suggest that Vienna sausages are good for you.

5. When the poet wrote the second and third stanzas, he must have felt despair.

6. This is a fine horse.

7. Government regulatory agencies were not honest in their press releases about the recent railway accident.

Answers to Exercise 11: Subject-Verb Agreement

1. The logical structure of his complicated and rather tortuous arguments is always the same.

2. The majority of the organization's members are over 60 years old.

3. A case of bananas has been sent to the local distributor in compensation for the fruit that was damaged in transit.

4. A total of fifty editors reads each article, a process that takes at least a week, sometimes six months.

5. Neither the shipping clerk who packed the equipment nor the truckers who transported it admit responsibility for the dented circuit box.

6. I can never decide whether to eat an orange or a Belgian chocolate; each of them has its wondrous qualities. (Note that you must also change the possessive pronoun to the singular form.)

7. Everyone in the United States, as well the Canadians, expects the timber agreement to fall through.

Answers to Exercise 12: Faulty Modification
1. (*Quickly* is sandwiched between two verbs and could refer to either one.) Mr. Bentley advised him to make up his mind quickly.

2. (Was the student protest in the auditorium, or was the conference merely held there?) The Governor's conference met in the auditorium to discuss student protest.

3. (If none of his friends came, it must have been a small party indeed!) Not all of his friends were able to come, but he decided that he preferred small parties anyway.

4. (Did she remember when she got home? Or did she have to call when she got home?) When she got home, Madeleine remembered she had to place a telephone call.

5. (Either he didn't like discussing politics in the museum, or he didn't like discussing it at all.) As they walked through the museum, George told Suzette he did not like to discuss politics.

6. (Was it Spencer's resume that worked in publishing for ten years?) Spencer, who has worked in publishing for ten years, appears from his resume to be well qualified.

7. (It is the person holding the job, not the job itself, that requires experience in community service.) A politician without experience in community service would fail to serve her constituents.

Answers to Exercise 13: Faulty Pronoun Reference
1. (The structure of the sentence might leave us wondering whether Clausen or his dog was well bred. Instead, use the impersonal *it*.) Clausen's dog won first place at the show because it was well bred.

2. (It's not clear who *he* is: No antecedent exists in the sentence.) The critic's review made the novel a commercial success, and the novelist is now a rich man.

3. The military advisor was more conventional than his commander, but the advisor was a superior strategist.

4. (We do not know whether Bertha had not spent the night at home in weeks or whether she had not telephoned her friends in weeks.) Because she had not telephoned her California friends in weeks, Bertha called them before she went home for the night.

5. (Referring to some ambiguous *they* without identifying who *they* are beforehand is incorrect.) John wanted the job badly, but when he called the employer the next morning, he found that the company had hired someone else.

6. (We don't know exactly what *it* is, but we can assume that *it* is a fish.) You must pay attention when fishing—otherwise, you might lose your catch.

7. Zolsta Karmagi is the better musician, but Sven Wonderup had more formal training.

Answers to Exercise 14: Parallelism
1. The dancer taught her understudy how to move, dress, work with choreographers, and deal with professional competition.

2. Merrill based his confidence on the futures market, the bond market, and the strength of the President's popularity.

3. The grocery baggers were ready, able, and quite determined to do a great job.

4. The requirements for a business degree are not as stringent as those for a law degree.

Answers to Exercise 15: Shifting Narrative Voice
1. I am disgusted with the waste we tolerate in this country. We cannot simply stand by without adding to such waste: Living here makes all of us wasteful.

2. You must take care not to take these grammar rules too seriously, since you can often become bogged down in details and forget why you are writing at all. (Or use *one* consistently.)

3. We must all take a stand against waste in this country; or how can we look at ourselves in the mirror? (When using *we*, make sure to use the plural form of verbs and pronouns.)

Kaplan Tip

Don't worry if you aren't comfortable with complex sentence structures; just avoid using them. You can still earn top scores with a simple, but interesting, writing style.

Answers to Exercise 16: Slang and Colloquialisms

1. Cynthia Larson is an expert.

2. The crowd was absorbed in watching the fire-eating juggler, but then the dancing horse caught their attention.

3. As soon as the personnel department tries to verify his resume, I am sure we will hear gales of laughter issuing from the office.

4. The chef prepares salmon skillfully: His sauce was simple but the effect was sublime.

5. Normal human beings cannot tolerate repeated humiliation.

6. If you want a good cheesecake, you must make a superb crust.

7. The environmentalists are not involved in the project for prestige; they truly care about protecting the yellow-throated hornswoggler.

Answers to Exercise 17: Sentence Fragments and Run-On Sentences

1. The private academy has all the programs Angie will need, except that the sports program has been phased out.

2. Leadership ability is the elusive quality that our current government employees have yet to capture.

3. Antonio just joined the athletic club staff this year, but Barry has been with us since 1975; therefore, we would expect Barry to be more skilled with the weight-lifting equipment. It was quite a surprise to find Barry pinned beneath a barbell on the weight-lifting bench with Antonio struggling to lift the three-hundred-pound weight from poor Barry's chest.

4. However much she tries to act like a Southern belle, she cannot hide her roots. She will always be the daughter of a Yankee fisherman, taciturn and ever polite.

5. There is time to invest in property, but only after one has established oneself in the business world.

6. (Since transitional words like *however* do not subordinate a clause, this is a run-on sentence. You could either change the first comma to a semicolon or separate the clauses with a period.) Sentence fragments are often used in casual conversation. They should not, however, be used in written English under normal circumstances.

Answers for Exercise 18: Commas
1. Peter wants me to bring records, games, candy, and soda to his party.

2. I need lumber, nails, a hammer and a saw to build the shelf. (OR: a hammer, and a saw...)

3. It takes a friendly, energetic person to be a successful salesman.

4. I was shocked to discover that a large, modern, glass-sheathed office building had replaced my old school.

5. The country club, a cluster of ivy-covered whitewashed buildings, was the site of the president's first speech.

6. Pushing through the panicked crowd, the security guards frantically searched for the suspect.

7. Despite careful analysis of the advantages and disadvantages of each proposal, Harry found it hard to reach a decision.

Kaplan Tip

Use sentences that are as sophisticated in structure as possible without sacrificing clarity or risking excessive errors.

Answers for Exercise 19: Semicolons
1. Morgan has five years' experience in karate, but Tyler has even more.

2. Very few students wanted to take the class in physics; only the professor's kindness kept it from being canceled.

3. You should always be prepared when you go on a camping trip; however, you must avoid carrying unnecessary weight.

Answers to Exercise 20: Colons
1. I am sick and tired of your whining, your complaining, your nagging, your teasing, and, most of all, your barbed comments.

2. The chef has created a masterpiece: The pasta is delicate yet firm, the mustard greens are fresh, and the medallions of veal are melting in my mouth.

3. In order to write a good essay, you must do the following: practice, get plenty of sleep, and eat a good breakfast.

Answers to Exercise 21: Hyphens and Dashes
1. The child was able to count from one to ninety-nine.

2. The adults-only movie was banned from commercial TV.

3. It was the first time she had seen a movie that was for adults only.

4. John and his ex-wife remained on friendly terms.

5. A two-thirds majority would be needed to pass the budget reforms.

6. The house—and it was the most dilapidated house that I had ever seen—was a bargain because the land was so valuable.

Answers to Exercise 22: Apostrophes
1. The president's limousine had a flat tire.

2. Your tickets for the show will be at the box office.

3. The opportunity to change one's lifestyle does not come often.

4. The desk's surface was immaculate, but its drawers were messy.

5. The cat on the bed is hers.

Practice Essays

Now that you've learned the principles behind effective writing, it's time to put what you've learned to good use.

Write an essay on each of the topics below. While writing, pay particular attention to making your essay concise, forceful, and grammatically correct. Allow yourself 45 minutes to complete each Issue essay and 30 minutes to complete each Argument essay.

After you've finished with each essay, proofread to catch your errors. Then evaluate your essay, using the holistic scoring system that was explained at the beginning of this chapter. For this exercise, it's not critical that you assign yourself the "right" grade at the end. It's more important that you understand whether your essays are well written and how well they fulfill the required tasks.

Note

Remember, on the actual exam, you will be asked to write **one** Analysis of an Issue essay and **one** Analysis of an Argument essay.
- For the Issue essay, you'll choose one topic from the two topics that are presented to you.
- For the Argument essay, you'll be presented with only one topic.

Essay 1: Present Your Perspective on an Issue

Present your perspective on each of the issues below, using revelant reasons and/or examples to support your view:

> *Elementary schools should not waste their limited resources by teaching children a second language, especially since so many children are still struggling to master the most basic reading, writing, and arithmetic skills.*

> * * *

> *A nation's greatness can be measured by looking at the achievements of its individual rulers, scientists, and artists.*

> * * *

> *People can learn as much from watching television news programs as they can from reading newspapers.*

_____

_____

_____

_____

_____

_____

_____

_____

_____

_____

_____

_____

_____

_____

_____

_____

_____

Essay 2: Analyze an Argument

Discuss how well-reasoned you find each of the following arguments:

Many lives might be saved if inoculations against cow flu were routinely administered to all people in areas in which the disease is detected. However, since there is a small possibility that a person will die as a result of the inoculations, we cannot permit inoculations against cow flu to be routinely administered.

* * *

The following is a recommendation from the mayor of Sunny Harbor to the town council:

Three years ago, the neighboring town of Cedar Grove built a new shopping mall. During the past three years, Cedar Grove's tax revenues have risen by 40 percent. The best way to improve Sunny Harbor's economy and generate additional tax revenues is to build a bigger shopping mall than the one in Cedar Grove.

* * *

The following appeared in a report to the governor of the state of New Manchester:

Of the 500 serious traffic accidents that have occurred in our state over the past 10 months, 65 percent have involved 16-year-old drivers. Obviously, 16-year-olds do not have the emotional maturity needed to be safe drivers. The best solution is to pass a law requiring our citizens to be at least 18 years old before they can obtain a driver's license.

_____

_____

_____

_____

_____

_____

_____

_____

CHAPTER FIVE

Test Mechanics

HIGHLIGHTS

- Understand how the GRE CAT works and how it affects YOU
- Learn how to easily navigate through the test on your computer
- Study Kaplan's exclusive CAT-specific test-taking strategies

The first year of graduate school is a frenzied experience for many students. It's no surprise, then, that the GRE, the test specifically designed to predict success in the first year of graduate school, is a speed-intensive test that demands good time-management skills.

So when you're comfortable with the content of the test, namely, the type of material discussed in the previous chapters, your next challenge will be to take it to the next level—test mechanics—which will enable you to manage an entire section at a time.

On most of the tests you take in school, you wouldn't dream of not making at least a try at every single one of the questions. If a question seems particularly difficult, you spend significantly more time on it, because you'll probably be given more points for answering a hard question correctly. Not so on the GRE.

You've got to develop a way of handling the test sections to make sure you get as many points as you can as quickly and easily as you can. The following principles will help you do just that.

Teacher Tip

"One worry many students have is the fact that you can't skip questions on the CAT. I tell them the difference between a good score and a great score is recognizing the tougher questions, using Kaplan's methods for making an educated guess, and moving on to questions where they can focus their strengths. A great score is nothing but a good score topped with smart guesses."
—Jason Anderson
Chicago, Illinois

Mechanics of the GRE CAT

The CAT is in some ways quite different from the traditional paper-and-pencil tests you've probably taken in the past. In fact, it's pretty weird at first. Here's how it works. You will only see one question at a time. Instead of having a predetermined mixture of basic, medium, and hard questions, the computer will select questions for you based on how well you are doing. The first question will be of medium difficulty. If you get it right, the second question will be a little harder; if you get the first question wrong, the second will be a little more basic.

If you keep getting questions right, the test will get harder and harder; if you slip and make some mistakes, the test will adjust and start giving you easier problems, but if you answer them correctly, it will go back to the hard ones. Ideally, the test gives you enough questions to ensure that scores are not based on luck. If you get one hard question right you might just have been lucky, but if you get 10 hard questions right, then luck has little to do with it. So the test is self-adjusting and self-correcting.

Because of this format, the CAT is very different structurally from a paper-and-pencil test. After the first problem, every problem that you see is based on how you answered the prior problem. That means you cannot return to a question once you've answered it, because that would throw off the sequence. Once you answer a question, it's part of your score, for better or worse. That means you can't skip around within a section and do questions in the order that you like.

Another major consequence is that hard problems count more than easy ones. It has to be this way, because the very purpose of this adaptive format is to find out at what level you reliably get about *half* the questions right; that's your scoring level. It actually makes a lot of sense. Imagine two students—one who does 10 basic questions, half of which she gets right and half of which she gets wrong, and one who does 10 very difficult questions, half of which she gets right and half of which she gets wrong. The same number of questions have been answered correctly in each case, but this does not reflect an equal ability on the part of the two students.

In fact, the student who answered five out of ten very difficult questions incorrectly could still get a very high score on the CAT GRE. But in order to get to these hard questions, she first had to get medium-difficulty questions right. So, no matter how much more comfortable you might be sticking to the basic questions, you definitely want to get to the hard questions if you can, because that's where the points are.

Kaplan Tip

The CAT doesn't allow you to skip questions. If a question has you stumped, make an intelligent guess and just move on.

Teacher Tip

"On the first question, the CAT assumes that you have exactly average ability. If you get the first question right, the CAT raises its estimate of your test-taking ability; if you get the first question wrong, it lowers its estimate. Ideally, you want to convince the CAT that every estimate it makes of your test-taking ability is too low."
—Vince LoCascio
New Brunswick, New Jersey

First Impressions Count

One of the most important things to know is that the early questions are vital for a good score on the CAT. As in life, first impressions make a big difference.

Why? Because the computer doesn't have information about you at the start of the test, and its goal is to get an accurate estimate of your score as quickly as possible. In order to do that, the computer has to make large jumps in the estimation of your score for each of the first few questions.

It's a lot like how you would act if you were trying to guess which number a person had picked from one to 10, and the only thing you could be told was whether the number was higher, lower, or the same as what you guessed. To do this most efficiently, you'd guess five first, since if the right number were higher or lower you could eliminate about half the choices. If you were told the actual number was lower than five, you'd guess three next, since that cuts the possibilities down the most. If the number were higher than three, it would have to be four. If it were lower, it would have to be one or two. Using this method, at most you would have to take three guesses before you knew the answer, whereas if you just started guessing randomly, or started from one and worked your way up, you could guess as many as 10 times before getting the right answer.

Like the efficient guesser, the computer doesn't use intuition to find the right answer, but uses the most effective method. Instead of using numbers to "guess" your score, though, the computer gives you questions that have a precise difficulty level assigned to them. In effect, you tell it whether your score is higher or lower than this difficulty level by getting the question right or wrong.

What's the upshot of all this? Simple: *Pay extra attention to the first few questions, and do all that you can to get them right!* Feel free to spend a little extra time double-checking the first five problems or so, and make sure you try every elimination technique you know before guessing on one of these problems if you don't know the answer.

Three More Section Management Techniques

First, if you get a lot of mileage from the strategy of eliminating answer choices based on difficulty level, you can apply it on the CAT, though in a different and limited way. It won't be spelled out for you as it would be on a paper-and-pencil test, but as you progress through the questions, you should have a good idea of how you're doing. If you've practiced a lot on real questions, it's fairly easy to maintain a pretty clear sense of the difficulty level of your questions and to eliminate answer choices accordingly. For instance, if you're confident that you've been answering most of the questions correctly, then you should be seeing harder and harder questions. If that seems to be the case, you can safely eliminate answer choices that look too obvious or basic for a difficult question.

Kaplan Tip

It's difficult for some of us to give up on a tough, time-consuming question, but it must be done occasionally. Remember, there's no point of honor at stake here, but there are GRE points at stake.

Kaplan Tip

Use your one-minute break between sections to replenish your supply of scratch paper, if necessary.

Secondly, if crossing off answer choices on paper tests really helps to clarify your thinking (using a process of elimination), you may want to consider making a grid on your scratch paper before you begin the CAT. Use it to mark off answer choices that you have eliminated, as shown below. That way you can tell at a glance which answer choices are still in the running. If you end up using it often, it will be worth the 10 seconds it takes to draw a simple grid, like this one:

A	X	X		X		X			X		X		
B		X	X	X			X	X	X	X		X	
C					X				X				X
D	X		X		X			X		X		X	
E	X	X		X			X			X			

Finally, the timer in the corner can work to your advantage, but if you find yourself looking at it so frequently that it becomes a distraction, you should turn it off for 10 or 15 minutes and try to refocus your attention on the test, even if you lose track of time somewhat. *The CAT rewards focus and accuracy more than it does raw speed.*

Navigating the CAT: Computer Basics

Let's preview the primary computer functions that you will use to move around on the CAT. ETS calls them "testing tools," but they're basically just boxes that you can click with your mouse. The following screen is typical for an adaptive test.

Here's what the various buttons do.

The Scroll Bar
Similar to that on a windows-style computer display, this is a thin, vertical column with up and down arrows at the top and bottom. Clicking on the arrows moves you up or down the page you're reading.

The Time Button
Clicking on this button turns the time display at the top of the screen on and off. When you have five minutes left in a section, the clock flashes and the display changes from Hours/Minutes to Hours/Minutes/Seconds.

Kaplan Tip

Use the computer tutorial to your advantage. Spend as much time as you need to make yourself comfortable with the computer *before* you begin the actual test. Once the test is under way, clicking on "Help" to review the directions or a summary of the tutorial will count against your allotted time for that section of the test.

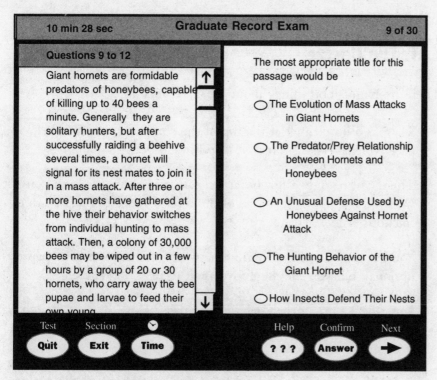

Typical screen display in the CAT.

The Section Exit Button
This allows you to exit the section before the time is up. If you budget your time wisely you should never have to use this button—time will run out just as you are finishing the section.

The Test Quit Button
Hitting this button ends the test prematurely. *Do not* use this button unless you want all of your scores canceled and your test invalidated.

The Help Button
This one leads to directions and other stuff from the tutorial. But beware: The test clock won't pause just because you click on Help.

The Confirm Answer Button
This button tells the computer you are happy with your answer and are really ready to move to the next question. You cannot proceed until you have hit this button.

The Next Button
Hit this when you want to move on to the next question. After you press Next, you must hit Confirm.

Note
For the Analytical Writing section of the GRE, the essay directions and prompts will be delivered on the computer screen, and then you have to word-process your essays. When you word-process your essays, the only functions you'll use are *insert text*, *delete text*, *cut and paste*, and *undo*.

CAT: The Upside

There are many good things about the CAT, such as:

- There is a little timer at the top of the computer screen to help you pace yourself (you can hide it if it distracts you).

- There will be only a few other test takers in the room with you—it won't be like taking it in one of those massive lecture halls with distractions everywhere.

- You get a pause of one minute between each section. The pause is optional, but you should always use it to relax and stretch.

- You can sign up for the GRE just two days before the test (though we recommend signing up much earlier!), and registration is very easy.

- The CAT is convenient to schedule. It's offered at more than 175 centers three to five days a week (depending on the center) all year long.

- You don't have to take it on the same day as a subject test, which can greatly reduce fatigue.

- Perhaps the CAT's best feature is that it gives you your Verbal and Quantitative scores immediately and will send them to schools just 10 to 15 days later.

CAT: The Downside

There are also not-so-good things about the CAT.

- You cannot skip around on this test; you must answer the questions one at a time in the order the computer gives them to you.

- If you realize later that you answered a question incorrectly, you can't go back and change your answer.

- You can't cross off an answer choice and never look at it again, so you have to be more disciplined about not reconsidering choices you've already eliminated.

- You may have to scroll through long reading comprehension passages and graphs, which means you won't be able to see the whole thing on the screen at once.

- You can't write on your computer screen the way you can on a paper test (though some have tried), so you have to use scratch paper they give you, which will be inconveniently located away from the computer screen.

- Lastly, many people find that computer screens tire them and cause eyestrain—especially after three hours.

Kaplan CAT Strategies

Using certain CAT-specific strategies can have a direct, positive impact on your score:

- At the beginning of the section, each question you get right or wrong will rapidly move the computer's estimate of your score up or down. A key strategy for doing well on the CAT is to get the computer's estimate of your score up to where you are handling the hard questions, because getting a hard question right will help your score a lot, but getting a hard question wrong will hurt your score only slightly. Thus it pays to spend more time on those early questions, double-checking each answer before you confirm it. Getting to the hard questions as quickly as possible can only help your final score.

- As you progress through the middle part of the section, try to avoid getting several questions in a row wrong, as this will sink your score on the CAT. If you know that the previous question you answered was a blind guess, spend a little extra time trying to get the next question right.

- The CAT will switch from one question type to another within a section (going from Reading Comp to Antonyms, for example) WITHOUT automatically showing the directions for each new question type. Knowing the format and directions of each GRE question type beforehand will save you a lot of time and avoid possible confusion during the exam.

> ### Teacher Tip
>
> "Because you can't skip questions and come back to them, it is essential that you make good judgments about how much time to invest in any one question."
> —Tiffany Sanders
> Downers Grove, Illinois

- The CAT does not begin with really easy questions that gradually get harder, as do many paper-based tests. Because the order of difficulty will not be predictable, always be on the lookout for answer-choice traps.

- Because each right or wrong answer directly affects the next question you get, the CAT does not allow you to go back to questions you've already answered to double-check your work. So be as certain as possible that you have answered a question correctly before moving on.

- The CAT does not allow you to skip questions. So if you are given a question you cannot answer, you'll have to guess. Guess intelligently and strategically—eliminating any wrong answer choices that you can spot and guessing among those remaining.

- Don't get rattled if you keep seeing really, really difficult questions. It just means you're doing very well on that section. Keep it up!

- At the end of the section, you are penalized more heavily for not getting to a question at all than for answering it wrong. So if you only have a minute or two left and several questions remaining, you should guess at random rather than leave anything unanswered. And if you're down to the very last question and have almost no time left, make sure to click on a response first and then attempt to answer the question. You can always change your answer, and you're allowed to confirm whatever answer you've clicked after the time has run out.

CHAPTER SIX

Test Mentality

- Learn Kaplan's Four Basic Principles of Good Test Mentality
- Find out how to handle stress leading up to and during the exam
- Know when and how you should cancel your scores

In this test prep section, we first looked at the content that makes up each specific section of the GRE, focusing on the strategies and techniques that you'll need to tackle individual questions, games, and passages. Then we discussed the mechanics involved in taking a computer-adaptive test. Now we're ready to turn our attention to the often overlooked attitudinal aspects of the test. We'll then combine these factors with what we learned in the chapters on test content and test mechanics to put the finishing touches on your comprehensive GRE approach.

Kaplan Tip

Remember that the GRE isn't like most tests you've taken. You can get a lot of questions wrong and still get a great score. So don't get rattled if you miss a few questions.

The Four Basic Principles of Good Test Mentality

We've already armed you with the weapons that you need to do well on the GRE. But you must wield those weapons with the right frame of mind and in the right spirit. This involves taking a certain stance toward the entire test. Here's what's involved.

Test Awareness

To do your best on the GRE, you must always keep in mind that the test is like no other test you've taken before, both in terms of its content and in terms of its scoring system. If you took a test in high school or college and got a quarter of the questions wrong, you'd probably receive a pretty lousy grade. Not so with the GRE CAT. The test is geared so that only the very best test takers are able to finish every section with time to spare. But even these people rarely get every question right.

What does this mean for you? Well, just as you shouldn't let one tough reading comp passage ruin an entire section, you shouldn't let what you consider to be a subpar performance on one section ruin your performance on the entire test. A lousy performance on one single section will not by itself spoil your score—unless you literally miss almost every question. If you allow that subpar section to rattle you, however, it can have a cumulative negative effect that sets in motion a downward spiral. It's that kind of thing that could potentially do serious damage to your score. Losing a few extra points won't do you in, but losing your head will.

Remember, if you feel that you've done poorly on a section, don't sweat it. It could be the experimental one. And even if it's not, you must remain calm and collected. Simply do your best on each section, and once a section is over, forget about it and move on.

Stamina

You must work on your test taking stamina. Overall, the GRE is a fairly grueling experience, and some test takers simply run out of gas on the final few sections. To avoid this, you must prepare by taking as many full-length practice tests as possible in the week or two before the test, so that on the test, five sections will seem like a breeze (well, maybe not a breeze, but at least not a hurricane).

When you register for the GRE, ETS will send you a free copy of its POWERPREP® software, including two computer-adaptive practice tests. Or if you prefer, you may download the POWERPREP software yourself at *www.gre.org*.

Another option, if you have enough time left before your exam, would be to take a Kaplan course, either classroom-based or online. You could also set up special one-on-one tutoring sessions with Kaplan experts. If you decide to go this route, visit *www.kaptest.com*, or call 1-800-KAP-TEST for a Kaplan center location near you.

Kaplan Tip

Losing a few extra points here and there won't do serious damage to your score but losing your head will. Keeping your composure is an important test-taking skill.

Kaplan Tip

Remember: You'll most likely be taking up to five full-length sections on Test Day (Verbal, Quantitative, Analytical Writing, Experimental, and Research). Don't run out of steam after your first couple of sections!

Confidence

Confidence feeds on itself, and unfortunately, so does the opposite of confidence—self-doubt. Confidence in your ability leads to quick, sure answers and an ease of concentration that translates into more points. If you lack concentration, you end up reading sentences and answer choices two, three, or four times. This leads to timing difficulties, which only continue the downward spiral, causing anxiety and a tendency to rush.

If you subscribe to the GRE mindset that we've described, however, you'll be ready and able to take control of the test. Learn our techniques and then practice them over and over again. That's the way to score your best on the test.

Attitude

Those who approach the GRE as an obstacle and who rail against the necessity of taking it usually don't fare as well as those who see the GRE as an opportunity to show off the reading and reasoning skills that graduate schools are looking for. Those who look forward to doing battle with the GRE—or, at least, who enjoy the opportunity to distinguish themselves from the rest of the applicant pack—tend to score better than do those who resent or dread it.

It may sound a little dubious, but take our word for it: attitude adjustment is proven to raise points. Here are a few steps you can take to make sure you develop the right GRE attitude:

- Look at the GRE as a challenge, but try not to obsess over it; you certainly don't want to psyche yourself out of the game.

- Remember that, yes, the GRE is obviously important, but, contrary to what some people think, this one test will not single-handedly determine the outcome of your life. In many cases, it's not even the most important piece of your graduate application.

- Try to have fun with the test. Learning how to match your wits against the test makers can be a very satisfying experience, and the reading and thinking skills you'll acquire will benefit you in graduate school as well as in your future career.

- Remember that you're more prepared than most people. You've trained with Kaplan. You have the tools you need, plus the know-how to use those tools.

Kaplan Tip

Still looking for more practice? Log on to **www.kaptest.com/ booksonline** to access a wide selection of GRE-like practice questions. Be sure to have this book handy when you log on: you'll be asked to input this book's ISBN number and a specific password that is derived from a passage in this book.

The Kaplan Advantage™ Stress Management System

Is it starting to feel as if your whole life is a buildup to the GRE? You've known about it for years, worried about it for months, and now spent at least a few weeks in solid preparation for it. As the test gets closer, you may find that your anxiety is on the rise. You shouldn't worry. Armed with the preparation strategies that you've learned from this book, you're in good shape for the day of the test.

To calm any pretest jitters that you may have, however, let's go over a few strategies for the couple of days before and after the test.

Quick Tips for the Days Just Before the Exam

- The best test takers do less and less as the test approaches. Taper off your study schedule and take it easy on yourself. Give yourself time off, especially the evening before the exam. By that time, if you've studied well, everything you need to know is firmly stored in your memory bank.

- Positive self-talk can be extremely liberating and invigorating, especially as the test looms closer. Tell yourself things such as "I will do well," rather than "I hope things go well"; "I can," rather than "I cannot." Replace any negative thoughts with affirming statements that boost your self-esteem.

- Get your act together sooner rather than later. Have everything (including choice of clothing) laid out in advance. Most important, make sure you know where the test will be held and the easiest, quickest way to get there. You'll have great peace of mind by knowing that all the little details—gas in the car, directions, etcetera—are set before the day of the test.

- Go to the test site a few days in advance, particularly if you are especially anxious. Better yet, bring some practice material and do at least a section or two.

- Forego any practice on the day before the test. It's in your best interest to marshal your physical and psychological resources for 24 hours or so. Even race horses are kept in the paddock and treated like princes the day before a race. Keep the upcoming test out of your consciousness; go to a movie, take a pleasant hike, or just relax. Don't eat junk food or tons of sugar. And, of course, get plenty of rest the night before—just don't go to bed too early. It's hard to fall asleep ear-

Kaplan Tip

Don't try to cram a lot of studying into the last day before the test. It probably won't do you much good, and it could bring on a case of test burnout.

Kaplan Tip

Don't study on your bed, especially if you have problems with insomnia. Your mind may start to associate the bed with work, and will make it even harder for you to fall asleep.

lier than you're used to, and you don't want to lie there worrying about the test.

Handling Stress During the Test

The biggest stress monster will be the test itself. Fear not; there are methods of quelling your stress during the test.

- Keep moving forward instead of getting bogged down in a difficult question. You don't have to get everything right to achieve a fine score. So, don't linger out of desperation on a question that is going nowhere even after you've spent considerable time on it.

- Don't be thrown if other test takers seem to be working more busily and furiously than you are. Don't mistake the other people's sheer activity as signs of progress and higher scores.

- Keep breathing! Weak test takers tend to share one major trait: They don't breathe properly as the test proceeds. They might hold their breath without realizing it, or breathe erratically or arrhythmically. Improper breathing hurts confidence and accuracy. Just as important, it interferes with clear thinking.

- Some quick isometrics during the test—especially if concentration is wandering or energy is waning—can help. Try this: Put your palms together and press intensely for a few seconds. Concentrate on the tension you feel through your palms, wrists, forearms, and up into your biceps and shoulders. Then, quickly release the pressure. Feel the difference as you let go. Focus on the warm relaxation that floods through the muscles. Now you're ready to return to the task.

- Here's another isometric that will relieve tension in both your neck and eye muscles: Slowly rotate your head from side to side, turning your head and eyes to look as far back over each shoulder as you can. Feel the muscles stretch on one side of your neck as they contract on the other. Repeat five times in each direction.

Test Day!

Let's now discuss what you can expect on the day of the test itself. The day should start with a moderate, high energy breakfast. Cereal, fruit, bagels, or eggs are good. Avoid donuts, danishes, or anything else with a

Teacher Tip

"Take care of yourself. Sounds simple, no? Sleep well, eat well, be nice to others, and drive safely before you take the test. Sick and injured people don't do well on exams!"
—Tanya Kormeili
Los Angeles, California

lot of sugar in it. Also, unless you are utterly catatonic without it, it's a good idea to stay away from coffee. Yeah, yeah, you drink two cups every morning and don't even notice it. But it's different during the test. Coffee won't make you alert (your adrenaline will do that much more effectively); it will just give you the jitters. Kaplan has done experiments in which test takers go into one exam having drunk various amounts of coffee and another exam without having drunk coffee. The results indicate that even the most caffeine-addicted test takers will lose their focus midway through the second section if they've had coffee, but they report no alertness problems without it.

When you get to the test center, you will be seated at a computer station. Some administrative questions will be asked before the test begins, and once you're done with those . . . it's showtime. While you're taking the test, a small clock will count down the time you have left in each section. The computer will tell you when you're done with each section, and when you're completed the test itself.

Finally, here are some last-minute reminders to help guide your work on the test:

- Give all five answer choices a fair shot in Verbal (especially reading comp), time permitting. For the Quantitative section, go with the objectively correct answer as soon as you find it, and just blow off the rest of the answers.

- Don't bother trying to figure out which section is unscored. It can't help you, and you might very well be wrong. Instead, just do your best on every section.

- Pay no attention to people who are chattering on their break. Just concentrate on how well prepared you are.

- Dress in layers for maximum comfort. This way, you can adjust to the room's temperature accordingly.

- Take a few minutes now to look back over your preparation and give yourself credit for how far you've come. Confidence is key. Accentuate the positives and don't dwell on the negatives! Your attitude and outlook are crucial to your performance on the test.

- During the exam, try not to think about how you're scoring. It's like a baseball player who's thinking about the crowd's cheers, the sportswriters, and his contract as he steps up to the plate. It's a great way to strike out. Instead, focus on the question-by-question task of picking the correct answer choice. After all, the correct answer is there (for the multiple-choice sections, at least). You don't have to come up with it; it's sitting right there in front of you! Concentrate on each question, each passage, each essay prompt—on the mechanics, in other words—and you'll be much more likely to hit a home run.

Cancellation and Multiple Scores Policy

Unlike many things in life, the GRE allows you a second chance. If, at the end of the test, you feel that you've definitely not done as well as you can, you have the option to cancel your score. The trick is, you must decide whether you want to keep your scores before the computer shows them to you. If you cancel, your scores will be disregarded. (You also won't get to see them.) Canceling a test means that it won't be scored. It will just appear on your score report as a canceled test. No one will know how well or poorly you really did—not even you.

Two legitimate reasons to cancel your test are illness and personal circumstances that cause you to perform unusually poorly on that particular day. Also, if you feel that you didn't prepare sufficiently, then it may be acceptable to cancel your score and approach your test preparation a little more seriously the next time.

But keep in mind that test takers historically underestimate their performance, especially immediately following the test. This underestimation is especially true on the CAT, which is designed to give you questions at the limits of your abilities. They tend to forget about all of the things that went right and focus on everything that went wrong. So unless your performance is terribly marred by unforeseen circumstances, don't cancel your test.

If you do cancel, your future score reports will indicate that you've canceled a previous score. But since the canceled test was never scored, you don't have to worry about bad numbers showing up on any subsequent score report. If you take more than one test without canceling, then all the scores will show up on each score report, so the graduate schools will see them all. Most grad schools average GRE scores, although there are a few exceptions. Check with individual schools for their policies on multiple scores.

Kaplan Tip

The key question to ask yourself when deciding whether to cancel is this: "Will I really do significantly better next time?"

Teacher Tip

"Students become so involved in the exam that they forget they must produce a flawless, professional application document in addition to jumping through the other hoops. I help students to balance their focus, so that they can meet effectively both the challenge of the test and the rigors of the application process.
—Chris Skinner
Santa Barbara, California

Post-GRE Festivities

After all the hard work that you've put in preparing for and taking the GRE, make sure you take time to celebrate afterwards. Plan to get together with friends the evening after the test. Relax, have fun, let loose. After all, you've got a lot to celebrate. You prepared for the test ahead of time. You did your best. You're going to get a great score.

CHAPTER SEVEN

The Subject Tests

- Learn about the various GRE Subject Tests and how they differ from the GRE General Test

Subject Tests are designed to test the fundamental knowledge most important for successful graduate study in a particular subject area. In order to do well on a GRE Subject Test, you basically need to have an extensive background in the particular subject area—the sort of background you would be expected to have if you majored in the subject. In this section, we'll answer the most common questions about the GRE Subject Tests.

Do You Have to Take a Subject Test?

Not every graduate school or program requires Subject Tests, so check admissions requirements at those schools in which you're interested.

What's the Purpose of Subject Tests?

Unlike the GRE General Test, which assesses skills that have been developed over a long period of time and are not related to a particular subject area, Subject Tests assess knowledge of a particular field of study. They enable admissions officers to compare students from different colleges with different standards and curricula.

Note

Online registration is available for Subject Tests (but not for the GRE General Test). Go to www.gre.org to fill out and submit your registration form electronically.

What Are Subject Tests Like?

All Subject Tests are administered in paper-and-pencil format and consist exclusively of multiple-choice questions that are designed to assess knowledge of the areas of the subject that are included in the typical undergraduate curriculum.

On Subject Tests, you'll earn one point for each multiple choice question that you answer correctly but lose one-quarter point for each incorrectly answered question. Unanswered questions aren't counted in the scoring. Your raw score is the number of correctly answered questions minus one-quarter of the incorrectly answered questions. This raw score is then converted into a scaled score, which can range from 200 to 900. The range varies from test to test.

Some Subject Tests also contain subtests, which provide more specific information about your strengths and weaknesses. The same questions that contribute to your subtest scores also contribute to your overall score. Subtest scores, which range from 20 to 99, are reported along with the overall score. For further information on scoring, you should consult the relevant Subject Test Descriptive Booklet, available from ETS.

Note

On a Subject Test, you gain one point for each correct answer—but lose one-quarter point for each wrong answer.

Are There Any Different Test-Taking Strategies for the Subject Tests?

Because the multiple-choice questions on Subject Tests have a wrong-answer penalty of one-quarter point, you should adopt a different test-taking strategy for your Subject Test than the one you're going to use for the GRE General Test. On the Subject Tests, you shouldn't attempt to fill in an answer for every question on the test, nor do you have to guess at every question you see if you want to get another question (like on the CAT). On Subject Tests, you should guess only if you can eliminate one or more of the answer choices.

When Should You Take the Subject Test?

Subject Tests are offered three times a year: in November, December, and April. Note that not all of the Subject Tests are offered on every test date; consult the relevant Subject Test Descriptive Booklet, available from ETS, for upcoming test dates and registration deadlines.

How Many Subject Tests Are There and What Fields Do They Cover?

Over the past few years, ETS has eliminated several of the GRE Subject Tests. Currently, only eight Subject Tests are offered. A list of them follows, along with a brief description of each.

Biochemistry, Cell, and Molecular Biology

This test consists of 180 questions and is divided among three subscore areas: biochemistry, cell biology, and molecular biology and genetics.

Biology

This test consists of about 200 questions divided among three subscore areas: cellular and molecular biology, organismal biology, and ecology and evolution.

Chemistry

This test consists of about 136 questions. There are no subscores, and the questions cover the following topics: analytical chemistry, inorganic chemistry, organic chemistry, and physical chemistry.

Computer Science

This test consists of approximately 70 questions. There are no subscores, and the questions cover the following topics: software systems and methodology, computer organization and architecture, theory, mathematical background, and other, more advanced topics, such as modeling, simulation, and artificial intelligence.

Literature in English

This test consists of 230 questions on literature in the English language. There are two basic types of questions: factual questions that test the student's knowledge of writers typically covered in the undergraduate curriculum, and interpretive questions that test the student's ability to read various types of literature critically.

Mathematics

This test consists of 66 questions on the content of various undergraduate courses in mathematics. Most of the test assesses the student's knowledge of calculus, abstract algebra, linear algebra, and real analysis. About a quarter of the test, however, requires knowledge in other areas of math.

Note

"Testing aids" are not allowed to be used, including calculators, rulers, translators, highlighters, etcetera.

Physics

This test consists of 100 questions covering mostly material covered in the first three years of undergraduate physics. Topics include classical mechanics, electromagnetism, atomic physics, optics and wave phenomena, quantum mechanics, thermodynamics and statistical mechanics, special relativity, and laboratory methods. About 9 percent of the test covers advanced topics, such as nuclear and particle physics, condensed matter physics, and astrophysics.

Psychology

This test consists of 220 questions drawn from courses most commonly included in the undergraduate curriculum. Questions fall into three categories. The experimental or natural science-oriented category includes questions in learning, cognitive psychology, sensation and perception, ethology and comparative psychology, and physiological psychology. The social or social science-oriented category includes questions in abnormal psychology, developmental psychology, social psychology, and personality. Together, these make up about 85 percent of the test, and each of the two categories provides its own subscore. The other 15 percent or so of the questions fall under the "general" category, which includes the history of psychology, tests and measurements, research design and statistics, and applied psychology.

For more information, you should consult the relevant Subject Test Descriptive Booklet, available from ETS.; you can download these free booklets now at *www.gre.org*. You can also visit the Kaplan website (*kaptest.com*) for a more detailed description of each subject test and some free sample questions.

The GRE Practice Test

How to Take This Practice Test

Before taking this Practice Test, find a quiet place where you can work uninterrupted for three hours. Make sure you have a comfortable desk and several pencils. Time yourself according to the time limits shown at the beginning of each section. It's okay to take a short break between sections, but for the most accurate results, you should go through all three sections in one sitting. Use the answer grid on the following page to record your answers to the multiple-choice sections. You'll find the answer key and score converter following the test. Good luck.

Note that the time limits and section lengths for this paper-based Practice Test differ from those of the actual GRE exam. (This compensates for the fact that on the actual exam, the level of difficulty will change based on your previous answers, and you will not be able to skip or return to any questions.) While the interactive test-taking experience is impossible to reproduce in a book, this normed Practice Test is designed to produce an accurate score.

If you purchased the edition of this book that is bundled with a CD-ROM, you will find three realistic CATs to practice with in the software. If you purchased the edition that doesn't come with a CD-ROM, you can take a practice CAT on Kaplan's website (www.kaptest.com), or purchase Kaplan's test-prep software separately at your local software store.

KAPLAN

Practice Test

Remove or photocopy this answer sheet and use it to complete the Verbal and Quantitative sections of the Practice Test. See the answer key at the end of the test to correct your answers when finished.

SECTION 1 VERBAL

1	A B C D E	20	A B C D E	39	A B C D E	58	A B C D E
2	A B C D E	21	A B C D E	40	A B C D E	59	A B C D E
3	A B C D E	22	A B C D E	41	A B C D E	60	A B C D E
4	A B C D E	23	A B C D E	42	A B C D E	61	A B C D E
5	A B C D E	24	A B C D E	43	A B C D E	62	A B C D E
6	A B C D E	25	A B C D E	44	A B C D E	63	A B C D E
7	A B C D E	26	A B C D E	45	A B C D E	64	A B C D E
8	A B C D E	27	A B C D E	46	A B C D E	65	A B C D E
9	A B C D E	28	A B C D E	47	A B C D E	66	A B C D E
10	A B C D E	29	A B C D E	48	A B C D E	67	A B C D E
11	A B C D E	30	A B C D E	49	A B C D E	68	A B C D E
12	A B C D E	31	A B C D E	50	A B C D E	69	A B C D E
13	A B C D E	32	A B C D E	51	A B C D E	70	A B C D E
14	A B C D E	33	A B C D E	52	A B C D E	71	A B C D E
15	A B C D E	34	A B C D E	53	A B C D E	72	A B C D E
16	A B C D E	35	A B C D E	54	A B C D E	73	A B C D E
17	A B C D E	36	A B C D E	55	A B C D E	74	A B C D E
18	A B C D E	37	A B C D E	56	A B C D E	75	A B C D E
19	A B C D E	38	A B C D E	57	A B C D E	76	A B C D E

SECTION 2 QUANTITATIVE

1	A B C D E	16	A B C D E	31	A B C D E	46	A B C D E
2	A B C D E	17	A B C D E	32	A B C D E	47	A B C D E
3	A B C D E	18	A B C D E	33	A B C D E	48	A B C D E
4	A B C D E	19	A B C D E	34	A B C D E	49	A B C D E
5	A B C D E	20	A B C D E	35	A B C D E	50	A B C D E
6	A B C D E	21	A B C D E	36	A B C D E	51	A B C D E
7	A B C D E	22	A B C D E	37	A B C D E	52	A B C D E
8	A B C D E	23	A B C D E	38	A B C D E	53	A B C D E
9	A B C D E	24	A B C D E	39	A B C D E	54	A B C D E
10	A B C D E	25	A B C D E	40	A B C D E	55	A B C D E
11	A B C D E	26	A B C D E	41	A B C D E	56	A B C D E
12	A B C D E	27	A B C D E	42	A B C D E	57	A B C D E
13	A B C D E	28	A B C D E	43	A B C D E	58	A B C D E
14	A B C D E	29	A B C D E	44	A B C D E	59	A B C D E
15	A B C D E	30	A B C D E	45	A B C D E	60	A B C D E

Section 3: Analytical Writing
Essay 1

_____

_____

_____

_____

_____

_____

_____

_____

_____

_____

_____

_____

_____

_____

_____

_____

_____

_____

_____

_____

_____

_____

GO ON TO THE NEXT PAGE

Essay 2

_____

_____

_____

_____

_____

_____

_____

_____

_____

_____

_____

_____

_____

_____

_____

_____

_____

_____

_____

_____

GO ON TO THE NEXT PAGE

SECTION ONE: VERBAL
Time—60 minutes   76 questions

Directions: Each of the following questions begins with a sentence that has either one or two blanks. The blanks indicate that a piece of the sentence is missing. Each sentence is followed by five answer choices that consist of words or phrases. Select the answer choice that completes the sentence best.

1. The fundamental _____ between dogs and cats is for the most part a myth; members of these species often coexist _____.

   Ⓐ antipathy . . amiably
   Ⓑ disharmony . . uneasily
   Ⓒ compatibility . . together
   Ⓓ relationship . . peacefully
   Ⓔ difference . . placidly

2. His desire to state his case completely was certainly reasonable; however, his lengthy technical explanations were monotonous and tended to _____ rather than _____ the jury.

   Ⓐ enlighten . . inform
   Ⓑ interest . . persuade
   Ⓒ provoke . . influence
   Ⓓ allay . . pacify
   Ⓔ bore . . convince

3. In some countries, government restrictions are so _____ that businesses operate with nearly complete impunity.

   Ⓐ traditional
   Ⓑ judicious
   Ⓒ ambiguous
   Ⓓ exacting
   Ⓔ lax

4. The recent Oxford edition of the works of Shakespeare is _____ because it not only departs frequently from the readings of most other modern editions, but also challenges many of the basic _____ of textual criticism.

   Ⓐ controversial . . conventions
   Ⓑ typical . . innovations
   Ⓒ inadequate . . norms
   Ⓓ curious . . projects
   Ⓔ pretentious . . explanations

5. The early form of writing known as Linear B was _____ in 1952, but no one has yet succeeded in the _____ of the still more ancient Linear A.

   Ⓐ superseded . . explanation
   Ⓑ encoded . . transcription
   Ⓒ obliterated . . analysis
   Ⓓ deciphered . . interpretation
   Ⓔ discovered . . obfuscation

6. Considering everything she had been through, her reaction was quite normal and even _____ ; I was therefore surprised at the number of _____ comments and raised eyebrows that her response elicited.

    (A) commendable . . complimentary
    (B) odious . . insulting
    (C) apologetic . . conciliatory
    (D) commonplace . . typical
    (E) laudable . . derogatory

7. The purpose of the proposed insurance policy is to _____ the burden of medical costs, thereby removing what is for many people a major _____ medical care.

    (A) augment . . problem with
    (B) eliminate . . perquisite of
    (C) ameliorate . . study of
    (D) assuage . . impediment to
    (E) clarify . . explanation for

GO ON TO THE NEXT PAGE

Directions: Each of the following questions consists of a pair of words or phrases that are separated by a colon and followed by five answer choices. Choose the pair of words or phrases in the answer choices that are most similar to the original pair.

8. NOVEL : BOOK ::

   Ⓐ epic : poem
   Ⓑ house : library
   Ⓒ tale : fable
   Ⓓ number : page
   Ⓔ play : theater

9. HUNGRY : RAVENOUS ::

   Ⓐ thirsty : desirous
   Ⓑ large : titanic
   Ⓒ famous : eminent
   Ⓓ dizzy : disoriented
   Ⓔ obese : gluttonous

10. BOUQUET : FLOWER ::

   Ⓐ humidor : tobacco
   Ⓑ mosaic : tile
   Ⓒ tapestry : color
   Ⓓ pile : block
   Ⓔ sacristy : vestment

11. REALIST : QUIXOTIC ::

   Ⓐ scholar : pedantic
   Ⓑ fool : idiotic
   Ⓒ idler : lethargic
   Ⓓ tormentor : sympathetic
   Ⓔ diner : dyspeptic

12. SHARD : GLASS ::

   Ⓐ grain : sand
   Ⓑ morsel : meal
   Ⓒ strand : rope
   Ⓓ scrap : quilt
   Ⓔ splinter : wood

13. FILTER : IMPURITY ::

   Ⓐ expurgate : obscenity
   Ⓑ whitewash : infraction
   Ⓒ testify : perjury
   Ⓓ perform : penance
   Ⓔ vacuum : carpet

14. PARAPHRASE : VERBATIM ::

   Ⓐ approximation : precise
   Ⓑ description : vivid
   Ⓒ quotation : apt
   Ⓓ interpretation : valid
   Ⓔ significance : uncertain

15. ONCOLOGY : TUMOR ::

   Ⓐ chronology : time
   Ⓑ theology : tenet
   Ⓒ oral : sound
   Ⓓ philology : religion
   Ⓔ taxonomy : classification

16. INTRANSIGENT : FLEXIBILITY ::

   Ⓐ transient : mobility
   Ⓑ disinterested : partisanship
   Ⓒ dissimilar : variation
   Ⓓ progressive : transition
   Ⓔ ineluctable : modality

GO ON TO THE NEXT PAGE

Directions: After each reading passage you will find a series of questions. Select the best choice for each question. Answers are based on the contents of the passage or what the author implies in the passage.

There can be nothing simpler than an elementary particle: it is an indivisible shard of matter, without internal structure and without detectable shape or size. One might expect
(5) commensurate simplicity in the theories that describe such particles and the forces through which they interact; at the least, one might expect the structure of the world to be explained with a minimum number of
(10) particles and forces. Judged by this criterion of parsimony, a description of nature that has evolved in the past several years can be accounted a reasonable success. Matter is built out of just two classes of elementary particles:
(15) the leptons, such as the electron, and the quarks, which are constituents of the proton, the neutron, and many related particles. Four basic forces act between the elementary particles. Gravitation and electromagnetism have long
(20) been familiar in the macroscopic world; the weak force and the strong force are observed only in subnuclear events. In principle this complement of particles and forces could account for the entire observed hierarchy of material structure,
(25) from the nuclei of atoms to stars and galaxies. An understanding of nature at this level of detail is a remarkable achievement; nevertheless, it is possible to imagine what a still simpler theory might be like. The existence of two disparate
(30) classes of elementary particles is not fully satisfying; ideally, one class would suffice. Similarly, the existence of four forces seems a needless complication; one force might explain all the interactions of elementary particles. An
(35) ambitious new theory now promises at least a partial unification along these lines.

The theory does not embrace gravitation, which is by far the feeblest of the forces and may be fundamentally different from the
(40) others. If gravitation is excluded, however, the theory unifies all elementary particles and forces. The first step in the construction of the unified theory was the demonstration that the weak, the strong,
(45) and the electromagnetic forces could all be described by theories of the same general kind. The three forces remained distinct, but they could be seen to operate through the same mechanism. In the course of this
(50) development a deep connection was discovered between the weak force and electromagnetism, a connection that hinted at a still grander synthesis. The new theory is the leading candidate for accomplishing
(55) the synthesis. It incorporates the leptons and the quarks into a single family and provides a means of transforming one kind of particle into the other. At the same time the weak, the strong, and the electro-
(60) magnetic forces are understood as aspects of a single underlying force. With only one class of particles and one force (plus gravitation), the unified theory is a model of frugality.

17. All of the following are differences between the two theories described by the author EXCEPT

Ⓐ the second theory is simpler than the first
Ⓑ the first theory encompasses gravitation while the second does not
Ⓒ the second theory includes only one class of elementary particles
Ⓓ the first theory accounts for only part of the hierarchy of material structure
Ⓔ the second theory unifies forces that the first theory regards as distinct

GO ON TO THE NEXT PAGE

18. The primary purpose of the passage is to

Ⓐ correct a misconception in a currently accepted theory of the nature of matter

Ⓑ describe efforts to arrive at a simplified theory of elementary particles and forces

Ⓒ predict the success of a new effort to unify gravitation with other basic forces

Ⓓ explain why scientists prefer simpler explanations over more complex ones

Ⓔ summarize what is known about the basic components of matter

19. According to the passage, which of the following are true of quarks?

   I. They are the elementary building blocks for neutrons.

   II. Scientists have described them as having no internal structure.

   III. Some scientists group them with leptons in a single class of particles.

Ⓐ I only

Ⓑ III only

Ⓒ I and II only

Ⓓ II and III only

Ⓔ I, II, and III

20. The author considers which of the following in judging the usefulness of a theory of elementary particles and forces?

   I. The simplicity of the theory

   II. The ability of the theory to account for the largest possible number of known phenomena

   III. The possibility of proving or disproving the theory by experiment

Ⓐ I only

Ⓑ II only

Ⓒ I and II only

Ⓓ I and III only

Ⓔ II and III only

21. It can be inferred that the author considers the failure to unify gravitation with other forces in the theory he describes to be

Ⓐ a disqualifying defect

Ⓑ an unjustified deviation

Ⓒ a needless oversimplification

Ⓓ an unfortunate oversight

Ⓔ an unavoidable limitation

22. The author organizes the passage by

Ⓐ enumerating distinctions among several different kinds of elementary particles

Ⓑ stating a criterion for judging theories of nature, and using it to evaluate two theories

Ⓒ explaining three methods of grouping particles and forces

Ⓓ criticizing an inaccurate view of elemental nature and proposing an alternative approach

Ⓔ outlining an assumption about scientific verification, then criticizing the assumption

23. It can be inferred that the author would be likely to consider a new theory of nature superior to present theories if it were to

Ⓐ account for a larger number of macroscopic structures than present theories

Ⓑ reduce the four basic forces to two more fundamental, incompatible forces

Ⓒ propose a smaller number of fundamental particles and forces than current theories

Ⓓ successfully account for the observable behavior of bodies due to gravity

Ⓔ hypothesize that protons but not neutrons are formed by combinations of more fundamental particles

The majority of white abolitionists and the majority of suffragists worked hard to convince their compatriots that the changes they advocated were not revolutionary, that far from
(5) undermining the accepted distribution of power they would eliminate deviations from the democratic principle it was supposedly based on. Non-Garrisonian abolitionists repeatedly disavowed miscegenationist or revolutionary
(10) intentions. And as for the suffragists, despite the presence in the movement of socialists, and in the final years of a few blacks, immigrants, and workers, the racism and nativism in the movement's thinking were not an aberration and
(15) did not conflict with the movement's objective of suffrage. Far from saying, as presentist historians do, that the white abolitionists and suffragists compromised the abiding principles of equality and the equal right of all to life, liberty, and the
(20) pursuit of happiness, I suggest just the opposite: the non-Garrisonian majority of white abolitionists and the majority of suffragists showed what those principles meant in their respective generations, because they traced the
(25) farthest acceptable boundaries around them.

24. The author's main point is that

   (A) the actions of the abolitionist and suffragist movements compromised their stated principles
   (B) the underlying beliefs of abolitionists and suffragists were closer than is usually believed
   (C) abolitionists' and suffragists' thinking about equality was limited by the assumptions of their time
   (D) presentist historians have willfully misrepresented the ideology of abolitionists and suffragists
   (E) historians should impose their own value systems when evaluating events of the past

25. Which of the following does the author imply about the principle of equality?

   I. It does not have a fixed meaning.
   II. Suffragists applied it more consistently than abolitionists.
   III. Abolitionists and suffragists compromised it to gain their political objectives.

   (A) I only
   (B) II only
   (C) III only
   (D) I and II only
   (E) II and III only

26. The author takes exception to the views of presentist historians by

   (A) charging that they ignore pertinent evidence
   (B) presenting new information that had not been available before
   (C) applying a different interpretation to the same set of facts
   (D) refuting the accuracy of their historical data
   (E) exposing a logical contradiction in their arguments

27. Which of the following is suggested about the abolitionist movement?

   (A) Its members disguised their objectives from the public.
   (B) It contained different groupings characterized by varied philosophies.
   (C) It undermined its principles by accommodating public concerns.
   (D) A majority of its members misunderstood its objectives.
   (E) Its progress was hindered by the actions of radical factions within it.

GO ON TO THE NEXT PAGE

Directions: Each of the following questions begins with a single word in capital letters. Five answer choices follow. Select the answer choice that has the most opposite meaning of the word in capital letters.

Since some of the questions require you to distinguish fine shades of meaning, be sure to consider all the choices before deciding which one is best.

28. UNDERMINE:

    Ⓐ appreciate
    Ⓑ donate
    Ⓒ bolster
    Ⓓ decay
    Ⓔ simplify

29. OBSEQUIOUS:

    Ⓐ original
    Ⓑ haughty
    Ⓒ casual
    Ⓓ virtuous
    Ⓔ informative

30. BLANCH:

    Ⓐ stand
    Ⓑ repay
    Ⓒ flush
    Ⓓ relax
    Ⓔ cope

31. DISSIPATED:

    Ⓐ temperate
    Ⓑ pleased
    Ⓒ inundated
    Ⓓ encouraged
    Ⓔ planned

32. FECUNDITY:

    Ⓐ levity
    Ⓑ sanity
    Ⓒ cowardice
    Ⓓ sterility
    Ⓔ ventilation

33. ENCUMBER:

    Ⓐ animate
    Ⓑ inaugurate
    Ⓒ bleach
    Ⓓ disburden
    Ⓔ obliterate

34. DISSEMINATE:

    Ⓐ fertilize
    Ⓑ ordain
    Ⓒ suppress
    Ⓓ explain thoroughly
    Ⓔ make an impression

GO ON TO THE NEXT PAGE

35. RESTIVE:

    (A) morose
    (B) intangible
    (C) fatigued
    (D) patient
    (E) curious

36. SYNCOPATED:

    (A) carefully executed
    (B) normally accented
    (C) brightly illuminated
    (D) easily understood
    (E) justly represented

37. VITUPERATIVE:

    (A) lethal
    (B) incapacitated
    (C) laudatory
    (D) insulated
    (E) prominent

38. SATURNINE:

    (A) magnanimous
    (B) ebullient
    (C) finicky
    (D) unnatural
    (E) impoverished

GO ON TO THE NEXT PAGE

Directions: Each of the following questions begins with a sentence that has either one or two blanks. The blanks indicate that a piece of the sentence is missing. Each sentence is followed by five answer choices that consist of words or phrases. Select the answer choice that completes the sentence best.

39. Her concern for the earthquake victims _____ her reputation as a callous person.

- (A) restored
- (B) rescinded
- (C) created
- (D) proved
- (E) belied

40. Due to unforeseen circumstances, the original plans were no longer _____ and were therefore _____ .

- (A) relevant . . adaptable
- (B) applicable . . rejected
- (C) expedient . . adopted
- (D) acceptable . . appraised
- (E) capable . . allayed

41. The microscopic cross section of a sandstone generally shows a _____ surface, each tiny layer representing an _____ of deposition that may have taken centuries or even millennia to accumulate.

- (A) ridged . . enlargement
- (B) multifaceted . . angle
- (C) distinctive . . area
- (D) stratified . . interval
- (E) coarse . . episode

42. The convict has always insisted upon his own _____ and now at last there is new evidence to _____ him.

- (A) defensiveness . . incarcerate
- (B) culpability . . exonerate
- (C) blamelessness . . anathematize
- (D) innocence . . vindicate
- (E) contrition . . condemn

43. The theory of plate tectonics was the subject of much _____ when it was first proposed by Alfred Wegener, but now most geophysicists _____ its validity.

- (A) opposition . . grant
- (B) consideration . . see
- (C) acclamation . . boost
- (D) prognostication . . learn
- (E) contention . . bar

44. Despite her professed _____ , the glint in her eyes demonstrated her _____ with the topic.

- (A) intelligence . . obsession
- (B) interest . . concern
- (C) obliviousness . . confusion
- (D) indifference . . fascination
- (E) expertise . . unfamiliarity

45. Lacking sacred scriptures or _____ , Shinto is more properly regarded as a legacy of traditional religious practices and basic values than as a formal system of belief.

- (A) followers
- (B) customs
- (C) dogma
- (D) relics
- (E) faith

GO ON TO THE NEXT PAGE

Directions: Each of the following questions consists of a pair of words or phrases that are separated by a colon and followed by five answer choices. Choice the pair of words or phrases in the answer choices that are most similar to the original pair.

46. IMPECCABLE : FLAW ::

(A) impeachable : crime
(B) obstreperous : permission
(C) impetuous : warning
(D) moribund : living
(E) absurd : sense

47. SEISMOGRAPH : EARTHQUAKE ::

(A) stethoscope : health
(B) speedometer : truck
(C) telescope : astronomy
(D) thermometer : temperature
(E) abacus : arithmetic

48. GUZZLE : DRINK ::

(A) elucidate : clarify
(B) ingest : eat
(C) boast : describe
(D) stride : walk
(E) admonish : condemn

49. ORATOR : ARTICULATE ::

(A) soldier : merciless
(B) celebrity : talented
(C) judge : unbiased
(D) novice : unfamiliar
(E) dignitary : respectful

50. BADGE : POLICEMAN ::

(A) placard : demonstrator
(B) tattoo : sailor
(C) dog-tag : soldier
(D) pedigree : dog
(E) fingerprint : defendant

51. SCRUTINIZE : OBSERVE ::

(A) excite : pique
(B) beseech : request
(C) search : discover
(D) smile : grin
(E) dive : jump

52. INDULGE : EPICUREAN ::

(A) frighten: ugly
(B) retract : revocable
(C) hesitate : unproductive
(D) revenge : vindictive
(E) understand : comprehensible

53. FLOOD : DILUVIAL ::

(A) punishment : criminal
(B) bacteria : biological
(C) verdict : judicial
(D) light : candescent
(E) heart : cardiac

54. SPHINX : PERPLEX ::

(A) oracle : interpret
(B) prophet : prepare
(C) siren : lure
(D) jester : astound
(E) minotaur : anger

GO ON TO THE NEXT PAGE

Directions: After each reading passage you will find a series of questions. Select the best choice for each question. Answers are based on the contents of the passage or what the author implies in the passage.

Although the schooling of fish is a familiar form of animal social behavior, how the school is formed and maintained is only beginning to be understood in detail. It had been thought that (5) each fish maintains its position chiefly by means of vision. Our work has shown that, as each fish maintains its position, the lateral line, an organ sensitive to transitory changes in water displacement, is as important as vision. In each (10) species a fish has a "preferred" distance and angle from its nearest neighbor. The ideal separation and bearing, however, are not maintained rigidly. The result is a probabilistic arrangement that appears like a random aggregation. The (15) tendency of the fish to remain at the preferred distance and angle, however, serves to maintain the structure. Each fish, having established its position, uses its eyes and its lateral lines simultaneously to measure the speed of all the (20) other fish in the school. It then adjusts its own speed to match a weighted average that emphasizes the contribution of nearby fish.

55. According to the passage, the structure of a fish school is dependent upon which of the following?

   I. rigidly formed random aggregations
   II. the tendency of each fish to remain at a preferred distance from neighboring fish
   III. measurements of a weighted average by individual fish

   (A) II only
   (B) III only
   (C) I and II only
   (D) I and III only
   (E) II and III only

56. Which of the following best describes the author's attitude toward the theory that the structure of fish schools is maintained primarily through vision?

   (A) heated opposition
   (B) careful neutrality
   (C) considered dissatisfaction
   (D) cautious approval
   (E) unqualified enthusiasm

57. The passage suggests that, after establishing its position in the school formation, an individual fish will subsequently

   (A) maintain its preferred position primarily by visual and auditory means
   (B) rigorously avoid changes that would interfere with the overall structure of the school
   (C) make continuous sensory readjustments to its position within the school
   (D) make unexpected shifts in position only if threatened by external danger
   (E) surrender its ability to make quick, instinctive judgments

GO ON TO THE NEXT PAGE

Whether as a result of some mysterious tendency in the national psyche or as a spontaneous reaction to their turbulent historical experience after the breakup of the Mycenaean
(5) world, the Greeks felt that to live with changing, undefined, unmeasured, seemingly random impressions—to live, in short, with what was expressed by the Greek word *chaos*—was to live in a state of constant anxiety.

(10)   If the apparent mutability of the physical world and of the human condition was a source of pain and bewilderment to the Greeks, the discovery of a permanent pattern or an unchanging substratum by which apparently chaotic experi-
(15) ence could be measured and explained was a source of satisfaction, even joy, which had something of a religious nature. For the recognition of order and measure in phenomena did more than simply satisfy their intellectual
(20) curiosity or gratify a desire for tidiness; it also served as the basis of a spiritual ideal. "Measure and commensurability are everywhere identified with beauty and excellence," was Plato's way of putting it in a dialogue in which measure is
(25) identified as a primary characteristic of the ultimate good. Rational definability and spirituality were never mutually exclusive categories in Greek thought. If the quest for order and clarity was in essence the search for a kind of spiritual
(30) ideal, it was not an ideal to be perceived in rapturous emotional mysticism but rather one to be arrived at by patient analysis.

We see this process at work especially in Greek philosophy, which in various ways was
(35) aimed at alleviating the anxiety that is inherent in the more spontaneous expression of lyric poetry. The Milesian philosophers of the sixth century were interested above all in discovering a primary substance from which all other phe-
(40) nomena could be explained. Neat, clear, and sub-

limely undisturbed by the social world of humanity, which took shape and dissolved within the natural order of things, it was an austere ideal, an astringent antidote to the appar-
(45) ent senselessness of life. The person who contemplated it deeply could feel a part of a great system that was impersonal but predictable, and, like Lucretius, who revived the Milesian attitude in a later age, he or she could derive a
(50) peculiar peace from it. As time passed and Greek philosophy developed, the urge to find order in experience was shifted from physics to the realm of mathematical abstraction by the Pythagoreans, and to the world of human
(55) behavior by various thinkers of the later fifth century; and, finally, Plato and Aristotle attempted to weave all these foci of interest into comprehensive pictures of the relationship between human life and the world as a whole.
(60) But in all these epochs the basic quest—the search for a "kosmos"—remained the same.

58. The author's primary purpose is to

(A) evaluate conflicting viewpoints
(B) challenge an accepted opinion
(C) question philosophical principles
(D) enumerate historical facts
(E) describe a cultural phenomenon

GO ON TO THE NEXT PAGE

KAPLAN

59. The author indicates that the discovery of "an unchanging substratum" (lines 13–14) served primarily to

    (A) alter the Greeks' perception of the mutability of existence
    (B) help eradicate severe social problems
    (C) alleviate painful memories of national suffering
    (D) calm a restless intellectual curiosity
    (E) foster a more mystical understanding of the physical world

60. It can be inferred from the passage that rational thought and spiritual ideals were categories of experience that were

    (A) unimportant and unfamiliar to most ordinary Greeks
    (B) advocated by the Milesians and rejected by the Pythagoreans
    (C) neglected by most philosophers before Plato and Aristotle
    (D) seen by the Greeks as essentially compatible
    (E) embraced mainly by Greek poets

61. All of the following can be inferred about the Greeks' anxiety over the possibility of "chaos" EXCEPT that it

    (A) had sources in their national consciousness
    (B) was reflected in specific aspects of their religion
    (C) was related to their sense of change in the physical world
    (D) led to a striving for order in their philosophy
    (E) was expressed in their lyric poetry

62. The author implies that the Milesian philosophers of the sixth century sought relief from worldly anxiety by

    (A) focusing narrowly on inherently human questions
    (B) establishing sharp distinctions between spiritual and rational understanding
    (C) focusing primarily on an impersonal natural order
    (D) attempting to integrate rational and mystical worldviews
    (E) withdrawing from the physical world into the realm of mathematical abstraction

63. Which of the following best describes the organization of lines 17–28 of the passage ("For the recognition of order . . . in Greek thought.")?

    (A) The author summarizes two viewpoints, cites historical evidence, and then declines to support either of the viewpoints.
    (A) The author makes an observation, admits to evidence that weakens the viewpoint, and then revises his observation.
    (C) The author specifies two distinct arguments, examines both in detail, then advances a third argument that reconciles the other two.
    (D) The author clarifies a previous statement, offers an example, and then draws a further conclusion based on these ideas.
    (E) The author states a thesis, mentions an opposed thesis, and cites evidence supporting it, and then restates his original thesis.

GO ON TO THE NEXT PAGE

64. According to the passage, the Pythagoreans differed from the Milesians primarily in that the Pythagoreans

   (A) focused on mathematical abstractions rather than physical phenomena
   (B) placed a renewed emphasis on understanding human behavior
   (C) focused primarily on a rational means to understanding truth
   (D) attempted to identify a fundamental physical unit of matter
   (E) stressed concrete reality over formal theory

65. In the context of the author's overall argument, which of the following best characterizes the Greeks' "search for a 'kosmos'" (line 61)?

   (A) a mystical quest for a strong national identity
   (B) efforts to replace a sterile philosophical rationalism with revitalized religious values
   (C) attempts to end conflict among key philosophical schools
   (D) a search for order and measure in an unpredictable world
   (E) a search for an alternative to a narrow preoccupation with beauty and excellence

GO ON TO THE NEXT PAGE

Directions: Each of the following questions begins with a single word in capital letters. Five answer choices follow. Select the answer choice that has the most opposite meaning of the word in capital letters.

Since some of the questions require you to distinguish fine shades of meaning, be sure to consider all the choices before deciding which one is best.

66. ENMITY:

- (A) friendship
- (B) reverence
- (C) boredom
- (D) stylishness
- (E) awkwardness

67. DILATE:

- (A) enclose
- (B) shrink
- (C) hurry
- (D) inflate
- (E) erase

68. CHARLATAN:

- (A) genuine expert
- (B) powerful leader
- (C) false idol
- (D) unknown enemy
- (E) hardened villain

69. PERIPHERAL:

- (A) civilized
- (B) partial
- (C) central
- (D) unharmed
- (E) stable

70. MERITORIOUS:

- (A) effulgent
- (B) stationary
- (C) uneven
- (D) narrow-minded
- (E) unpraiseworthy

71. DISCHARGE:

- (A) heal
- (B) advance
- (C) enlist
- (D) penalize
- (E) delay

72. MALEDICTION:

- (A) blessing
- (B) preparation
- (C) good omen
- (D) liberation
- (E) pursuit

GO ON TO THE NEXT PAGE

73. MAWKISH:

    Ⓐ unsentimental
    Ⓑ sophisticated
    Ⓒ graceful
    Ⓓ tense
    Ⓔ descriptive

74. TEMERITY:

    Ⓐ blandness
    Ⓑ caution
    Ⓒ severity
    Ⓓ strength
    Ⓔ charm

75. JEJUNE:

    Ⓐ morose
    Ⓑ natural
    Ⓒ mature
    Ⓓ contrived
    Ⓔ accurate

76. VITIATE:

    Ⓐ deaden
    Ⓑ trust
    Ⓒ rectify
    Ⓓ drain
    Ⓔ amuse

END OF SECTION

GO ON TO THE NEXT PAGE

SECTION TWO—QUANTITATIVE
Time—60 minutes   60 questions

Numbers: The numbers in this section are real numbers.

Figures: You may assume that the position of points, lines, angles, etcetera are in the order shown and that all lengths and angle measures may be assumed to be positive.

You may assume that lines that look straight are straight.

Figures are in a plane unless otherwise stated.

Figures are not drawn to scale unless otherwise stated.

Directions: Questions 1–15 provide two quantities, one in Column A and another in Column B. Compare the two quantities and answer

- Ⓐ if the quantity in Column A is greater
- Ⓑ if the quantity in Column B is greater
- Ⓒ if the two quantities are equal
- Ⓓ if the relationship cannot be determined from the information given

Common
Information: In each question, information relating to one or both of the quantities in Column A and Column B is centered above the two columns. A symbol that appears in both columns represents the same thing in Column A as it does in Column B.

Column A	Column B	Sample Answers

Example 1: 3×4 $3 + 4$ ● Ⓑ Ⓒ Ⓓ

GO ON TO THE NEXT PAGE

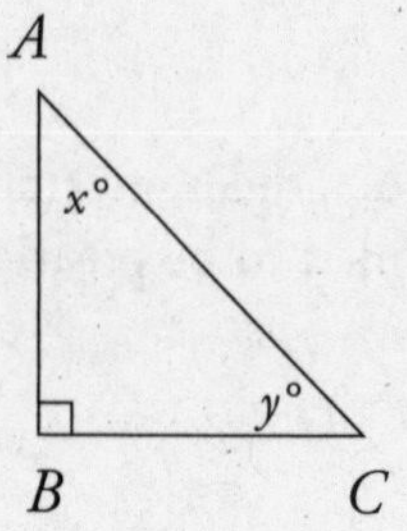

Column A	Column B	Sample Answers

Examples 2–4 refer to the figure below.

Example 2: x y

ⒶⒷⒸ⬤

(Because we cannot assume the angles are equal, even though they appear that way.)

Example 3: $x + y$ 90

ⒶⒷ⬤Ⓓ

(Because the sum of the angles is 180°.)

Example 4: x 90

Ⓐ⬤ⒸⒹ

(Since $\triangle ABC$ is a right triangle, x is less than 90°.)

GO ON TO THE NEXT PAGE

Column A	Column B
1. 0.0260	0.0256

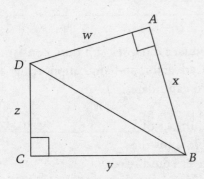

$\triangle ABD$ and $\triangle CDB$ are right triangles.

2. $w^2 + x^2$	$y^2 + z^2$

$$x + 4y = 6$$
$$x = 2y$$

3. x	y

4. $\sqrt{4^2 + 5^2}$	$\sqrt{3^2 + 6^2}$

Column A	Column B

In a certain accounting firm, there are exactly three types of employees: managerial, technical, and clerical. The firm has 120 employees and 25 percent of the employees are managerial.

5. The number of managerial employees	Two-thirds of the number of clerical employees

6. $\dfrac{12 \times 1}{12 + 1}$	$\dfrac{12 + 1}{12 \times 1}$

7. $(a + 1)(b + 1)$	$ab + 1$

In the two-digit number jk, the value of the digit j is twice the value of the digit k.

8. k	6

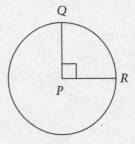

P is the center of the circle and the area of sector PQR is 4.

9. The area of circle P	4π

GO ON TO THE NEXT PAGE

Column A	Column B

Henry purchased x apples and Jack purchased 10 apples fewer than one-third of the number of apples Henry purchased.

10. The number of apples Jack purchased $\dfrac{x-30}{3}$

11. The volume of a rectangular solid with a length of 5 feet, a width of 4 feet, and a height of x feet   The volume of a rectangular solid with a length of 10 feet, a width of 8 feet, and a height of y feet

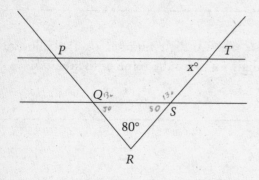

$$PQ = ST$$
$$QR = RS$$

12. x 50

Column A	Column B

$$2 \times 16 \times 64 = 2 \times 4n \times 256$$

13. n 2

A producer must select a duo, consisting of one lead actor and one supporting actor, from 6 candidates.

14. The number of possible duos the producer could select.   30

The perimeter of isosceles $\triangle ABC$ is 40 and the length of side BC is 12.

15. The length of side AB 14

GO ON TO THE NEXT PAGE

Directions: Questions 16–30 each have five answer choices. For each of these questions, select the best of the answer choices given.

16. If $\dfrac{p-q}{p} = \dfrac{2}{7}$, then $\dfrac{q}{p} =$

(A) $\dfrac{2}{5}$

(B) $\dfrac{5}{7}$

(C) 1

(D) $\dfrac{7}{5}$

(E) $\dfrac{7}{2}$

17. Jane must select three different items for each dinner she will serve. The items are to be chosen from among 5 different vegetarian and 4 different meat selections. If at least one of the selections must be vegetarian, how many different dinners could Jane create?

(A) 30
(B) 40
(C) 60
(D) 70
(E) 80

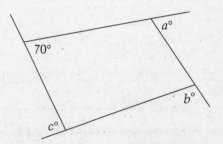

18. In the figure above, what is the value of $a + b + c$?

(A) 110
(B) 250
(C) 290
(D) 330
(E) 430

19. John has four ties, 12 shirts, and three belts. If each day he wears exactly one tie, one shirt, and one belt, what is the maximum number of days he can go without repeating a particular combination?

(A) 12
(B) 21
(C) 84
(D) 108
(E) 144

20. Which of the following is the greatest?

(A) $\dfrac{0.00003}{0.0007}$

(B) $\dfrac{0.0008}{0.0005}$

(C) $\dfrac{0.007}{0.0008}$

(D) $\dfrac{0.006}{0.0005}$

(E) $\dfrac{0.01}{0.008}$

GO ON TO THE NEXT PAGE

Questions 21–25 refer to the charts below.

U.S. PHYSICIANS IN SELECTED SPECIALTIES BY SEX, 1986

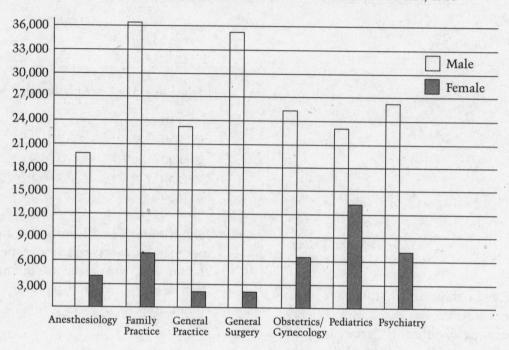

GENERAL SURGERY PHYSICIANS BY AGE, 1986

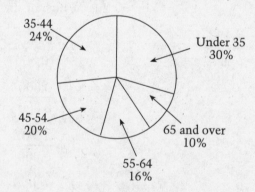

GO ON TO THE NEXT PAGE

21. Approximately what percent of all general practice physicians in 1986 were male?

    Ⓐ 23%
    Ⓑ 50%
    Ⓒ 75%
    Ⓓ 82%
    Ⓔ 90%

22. Which of the following physician specialties had the lowest ratio of males to females in 1986?

    Ⓐ Family practice
    Ⓑ General surgery
    Ⓒ Obstetrics/gynecology
    Ⓓ Pediatrics
    Ⓔ Psychiatry

23. In 1986, approximately how many general surgery physicians were between the ages of 45 and 54, inclusive?

    Ⓐ 5,440
    Ⓑ 6,300
    Ⓒ 7,350
    Ⓓ 7,800
    Ⓔ 8,900

24. If in 1986 all the family practice physicians represented 7.5 percent of all the physicians in the United States, approximately how many physicians were there total?

    Ⓐ 300,000
    Ⓑ 360,000
    Ⓒ 430,000
    Ⓓ 485,000
    Ⓔ 570,000

25. If the number of female general surgeon physicians in the under-35 category represented 3.5 percent of all the general surgeon physicians, approximately how many male general surgeon physicians were under 35 years?

    Ⓐ 9,200
    Ⓑ 9,800
    Ⓒ 10,750
    Ⓓ 11,260
    Ⓔ 11,980

GO ON TO THE NEXT PAGE

26. $|3| + |-4| + |3 - 4| =$

   Ⓐ 14
   Ⓑ 8
   Ⓒ 7
   Ⓓ 2
   Ⓔ 0

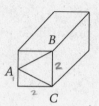

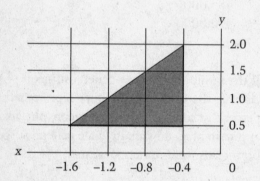

27. What is the area of the shaded region in the figure above?

   Ⓐ 0.5
   Ⓑ 0.7
   Ⓒ 0.9
   Ⓓ 2.7
   Ⓔ 4.5

28. A computer can perform 30 identical tasks in six hours. At that rate, what is the minimum number of computers that should be assigned to complete 80 of the tasks within three hours?

   Ⓐ 6
   Ⓑ 7
   Ⓒ 8
   Ⓓ 12
   Ⓔ 16

29. The volume of the cube in the figure above is 8. If point A is the midpoint of an edge of this cube, what is the perimeter of $\triangle ABC$?

   Ⓐ 5
   Ⓑ $2 + 2\sqrt{3}$
   Ⓒ $2 + 2\sqrt{5}$
   Ⓓ 7
   Ⓔ $6 + \sqrt{5}$

30. Which of the following is 850 percent greater than 8×10^3 ?

   Ⓐ 8.5×10^3
   Ⓑ 6.4×10^4
   Ⓒ 6.8×10^4
   Ⓓ 7.6×10^4
   Ⓔ 1.6×10^5

GO ON TO THE NEXT PAGE

Column A	Column B		Column A	Column B

$$y = (x + 3)^2$$

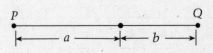

31. The value of y when $x = 1$ | 9

35. The length of segment PQ | 2

$$8a + 8b = 24$$

32. The number of miles traveled by a car that traveled for four hours at an average speed of 40 miles per hour | The number of miles traveled by a train that traveled for two and a half hours at an average speed of 70 miles per hour

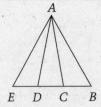

$$x < y$$

36. $y - x$ | $x - y$

33. The number of cookies in a bag that weighs 3 kilograms | The number of grapes in a bag that weighs 2 kilograms

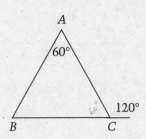

The area of triangular region ABE is 75.

37. The area of $\triangle ABC$ | The area of $\triangle ADE$

34. AB | BC

GO ON TO THE NEXT PAGE

Column A	Column B

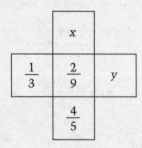

The sum of the numbers in the horizontal row of boxes equals the sum of the numbers in the vertical row of boxes.

38. x y

39. $\dfrac{\frac{1}{3} \times \frac{1}{4}}{\frac{2}{3} \times \frac{1}{2}}$ $\dfrac{\frac{2}{3} \times \frac{1}{2}}{\frac{1}{3} \times \frac{1}{4}}$

Eileen drives due north from town A to town B for a distance of 60 miles, then drives due east from town B to town C for a distance of 80 miles.

40. The distance from town   120
    A to town C in miles

41. $(\sqrt{7} - 2)(\sqrt{7} + 2)$ $(2 - \sqrt{7})(-\sqrt{7} - 2)$

Column A	Column B

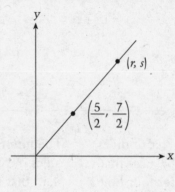

42. r s

x is an integer greater than 0.

43. $1 - \left(\dfrac{1}{4}\right)^x$ 0.95

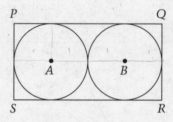

The two circles with centers A and B have the same radius.

44. The sum of the   The perimeter of
    circumferences of   rectangle $PQRS$
    of the two circles

45. $3^{17} + 3^{18} + 3^{19}$ 3^{20}

GO ON TO THE NEXT PAGE

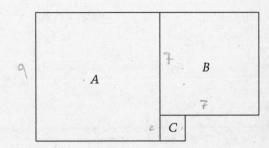

Directions: Questions 46–60 each have five answer choices. For each of these questions, select the best of the answer choices given.

46. If $4 + y = 14 - 4y$, then $y =$

   (A) -4

   (B) 0

   (C) $\dfrac{5}{8}$

   (D) $\dfrac{4}{5}$

   (E) 2

47. $\dfrac{4}{5} + \dfrac{5}{4} =$

   (A) 1

   (B) $\dfrac{9}{8}$

   (C) $\dfrac{6}{5}$

   (D) $\dfrac{41}{20}$

   (E) $\dfrac{23}{10}$

48. If $3^m = 81$, then $m^3 =$

   (A) 9
   (B) 16
   (C) 27
   (D) 54
   (E) 64

49. In the figure above, there are three square gardening areas. The area of square A is 81 square meters and the area of square B is 49 square meters. What is the area, in square meters, of square C?

   (A) 2
   (B) 4
   (C) 9
   (D) 27
   (E) 32

50. In a certain history class, all except 23 students scored under 85 on a test. If 18 students scored over 85 on this test, how many students are there in this history class?

   (A) 33
   (B) 37
   (C) 39
   (D) 41
   (E) It cannot be determined from the information given.

GO ON TO THE NEXT PAGE

Questions 51–55 refer to the following graphs

ENERGY USE BY YEAR, COUNTRY Y, 1950–1980
(in millions of kilowatt-hours)

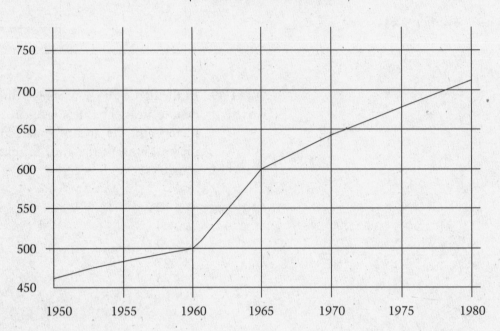

ENERGY USE BY TYPE, COUNTRY Y

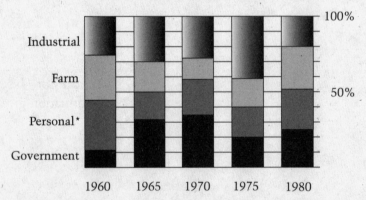

Total personal use = population × per-capita personal use

GO ON TO THE NEXT PAGE

KAPLAN

51. In which of the following years was the energy use in country *Y* closest to 650 million kilowatt-hours?

   (A) 1960
   (B) 1965
   (C) 1970
   (D) 1975
   (E) 1980

52. In 1965, how many of the categories shown had energy use greater than 150 million kilowatt-hours?

   (A) none
   (B) one
   (C) two
   (D) three
   (E) four

53. In which of the following years was industrial use of energy greatest in country *Y*?

   (A) 1960
   (B) 1965
   (C) 1970
   (D) 1975
   (E) 1980

54. If the population of country *Y* increased by 20 percent from 1960 to 1965, approximately what was the percent decrease in the per-capita personal use of energy between those two years?

   (A) 0%
   (B) 17%
   (C) 25%
   (D) 40%
   (E) It cannot be determined from the information given.

55. Which of the following can be inferred from the graphs?

   I. Farm use of energy increased between 1960 and 1980.
   II. In 1980, industrial use of energy was greater than industrial use of energy in 1965.
   III. More people were employed by the government of country *Y* in 1980 than in 1960.

   (A) I only
   (B) II only
   (C) I and II only
   (D) II and III only
   (E) I, II, and III

GO ON TO THE NEXT PAGE

56. If the average of two numbers is $3y$ and one of the numbers is $y - z$, what is the other number, in terms of y and z?

(A) $y + z$
(B) $3y + z$
(C) $4y - z$
(D) $5y - z$
(E) $5y + z$

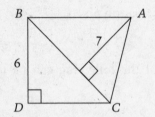

57. In the figure above, the area of $\triangle ABC$ is 35. What is the length of DC?

(A) 6
(B) 8
(C) $6\sqrt{2}$
(D) 10
(E) $6\sqrt{3}$

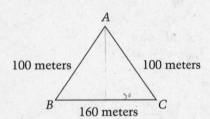

58. In the figure above is a triangular field. What is the minimum distance, in meters, that a person would have to walk to go from point A to a point on side BC?

(A) 60
(B) 80
(C) 100
(D) 140
(E) 180

59. If the ratio of $2a$ to b is 8 times the ratio of b to a, then $\dfrac{b}{a}$ could be

(A) 4
(B) 2
(C) 1
(D) $\dfrac{1}{2}$
(E) $\dfrac{1}{4}$

60. A certain dentist earns n dollars for each filling she puts in, plus x dollars for every 15 minutes she works. If in a certain week she works 14 hours and puts in 21 fillings, how much does she earn for the week, in dollars?

(A) $\dfrac{7}{2}x + 21n$
(B) $7x + 14n$
(C) $14x + 21n$
(D) $56x + 21n$
(E) $56x + \dfrac{21}{4}n$

END OF SECTION

SECTION THREE—ANALYTICAL WRITING
Time—75 minutes   2 questions

Essay 1

Directions: You will have 45 minutes to plan and write an essay that communicates your perspective on a given topic. Choose one of the two topics provided. No other topics are admissible for this essay.

The topic is a short quotation that expresses an issue of general interest. Write an essay that agrees with, refutes, or qualifies the quotation, and support your opinion with relevant information drawn from your academic studies, reading, observation, or other experiences.

Feel free to consider the issue for a few minutes before you beginning your writing. Be certain that your ideas are fully developed and organized logically and make sure you have enough time left to review and revise what you've written.

1. "Scientific theories, which most people consider 'fact,' almost invariably prove to be inaccurate. Thus, one should look upon any information described as 'factual' with skepticism since it may well be proven false in the future."

2. "In bygone days, many people received whatever musical education they acquired by singing around the parlor piano. In the age of recorded music and the Internet, people can learn as much by listening as they can by singing."

GO ON TO THE NEXT PAGE

Essay 2
The following appeared in a memo written by a member of the booster club at Tusk University:

"Tusk University should build a new recreational facility, both to attract new students and to better serve the needs of our current student body. Tusk projects that enrollment will double over the next ten years, based on current trends. The new student body is expected to reflect a much higher percentage of commuter students than we currently enroll. This will make the existing facilities inadequate. Moreover, the cost of health and recreation club membership in our community has increased rapidly in recent years. Thus, students will find it much more advantageous to make use of the facilities on campus. Finally, an attractive new recreation center would make prospective students, especially athletically gifted ones, more likely to enroll at Tusk."

Directions: You will have 30 minutes to explain how logically persuasive you find this argument. In discussing your viewpoint, analyze the argument's line of reasoning and its use of evidence. Also explain what, if anything, would make the argument more valid and convincing or help you to better evaluate its conclusion.

END OF SECTION

Practice Test
Answers And
Explanations

Practice Test Answer Key

VERBAL

1. A	14. A	27. B	40. B	53. E	66. A
2. E	15. E	28. C	41. D	54. C	67. B
3. E	16. B	29. B	42. D	55. E	68. A
4. A	17. D	30. C	43. A	56. C	69. C
5. D	18. B	31. A	44. D	57. C	70. E
6. E	19. E	32. D	45. C	58. E	71. C
7. D	20. C	33. D	46. E	59. A	72. A
8. A	21. E	34. C	47. D	60. D	73. A
9. B	22. B	35. D	48. D	61. B	74. B
10. B	23. C	36. B	49. C	62. C	75. C
11. D	24. C	37. C	50. C	63. D	76. C
12. E	25. A	38. B	51. B	64. A	
13. A	26. C	39. E	52. D	65. D	

QUANTITATIVE

1. A	11. D	21. E	31. A	41. C	51. C
2. C	12. C	22. D	32. B	42. B	52. C
3. A	13. B	23. C	33. D	43. D	53. D
4. B	14. C	24. E	34. C	44. A	54. D
5. D	15. D	25. B	35. A	45. B	55. A
6. B	16. B	26. B	36. A	46. E	56. E
7. D	17. E	27. C	37. D	47. D	57. B
8. B	18. B	28. A	38. B	48. E	58. A
9. A	19. E	29. C	39. B	49. B	59. D
10. C	20. D	30. D	40. B	50. E	60. D

Calculate Your Score

Step 1

Using the Answer Key to check your answers, award yourself one point for each correct answer in the Verbal and Quantitative sections. This is your raw score for each measure.

Verbal

Total Correct ☐ (raw score)

Quantitative

Total Correct ☐ (raw score)

Step 2

Find your raw score on the following tables and read across to find your scaled score and your percentile.

Verbal

Raw Score	Scaled Score	Percentile Rank	Raw Score	Scaled Score	Percentile Rank
0	200	1	39	420	41
1	200	1	40	420	41
2	200	1	41	430	44
3	200	1	42	440	48
4	200	1	43	450	51
5	200	1	44	460	54
6	200	1	45	470	56
7	200	1	46	470	59
8	200	1	47	480	61
9	200	1	48	490	67
10	200	1	49	510	69
11	200	1	50	520	72
12	200	1	51	530	74
13	220	1	52	530	76
14	230	1	53	540	78
15	240	1	54	550	80
16	250	1	55	560	82
17	260	1	56	570	84
18	270	2	57	580	85
19	270	3	58	590	87
20	280	4	59	590	89
21	290	5	60	600	90
22	300	6	61	610	92
23	310	7	62	620	93
24	320	9	63	630	94
25	320	10	64	640	95
26	330	12	65	650	95
27	330	14	66	660	96
28	340	16	67	670	97
29	350	16	68	680	98
30	360	20	69	690	98
31	360	22	70	700	99
32	360	24	71	710	99
33	370	24	72	720	99
34	380	26	73	740	99
35	390	30	74	760	99
36	400	33	75	780	99
37	410	36	76	800	99
38	420	38			

Quantitative

RAW SCORE	SCALED SCORE	PERCENTILE RANK	RAW SCORE	SCALED SCORE	PERCENTILE RANK
0	200	1	31	430	24
1	200	1	32	440	26
2	200	1	33	460	28
3	200	1	34	470	32
4	200	1	35	480	35
5	200	1	36	490	37
6	200	1	37	500	40
7	200	1	38	510	42
8	200	1	39	520	45
9	200	1	40	530	48
10	210	1	41	540	49
11	220	1	42	540	51
12	240	1	43	560	57
13	260	1	44	570	59
14	270	1	45	580	61
15	280	2	46	600	66
16	290	2	47	610	68
17	300	3	48	630	72
18	310	4	49	640	74
19	310	5	50	660	78
20	320	5	51	670	80
21	330	6	52	690	84
22	340	7	53	690	86
23	360	9	54	700	89
24	370	10	55	720	92
25	380	13	56	730	94
26	390	14	57	750	97
27	400	16	58	770	97
28	410	18	59	780	97
29	420	20	60	800	97
30	420	22			

Step 3

Use the holistic scoring guide below to determine your score on the essays. (Also see the sample "6" essays in the next section as a basis for comparison.)

Analytical Writing

6: "Outstanding" Essay
- Insightfully presents and convincingly supports an opinion on the issue or a critique of the argument
- Ideas are very clear, well organized and logically connected
- Shows superior control of language: grammar, stylistic variety, and accepted conventions of writing; minor flaws may occur

5: "Strong" Essay
- Presents well-chosen examples and strongly supports an opinion on the issue or a critique of the argument
- Ideas are generally clear and well organized; connections are logical
- Shows solid control of language: grammar, stylistic variety, and accepted conventions of writing; minor flaws may occur

4: "Adequate" Essay
- Presents and adequately supports an opinion on the issue or a critique of the argument
- Ideas are fairly clear and adequately organized; logical connections are satisfactory
- Shows satisfactory control of language: grammar, stylistic variety, and accepted conventions of writing; some flaws may occur

3: "Limited" Essay
- Succeeds only partially in presenting and supporting an opinion on the issue or a critique of the argument
- Ideas may be unclear and poorly organized
- Shows less than satisfactory control of language: contains significant mistakes in grammar, usage, and sentence structure

2: "Weak" Essay
- Shows little success in presenting and supporting an opinion on the issue or a critique of the argument
- Ideas lack clarity and organization
- Meaning is impeded by many serious mistakes in grammar, usage, and sentence structure

1: "Fundamentally Deficient" Essay
- Fails to present a coherent opinion and/or evidence on the issue or a critique of the argument
- Ideas are seriously unclear and disorganized
- Lacks meaning due to widespread, severe mistakes in grammar, usage, and sentence structure

0: "Unscorable" Essay
- Completely ignores topic

Section One Explanations—Verbal

1 **(A)** We're told that the fundamental (blank) between cats and dogs is a myth, that the species actually coexist quite (blankly). We need a contrast, and we find it in (A)—*antipathy* means aversion or dislike, and *amiably* means agreeably.

In (B), if the members of the species coexisted "uneasily," their "disharmony" wouldn't be a myth. In (C), both *compatibility* and *together* imply that dogs and cats are good friends. In (D), it doesn't make sense to say that the "relationship" between dogs and cats is a myth. In (E), no one could claim that there's no "difference" between dogs and cats.

2 **(E)** The clue is the signal *rather than*: We need a contrast between what the speaker intended and what he achieved. The word *monotonous* clues you into boredom, and *bore* in (E), followed by *convince* makes the contrast we need. In (A), *enlighten* and *inform* are similar. *Interest* and *persuade*, (B), don't show contrast. In (C), *provoke* and *influence* don't express a contrast. *Allay* in (D) means to relieve, which is similar to *pacify*, which means to calm or to make peace. No contrast here, and again, it's (E) for this question.

3 **(E)** The blank is part of a cause-and-effect structure as the keyword *that* indicates. Because government restrictions are so something, businesses can operate with nearly complete impunity. There's an absence of restrictions, so we need a word that cancels out restrictions. Would a "traditional" restriction, (A), be canceled out? No. (B), *judicious*, means wise or having sound judgment, but a wise restriction would probably be effective. In (C), *ambiguous* means unclear, but though ambiguity might interfere with the effectiveness of restrictions, it doesn't cancel them out. (D), *exacting*, means very strict, which is the opposite of what we want. (E), *lax*, means loose, careless, or sloppy. This describes restrictions that aren't very strict, and it's correct for this question.

4 **(A)** The first blank describes a book—the recent Oxford edition of the works of Shakespeare is (blank). The word *because* tells us that what follows is an explanation of why this book is whatever it is. The "not only but also" structure tells us that there are *two* reasons why: it departs from the readings of other editions, and it challenges basic (blanks) of textual criticism. In (A), we could say that challenging conventions could make a book "controversial." Conventions are accepted practices, so challenging conventions would make a book controversial. What else have we got? (B) gives us the book is typical because it challenges innovations. *Typical* doesn't fit in with *departs from other editions*. How about (C)? Challenging norms, which are rules or patterns, wouldn't make something "inadequate." (D)—a book that is different might be called curious, but could you call a book curious for challenging projects? Finally, (E) says the book is pretentious because it challenges explanations—no good. So the best answer is (A).

5 **(D)** We learn that an early form of writing, Linear B, was (blank) in 1952. The keyword *but* tells us that Linear A, an older form, met with a contrasting fate, so we'll look for a pair of contrasting words. The words *no one has yet succeeded in* precede the second blank, so instead of a word that is contrasted with the first blank, we need a word that means about the same thing. That leads us to pick (D)—the words *deciphered* and *interpretation* are similar since both imply understanding.

The word *superseded* in (A) means replaced by something more up to date—not giving an explanation of something. (B)—in the context of ancient languages, a *transcription* would probably be a decoded version of something. That would be the opposite of *encoding* something. (C)'s *obliterated* and *analysis* imply a contrast—wiping something out is different from figuring it out. In (E) *discovered* and *obfuscation* are more at odds than they are alike. Obfuscation means confusion, while a discovery usually sheds light on a situation.

6 **(E)** The clue here is the structure "quite normal and even (blank)"—the missing word has a more positive meaning than the word *normal*. Then we get, "I was therefore surprised," which tips us off to look for contrast. *Commendable* and *complimentary* in (A) are both positive. In (B), *odious* means hateful, so *odious* and *insulting* are both negative. *Conciliatory* in (C) means placating or reconciling, which fits in with *apologetic*. *Commonplace* and *typical* in (D) mean the same thing. Only correct choice (E) is left—*laudable* means praiseworthy while *derogatory* means belittling or detracting.

7 **(D)** Whatever we're doing to the burden of medical costs is causing the removal of the second blank, signaled by *thereby*. In (A), it doesn't make sense to say that to *augment* or add to the burden would remove a problem—it could make the problem worse. In (B), a *perquisite* is a reward over and above one's salary. But would eliminating a burden remove a perquisite? In (C), to *ameliorate* means to improve, but you can't talk about removing a major study of medical care. (D) is perfect. To *assuage* means to make less severe and an *impediment* is an obstacle. Assuaging the burden would remove an impediment to medical care, so (D)'s correct. As for (E), to *clarify* means to explain or make clear, and explaining the burden of medical costs wouldn't remove an explanation.

8 **(A)** A *novel* is a type of *book*. That's an easy bridge. In (A), is an *epic* a type of *poem*? Yes, an epic is a long narrative poem, so (A) is right. In (B), a *house* isn't a type of *library*. (C) is tempting—*tales* and *fables* are related—but a fable is a kind of tale, not vice versa, so it's not parallel. In (D), a *number* is not a type of *page*, and in (E), a *play* isn't a type of *theater*.

9 **(B)** *Ravenous* means extremely *hungry*—the second word is an extreme version of the first word. In (A), *desirous* means desiring or wanting something—it's not an extreme form of *thirsty*. (B) is perfect—*titanic* is an amplification of *large*. *Titanic*

means gigantic, so (B) is the answer.

Eminent and *famous* in (C) mean the same thing. (D)'s *disoriented* and *dizzy* are close in meaning. To be disoriented means to have lost your bearings, and when you're dizzy, you feel as if you're going to fall down. (E)'s *obese* and *gluttonous* could be related, but don't have to be. *Gluttonous* comes from *gluttony*—it means excessive eating or drinking. Gluttony doesn't have to result in obesity and it's not an extreme form of it.

10 **(B)** A *bouquet* is an arrangement of *flowers*, so the first word will be an arrangement of the second word. In (A), a *humidor* is a container for *tobacco*—a container for tobacco is not the same as a formal arrangement of it. The next choice, (B), is more like it. A *mosaic* is made of *tiles,* just as a bouquet is made up of flowers. That's a good match. In (C), a *tapestry* is not made of *color*, it's made of threads woven to make a design. You can't argue that a tapestry is an arrangement of colors. (D) also has problems. A *pile* of *blocks* could be an arrangement. But a bouquet isn't just a group of flowers—it's a formal arrangement. In the same way, a mosaic is an orderly arrangement of tiles. A pile isn't a formal arrangement. What about *sacristy* and *vestment* in (E)? A sacristy is a room in a church where priests' clothes or vestments are kept, so vestments are stored in a sacristy. The correct answer is (B).

11 **(D)** *Quixotic* means impractical, after the hero of *Don Quixote*. A *realist* is a person who is especially realistic. *Realistic* is the opposite of *quixotic*, so a realist is never quixotic. In (A), *pedantic* people show off their learning. Many scholars are pedantic, so this won't work. In (B), a *fool* is foolish—a synonym for *idiotic*. The same relationship holds true for (C)—an *idler* is a *lethargic* person. (D) looks good—a *tormentor* is vicious or cruel. The opposite sort of person would be kinder and more *sympathetic*—a tormentor is never sympathetic. (E) *dyspeptic* means suffering from indigestion. A *diner* is someone who eats—some diners get dyspeptic, some don't, so (D)'s correct.

12 **(E)** A *shard* is a broken fragment of *glass* or crockery. Glass, when it shatters, creates shards, so a shard is a piece of broken glass. (E) shows the same analogy—a *splinter* is a piece of broken *wood*. As for the wrong choices, in (A), a *grain* is the basic unit that *sand* comes in, but you can't talk about breaking sand. (B)'s *morsel* means a bit of food, but a *meal* doesn't shatter into morsels. In (C), a *rope* is composed of *strands,* and in (D), a *quilt* is made from *scraps*. The correct answer is (E).

13 **(A)** The word *filter* is used as a verb. When you use a filter, an *impurity* is removed, so you *filter* to remove an *impurity*. The word *expurgate* in (A) means to censor, to remove *obscenities*—you *expurgate* to remove an *obscenity*. To *whitewash*, (B), is to misrepresent a bad thing to make it look better. An *infraction* isn't removed by *whitewashing* it, it's only covered up, so (B) isn't parallel. In (C), *perjury* is the crime of lying under oath. To *testify* doesn't mean to remove a false statement. In (D), *penance* is something you do to atone for a sin, but you don't *perform* to remove *penance*. And in (E), you don't *vacuum* to remove a *carpet*. So (A) is correct.

14 **(A)** *Paraphrase* means restatement of a text using different words. *Verbatim* means word for word or exact. A paraphrase is not verbatim—the words are near opposites. The only choices opposite in meaning are *approximation* and *precise,* in (A). An approximation is an estimate, while something that's precise is exact, so an approximation is not precise. A description might or might not be vivid in (B). In (C), *apt* means appropriate, so a quotation could be apt. There's no relationship in (D), *interpretation* and *valid,* or in (E), *significance* and *uncertain.* (A) is correct.

15 **(E)** Even if you didn't know what *oncology* means, you might have guessed the study of something because of the *ology* ending, and judging from the other word it's probably the study of tumors. The choices look like sciences too. (A)'s pairing of *chronology* and *time* looks okay, but not dead on. There's a science called chronology, the science of arranging time into periods. Chronology is not exactly the study of time—it's a science involved with mapping events in time. Likewise, (B) is almost there. The *theo* in *theology* comes from the Greek word for god, and *theology* means the study of gods or religious beliefs. *Tenet,* on the other hand, means a particular belief or principle. It's too narrow to say theology is the study of tenets. We can eliminate (C) because *aural* is not the study of sound—that would be closer to *acoustics*. In (D), *philology* is a field that includes the study of literary history, language history, and systems of writing, not the study of religion. *Taxonomy,* (E), is the study of *classification*, the correct answer. *Taxonomy* is also used to refer specifically to the classification of organisms.

16 **(B)** *Intransigent* means unyielding—the opposite of *flexible*. Our bridge is "a person who is intransigent is lacking in flexibility." The only pair that looks good is (B), *disinterested* and *partisanship*. One who's disinterested is unbiased—he doesn't have an interest in either side of a dispute. *Partisan* means partial to a particular party or cause. That's the opposite of disinterested. So partisanship, the quality of being biased, is lacking in a person who could be described as disinterested.

In (A), *transient* means transitory, so you wouldn't say that someone transient lacks *mobility*. In (C), *dissimilar* means not similar, along the same lines as *variation*. You can't say that something progressive lacks transition, so (D) is no good. The word *ineluctable* in (E) means inescapable, while *modality* is a longer way of saying mode.

Reading Passage: Questions 17–23

The longer of the two reading comp passages appears first. The author's main concern, the aim of science to derive a theory which describes particles and their forces as simply as possible, becomes apparent early in the first paragraph. Simplicity is so important that the author sets it up as a criterion for judging the specific theory of nature. Then the author outlines a recently developed theory which he considers to be a remarkable achievement for its frugality and level of detail. He then asserts that an even simpler theory is conceivable and goes on to mention one that promises at least a partial unification of elementary particles and forces. The last half of the second paragraph and the final paragraph describe this theory in greater detail.

17 **(D)** We need either a choice that describes the similarity between the theories, or one that falsifies information about them. (D) should raise your suspicions. The author acknowledged at the end of the first paragraph that the first theory could account for the entire observed hierarchy of material structure. (D) is right, but let's look at the others.

(A) is a valid difference between the two theories—the second is presented as a simpler alternative to the first. (B) is also a real difference. The first theory encompass gravitation and the second unifies three of the four forces, which makes it a better theory, but it doesn't account for gravitation. The first theory includes leptons and quarks, while the second combines these two classes into just one, so (C) is valid. In a similar way, the second theory unifies three of the four forces outlined in the first theory, so (E) is valid. Again, it's (D).

18 **(B)** This question asks for the primary purpose, and we know that the author is concerned with theories that describe, simply and precisely, particles and their forces. The author's primary pur-

pose is to describe attempts to develop a simplified theory of nature. Skimming through the choices, (B) looks good. (E) doesn't fit at all. You might say the author summarizes the theories describing matter, but he doesn't summarize all that is known about matter itself. As for (A), the author doesn't cite a misconception in either of the theories he describes. At most, he mentions ways in which the first could be simplified but this doesn't imply that there's a misconception. The author does refer to the second theory as a leading candidate for achieving unification, but predicting its success, (C), is far from his primary purpose. As for (D), although it's implied that scientists in general do prefer simpler theories, their reasons for this preference are never discussed. Again, it's (B) for Question 18.

19 **(E)** This question is a scattered detail question concerning quarks. In the first paragraph we're told that quarks are constituents of the proton and the neutron. It's reasonable, then, to say that quarks are the elementary building blocks of protons and neutrons, option I. Since option I is correct, we can eliminate choices which exclude it, (B) and (D). The remaining choices are either I only, I and II only, or I, II, and III. You could skip II and go to III. If you're sure III is right, you can assume that II is also and pick (E). It turns out that III can be easily checked at the end of paragraph three, where the author states that a new theory incorporates the leptons and quarks into a single family or class, so option III is correct. For a complete list, let's look at option II. In the very first sentence the author tells us that elementary particles don't have an internal structure and since quarks are elementary particles, option II is indeed correct, and (E) is our answer.

20 **(C)** It should be clear that the author has some very definite criteria for judging the usefulness or worth of various theories of nature. As for option I, *simplicity* should leap off the page at you—it's what this passage is all about. We can eliminate (B) and (E). The author also takes the theory's completeness into consideration. He commends the first theory he describes because it accounts for the entire observed hierarchy of material structure and therefore option II is correct. We know that (C) must be correct because there is no I, II, and III choice. But let's look at III anyway. Does the author ever mention proving either of those two theories he describes? Proof is of no concern to him—there's no mention in the passage of any experiments, or of wanting to find experimental proof. So III is out and (C) it is.

21 **(E)** We've mentioned that the second theory doesn't include gravitation in its attempt to unify the four basic forces. We need the author's opinion about this omission. The author introduces the theory in the second paragraph, describing it as an ambitious theory that promises at least a partial unification of elementary particles and forces. The failure to include gravitation and achieve complete unification doesn't dampen the author's enthusiasm and he seems to suggest that gravitation's omission can't be helped, at least at this stage. So, although the omission is a limitation—it prevents total unification—it is also unavoidable. It looks like (E) does the trick.

You could see the limitation as a defect, (A), but the author never gives the impression that the omission of gravitation disqualifies the theory. As for (B), *deviation* is a funny word—deviation from what? More important, we've already seen that the author doesn't consider the omission to be unjustified. For the same reason, (C) can be eliminated. If the omission of gravitation can't be avoided, then it certainly isn't a needless oversimplification. Finally (D) is out because there's no way that gravitation's omission could be an oversight. A scientist just forgot about one of the four basic forces when developing a theory of nature? No, the idea is that, for now at least, gravitation just can't be fit in, and (E) is correct.

22 **(B)** The passage begins with the author's discussion of the simplicity of elementary particles and the theories which describe them. In the third sentence, the author sets forth simplicity as a standard for judging theories of nature. In the rest of the passage, the author measures two specific theories against this standard. (B) summarizes this setup nicely and it's our answer. (A) is way off base. Although the author might be said to enumerate distinctions between how the two theories treat elementary particles, he doesn't enumerate distinctions among the particles. (C) is easy to eliminate—the author describes only two methods of grouping particles and forces—not three. As for (D), the author doesn't criticize the first theory he describes or call it inaccurate—he commends it. Finally, (E) goes overboard. As we mentioned in our discussion of option III in Question 20, the author is not interested in scientific verification. Nothing is ever mentioned about proving or verifying either of the theories he describes. Again, (B) is correct.

23 **(C)** This question shouldn't be difficult. It asks us to put ourselves in the author's shoes and figure out what sort of theory he would find superior to present theories. We already know—a simpler theory. The author's criteria for judging a theory are its simplicity and its ability to account for the largest possible number of known phenomena. Which choice represents a theory with one or both of these characteristics? (A) misrepresents the two theories described in the passage. The author says that the first theory could account for the entire observed hierarchy of material structure. The second does also, even though gravitation must be thrown in as a separate force. A theory that could account for a larger number of structures isn't what's needed.

As for (B), why would the author approve of a theory that reduces the four basic forces to two which are incompatible? (C) is on the right track. The author would prefer a theory that accounts for all matter with the fewest particles and forces and this is offered by (C), the correct answer. (D) is out because it wouldn't represent an improvement on currently existing theories. They account for gravitation, although they haven't yet unified it with the other three forces. Finally, (E) represents a step backwards.

The current theories hypothesize that both protons and neutrons are formed by combinations of elementary particles. Again, it's (C).

Reading Passage: Questions 24–27

The second passage is short but dense, and the author doesn't arrive at her main point until the last sentence. We see that the author sets herself in opposition to presentist historians, people who believe that white abolitionists and suffragists comprise the abiding principles of equality and the equal right of all to life, liberty, and the pursuit of happiness.

Their evidence is presented in the first three sentences. First, a majority of both groups tried to assure people that the changes they advocated weren't revolutionary and served to support rather than to undermine the status quo. A certain group of abolitionists disclaimed miscegenationist intentions—they were careful to assert that their interest in obtaining freedom for blacks didn't mean they were advocating mixing of races. And finally, suffragists saw no conflict between racism or nativism and their movement's objectives. Presentist historians apparently think that, by denying any revolutionary intentions and miscegenationist intentions, and by justifying nativism and racism, both groups were undermining their own principles. And, because their objectives—the abolition of slavery and voting rights for all—go hand in hand with our present conception of equality, presentist historians think that both groups undermine the principle of equality at the same time. The author uses the same evidence to argue that the actions of both groups served not to show how far these groups deviated from a fixed principle of equality, but to show what the principle meant in their own generations. The author thinks that the principle of equality is not unchanging, but means different things for different generations and that presentist historians err when they judge these movements by our conception of equality.

24 **(C)** We need the author's main point, which we just formulated—the actions of abolitionists and suffragists demonstrate the meaning that equality had in their time. (C) expresses this, and it's the correct answer. (A) is wrong because it's the presentist historians who believe that the actions of the abolitionists and suffragists compromised their principles. (B) has nothing to do with the author's discussion. A comparison of beliefs never occurs. As for (D), the author charges presentist historians with misinterpreting abolitionist and suffragist ideology, not with willfully misrepresenting it. Finally, (E) constitutes a criticism the author makes about presentist historians—that they impose their own value systems on the past, rather than interpreting actions in the appropriate historical context. Again, it's (C) for this question.

25 **(A)** We can infer something about the author's concept of the principle of equality—it's clear that the author thinks the principle of equality is not abiding. Rather, she thinks, it encompasses different things for people at different times. We can give the nod to option I, which eliminates (B), (C), and (E). Since the only choices left include option I only or options I and II only, option III can be eliminated. Option II—does the author suggest that the suffragists applied the principle of equality more consistently than abolitionists? No, if anything, she implies that they applied it equally consistently. We're left with (A) as our answer. We know option III can't be true—presentist historians say that abolitionists and suffragists compromised the principle of equality, not the author, who thinks their actions conform to their generation's conception of equality.

26 **(C)** This question deals with the logical structure of the author's argument, how she argues her case against the presentist historians. She uses the same evidence to support her views that they do, cites the actions of the suffragists and abolitionists, states that the presentist historians knew of these actions, then presents her own interpretation of these same actions. She's applying a different interpretation to the same set of facts, and (C) is our answer. The author doesn't cite any new evidence, so both (A) and (B) can be ruled out. As for (D), the author refutes not the accuracy of the historians' data but the accuracy of their interpretation. Finally, the author doesn't claim that the historians' argument is flawed by a logical contradiction, (E). She claims instead that they erred by assuming that equality is an abiding value and by measuring the actions of past groups against this concept of equality. Again, it's (C) for this question.

27 **(B)** We need to know what the author suggests about the abolitionist movement. Well, in her references to this movement, the author mentions the non-Garrisonian abolitionists. If there were non-Garrisonian abolitionists, it seems reasonable to assume that Garrisonian abolitionists existed. Also, the author refers to a majority of white abolitionists who made certain denials. This implies that there was a minority of abolitionists who didn't make such denials and also that there were black abolitionists. In other words, the abolitionist movement was subdivided into different groups and these groups didn't always share identical ideologies. This corresponds closely to (B), the correct answer. As for (A), the passage does state that some abolitionists denied that they had revolutionary or miscegenationist intentions, but these denials don't seem to be an attempt to disguise their real intentions. (C) is wrong because the author thinks the abolitionists did live by their principles. As for (D), presentist historians might claim that abolitionists undermined their objectives by making certain disclaimers to the public. But even they wouldn't say that these disclaimers were the result of abolitionists misunderstanding their objectives. Finally, the passage makes no mention of radical factions within the abolitionist movement and the effects of abolitionists' actions on their movement's progress is never discussed, so (E) is out. Again, (B) is correct.

28 **(C)** Our first word is *undermine,* which means to weaken or cause to collapse, especially by secret means. The opposite would be something like *build up* or make *stronger.* The best choice here is (C), *bolster,* meaning to support. The only other tempting choice was (A), *appreciate,* but a better opposite for appreciate would be *resent.*

29 **(B)** *Obsequious* means servile or submissive. The opposite of *obsequious* would be something like *snooty* or *arrogant. Haughty,* (B), fits perfectly. A haughty person is overly arrogant while an obsequious person is overly eager to please. None of the other choices comes close.

30 **(C)** The word *blanch* may be familiar to you if you cook. Foods like broccoli are blanched by plunging them in boiling water so they lose color. In the same way, a person might blanch from fear, shock, or dismay. Since *blanch* means to whiten or turn pale, the opposite would be to redden or blush. (C), *flush* is what we need. None of the other answer choices are particularly colorful.

31 **(A)** The word *dissipated* can be a pejorative reference to someone devoted to the pursuit of pleasure—the opposite of dissipation is restraint or moderation. (A) is correct because *temperate* means moderate or self-restrained. None of the other answer choices have to do with moderation. *Inundated* means overwhelmed or deluged.

32 **(D)** *Fecundity* means fertility, the capacity for producing life, whether it be children or vegetation. Clearly the opposite would be (D), *sterility,* which refers to an inability to reproduce. None of the other choices comes close, and the only unusual word is (A)'s *levity,* which means silliness or frivolity.

33 **(D)** In Question 33, *encumber* means to block or weigh down. A good synonym would be *oppress*. The best opposite is (D), *disburden*, which means to free from oppression. *Animate* (A), means to make alive—its opposite would be something like deaden. To *inaugurate*, (B), is to begin or commence. To *bleach* is to pale or whiten and to *obliterate* means to erase or remove.

34 **(C)** The word *disseminate* isn't easy to figure out if you don't know it—it means to spread widely. Ideas, theories, and beliefs can all be disseminated. The opposite of spreading an idea is *suppressing* it, (C). None of the other choices work.

35 **(D)** *Restive* looks like the word rested, but the two don't mean the same thing at all. Restive can mean stubborn or restless. A mule that won't move is restive, as is a fidgety child. We need something like *obedient, quiet,* or *settled,* and it's *patient,* (D). *Morose* in (A) means gloomy. *Intangible* means untouchable or elusive. *Fatigued* means tired and the opposite of *curious* would be *indifferent*.

36 **(B)** If you didn't know what *syncopated* means, you might have guessed it had something to do with rhythm from the expression *out of sync*. That would lead you to (B), *normally accented*. *Syncopation* refers to a pattern or rhythm in which stress is shifted onto normally unaccented beats.

The opposite of (A)'s *carefully executed* would be *haphazard,* and (C)'s *brightly illuminated* is the opposite of *dim*. *Obscure* would be an antonym for (D)'s *easily understood*. *Justly represented,* in (E) isn't easy to match, but even if you couldn't eliminate all the choices, you could have at least narrowed the field.

37 **(C)** *Vituperative* means verbally abusive. The opposite of defaming someone with vituperative remarks would be praising them—(C)'s *laudatory* means expressing praise. As for the other choices, *lethal* means deadly and *incapacitated* means incapable or unfit. In (D), *insulated* means protected, as in *insulation,* and *prominent,* (E), means famous.

38 **(B)** *Saturnine* is probably the hardest word in the section. It means heavy, gloomy, sluggish, so its opposite is *cheerful* or *lively*. The answer is (B), *ebullient* which means bubbling with enthusiasm or high spirited. (A)'s *magnanimous* means generous or high minded. *Finicky,* (C), means fussy or picky. The opposite of (D), *unnatural* is natural and (E), *impoverished* means poor.

39 **(E)** *Callous* means unfeeling, uncaring, but if this person has concern for the earthquake victims, her reputation must be an unfounded one, so the correct choice will mean *contradicted* or *proved false*. This is one of the meanings of *belied,* correct choice (E). (B), *rescinded,* is the second best answer. It means revoked or withdrawn, but you don't say that a reputation is rescinded. (A), (C), and (D) are the opposite of what we're looking for—they don't make sense in this context.

40 **(B)** *No longer* and *therefore* show strong contrast—something is done with the original plans because they are no longer something else. (B) expresses this contrast, *applicable . . . rejected,* and if we plug in these words, the plans could no longer be applied so they were tossed aside. In (A), there's no contrast between something being *relevant,* or pertinent, and its being *adaptable,* capable of being changed to fit a new situation. In (C), *expedient* means convenient—it makes no sense for something not expedient to be *adopted* or taken up. In (D), *appraised* means judged or rated, which doesn't follow from no longer being *acceptable*. In (E) it doesn't make sense to say that the plans were no longer *capable* or that the plans were *allayed,* or minimized—again, (B) is the best choice.

41 **(D)** The second half of the sentence is about each tiny layer of the surface of the cross-section of the sandstone. This must explain what the first part alludes to, so the first blank must mean *layered*—otherwise, what tiny layers is the author talking about? On this basis, (D) is the best answer since *stratified* means layered. In (A), a ridge isn't really a layer. In (B), a facet is a face or flat surface, so *multifaceted* can't be right. *Distinctive*, in (C) means distinguishing or individual. And *coarse* in (E) means rough. Looking at the second blank, *enlargement*, in (A), has nothing to do with the formation of the stone. In (B), if the phrase *angle of deposition* means anything at all, it's an obscure geological term and can't be what we want here. The remaining choices could refer to the time or place in which material is deposited. Since (D) has the best answer for the first blank and a possible answer for the second blank, it's correct.

42 **(D)** The phrase *and now* suggests that the second part of the sentence will say something consistent with the first part. Whatever the convict has always insisted upon, the new evidence must support his claim. (D) gets this connection right—*innocence . . vindicate*. To vindicate means to clear from an accusation, to prove innocent. The convict has always insisted upon his own innocence and now at last there is new evidence to vindicate him—this makes perfect sense and it's the answer. In (A), *defensiveness* means a tendency to defend oneself and *incarcerate* means to put in prison. In (B), *culpability* is guilt, as in the word *culprit*, and *exonerate* means to clear from guilt. In (C), to *anathematize* someone means to curse him or pronounce a strong sentence against him but that doesn't go with *blamelessness*. In (E) *contrition* is a sense of remorse, while to *condemn* someone means to pass judgment against him. This is probably second best, but it doesn't follow as logically as (D), so (D) is correct.

43 **(A)** The word *but* signals a contrast between the opinion of plate tectonics when the theory was first proposed, and the opinion of it now—either people disbelieved the theory at first and believe it now or vice versa. (A), *opposition . . grant* provides the contrast. If most geophysicists now grant its validity, they believe in it. That's the opposite of opposing it, so (A) is the answer. In (B), *consideration* is a neutral term—people are thinking about the theory, but it doesn't provide the necessary contrasts with *see*, which implies that physicists now recognize the validity of the theory. In (C), *acclamation* means loud praise and *boost* means to support enthusiastically—no contrast there. In (D), a *prognostication* is a prediction of the future, which doesn't make sense in this context and *learn its validity* doesn't make sense either, so (D) isn't a good choice. In (E), *contention* is argument and to *bar* means to exclude or forbid—there is no contrast with this pair. Again, (A) is the correct answer.

44 **(D)** *Despite* clues you in to a contrast between something professed, claimed or pretended, and reality, indicated by the glint in her eyes. A glint in someone's eye is a sign of strong interest, so *obsession* and *fascination,* in (A) and (D) are tempting. We want a contrast with strong interest, so the first word is something like *disinterest*. We find *indifference* in (D) and *obliviousness* in (C). Since both words in (D) fit, it must be correct. None of the others offers the kind of contrasts we need. There's no contrast between *intelligence* and *obsession,* in (A), between *interest* and *concern* in (B), or between *obliviousness* and *confusion* in (C). We get a contrast in (E) between *expertise* and *unfamiliarity,* but the words don't make sense—a glint in someone's eye isn't a sign of unfamiliarity.

45 **(C)** We're looking for something that goes with sacred scriptures and implies a formal system of belief, but something whose absence doesn't rule out a legacy of traditional religious practices and basic values. We can eliminate choices (A), (B), and (E) because if Shinto lacked *followers*, *customs*, or *faith* it wouldn't be a legacy of traditional religious practices and basic values. *Relics*, (D), are sacred objects but relics don't make something a formal system of beliefs. The best choice is (C)—a *dogma* is a formal religious belief.

46 **(E)** Something *impeccable* is perfect, it doesn't have a *flaw*. In (A) *impeachable* means subject to accusation, so something impeachable is not necessarily without *crime*. *Obstreperous,* in (B) means loud or unruly, not without *permission*. *Impetuous,* in (C) means rash or without care, rather than without *warning*. In (D), *moribund* means in the process of dying, so it's inappropriate to use *living*. In (E), *absurd* means without *sense*, so this is the correct answer.

47 **(D)** A *seismograph* is an instrument used to measure an earthquake, so we need another instrument used to measure something. In (A), a *stethoscope* is an instrument used to listen to a patient's chest. Only indirectly can this be used to measure a patient's *health*. In (B), a *speedometer* doesn't measure a *truck*—it measures the speed of any kind of vehicle. In (C), a *telescope* doesn't measure *astronomy*. A telescope is an instrument used to observe far away objects. In (D), a *thermometer* measures *temperature*, so this looks like a promising answer. In (E), an *abacus* is used in *arithmetic* as a calculator but it doesn't measure arithmetic. So (D) is the best answer.

48 **(D)** To *guzzle* is to *drink* very quickly, taking big gulps, so the relationship is one of speed or degree. In (A), *elucidate* and *clarify* mean to make clearer. One doesn't imply greater speed or volume than the other. Similarly, with (B) to *ingest* is to *eat* or drink—it doesn't mean to eat in big bites. In (C), to *boast* and to *describe* are two unrelated ways of talking. In (D), to *stride* is to *walk* quickly, taking big steps, so this may be the answer. In (E), *condemn* is stronger than the first word *admonish,* meaning to rebuke—the opposite of how the stem pair is presented. So (D) is the best answer.

49 **(C)** An *orator* is a public speaker and *articulate* means able to express oneself well. You can form the bridge, "A successful orator is one who is articulate." With that in mind, (A) may seem tempting but the profession of *soldier* isn't defined as aspir-

ing towards being *merciless*. In (B) a *celebrity* is a famous person, not by definition a *talented* one. (C) is good—a good *judge* has to be *unbiased*. It's safe to say that a biased judge is a bad judge in the same way that an inarticulate orator is a bad orator. In (D), a *novice* is a beginner—it wouldn't be unusual for a novice to be *unfamiliar* but that's not what makes a good novice. In (E), a *dignitary* is a person of high rank, and such a person doesn't need to be *respectful*. (C) is correct.

50 **(C)** A *badge* is the identification worn by a *policeman*. In (A), a *placard* is a sign carried by a *demonstrator*. There's a link here but a placard isn't an official ID and a demonstrator doesn't necessarily carry a placard. (B) is wrong because although there is a tradition for a *sailor* to have a *tattoo*, a tattoo isn't an official identification of a sailor. In (C), a *soldier* wears a *dog-tag* on his uniform to identify him, so this is plausible. In (D), the *pedigree* of a *dog* is the dog's lineage or genealogy, not something worn by the dog as identification. In (E), even though a *fingerprint* may be used to identify a *defendant*, everybody has fingerprints. So the best answer is (C).

51 **(B)** To *scrutinize* means to *observe* intently, so the relationship is one of degree. In (A), to *pique* interest is to *excite* interest. The words mean the same thing. In (B), to *beseech* means to *request* with great fervor—this is more like it. In (C), to *search* is the process you go through to *discover* something. That's different from the stem pair. In (D) to *grin* is to *smile* broadly—this reverses the original pair. And in (E), to *dive* means to *jump* in a certain way or under certain conditions, not to jump intently. The best answer is (B).

52 **(D)** If you didn't know what *epicurean* means, you might have had trouble here, but you can still eliminate some choices. There must be some relationship between *epicurean* and *indulge*. Could (A) have the same relationship? No, because there really is no relationship between *frightened* and *ugly*. Something ugly doesn't necessarily frighten people.

Same with (C)—there's no relationship between *hesitate* and *unproductive*. There are good relationships for the other choices but let's see if we can eliminate them. In (E), the relationship is that something *comprehensible* can be *understood*. Do you think that something *epicurean* can be *indulged*? That sounds odd—just about everyone and everything can be indulged.

In (B), *revocable* means something can be taken back, so the relationship is, "Something *revocable* can be *retracted*." That's the same relationship that we just saw in (E), another clue that they must be wrong. If (B) and (E) share the same relationship, they can't both be right, so they must both be wrong. That leaves us with (D), and there our relationship is something like, "someone *vindictive* is likely to *revenge* himself," and that sounds better. In fact, an epicurean person is one who is likely to indulge himself, so (D) is correct here.

53 **(E)** *Diluvial* means having to do with a *flood*. You may have heard the word *antediluvian*, meaning before the flood, Noah's flood, that is—in other words, a long time ago. So our bridge is "having to do with." In (A), *criminal* can mean "having to do with crime" but it doesn't mean having to do with *punishment*. In (B), *biological* means "having to do with living things." *Bacteria* are living things but to define *biological* as "having to do with bacteria" would be too narrow. In (C), *judicial* means "having to do with the administration of justice." A *verdict* is the decision about the guilt or innocence of a defendant, a small part of the judicial process. (D)'s *candescent* means "giving off *light*" rather than "having to do with light." This leaves (E) and *cardiac* means "having to do with the *heart*," so (E) is correct.

54 **(C)** It is in the nature of a *sphinx* to *perplex*. This comes from Greek mythology—the sphinx was a monster that asked a riddle that no one could answer. *Sphinx* can be used to mean anything that is difficult to understand, so our bridge is: "A sphinx is known for perplexing." In (A), an *oracle* is a soothsayer, someone who predicts the future—an oracle doesn't

interpret. In (B), a *prophet* is someone who foretells the future. This may help someone to *prepare* but you don't say that a prophet is known for preparing. In (C), a *siren* can be a beautiful or a seductive woman who *lures* men. So (C) looks good—a siren lures in the same way that a sphinx perplexes. In (D), the role of a *jester* is to amuse, not necessarily to *astound*. In (E), a *minotaur* is a mythological monster—it didn't, by definition, *anger* someone. So (C) is correct.

Reading Passage: Questions 55–57

This reading comp passage is short and it's followed by three questions—the remaining passage will be long with eight questions. The style of this natural science passage is factual, descriptive and straightforward, although the discussion does get fairly detailed. The topic is clear from the first sentence: our knowledge of how fish schools are formed and how their structure is maintained. The next two sentences get more specific and express the author's main point—that, contrary to the previous theory, the structure of fish schools is not primarily dependent on vision.

The tone is objective, but it's worth noting that since the author is contrasting the new knowledge about lateral lines with older, outdated knowledge, he must be skeptical of the notion that vision is the primary means of forming and maintaining fish schools. The rest of the passage is a more technical report of how the schools are structured, how individual fish actually behave in forming schools—this is detail and the best way to deal with it is to read it attentively but more quickly than the earlier lines.

55 **(E)** This Roman numeral-format question focuses on detail. The stem is asking what the structure of fish schools depends on, and the options focus on the more technical elements in the last half of the passage. The author states that ideal positions of individual fish aren't maintained rigidly and this contradicts option I right away. The idea of random aggregation appears: the school formation results from a probabilistic arrangement that appears like a random aggregation, so the idea is that fish are positioned probabilistically, but not rigidly. Option II is true, repeating the idea in the next sentence that fish school structure is maintained by the preference of fish to have a certain distance from their neighbors. Option III is true, too. It's a paraphrase of the last two sentences, that each fish uses its vision and lateral line first to measure the speed of the other fish, then to adjust its own speed to conform, based primarily on the position and movements of other fish. So options II and III are true and (E) is the right choice.

56 (C) You know the primary purpose here is to present new ideas that challenge the emphasis of the old theory. So you're probably safe in assuming that the author's attitude toward the old idea will be at least somewhat negative. You can therefore cross off choices that sound neutral or positive, (B), (D), and (E). The negative choices are (A) and (C). (A) is out because it is much too extreme—the author is not offended or indignant, nor does he or she argue that vision is insignificant—quite the contrary. This leaves (C), the best choice. The author disagrees with the old theory since it overlooks the role of the lateral line, but the disagreement is tempered by an acknowledgment that the old theory did recognize the role of vision. So it's a qualified or measured disagreement—the adjective *considered* works well here. Again, the correct answer is (C).

57 (C) This question involves inference as the word *suggests* in the stem suggests. It refers to the latter, more detailed half of the passage, and that's where correct answer (C) is. It's logically suggested by the last couple of sentences where you're told that once it establishes its position, each fish uses its eyes and lateral line to measure the movements of nearby fish in order to maintain appropriate speed and position. Since the school is moving, each fish's adjustments must be ongoing and continuous, as (C) states. (A) is wrong because auditory organs aren't mentioned. Lateral lines correspond to a sense of touch,

not hearing. (B) and (D) both have words that should strike you as improbable. Nothing suggests that each fish rigorously avoids any disruptive movements, (B), or that the fish would make sudden unexpected movements only in the presence of danger, (D). The idea in (E) also isn't mentioned. It's never suggested that a fish, once part of a school, completely loses its ability to act on its own. Again, (C) is our answer for this question.

Reading Passage: Questions 58–65

This passage is divided into three paragraphs. If you figure out what each paragraph covers, you've understood the passage's handful of ideas, plus you've sketched out a rough mental map. In this passage, the first 10 or 15 lines take you through the first paragraph and into the second and if you were careful you picked up the author's broad topic area (ancient Greek social anxiety), the style of the writing (dense and scholarly) and the tone or attitude (expository and neutral).

The second paragraph gives you the central point—what the Greeks apparently succeeded in doing was discovering a way of measuring and explaining chaotic experience so that chaos was no longer so threatening and anxiety producing. This recognition of order in the midst of chaos served as the basis of a spiritual ideal for the Greeks. So by the end of the second paragraph you have the author's central idea plus all the information about style, tone, and topics in the beginning. The first sentence of the last paragraph tells you the search for order and clarity in the midst of chaos is reflected especially in Greek philosophy. The rest of the paragraph is a description of how various philosophers and schools of philosophy offered solutions to the problem of finding order and measure in a disorderly world.

58 (E) This kind of primary purpose question is common, and here the right answer is (E). In this case, both the noun and the verb are right on the money. The verb is exactly right for this author's expository neutral tone, and a cultural phenomenon, the Greeks' perception of chaos and their solution to the problem, is what the author is describing. The verbs in (B) and (C), *challenge* and *question* eliminate them right away—no opinion is given but the author's own, and philosophy in (C) is discussed only in the last paragraph. The noun phrase in (A), *conflicting viewpoints* is wrong. (D) is the most tempting—the author is looking at history and mentioning certain facts, but this misses the author's purpose, which is not to simply list facts but rather to describe and define something in the form of a thesis. Again, (E) is the correct answer.

59 **(A)** This is from the first sentence of the second paragraph and it's the central idea that's being focused on, that the discovery of this substratum helped bring a satisfying new sense of order into experience, thus reforming the Greeks' perception of worldly chaos. The choice that paraphrases this point is (A), the perception of constant change was altered by the idea of a permanent principle of order lying underneath it—this is the main point of the passage. (B) is out because severe social problems are never mentioned, at least not in any concrete way. As for (C), it misses the point made in the sentence the question refers to. The passage does refer to pain and bewilderment and to an earlier period of political turbulence, but this choice goes overboard with its notions of painful memories and national humiliation and so on. As for (D), a few lines into the second paragraph the author says directly that the discovery did much more than satisfy intellectual curiosity. And (E) also contradicts the author, distorting a detail at the end of the paragraph. It's not mysticism, but rationality and careful analysis that lead to order and clarity, so it's (A) for this question.

60 **(D)** The author is arguing in the second, third, and fourth sentences that the Greeks identified rational thought and spiritual ideals as inseparable. Rationality, order, measure, and so forth became equivalent to spiritual ideals for the Greeks.

Toward the end of the second paragraph the author states that rationality and spirituality are not mutually exclusive. The choice that's most clearly consistent with this is (D). As for (A), the passage never suggests that ordinary Greeks were unfamiliar with or uninterested in the concepts of rational thought and spiritual ideals. The passage suggests quite the contrary. (B) and (C) are both inconsistent with the passage as well. All the philosophers mentioned accepted the notion that rationality was the key, amounting to an ideal to understanding the world. (E) picks up on the mention of poetry at the beginning of the last paragraph, but the point there is that Greek poetry manifested the sense of cultural anxiety that philosophy tried to alleviate.

61 **(B)** This question is looking for the choice that isn't mentioned as reflecting the Greeks' anxieties about chaos. The one that's never mentioned is (B), that it was reflected in aspects of their religion. We don't actually learn anything about Greek religion in the passage—we just don't know and we certainly can't infer anything about specific aspects. Each of the other choices is mentioned specifically. (A) is implied in the long opening sentence of the first paragraph—the national psyche and historical experience both relate to national consciousness. (C), the sense of change in the physical world, is mentioned at the start of paragraph two. (D), the striving for order and philosophy, is discussed throughout the third paragraph. And finally (E), lyric poetry, is mentioned at the start of the paragraph as one place where the sense of anxiety was expressed directly.

62 **(C)** Your mental map should have taken you straight to the last paragraph—the Milesians are discussed in the first several sentences. (C) encapsulates what the passage says, that Milesians were interested primarily in understanding a fundamental order in nature, outside the disturbing world of human society. (A) gets it backwards—the Milesians apparently ignored questions that were inherently human. (B) and (D) contradict the passage. None of the philosophies mentioned did what these choices suggest, either to sharply distinguish between rationality and spirituality, (B), or to integrate rationality and mysticism, (D). (E), finally, describes the approach of the Pythagoreans who were absorbed by the logic and order of mathematics, rather than by attempts to explain physical phenomena.

63 **(D)** You're being asked not the actual content, but the logical progression of the contents. Is he or she making a series of disconnected assertions? Making a point and backing it up with factual evidence, or what? What's the author up to logically in the lines referred to? In the preceding sentence the author is talking about the Greeks' discovery of order and measure, and that it helped them get a secure handle on chaotic experience. The discovery was a relief—its impact was almost religious in nature. In the next sentence, the author says that this recognition, discovery, of order and measure was much more than merely intellectually satisfying—it served as a basic part of their spiritual values. The author quotes Plato to support his point, to give an idea of the significance of measure.

In the last of the three sentences the author finishes up with a statement that pulls the strands of the thesis together and puts the basic point into clear cultural perspective. Rational definability or measure was never regarded by the Greeks as inconsistent with spirituality—(D) is the choice that describes things best. The problem with (A) is that the author isn't summarizing two viewpoints but discussing one thesis. As for (B), the author neither mentions evidence that weakens his thesis nor revises it. (C) is out because the author is not discussing two separate arguments that need to be reconciled by a third. It's just one argument that's the topic here. (E), finally, is wrong for the same reason—the author discusses one thesis only and never suggests any other.

64 **(A)** We know from our rough map of the structure that except for one reference to Plato in the middle of the second paragraph, philosophy is discussed only in the last paragraph, so that's where you'll find out about the Pythagoreans. The main thing about them was that they concentrated on mathematical abstraction. They shifted the focus in philosophy from the physical realm to the mathematical. The Milesians focused on physical phenomena, and that's the idea you see immediately in (A), the correct choice. (B) lists an idea that mentions the Pythagoreans—thinkers who came *after* the Pythagoreans focused on human behavior. (C) won't work because both of these schools and all other philosophies mentioned used rationality as the means to truth. (D) picks up what characterized the Milesians—we want the Pythagorean side of the contrast. (E) gets things backward—the Pythagoreans stressed mathematical theory over physical matter. Again, it's (A).

65 **(D)** The last sentence is saying that in all these various periods of Greek history and philosophy, the basic preoccupation of the Greeks was with the search for a kosmos. The term *kosmos* hasn't been used before, but because this sentence is at the end of the passage and because it's phrased as a summary, you should realize that the basic quest here must be the same one the author has been talking about all along. So this refers to the central problem for Greek society—how to find order and measure in a seemingly confusing and disorderly world. This search for a kosmos then is the passage's main idea, and correct choice (D) restates it.

(A) is out because the word *mystical* is incorrect, since the author states at the end of paragraph two that the Greeks stressed rationalism over mysticism. (B) and (E) are inconsistent with some major points. In (B), the idea that the Greeks would have regarded rationalism as sterile is completely wrong. And in (E), the ideals of beauty and excellence, as mentioned in paragraph two, are preeminent and fundamental within the Greeks' world view. Finally, (C) talks about ending conflict among important schools of philosophy. This last sentence about the search for kosmos is talking about a quest you find in Greek thought as a whole, a much bigger topic than mere conflicts among philosophers.

66 **(A)** *Enmity* is the state of being an enemy—the opposite is *friendship*, (A). *Reverence*, (B), is great respect, the opposite of contempt. The opposite of *boredom*, (C), is interest. The opposite of (D), *stylishness*, is a lack of style, and the opposite of (E), *awkwardness*, is skillfulness.

67 **(B)** *Dilate* means expand and widen. The opposite is the word *contract*, so (B), *shrink*, is what we're looking for. (A), *enclose*, means to confine. The opposite of the word *hurry*, (C), is *delay*. *Inflate*, (D), means to expand or fill with air. The opposite of (E), *erase*, might be *preserve* or *set down*.

68 **(A)** A *charlatan* is a fraud or a quack. (A), *genuine expert*, is a possible answer. The opposite of a *powerful leader*, (B), is a follower or maybe a weak leader. The opposite of a *false idol*, (C), is a true god or a hero. The opposite of an *unknown enemy*, (D), is a known enemy, an unknown friend or a known friend. The opposite of (E), *hardened villain*, might be an innocent person or first offender. So it's (A).

69 **(C)** *Peripheral* means having to do with the periphery, the outer edge of something. The opposite of *peripheral* is *central*, (C). The opposite of (A), *civilized*, is *crude* or *savage*. (B), *partial*, means favoring or biased, or incomplete—it has lots of opposites but *peripheral* isn't one of them. *Harmed* is the opposite of *unharmed*, and the opposite of (E), *stable*, is *weak* or *inconstant*. (C) is correct.

70 **(E)** *Meritorious* means full of merit, deserving reward. Its opposite is *unpraiseworthy*, (E), the best choice. *Effulgent*, (A), means shiny—its opposite is *dull*. (B), *stationary*, means not moving. Neither (C), *uneven*, nor (D), *narrow-minded*, works, so (E) is correct.

71 **(C)** *Discharge* means to unburden, eject, or exude. However, it has a more specific meaning in military context: to release or remove someone from service. The opposite is to *enlist*, (C). The opposite of (A), *heal*, is *sicken*. The opposite of (B), *advance*, is *retreat*. (D) *penalize*, means to punish. The opposite of *delay*, (E), is *hasten*.

72 **(A)** A *malediction* is a curse. We want something like *benediction*, and we find *blessing* in (A). The opposite of *preparation*, (B), is *lack of preparation*. (C), *good omen*, has *bad omen* as its opposite. The opposite of (D), *liberation*, is *captivity*. The opposite of *pursuit*, (E), is tough, but it sure isn't *malediction*, so (A) is correct.

73 **(A)** *Mawkish* means sickeningly sentimental. *Unsentimental*, (A), is the answer here. The opposite of (B), *sophisticated*, is *naive* or *simple*. The opposite of *graceful*, (C), is *clumsy*. The opposite of *tense*, (D), is *relaxed*. There are various antonyms to *descriptive*, (E), but *mawkish* isn't one.

74 **(B)** *Temerity* is recklessness or foolish daring. Its opposite is *hesitancy* or *carefulness*. *Blandness*, (A), is a lack of character, not a lack of courage. (B), *caution*, fits—one with temerity lacks caution. The opposite of (C), *severity*, is *leniency*. The opposite of (D), *strength*, is *weakness*. *Charm*, (E), is personal appeal. The best answer is (B), caution.

75 **(C)** *Jejune* can mean immature or sophomoric. The opposite would be *adult* or correct choice (C), *mature*. *Morose*, (A), means sad or moody. The opposite of *natural*, (B), is *artificial*. (D), *contrived*, means deliberately planned. Its opposite is *natural*. *Accurate*, (E), means precise or exact.

76 **(C)** *Vitiate* means to corrupt, put wrong, spoil, or make worse, and the opposite is *improve* or *correct*. The closest choice is *rectify*, (C). (A), *deaden*, is way off. The opposite of *trust*, (B), is *distrust* or *suspect*. The opposite of *drain*, (D), is *fill*. And the opposite of *amuse*, (E), is *bore* or *upset*.

Section Two Explanations–Quantitative

1 **(A)** To compare these two quantities, work column by column starting with the decimal point and working to the right. Both have a 0 in the tenths column, so no difference there. In the hundredths column, both have a 2, so we go to thousandths. Column A has a 6 and Column B has a 5—there are more thousandths in A than in B, so Column A is larger and (A) is the correct answer.

2 **(C)** Right triangles *ABD* and *CDB* share a hypotenuse, segment *DB*. The squared quantities should clue you to use the Pythagorean theorem. See that w and x are lengths of the legs of right triangle *ABD*. Side *AD* has length w, side *AB* has length x. Also, y and z are lengths of the legs of right triangle *CDB*. Side *CD* has length z, side *CB* has length y. Where a and b are lengths of the legs of a right triangle, and C is the length of the hypotenuse, $a^2 + b^2 = c^2$, so $w^2 + x^2 =$ length BD^2. $y^2 + z^2$ also equals length DB^2, the quantities are equal and the answer is (C).

3 **(A)** We have $x + 4y = 6$ and $x = 2y$, and we want to compare x and y, so substitute $2y$ for x in the first equation. Using that information, solve for the other variable. Substitute $2y$ for x into $x + 4y = 6$ and get $2y + 4y = 6$ or $6y = 6$. Divide both sides by 6 and we get $y = 1$. If $y = 1$ and $x = 2y$ as the second equation tells us, x must equal 2. Since 2 is greater than 1, the quantity in Column A is greater.

4 **(B)** Question 4 looks hard—but you don't have to simplify to find the relationship. With positive numbers, you can square both without changing the relationship. That leaves you with $4^2 + 5^2$ in Column A and $3^2 + 6^2$ in Column B. 4^2 is 16, 5^2 is 25, 16 + 25 is 41. In Column B we have 3^2, that's $9 + 6^2$, that's 36, 9 + 36 is 45. 45 is greater than 41, Column B is greater than Column A, and the answer is (B).

5 **(D)** Column A asks for the number of managerial employees—that's easy. There are 120 employees in the firm, and 25 percent of them are managerial. One-fourth of 120 is 30, the value of Column A.

Column B asks for two-thirds of the clerical employees. But we can't figure out how many workers are clerical workers, so we can't find two-thirds of that number. We can't determine a relationship, and the answer is choice (D).

6 **(B)** We have 12×1 over $12 + 1$ in Column A: 12×1 is 12 and $12 + 1$ is 13. So we have $\frac{12}{13}$ in Column A. In Column B we have $12 + 1 = 13$ in the numerator, and $12 \times 1 = 12$ in the denominator. So $\frac{12}{13}$ in Column A versus $\frac{13}{12}$ in Column B. Of course, $\frac{12}{13}$ is less than 1 while $\frac{13}{12}$ is greater than 1, and the answer is (B).

7 **(D)** You might suspect (D) because there are no variable restrictions. To make the columns look as much alike as you can, multiply out Column A. You'll get $a \times b$ or ab, plus $1 \times b$, plus $1 \times a$, plus 1×1 or 1. So you get $ab + a + b + 1$. Column B has $ab + 1$. We can subtract ab from both sides, and it won't change the relationship and we have $1 + a + b$ in Column A, and 1 in Column B. Subtract 1 from both sides and we have $a + b$ in Column A and 0 in Column B. But consider that a and b could be negative numbers. Since $a + b$ could be positive, negative, or zero, the answer is (D).

8 **(B)** In the two-digit number jk the value of digit j is twice the value of digit k. We have to compare the value of k in Column A with 6 in Column B. If you plug in 6 for k, then go back, you see that the value of digit j is twice digit k. We know that j isn't just a number—it's a digit, which means it's 0, 1, 2, 3, 4, 5, 6, 7, 8, or 9. So 12, twice the value of 6, can't be j. In other words, k has to be something less than 6, so the answer must be (B), the value in Column B is greater.

9 **(A)** We have a circle with right angle QPR as a central angle. The area of sector PQR is 4 and we're asked to compare the area of the circle with 4π. There's a shortcut—the right angle defines the sector, and you have the area of that sector. A 90° angle cuts off one-fourth of the circle. If you multiply by four, you have the area of the circle. So in Column A you have 4×4, and in Column B, you have 4π. π is about 3.14, and 4 is bigger than that, so Column A, 4×4, must be bigger than 4π, and the answer is (A).

10 **(C)** Henry purchased x apples and Jack purchased 10 apples less than one-third the number of apples Henry purchased. *One-third of* means the same as *one-third times* and the number of apples Henry purchased is x. So this boils down to $j = \frac{1}{3}x - 10$. You can plug this in for Column A. We have $\frac{1}{3}x - 10$ in Column A and in Column B we have $x - \frac{30}{3}$. Now you can clear the fraction in Column B. Let's split Column B to two fractions. $\frac{x}{3} - \frac{30}{3}$. We leave the $\frac{x}{3}$ alone and cancel the factor of 3 from the numerator and denominator of $\frac{30}{3}$ and we're left with $\frac{x}{3} - 10$. What's $\frac{x}{3}$? It's one-third of x, so these two quantities are equal. Column A equals $\frac{1}{3}x - 10$, while Column B also equals $\frac{1}{3}x - 10$, so the answer is (C).

11 **(D)** You can suspect (D) because there are unrestricted variables. In Column A we have the volume of a rectangular solid with length 5 feet, width 4 feet, and height x feet. The formula is length times width times height, so we have 5 times 4 times x, or $20x$. In Column B we need the volume of rectangular solid with length 10 feet, width 8 feet, and height y feet. 10 times 8 times y gives you a volume of $80y$. Now you may think, I've got $20x$, and $80y$, so $80y$ must be bigger because there are more ys than xs. That would be true if x and y were close together, but the variables are unrestricted, and the answer is (D).

12 **(C)** We want to compare 50 with x, one of the angles formed by the intersection of ST and PT. Now angle QRS is labeled 80. We also know PQ and ST have the same length and QR and RS have the same length. If you add PQ and QR, you get PR. If you add ST and RS, you get RT. If you add equals to equals, you get equals, so $PQ + QR$ must be the same as $ST + RS$, which means that PR and RT are the same. You have isoceles triangle PRT and we're given one angle that has measure 80 and the second angle that has measure x. The angle measuring x is opposite equal side PR. That means the other angle must have the same measure, because it's opposite the other equal side. The sum of the interior angles in a triangle always equals 180°. $x + x + 80$ must equal 180, $2x$ must equal 100, $x = 50$. So x and 50 are equal, and the answer is (C).

13 **(B)** First we can cancel factors of 2 from $2 \times 16 \times 64$ on the left, and $2 \times 4n \times 256$ on the right. If we cancel a factor of 2 we have 16×64 on the left, $4n \times 256$ on the right. 64 goes into 256 four times, so let's cancel a factor of 64. That leaves us 16 on the left and $4n \times 4$ on the right. We can cancel a factor of 4 and we're left with 4 on the left and $4n$ on the right. If $4 = 4n$, n must equal 1, so we have $n = 1$ for Column A. Column B is 2, so the answer is (B).

14 **(C)** For each unordered group of two people selected, there are two ways to arrange the people (depending on which one is the lead). Hence, this is a permutation problem: order matters. For the lead role, there are 6 people to choose from. For the supporting role, there will be 5. So the number of possible duos is $6 \times 5 = 30$. The columns are equal.

15 **(D)** The perimeter of *ABC* is 40 and the length of *BC* is 12, and we want to compare the length of *AB* with 14. In an isosceles triangle there are two sides with equal length, but we don't know whether side *BC* is one of those sides or not. If side *BC* is the unequal side, we have two unknown sides plus 12 and they have a sum of 40, the perimeter. The two remaining sides have a sum of 28, so each is 14. That would mean that *AB* and *AC* would have length 14. Then the answer would be (C). If *BC* is one of the equal sides, we have two sides length 12 and a third unknown side, and the sum is 40. 12 + 12 is 24, so that the third side has length 16. *AB* could be one of the sides length 12, or the side length 12. There are three possible lengths for side *AB*—16, 14, and 12—so the answer is (D).

16 **(B)** Isolate $\frac{q}{p}$. Multiplying both sides of the equation by p gives $p - q = \frac{2p}{7}$. Subtracting p from both sides gives $-q = \frac{2p}{7} - p = \frac{2p}{7} - \frac{7p}{7} = -\frac{5p}{7}$. So $-q = \frac{5p}{7}$, or $q = \frac{5p}{7}$. Dividing both sides by p gives $\frac{q}{p} = \frac{5}{7}$.

17 **(E)** The question asks for the number of different dinners Jane could make. Since the order of the selections in the dinner doesn't matter, this presents itself as a combination problem. But it involves three possible combination types: Veg, Meat, Meat; Veg, Veg, Meat; or Veg, Veg, Veg. We must calculate the possibilities for each type of combination and then add the results to find the total number of different combinations possible.

Let V represent vegetarian and M represent meat.

Then with V, M, M, she has 5 choices for the vegetarian and she must choose 1, times 4 choices for meat among which she must choose 2.

For V, V, M, she will choose 2 from among 5 for the vegetarian, and 1 among 4 for the meat.

If she goes with V, V, V, the all-vegetarian menu, she will choose a subgroup of 3 from among 5 vegetarian choices (or 5 choose 3).

If n and k are positive integers where $n \geq k$, then the number of different subgroups consisting of k objects that can be selected from a group consisting of n different objects, denoted by $_nC_k$, is given by the formula $_nC_k = \frac{n!}{k!(n-k)!}$.

Here the total number of different possible servings for a plate is $(_5C_1)(_4C_2) + (_5C_2)(_4C_1) + (_5C_3)$

Now $_5C_1$ represents choosing 1 type of vegetable selection from 5 different types, so $_5C_1 = 5$. The formula also gives this result.

$$_4C_2 = \frac{4}{2!(4-2)!} = \frac{4!}{2! \times 2!} = \frac{4 \times 3 \times 2 \times 1}{2 \times 1 \times 2 \times 1} = 6$$

$$_5C_2 = \frac{5!}{2!(5-2)!} = \frac{5!}{2! \times 3!} = \frac{5 \times 4 \times 3 \times 2 \times 1}{2 \times 1 \times 3 \times 2 \times 1} = 10$$

Here $_4C_1$ corresponds to choosing 1 type of meet selection from 4 different types, so $_4C_1 = 4$.

$$_5C_3 = \frac{5!}{3!(5-3)!} = \frac{5!}{3! \times 2!} = \frac{5 \times 4 \times 3 \times 2 \times 1}{3 \times 2 \times 1 \times 2 \times 1} = 10$$

So the number of different possible servings that can be made for a plate is $5 \times 6 + 10 \times 4 + 10 = 80$.

18 **(B)** We need the value of $a + b + c$. We know that a, b, and c are exterior angles of our quadrilateral in the diagram and there's a fourth exterior angle which isn't labeled. But the measure of the interior angle next to it is given to us—it's 70°. The sum of the exterior angles of any figure is always 360°. So we can figure out the measure of the missing angle, then subtract it from 360 and get the sum of the other three. The unlabeled angle must be 110°. Now we know $110 + a + b + c = 360$, we subtract to get the sum of a, b, and c and we get 250, (B) as the correct answer.

19 **(E)** John has four ties, 12 shirts and three belts, and we need the number of days he can go without repeating. So we multiply the number of ties times the number of shirts times the number of belts. Four ties, 12 shirts—48 combinations. Multiply by three choices of belt, and you get 3×48 or 144 combinations, (E).

20 **(D)** Move the decimal points to the right until they disappear—but keep track of how many places you move the decimal. In (A) we have .00003 in the numerator. Move five places to the right to change it to 3. Then we change from .0007 to 70 in the denominator and we end up with $\frac{3}{70}$. In (B) we have .0008 on top, .0005 on the bottom—we get $\frac{8}{5}$. We have $\frac{70}{8}$ for (C). In (D), we end up with $\frac{60}{8}$ and $\frac{10}{8}$ in (E). Clearly (D), 12, is the largest value.

Graphs: Questions 21–25

21 **(E)** The bar graph doesn't give us the total number of general practice physicians, but if we add the number of males to the number of females, we get the total number of g.p. physicians. To find the percent who are male, we take the number of males and put it over the total number and that will give us our percent. We have about 2,000 women and about 23,000 men, making the total about 25,000. Well, if there are around 25,000 g.p. physicians altogether and 2,000 to 3,000 of them are female, that's what percent of 25,000? It's around 10 percent. About 22,500 are male, which gives us 90 percent, (E).

22 **(D)** We're looking for the lowest ratio of males to females so we have to get the smallest number of males and the largest number of females. Skimming the bar graphs, we can see that in pediatrics the female graph and the male graph are closer than any of the others. Pediatrics is (D), the correct answer.

23 **(C)** To refer to ages of physicians, we need to find the slice of the pie that goes from 45 to 54. It's 20 percent, but 20 percent of what? We're not looking for a percent, we're looking for a number of doctors. For general surgery the male bar goes up to about 35,000 and the female bar goes up to about 2,000—about 37,000 total. So 20 percent of 37,000 is the number of general surgery physicians between ages 45 and 54, inclusive. What's 20 percent of 37,000, or $\frac{1}{5}$ of 37,000? Well, let's see, $\frac{1}{5}$ of 35,000 is 7,000, $\frac{1}{5}$ of 2,000 is 400, making 7,400. (C) is 7,350, the correct answer.

24 **(E)** We'll have to find the total number of family practice physicians, which represents 7.5 percent of all the physicians in the United States, then we can find 100 percent of that number. The male bar of family practice physicians goes just over 36,000, so we'll say it's 36,000 plus. The number of females goes just over 6,000 so we'll call that 6,000 plus, so we have about 43,000 all together. This is 7.5 percent of all the physicians. 7.5 percent is awkward—it's three-quarters of 10 percent, which is $\frac{3}{4} \times \frac{1}{10}$, or $\frac{3}{40}$. So 43,000 is $\frac{3}{40}$ of the total number of doctors. To change 43,000 into the number of total physicians, we multiply it by $\frac{40}{3}$. Think of it this way: we have an equation now, $\frac{3}{40}$ of the number we're looking for, we'll call it N, the number of physicians, equals 43,000. We want to get N by itself, so we have to get rid of that $\frac{3}{40}$. So we multiply by the reciprocal, $\frac{40}{3}$, and that leaves us N by itself on the left. But the hard part is multiplying $\frac{40}{3} \times 43,000$. What's $\frac{40}{3}$? It's $13\frac{1}{3}$ and that's easier to multiply. 13×43 is 559, so $13 \times 43,000$ is 559,000—you can look at your choices and estimate. Only one is close to 559,000—(E), 570,000, and we're going to add on to that, so (E) is the correct answer.

25 **(B)** How many male general surgeon physicians were under 35 years old? The pie chart breaks down general surgery physicians by age, so we'll be working with it. And, since we're looking for a number of general surgery physicians, we know that we're going to have to find the total number of general surgery physicians, then break it down according to the percentages on the pie chart.

We're told the number of female general surgery physicians in the under-35 category represented 3.5 percent of all the general surgery physicians. What this does is break that slice of the pie for under-35 into two smaller slices, one for men under 35 and one for women under 35. Now we know that the whole slice for under-35-year-olds is 30 percent of the total and we've just been told that the number of females under 35 is 3.5 percent of the total. So the difference between 30 percent and 3.5 percent must be the men in the under-35 category, which leaves 26.5 percent, which we have to multiply by the total number of general surgery physicians.

We figured out in Question 23 that there were 37,000 total general surgery physicians, and 26.5 percent of those are men under 35. What's 26.5 percent of 37,000? One-quarter of 37,000 is 9,250 and that's very close to (A), but remember we've still got another 1.5 percent to go. One percent of 37,000 is 370 and half of that, or .5 percent will be 185, so if you add 370 and 185 to 9,250 you end up with a total of 9,805 which is very close to (B), the correct answer.

26 **(B)** We want to find the sum of the absolute value of three, the absolute value of −4 and the absolute value of 3 − 4. Well, the absolute value of 3 is 3, the absolute value of −4 is 4. What's the absolute value of 3 − 4? Do the subtraction inside the absolute value sign first, and we get −1. What's the absolute value of −1? It's 1, so we have 3 + 4 + 1 or 8 as our sum for Question 26, (B).

27 **(C)** This looks like a right triangle on a coordinate grid, but it's not a normal coordinate grid—the lines on the grid don't represent integer units, they represent units of less than an integer. Going up on the y-axis, we have .5, 1.0, 1.5, and 2.0, so the lines each represent half an integer and, going to the left, the lines are labeled -0.4, -0.8, -1.2, so these each represent .4, and yet the diagram's not drawn to scale. Going left to right, the vertical lines are actually farther apart than the horizontal lines, which represent more value on the number line. Now, to find the area of the shaded region, a triangle, we need a base and a height. This is a right triangle because its base lies on the horizontal line on our grid and its height, the side to the right, lies right on a vertical line on the grid. What's the length of the bottom side? The far right end point is at -0.4 and the far left end point is at -1.6, and the difference is 1.2 units, so the base is 1.2. The lower right vertex has value .5 and the upper right vertex has value 2.0—the difference is 1.5, so that's the height. The base is 1.2 and the height is 1.5, and the formula for the area of a right triangle is one half base times height. We have 1.2 as our base, we can call that $\frac{6}{5}$, 1.5 is $\frac{3}{2}$ so the area is $\frac{1}{2} \times \frac{6}{5} \times \frac{3}{2}$—that's $\frac{9}{10}$ or .9, choice (C).

28 **(A)** You could find the number of tasks per hour from one computer, but that would add extra steps, because you want to find out how many computers you need to do a certain number of tasks in three hours. Well, if it can do 30 tasks in six hours, it can do 15 tasks in three hours. So, if you have two computers, that's 30 tasks, three is 45, four is 60, five is 75, six is 90. You can't get by with five because you have to get 80 tasks done, so you'll need six computers, (A).

29 **(C)** One side of triangle ABC is an edge of our cube, segment BC. But segments AB and AC aren't lengths of the edge of the cube or fractions of a length of an edge of the cube. Well, let's find the length of an edge of the cube. If the cube has volume 8, that's the length of an edge to the third power. Since 2 cubed is 8, the length of an edge of this cube is 2. We need AB and AC, and so we have to concentrate on smaller right triangles on the same face of the cube that includes triangle ABC.

On the upper left, directly above point A is an unlabeled vertex—let's call that point Y—and down below point A is an unlabeled vertex—we'll call that point X. Look at triangle AXC. It's a right triangle because angle AXC is one of the angles formed by two edges of a cube—and AC is its hypotenuse. AX is half an edge of the cube because point A's the midpoint of edge XY. That means that AX has length 1 and XC is an edge of the cube, so it has length 2 . The legs of this right triangle are 1 and 2, so we can use the Pythagorean theorem to find the length of AC. AX^2 is 1^2, XC^2 is 2^2, 1^2 is 1, 2^2 is 4, the sum of 1 and 4 is 5, AC^2 is 5 and AC has length $\sqrt{5}$. AB is identical to AC because triangle AYB is identical to triangle AXC, so AB also has length $\sqrt{5}$ and the perimeter of ABC is $2 + 2\sqrt{5}$, choice (C).

30 **(D)** The catch here is that it's not which of the following is 850 percent *of* 8×10^3, it's which of the following is 850 percent *greater than* 8×10^3. Well, what's bigger, 850 percent of 1 or a number that's 850 percent greater than 1? 850 percent of 1 is 8.5×1 or $8\frac{1}{2}$. But a number that's 850 percent greater than 1 is $1 + 850$ percent of 1, it's $1 + 8.5$ or 9.5. So the number we want is $9.5 \times 8 \times 10^3$. $9.5 \times 8 = 76$, so the answer is 76×10^3, or 7.6×10^4, in scientific notation.

31 **(A)** We have to plug 1 in for x and solve the equation for y. Well, $x + 3$ is $1 + 3$—that's what's inside the parentheses and we do that first. We have $1 + 3 = 4$ inside the parentheses. $y = 4^2$, 4^2 is 16, and 16 is greater than 9, so the answer is (A).

32 **(B)** In both columns we'll use the basic formula: rate $\times$ time = distance. In Column A, 40 mph $\times$ 4 hours traveled gives you 160 miles. In Column B, 70 mph $\times 2\frac{1}{2}$ hours, $2 \times 70 = 140$, half of 70 is 35, and $140 + 35 = 175$ miles in Column B. 175 is greater than 160, so the answer is (B).

33 **(D)** This is intended to conjure up a picture of heavy cookies in one bag and light grapes in the other, but you can't assume that because cookies are usually bigger than grapes, these cookies weigh more than these grapes. Since you don't know how much each cookie and each grape weighs, you can't find the number of cookies or grapes, so it's (D).

34 **(C)** Here we have triangle ABC—base BC has been extended on one side so we have an exterior angle drawn in and labeled 120°. We want to compare side lengths AB and BC—in any triangle, the largest side will be opposite the largest angle, so we want to see which of these sides is opposite a larger angle. Since angle A is labeled 60°, is angle C less

than, equal to, or greater than 60? Notice that the adjacent angle is 120°—the two together form a straight line, so their sum is 180°. $180 - 120 = 60$, so angle C is a 60° angle. Since the angles are equal, the sides are equal, and the answer is (C).

35 **(A)** Notice the way the diagram is set up—$a + b$ is the same as PQ. Our equation is $8a + 8b = 24$. Divide by 8. We end up with $a + b = 3$. PQ is 3 and since 3 is greater than 2, the answer is (A).

36 **(A)** All we know is that x is less than y but though we don't know their values, we may know enough to determine a relationship. In Column A we have $y - x$, the larger number minus the smaller number, so you must get a positive difference, even if both numbers are negative. In Column B you have the smaller number minus the larger number—the difference is the same except this time it is negative. So you can determine a relationship—you know the answer is (A), the quantity in Column A is always greater than the quantity in Column B.

37 **(D)** Remember, area equals $\frac{1}{2} \times$ base $\times$ height. Both triangles have the same height, because they have the same apex point A and each of them has as its base a part of line EB. So the one with the larger base has the larger area. Which is bigger, CB or DE? We have no way to figure it out. We are not given any relationships or lengths for any of those segments, so the answer is (D).

38 **(B)** There's one box that's in both rows—the one in the middle with value $\frac{2}{9}$. In

KAPLAN

fact, we have $\frac{1}{3} + \frac{2}{9} + y$ in the horizontal row, $x + \frac{2}{9} + \frac{4}{5}$ in the vertical row, and we are comparing x and y. Since $\frac{2}{9}$ is part of both rows, we can throw it out. So we have $\frac{1}{3} + y = \frac{4}{5} + x$. We have $\frac{1}{3} + y$ and that is the same as $\frac{4}{5} + x$. Since $\frac{4}{5}$ is greater than $\frac{1}{3}$, the number we add to $\frac{4}{5}$ has to be less than the number we add to $\frac{1}{3}$ for the sums to be the same. Since $\frac{4}{5}$ is greater than $\frac{1}{3}$, x must be less than y. The answer is (B).

39 **(B)** Looking at the fraction in Column A we have $\frac{1}{3} \times \frac{1}{4}$ in the numerator, $\frac{2}{3} \times \frac{1}{2}$ in the denominator. We can cancel the factor of $\frac{1}{3}$ from the numerator and denominator, right? Cancel a $\frac{1}{3}$ from each and you end up with $1 \times \frac{1}{4}$ in the numerator, $2 \times \frac{1}{2}$ in the denominator. Using the same approach, we can cancel a factor of $\frac{1}{4}$, so we're left with 1×1 in the numerator and 2×2 in the denominator, so the value of Column A is $\frac{1}{4}$. Now take a look at Column B. It's the reciprocal of the value in Column A. You have $\frac{2}{3} \times \frac{1}{2}$ in the numerator and $\frac{1}{3} \times \frac{1}{4}$ in the denominator. So you have $\frac{4}{1}$ as your value for Column B. With 4 in Column B and $\frac{1}{4}$ in Column A, the answer is (B).

40 **(B)** Make a map—if you have trouble with geometry, this will make it much easier. Eileen drives due north from town A to town B for 60 miles. Start at a point and draw a line straight up. Label the point you started at A and the point above it, B. Label 60 as the length of the distance from A to B. Next she drives due east from town B to town C for a distance of 80 miles. Start at point B, draw a line straight over to the right, call the right endpoint C, and label as 80 the distance BC. You have a right angle, angle ABC. Well, the distance from town A to town C is the hypotenuse of a right triangle if you draw line AC. The two legs are 60 and 80 and this is one of our Pythagorean ratios. It is a 6-8-10 triangle except this time it is 60-80-100. So the distance from A to C is 100 miles, the same as our value for Column A, so the answer is (B).

41 **(C)** Let's see if we can do something to make these look more alike by getting both sets of binomials so the $\sqrt{7}$s are in the front. We have $\sqrt{7} - 2$. Is that a positive or negative quantity? 2^2 is 4, 3^2 is 9 so $\sqrt{7}$ is between 2 and 3. We have $\sqrt{7} - 2$, that is positive, times $\sqrt{7} + 2$, that is positive again. Two positives in Column A and the product of two positives is always positive. What do we have in Column B? $2 - \sqrt{7}$, that is a negative number times negative $\sqrt{7} - 2$. $-\sqrt{7}$ is a negative, -2 is negative, that quantity is negative. You have the product of two negatives in Column B, but a product of two negatives is positive also, so you can't tell which is greater. Let's see if we can make these quantities look more alike. With the last one on the right, $-\sqrt{7} - 2$, if we divide the whole thing by -1, we're left with a positive $\sqrt{7}$ and a positive 2, $\sqrt{7} + 2$. On the right in Column B we have $(2 - \sqrt{7}) \times (-1) \times (\sqrt{7} + 2)$, and $(\sqrt{7} + 2)$ is also in Column A, so we can cancel. Those two factors are the same, right? We have $-1 \times (2 - \sqrt{7})$. Let's distribute again. What is -1×2? It's -2. What is $-1 \times -\sqrt{7}$? It's $+\sqrt{7}$ so we end up with $+\sqrt{7} + -2$ or $\sqrt{7} - 2$. It's exactly the same as the factor in Column A. So the quantities are equal and the answer is (C).

42 **(B)** We can see from our diagram that r and s are the coordinates of a point on our line. We have a line on the graph with one point with coordinates $(\frac{5}{2}, \frac{7}{2})$. The line also goes through the origin $(0, 0)$, so what can we figure out about this line? Well, draw in the line $x = y$, a line which makes a 45° angle with the x-axis that goes from the lower left to the upper right—you notice that it goes through the point $(\frac{5}{2}, \frac{5}{2})$, because any point on line $x = y$ has the same x coordinate and y coordinate. Point $(\frac{5}{2}, \frac{7}{2})$ falls above point $(\frac{5}{2}, \frac{5}{2})$, because the y coordinate is greater, it's above the $x = y$ line. Similarly, point (r, s) lies above the $x = y$ line so the y coordinate is greater than the x coordinate and the y coordinate of that point is s. Where we have coordinates (r, s), r is the x coordinate, s is the y coordinate; s is greater than r in this case. The answer is (B), the quantity in Column B is greater.

43 **(D)** We have $1 - \left(\frac{1}{4}\right)$ to the x power in Column A and we have 0.95 in Column B. That's a bizarre comparison, isn't it? Converting Column B, 0.95 into fraction form, $0.95 = \frac{95}{100} = \frac{19}{20}$. What do we have in Column A if $x = 1$? We have $1 - \frac{1}{4}$ or $\frac{3}{4}$. $\frac{19}{20}$ is greater than $\frac{3}{4}$. What happens if we have $x = 2$? Column A becomes $1 - \left(\frac{1}{4}\right)^2$. $\frac{1}{4}^2$ is $\frac{1}{4} \times \frac{1}{4}$ or $1 - \frac{1}{16}$ is $\frac{15}{16}$. So what's bigger, $\frac{15}{16}$ or $\frac{19}{20}$? Still $\frac{19}{20}$, but as x gets larger and we multiply $\frac{1}{4}$ times itself more times, the amount that we're taking away from 1 is going to get smaller and we'll be taking less than $\frac{1}{20}$ away from 1 as soon as we get to

$x = 3$. $\frac{1}{4}$ to the third power is $\frac{1}{64}$ and at that point Column A becomes $\frac{63}{64}$. What is bigger, $\frac{19}{20}$ or $\frac{63}{64}$? Well, $\frac{63}{64}$ is bigger, it is closer to 1, and there are two possible relationships here. If x is 1 or 2, Column B is greater. If x is 3 or larger, Column A is greater. The answer is choice (D).

44 **(A)** If you draw in some diameters in the circles, you will see that PS is equal to one diameter, and PQ is equal to two diameters. Let one diameter be d. The perimeter of $PQRS$ is then $PS + PQ + SR + QR = 6d$. The circumference of a circle is πd, where d is a diameter. Since we have two circles, the combined circumferences is $2 \times \pi d = 2\pi d$. Since π is greater than 3 (it's about 3.14), the value in Column A is greater than $6d$ in Column B.

45 **(B)** I hope you didn't try to figure out the exact values of each of these. Instead, if you look at Column B and Column A, they look sort of alike because they both have 3 in terms of a power. What is 3^{20}? It's 3×3^{19} right? So we can have $3^{19} + 3^{19} + 3^{19}$ in Column B. In Column A we have $3^{17} + 3^{18} + 3^{19}$. We can subtract 3^{19} from both sides and we're left with $3^{17} + 3^{18}$ in Column A and $3^{19} + 3^{19}$ in Column B. We know that 3^{19} is bigger than 3^{17} or 3^{18} so we know that $3^{19} + 3^{19}$ is bigger than $3^{17} + 3^{18}$. The answer is (B), the quantity in Column B is greater.

46 **(E)** We have $4 + y = 14 - 4y$ and we want to solve for y. We can isolate the ys on one side of the equal sign by adding $4y$ to both sides, giving us $4 + 5y = 14$. Subtracting the 4 from both sides we get $5y = 10$. Divide both sides by 5 and get $y = 2$, (E).

KAPLAN

47 **(D)** Let's go the quickest, most obvious route and use the common denominator method. With $\frac{4}{5}$ and $\frac{5}{4}$, the denominator that we will use is easy to find; just use 5×4 or 20. $\frac{4}{5}$ is $\frac{16}{20}$ and $\frac{5}{4}$ is $\frac{25}{20}$. $\frac{16}{20} + \frac{25}{20}$ is $\frac{41}{20}$, which is (D).

48 **(E)** First we need to find m. We are told that 3^m is 81. Well, 81 is 9×9. 9 is 3^2. So we have $3^2 \times 3^2 = 81$ or $3 \times 3 \times 3 \times 3 = 81$. How many factors of 3 are there in 81? There are 4, so m has the value 4. Now what's 4^3? 4×4 is 16. 16×4 is 64. So (E) is correct, 64 is m^3.

49 **(B)** We are looking for the area in square meters of square C. Now notice we have one side of square B butted up against one side of square A—they're not the same length, but the difference in their lengths is made up by the length of a side of square C. One side of square B + one side of square C = one side of square A. We can figure out the length of the side of A and length of the side of B, which will let us figure out the length of side of C. That is what we need to figure out the area of square C. The area of a square is its side squared. The area of square A is 81, so it has a side of $\sqrt{81} = 9$. The area of square B is 49, so it has sides of length $\sqrt{49} = 7$. So $9 = 7 + C$, so C must have length 2. So we have 2 as the length of the side of square C, 2^2 is 4, there are 4 square meters in gardening area C, and the answer is (B).

50 **(E)** We can figure out how many students scored exactly 85. Twenty-three scored 85 or over, and 18 scored over 85. So $23 - 18$ or 5 students scored exactly 85 on the exam, but that's no help. How many students scored less than 85? We don't know—we can't answer this question. It's (E), it can't be determined.

51 **(C)** We're asked in which year the energy use in country Y was closest to 650 million kilowatt hours, so we just have to follow the jagged line which represents energy use from left to right until we encounter a vertical line representing a year in which we're close to 650 million. The one year in which this is true is 1970. In no other year are we as close, so (C), 1970, is our answer.

52 **(C)** In order to find how many categories had energy use greater than 150 million kilowatts, you have to find out how many total kilowatts were used in that year using the line graph. You see that there were 600 million kilowatts used in 1965. What is the relationship of 150 million kilowatts to 600 million kilowatts? It's 25 percent of 600 million kilowatts, so we're looking for categories with more than 25 percent of the energy use for 1965. How many categories exceeded 25 percent? Just two, government and industrial. So our answer is (C).

53 **(D)** We can estimate quite a bit from our graph. If we look at our line chart, we can see that as time goes on, energy use goes up pretty steadily. It went up sharply between 1960 and 1965, then more gradually from 1965 to 1980. Because in more recent years the overall use was much greater, if the percent of industrial use was about the same over all the years, then as the overall use increases, the amount used for industrial purposes will increase also. Let's take a quick look at the bar graph and see if that is the case. Was the percent being used for industrial use about the same? Well, it didn't fluctuate much from 1960 to 1970, but in 1975 industrial use jumped significantly as a percent of the total, then shrank significantly going to 1980. The most likely answer is 1975, and if you find 40 percent of 690 million, your amount for 1975, you get 276 million kilowatt hours. Then if you find 20 percent of 710 million, your amount for 1980, you only get 142 million kilowatt hours, so (D), 1975, is the correct answer.

54 **(D)** What we are going to do for 1960 and 1965 is find the per capita personal use, then find the percent decrease from 1960 to 1965. To do that, we have to plug in a value for the population of country Y for 1960. Let's use 100 million for the '60s population. The per capita use in 1960 is the total personal use, which is 30 percent of 500 million, that's 150 million. We know that 150 million, the total personal use, equals 100 million, the population × the per capita use. The per capita use is $\frac{3}{2}$ or 1.5. Going on to 1965, we are told the population increased by 20 percent, so in 1965 the population was 120 million people. What was the total personal use of energy? It was a little bit less than 20 percent of our total 600 million so we'll call it 20 percent of 600 million, or 120 million. If total personal use is 120 million and we have 120 million people, that's one kilowatt hour per person. What's the percent decrease? It's a decrease of $\frac{1}{3}$, $33\frac{1}{3}$ percent. But remember, in 1965, they were using a little more energy for personal use than we figured. The correct answer must be a little greater than $33\frac{1}{3}$ percent, so 40 percent, (D), is the correct answer.

55 **(A)** Statement I says farm use of energy increased between 1960 and 1980. In 1960, 500 million. In 1980, 710 million kilowatt hours were used. What was the percent of farm use in 1960? It was 30 percent of the total in 1960 and a little bit less than 30 percent, around 28 percent, in 1980. The percent is very close together while the whole has become much larger from 1960 to 1980, so 30 percent of 500 million is less than 28 percent of 710 million. Farm use of energy did go up in that 20-year period and Statement I is going to be part of our answer. That eliminates two answer choices, (B) and (D).

How about Statement II? This one is harder. It says that in 1980, industrial use of energy was greater than industrial use of energy in 1965. But what was it in 1965? Industrial use of energy in 1965 was 30 percent of 600 million. We got the percent from the bar graph, the total from the line chart. Okay, 30 percent of 600 million is 180 million. But what about 1980? In 1980 industrial use of energy was 20 percent of a larger whole, 710 million kilowatt hours. Well, 20 percent of 710 is 142 million. That's less than 180 million, isn't it? In fact, industrial use of energy went down from 1965 to 1980, so this can't be inferred from the graph and it's not part of our answer. That cuts out (C) and (E), leaving choice (A), I only. Statement III is another easy one to eliminate because it says more people were employed by the government of country Y in 1980 than in 1960. These graphs deal only with energy use, not with employment, so it's irrelevant and we can eliminate it. Only Statement I can be inferred, and (A) is correct.

56 **(E)** The average is $\frac{\text{The sum of terms}}{\text{The number of terms}}$. Here we have $y - z$ and the other number, which we will call x. The average of x and $y - z$ is $3y$, so $3y = \frac{x + y - z}{2}$. Multiplying both sides by 2 gives $6y = x + y - z$. Subtracting $y - z$ from both sides gives $5y + z = x$. So the other number, x, is $5y + z$, answer choice (E).

57 **(B)** We're told that the area of triangle ABC is 35 and in our diagram we're given a height for triangle ABC. If we use BC as the base of the triangle, the perpendicular distance from segment BC up to point A is 7, so we can find the length of BC. When we find the length BC, the base of triangle ABC, what do we have? We have the hypotenuse of right triangle

BDC. Given the hypotenuse and the length of leg *BD*, which is given in the diagram as 6, we'll be able to find the third leg of the triangle, side *DC*, which is what we're looking for. Okay, going back to triangle *ABC* where we started, the area is 35 and the height is 7. The area of a triangle is $\frac{1}{2}$base × height, so $\frac{1}{2}$base × height is 35, $\frac{1}{2}$ × 7 × length *BC* is 35. That means 7 × length *BC* is 70, so *BC* must have length 10. Now we can look at right triangle *BDC*. Here is a right triangle with one leg of length 6, the hypotenuse of length 10 and the third side unknown; what we have is a 6-blank-10 right triangle. That's one of our famous Pythagorean ratios—it's a 6-8-10 triangle. So *DC* must have length 2 × 4, or 8, (B).

58 **(A)** We're trying to find the shortest distance in meters a person would have to walk to go from point *A* to a point on side *BC* of the triangular field represented in our diagram. In order to get the shortest distance from side *BC* up to point *A*, we want to draw a perpendicular line from point *A* down to side *BC*. That will divide up the triangular field into right triangles. Let's draw in the path from point *A* down to segment *BC* and call the new vertex we make point *D*. We just created two smaller right triangles, *ADC* and *ADB*. Now our diagram tells us that length *BC* is 160 meters and *AB* is 100 meters—*AC* is also 100 meters. Now each of these two right triangles has 100 meters as the length of its hypotenuse. What does that tell you about triangle *ABC* ? *AB* and *AC* have the same lengths, so this is an isosceles triangle. That means that when you drew in the perpendicular distance from *A* down to *D*, you split that isosceles triangle into two identical right triangles. Length *BD* is the same as length *BC*. So each of them is half of 160 meters, or 80 meters each. We have right trian-

gles with hypotenuses of length 100 meters each and one leg of each these right triangles is 80 meters. This is a 3-4-5 right triangle, with each member of the ratio multiplied by 80. So *AD* must have length 60, and the minimum distance is 60 meters, (A).

59 **(D)** We're told the ratio of 2*a* to *b* is eight times the ratio of *b* to *a*. That's awkward to keep track of in English—it's a little easier to write fractions. The ratio of 2*a*:*b* equals $2\frac{a}{b}$. So $2\frac{a}{b} = 8\left(\frac{b}{a}\right)$. We're asked to find what $\frac{b}{a}$ could be; that may tell you there's more than one possible value for $\frac{b}{a}$, but let's start with the equation we just put together using translation and isolate $\frac{b}{a}$. To do that, we'll divide both sides of the equation by 8, which is the same as multiplying by $\frac{1}{8}$. So now we have $\frac{1}{8} \times 2\frac{a}{b} = \frac{b}{a}$. Well, what is $\frac{1}{8} \times 2\frac{a}{b}$? It's $\frac{a}{4b}$. So $\frac{a}{4b} = \frac{b}{a}$. We need to multiply both sides of the equation right now on both sides by $\frac{b}{a}$. It'll be more complicated on the right side but simpler on the left because the *a*s and *b*s on the left side will cancel out, and you'll be left with $\frac{1}{4}$. On the right you have $\frac{b}{a} \times \frac{b}{a} = \frac{b^2}{a^2}$. So we have $\frac{1}{4} = \frac{b^2}{a^2}$. So $\frac{b}{a}$ could represent positive or negative $\frac{1}{2}$.

60

(D) A dentist earns n dollars for each filling plus x dollars for every 15 minutes. So the money is figured in two different ways; dollars for each filling and dollars per hour, represented in terms of 15 minutes. Our result will be a two-part answer choice. If you can figure out one part, it will let you eliminate some choices. She put in 21 fillings. She makes n dollars for each, so she gets $21n$ dollars for fillings. You can eliminate (B) and (E) because (B) has only $14n$ in it, and (E) has $\frac{21}{4}n$ dollars in it. That narrows our choices to (A), (C), and (D).

How about the hourly rate? The dentist works 14 hours in a week. Does that mean she makes $14x$ dollars? No, because the rate is dollars for every 15 minutes. Now if she makes x dollars for every 15 minutes and 15 minutes is $\frac{1}{4}$ of an hour, then we have to multiply that rate by 4 to get the rate per hour, it's $4x$ dollars per hour. Well, $4x$ times 14 hours is $56x$, so (D), $56x + 21n$, is correct.

Section Three Explanations– Analytical Writing

Present Your Perspective on an Issue
Sample Essay Response to prompt #1

At face value, the belief that "one should look upon any information described as 'factual' with skepticism since it may well be proven false in the future," seems ludicrous almost to the point of threatening anarchy. Yet not only does this belief prove well justified, it also amounts to the linchpin around which our complex, highly technical society creates and consolidates its advances.

Science itself provides the best evidence and example in support of this statement. One need look no further than contemporary medicine to see how far we have come from the days when illness was perceived as a sign of moral weakness or as a punishment from on high. In fact, the most outstanding characteristic of what we call "the scientific method" amounts to endless questioning of received theory in search of a more comprehensive explanation of what we perceive to be true. This inquiry extends even to the nature of perception itself. It demands the kind of creative madness perhaps epitomized in the rejoinder Nobel prize–winning physicist Enrico Fermi offered to fellow laureate Nils Bohr who had questioned Fermi on whether a new theory the Italian was presenting went far enough in its skepticism to meet the test of new science. "But think, Enrico, is this crazy enough," demanded Bohr. "Maybe," proffered Fermi, "but not really."

Furthermore, the advances made through constant questioning are not limited to the scientific arena: The skeptical attitudes of ancient Greek philosophers, as well as those of Renaissance mariners, 19th century suffragists, and 20th century civil rights activists, have left the world a richer and more hopeful place. By refusing to accept the world as explained by contemporary "fact," these doubters helped give birth to societies and cultures in which human potential and accomplishment have been enabled to an unprecedented degree.

In contrast, those societies that cultivate adherence to received belief and a traditional non-skeptical approach have advanced very little over the centuries. In Tibet, for instance, the prayer wheels spin endlessly around a belief system as secure and unquestioning as the Himalayas themselves. While there may very well be things worth learning from such a society, Tibet has proven to lack adaptability and expansiveness and prefers to turn inward, away from the modern world. Such introspection has not given Tibet immunity nor an array of defenses in the face of contemporary medical, social, and political problems.

It seems clear from the above discussion that a healthy skepticism remains the hallmark of Western faith and hope as we face the future. As the basis of our resiliency and creativity, this attitude offers the most positive prognosis for a society that revels in the solution of conundrums that its own constant questioning brings continually into view.

Assessment of Sample Essay: "6" (Outstanding)

An outstanding essay; this is well constructed and well written. The writer takes a clear position and supports it with evidence and several good examples. Organization, sentence structure, and language are also sound.

Analyze an Argument
Sample Essay Response

While it may prove to be a worthy project, the argument that Tusk University should build a new recreational facility to attract new students and to better serve the needs of its current student body appears to rely upon assumptions which lack conclusive supporting evidence. The writer would be well advised to address these issues in order to make the point of the argument more cogent and convincing.

First and foremost, the writer assumes, without providing any evidence, that recreational facilities will be a significant factor in attracting and serving students interested in Tusk. This begs the question of the role of recreation and/or athletic facilities in the matriculation and retention of students in institutions of higher learning. In the absence of any reference to the academic mission of the University, or even of the role that the facility might have in attracting, retaining or helping to fund areas more central to that mission, the writer's conclusion appears unsupported.

Secondly, the writer assumes, again without citing specific evidence, that the projected doubling of enrollment will by itself lead to an increase in demand and presumably in use for the new recreational facilities proposed. Even if the facilities would indeed be attractive relative to those available off-campus, the author has provided no proof that a substantial part of the increased or even current enrollment would be inclined to consider the new facilities an asset to their education. Suppose for a moment that this enlarged commuter-based enrollment turns out to be largely made up of part-time students with jobs and family demands away from the campus. Would such a student body see the new facility as a priority? Would the schedules of such students allow them to take advantage of the improvement?

Finally, the author fails to describe what specific services, programs, and amenities the proposed new facility will provide, how and at what cost relative to facilities available elsewhere these will be made available to the university community, and how the financial burden of both building and operating the new center will be offset. Beyond these issues endemic to the campus setting, the writer presents no overview of the environmental, social, and public relations aspects of the project in a larger context, either intra- or extracollegiate.

The issues raised here could easily be addressed by the provision of evidence that backs up the author's claim. By assembling sufficient and specific demographic and economic evidence to support the argument's questionable assumptions, the writer may not only be able to overcome the limitations of the present argument, but provide a rationale for the proposal beyond the terms offered here.

Assessment of Sample Essay: "6" (Outstanding)

An outstanding essay; not only does it thoroughly outline and critique the internal logic of the argument, but it also provides insightful suggestions for strengthening the connection between conclusion and evidence. It accomplishes all assigned tasks in an essay that's well written and clearly organized.

Appendixes

APPENDIX A

Root List

The Kaplan Root List can boost your knowledge of GRE-level words, and that can help you get more questions right. No one can predict exactly which words will show up on your test, but there are certain words that the test makers favor. The Root List gives you the component parts of many typical GRE words. Knowing these words can help you because you may run across them on your GRE. Also, becoming comfortable with the types of words that pop up will reduce your anxiety about the test.

Knowing roots can help you in two more ways. First, instead of learning one word at a time, you can learn a whole group of words that contain a certain root. They'll be related in meaning, so if you remember one, it will be easier for you to remember others. Second, roots can often help you decode an unknown GRE word. If you recognize a familiar root, you could get a good enough grasp of the word to answer the question.

Kaplan Tip

Most of the words we use every day have their origins in simple roots. Once you know the root, it's much easier to figure out what a strange word means.

Take a look through this appendix. Many of the roots are easy to learn, and they'll help you on the test.

A: without
amoral: neither moral nor immoral
atheist: one who does not believe in God
atypical: not typical
anonymous: of unknown authorship or origin
apathy: lack of interest or emotion
atrophy: the wasting away of body tissue
anomaly: an irregularity
agnostic: one who questions the existence of God

AB/ABS: off, away from, apart, down
abduct: to take by force
abhor: to hate, detest
abolish: to do away with, make void
abstract: conceived apart from concrete realities, specific objects, or actual instances
abnormal: deviating from a standard
abdicate: to renounce or relinquish a throne
abstinence: forbearance from any indulgence of appetite
abstruse: hard to understand; secret, hidden

AC/ACR: sharp, bitter
acid: something that is sharp, sour, or ill natured
acute: sharp at the end; ending in a point
acerbic: sour or astringent in taste; harsh in temper
acrid: sharp or biting to the taste or smell
acrimonious: caustic, stinging, or bitter in nature
exacerbate: to increase bitterness or violence; aggravate

ACT/AG: to do; to drive; to force; to lead
agile: quick and well coordinated in movement; active, lively
agitate: to move or force into violent, irregular action
litigate: to make the subject of a lawsuit
prodigal: wastefully or recklessly extravagant
pedagogue: a teacher
synagogue: a gathering or congregation of Jews for the purpose of religious worship

AD/AL: to, toward, near
adapt: adjust or modify fittingly
adjacent: near, close, or contiguous; adjoining
addict: to give oneself over, as to a habit or pursuit
admire: to regard with wonder, pleasure, and approval
address: to direct a speech or written statement to
adhere: to stick fast; cleave; cling
adjoin: to be close or in contact with
advocate: to plead in favor of

AL/ALI/ALTER: other, another
alternative: a possible choice
alias: an assumed name; another name
alibi: the defense by an accused person that he was verifiably elsewhere at the time of the crime with which he is charged
alien: one born in another country; a foreigner
alter ego: the second self; a substitute or deputy
altruist: a person unselfishly concerned for the welfare of others
allegory: figurative treatment of one subject under the guise of another

AM: love
amateur: a person who engages in an activity for pleasure rather than financial or professional gain
amatory: of or pertaining to lovers or lovemaking
amenity: agreeable ways or manners
amorous: inclined to love, esp. sexual love
enamored: inflamed with love; charmed; captivated
amity: friendship; peaceful harmony
inamorata: a female lover
amiable: having or showing agreeable personal qualities
amicable: characterized by exhibiting good will

AMB: to go; to walk
ambient: moving freely; circulating
ambitious: desirous of achieving or obtaining power
preamble: an introductory statement
ambassador: an authorized messenger or representative
ambulance: a wheeled vehicle equipped for carrying sick people, usually to a hospital
ambulatory: of, pertaining to, or capable of walking
ambush: the act of lying concealed so as to attack by surprise
perambulator: one who makes a tour of inspection on foot

AMB/AMPH: both, more than one, around
ambiguous: open to various interpretations
amphibian: any cold-blooded vertebrate, the larva of which is aquatic, and the adult of which is terrestrial; a person or thing having a twofold nature
ambidextrous: able to use both hands equally well

ANIM: of the life, mind, soul, spirit
unanimous: in complete accord
animosity: a feeling of ill will or enmity
animus: hostile feeling or attitude
equanimity: mental or emotional stability, especially under tension
magnanimous: generous in forgiving an insult or injury

ANNUI/ENNI: year
annual: of, for, or pertaining to a year; yearly
anniversary: the yearly recurrence of the date of a past event
annuity: a specified income payable at stated intervals
perennial: lasting for an indefinite amount of time
annals: a record of events, esp. a yearly record

ANTE: before
anterior: placed before
antecedent: existing, being, or going before
antedate: precede in time
antebellum: before the war (especially the American Civil War)
antediluvian: belonging to the period before the biblical Flood; very old or old-fashioned

ANTHRO/ANDR: man, human
anthropology: the science that deals with the origins of mankind
android: robot; mechanical man
misanthrope: one who hates humans or mankind
philanderer: one who carries on flirtations
androgynous: being both male and female
androgen: any substance that promotes masculine characteristics
anthropocentric: regarding man as the central fact of the universe

ANTI: against
antibody: a protein naturally existing in blood serum, that reacts to overcome the toxic effects of an antigen
antidote: a remedy for counteracting the effects of poison, disease, etcetera
antiseptic: free from germs; particularly clean or neat
antipathy: aversion
antipodal: on the opposite side of the globe

APO: away
apology: an expression of one's regret or sorrow for having wronged another
apostle: one of the 12 disciples sent forth by Jesus to preach the gospel
apocalypse: revelation; discovery; disclosure
apogee: the highest or most distant point
apocryphal: of doubtful authorship or authenticity
apostasy: a total desertion of one's religion, principles, party, cause, etcetera

ARCH/ARCHI/ARCHY: chief, principal, ruler
architect: the devisor, maker, or planner of anything
archenemy: chief enemy
monarchy: a government in which the supreme power is lodged in a sovereign
anarchy: a state or society without government or law
oligarchy: a state or society ruled by a select group

AUTO: self
automatic: self-moving or self-acting
autocrat: an absolute ruler
autonomy: independence or freedom

BE: to be; to have a particular quality; to exist
belittle: to regard something as less impressive than it apparently is
bemoan: to express pity for
bewilder: to confuse or puzzle completely
belie: to misrepresent; to contradict

BEL/BEL: war
antebellum: before the war
rebel: a person who resists authority, control, or tradition
belligerent: warlike, given to waging war

BEN/BON: good
benefit: anything advantageous to a person or thing
benign: having a kindly disposition
benediction: act of uttering a blessing
benevolent: desiring to do good to others
bonus: something given over and above what is due
bona fide: in good faith; without fraud

BI: twice, double
binoculars: involving two eyes
biennial: happening every two years
bilateral: pertaining to or affecting two or both sides
bilingual: able to speak one's native language and another with equal facility
bipartisan: representing two parties

CAD/CID: to fall; to happen by chance
accident: happening by chance; unexpected
coincidence: a striking occurrence of two or more events at one time, apparently by chance
decadent: decaying; deteriorating
cascade: a waterfall descending over a steep surface
recidivist: one who repeatedly relapses, as into crime

CANT/CENT/CHANT: to sing
accent: prominence of a syllable in terms of pronunciation
chant: a song; singing
enchant: to subject to magical influence; bewitch
recant: to withdraw or disavow a statement
incantation: the chanting of words purporting to have magical power
incentive: that which incites action

CAP/CIP/CEPT: to take; to get
capture: to take by force or stratagem
anticipate: to realize beforehand; foretaste or foresee
susceptible: capable of receiving, admitting, undergoing, or being affected by something
emancipate: to free from restraint
percipient: having perception; discerning; discriminating
precept: a commandment or direction given as a rule of conduct

CAP/CAPIT/CIPIT: head, headlong
capital: the city or town that is the official seat of government
disciple: one who is a pupil of the doctrines of another
precipitate: to hasten the occurrence of; to bring about prematurely
precipice: a cliff with a vertical face
capitulate: to surrender unconditionally or on stipulated terms
caption: a heading or title

CARD/CORD/COUR: heart

cardiac: pertaining to the heart
encourage: to inspire with spirit or confidence
concord: agreement; peace, amity
discord: lack of harmony between persons or
  things
concordance: agreement, concord, harmony

CARN: flesh

carnivorous: eating flesh
carnage: the slaughter of a great number of people
carnival: a traveling amusement show
reincarnation: rebirth of a soul in a new body
incarnation: a being invested with a bodily form

CAST/CHAST: cut

cast: to throw or hurl; fling
caste: a hereditary social group, limited to people
  of the same rank
castigate: to punish in order to correct
chastise: to discipline, esp. by corporal punishment
chaste: free from obscenity; decent

CED/CEED/CESS: to go; to yield; to stop

antecedent: existing, being, or going before
concede: to acknowledge as true, just, or proper;
  admit
predecessor: one who comes before another in an
  office, position, etcetera
cessation: a temporary or complete discontinuance
incessant: without stop

CENTR: center

concentrate: to bring to a common center; to
  converge, to direct toward one point
eccentric: off center
concentric: having a common center, as in circles
  or spheres
centrifuge: an apparatus that rotates at high
  speed that separates substances of different den-
  sities using centrifugal force
centrist: of or pertaining to moderate political or
  social ideas

CERN/CERT/CRET/CRIM/CRIT: to separate; to judge; to distinguish; to decide

discrete: detached from others, separate
ascertain: to make sure of; to determine
certitude: freedom from doubt
discreet: judicious in one's conduct of speech,
  esp. with regard to maintaining silence about
  something of a delicate nature
hypocrite: a person who pretends to have beliefs
  that she does not
criterion: a standard of judgment or criticism

CHRON: time

synchronize: to occur at the same time or agree
  in time
chronology: the sequential order in which past
  events occurred
anachronism: an obsolete or archaic form
chronic: constant, habitual
chronometer: a time piece with a mechanism to
  adjust for accuracy

CIRCU: around, on all sides

circumference: the outer boundary of a circular
  area
circumstances: the existing conditions or state of
  affairs surrounding and affecting an agent
circuit: the act of going or moving around
circumambulate: to walk about or around
circuitous: roundabout, indirect

CIS: to cut

scissors: cutting instrument for paper
precise: definitely stated or defined
exorcise: to seek to expel an evil spirit by ceremony
incision: a cut, gash, or notch
incisive: penetrating, cutting

CLA/CLO/CLU: shut, close

conclude: to bring to an end; finish; to terminate
claustrophobia: an abnormal fear of enclosed
  places
disclose: to make known, reveal, or uncover
exclusive: not admitting of something else; shut-
  ting out others
cloister: a courtyard bordered with covered walks,
  esp. in a religious institution
preclude: to prevent the presence, existence, or
  occurrence of

CLAIM/CLAM: to shout; to cry out
exclaim: to cry out or speak suddenly and vehemently
proclaim: to announce or declare in an official way
clamor: a loud uproar
disclaim: to deny interest in or connection with
reclaim: to claim or demand the return of a right or possession

CLI: to lean toward
decline: to cause to slope or incline downward
recline: to lean back
climax: the most intense point in the development of something
proclivity: inclination, bias
disinclination: aversion, distaste

CO/COL/COM/CON: with, together
connect: to bind or fasten together
coerce: to compel by force, intimidation, or authority
compatible: capable of existing together in harmony
collide: to strike one another with a forceful impact
collaborate: to work with another, cooperate
conciliate: to placate, win over
commensurate: suitable in measure, proportionate

CRE/CRESC/CRET: to grow
accrue: to be added as a matter of periodic gain
creation: the act of producing or causing to exist
increase: to make greater in any respect
increment: something added or gained; an addition or increase
accretion: an increase by natural growth

CRED: to believe; to trust
incredible: unbelievable
credentials: anything that provides the basis for belief
credo: any formula of belief
credulity: willingness to believe or trust too readily
credit: trustworthiness

CRYP: hidden
crypt: a subterranean chamber or vault
apocryphal: of doubtful authorship or authenticity
cryptology: the science of interpreting secret writings, codes, ciphers, and the like
cryptography: procedures of making and using secret writing

CUB/CUMB: to lie down
cubicle: any small space or compartment that is partitioned off
succumb: to give away to superior force; yield
incubate: to sit upon for the purpose of hatching
incumbent: holding an indicated position
recumbent: lying down; reclining; leaning

CULP: blame
culprit: a person guilty for an offense
culpable: deserving blame or censure
inculpate: to charge with fault
mea culpa: through my fault; my fault

COUR/CUR: running; a course
recur: to happen again
curriculum: the regular course of study
courier: a messenger traveling in haste who bears news
excursion: a short journey or trip
cursive: handwriting in flowing strokes with the letters joined together
concur: to accord in opinion; agree
incursion: a hostile entrance into a place, esp. suddenly
cursory: going rapidly over something; hasty; superficial

DE: away, off, down, completely, reversal
descend: to move from a higher to a lower place
decipher: to make out the meaning; to interpret
defile: to make foul, dirty, or unclean
defame: to attack the good name or reputation of
deferential: respectful; to yield to judgment
delineate: to trace the outline of; sketch or trace in outline

DEM: people
democracy: government by the people
epidemic: affecting at the same time a large number of people, and spreading from person to person
endemic: peculiar to a particular people or locality
pandemic: general, universal
demographics: vital and social statistics of populations

DI/DIA: apart, through
dialogue: conversation between two or more persons
diagnose: to determine the identity of something from the symptoms
dilate: to make wider or larger; to cause to expand
dilatory: inclined to delay or procrastinate
dichotomy: division into two parts, kinds, etcetera

DIC/DICT/DIT: to say; to tell; to use words
dictionary: a book containing a selection of the words of a language
predict: to tell in advance
verdict: judgment, decree
interdict: to forbid; prohibit

DIGN: worth
dignity: nobility or elevation of character; worthiness
dignitary: a person who holds a high rank or office
deign: to think fit or in accordance with one's dignity
condign: well deserved; fitting; adequate
disdain: to look upon or treat with contempt

DIS/DIF: away from, apart, reversal, not
disperse: to drive or send off in various directions
disseminate: to scatter or spread widely; promulgate
dissipate: to scatter wastefully
dissuade: to deter by advice or persuasion
diffuse: to pour out and spread, as in a fluid

DAC/DOC: to teach
doctor: someone licensed to practice medicine; a learned person
doctrine: a particular principle advocated, as of a government or religion
indoctrinate: to imbue a person with learning
docile: easily managed or handled; tractable
didactic: intended for instruction

DOG/DOX: opinion
orthodox: sound or correct in opinion or doctrine
paradox: an opinion or statement contrary to accepted opinion
dogma: a system of tenets, as of a church

DOL: suffer, pain
condolence: expression of sympathy with one who is suffering
indolence: a state of being lazy or slothful
doleful: sorrowful, mournful
dolorous: full of pain or sorrow, grievous

DON/DOT/DOW: to give
donate: to present as a gift or contribution
pardon: kind indulgence, forgiveness
antidote: something that prevents or counteracts ill effects
anecdote: a short narrative about an interesting event
endow: to provide with a permanent fund

DUB: doubt
dubious: doubtful
dubiety: doubtfulness
indubitable: unquestionable

DUC/DUCT: to lead
abduct: to carry off or lead away
conduct: personal behavior, way of acting
conducive: contributive, helpful
induce: to lead or move by influence
induct: to install in a position with formal ceremonies
produce: to bring into existence; give cause to

DUR: hard
endure: to hold out against; to sustain without yielding
durable: able to resist decay
duress: compulsion by threat, coercion
dour: sullen, gloomy
duration: the length of time something exists

DYS: faulty, abnormal
dystrophy: faulty or inadequate nutrition or development
dyspepsia: impaired digestion
dyslexia: an impairment of the ability to read due to a brain defect
dysfunctional: poorly functioning

EPI: upon
epidemic: affecting at the same time a large number of people, and spreading from person to person
epilogue: a concluding part added to a literary work
epidermis: the outer layer of the skin
epigram: a witty or pointed saying tersely expressed
epithet: a word or phrase, used invectively as a term of abuse

EQU: equal, even
equation: the act of making equal
adequate: equal to the requirement or occasion
equidistant: equally distant
iniquity: gross injustice; wickedness

ERR: to wander
err: to go astray in thought or belief, to be mistaken
error: a deviation from accuracy or correctness
erratic: deviating from the proper or usual course in conduct
arrant: downright, thorough, notorious

ESCE: becoming
adolescent: between childhood and adulthood
obsolescent: becoming obsolete
incandescent: glowing with heat, shining
convalescent: recovering from illness
reminiscent: reminding or suggestive of

EU: good, well
euphemism: pleasant-sounding term for something unpleasant
eulogy: speech or writing in praise or commendation
eugenics: improvement of qualities of race by control of inherited characteristics
euthanasia: killing person painlessly, usually one who has an incurable, painful disease
euphony: pleasantness of sound

E/EF/EX: out, out of, from, former, completely
evade: to escape from, avoid
exclude: to shut out; to leave out
extricate: to disentangle, release
exonerate: to free or declare free from blame
expire: to come to an end, cease to be valid
efface: to rub or wipe out; surpass, eclipse

EXTRA: outside, beyond
extraordinary: beyond the ordinary
extract: to take out, obtain against person's will
extradite: to hand over (person accused of crime) to state where crime was committed
extrasensory: derived by means other than known senses
extrapolate: to estimate (unknown facts or values) from known data

FAB/FAM: speak
fable: fictional tale, esp. legendary
affable: friendly, courteous
ineffable: too great for description in words; that which must not be uttered
famous: well known, celebrated
defame: attack good name of

FAC/FIC/FIG/FAIT/FEIT/FY: to do; to make
factory: building for manufacture of goods
faction: small dissenting group within larger one, esp. in politics
deficient: incomplete or insufficient
prolific: producing many offspring or much output
configuration: manner of arrangement, shape
ratify: to confirm or accept by formal consent
effigy: sculpture or model of person
counterfeit: imitation, forgery

FER: to bring; to carry; to bear
  offer: to present for acceptance, refusal, or consideration
  confer: to grant, bestow
  referendum: to vote on political question open to the entire electorate
  proffer: to offer
  proliferate: to reproduce; produce rapidly

FERV: to boil; to bubble
  fervor: passion, zeal
  fervid: ardent, intense
  effervescent: with the quality of giving off bubbles of gas

FID: faith, trust
  confide: to entrust with a secret
  affidavit: written statement on oath
  fidelity: faithfulness, loyalty
  fiduciary: of a trust; held or given in trust
  infidel: disbeliever in the supposed true religion

FIN: end
  final: at the end; coming last
  confine: to keep or restrict within certain limits; imprison
  definitive: decisive, unconditional, final
  infinite: boundless; endless
  infinitesimal: infinitely or very small

FLAG/FLAM: to burn
  flammable: easily set on fire
  flambeau: a lighted torch
  flagrant: blatant, scandalous
  conflagration: large destructive fire

FLECT/FLEX: to bend
  deflect: to bend or turn aside from a purpose
  flexible: able to bend without breaking
  inflect: to change or vary pitch of
  reflect: to throw back
  genuflect: to bend knee, esp. in worship

FLU/FLUX: to flow
  fluid: substance, esp. gas or liquid, capable of flowing freely
  fluctuation: something that varies, rising and falling
  effluence: flowing out of (light, electricity, etc.)
  confluence: merging into one
  mellifluous: pleasing, musical

FORE: before
  foresight: care or provision for future
  foreshadow: be warning or indication of (future event)
  forestall: to prevent by advance action
  forthright: straightforward, outspoken, decisive

FORT: chance
  fortune: chance or luck in human affairs
  fortunate: lucky, auspicious
  fortuitous: happening by luck

FORT: strength
  fortify: to provide with fortifications; strengthen
  fortissimo: very loud
  forte: strong point; something a person does well

FRA/FRAC/FRAG/FRING: to break
  fracture: breakage, esp. of a bone
  fragment: a part broken off
  fractious: irritable, peevish
  refractory: stubborn, unmanageable, rebellious
  infringe: to break or violate (law, etcetera)

FUS: to pour
  profuse: lavish, extravagant, copious
  fusillade: continuous discharge of firearms or outburst of criticism
  suffuse: to spread throughout or over from within
  diffuse: to spread widely or thinly
  infusion: infusing; liquid extract so obtained

GEN: birth, creation, race, kind
generous: giving or given freely
genetics: study of heredity and variation among animals and plants
gender: classification roughly corresponding to the two sexes and sexlessness
carcinogenic: producing cancer
congenital: existing or as such from birth
progeny: offspring, descendants
miscegenation: interbreeding of races

GN/GNO: know
agnostic: person who believes that existence of God is not provable
ignore: to refuse to take notice of
ignoramus: a person lacking knowledge, uninformed
recognize: to identify as already known
incognito: with one's name or identity concealed
prognosis: to forecast, especially of disease
diagnose: to make an identification of disease or fault from symptoms

GRAT: pleasing
grateful: thankful
ingratiate: to bring oneself into favor
gratuity: money given for good service
gracious: kindly, esp. to inferiors; merciful

GRAD/GRESS: to step
progress: forward movement
aggressive: given to hostile act or feeling
degrade: to humiliate, dishonor, reduce to lower rank
digress: to depart from main subject
egress: going out; way out
regress: to move backward, revert to an earlier state

HER/HES: to stick
coherent: logically consistent; having waves in phase and of one wavelength
adhesive: tending to remain in memory; sticky; an adhesive substance
inherent: involved in the constitution or essential character of something
adherent: able to adhere; believer or advocate of a particular thing
heredity: the qualities genetically derived from one's ancestors and the transmission of those qualities

(H)ETERO: different
heterosexual: of or pertaining to sexual orientation toward members of the opposite sex; relating to different sexes
heterogeneous: of other origin: not originating in the body
heterodox: different from acknowledged standard; holding unorthodox opinions or doctrines

(H)OM: same
homogeneous: of the same or a similar kind of nature; of uniform structure of composition throughout
homonym: one of two or more words spelled and pronounced alike but different in meaning
homosexual: of, relating to, or exhibiting sexual desire toward a member of one's own sex
anomaly: deviation from the common rule
homeostasis: a relatively stable state of equilibrium

HYPER: over, excessive
hyperactive: excessively active
hyperbole: purposeful exaggeration for effect
hyperglycemia: an abnormally high concentration of sugar in the blood

HYPO: under, beneath, less than
hypodermic: relating to the parts beneath the skin
hypochondriac: one affected by extreme depression of mind or spirits often centered on imaginary physical ailments
hypocritical: affecting virtues or qualities one does not have
hypothesis: assumption subject to proof

IDIO: one's own
idiot: an utterly stupid person
idiom: a language, dialect, or style of speaking particular to a people
idiosyncrasy: peculiarity of temperament; eccentricity

IM/IN/EM/EN: in, into
embrace: to clasp in the arms; to include or contain
enclose: to close in on all sides
intrinsic: belonging to a thing by its very nature
influx: the act of flowing in; inflow
implicit: not expressly stated; implied
incarnate: given a bodily, esp. a human, form
indigenous: native; innate, natural

IM/IN: not, without
inactive: not active
innocuous: not harmful or injurious
indolence: showing a disposition to avoid exertion; slothful
impartial: not partial or biased; just
indigent: deficient in what is requisite

INTER: between, among
interstate: connecting or jointly involving states
interim: a temporary or provisional arrangement; meantime
interloper: one who intrudes in the domain of others
intermittent: stopping or ceasing for a time
intersperse: to scatter here and there

JECT: to throw; to throw down
inject: to place (quality, etc.) where needed in something
dejected: sad, depressed
eject: to throw out, expel
conjecture: formation of opinion on incomplete information
abject: utterly hopeless, humiliating, or wretched

JOIN/JUNCT: to meet; to join
junction: the act of joining; combining
adjoin: to be next to and joined with
subjugate: to conquer
rejoinder: to reply, retort
junta: (usually military) clique taking power after a coup d'état.

JUR: to swear
perjury: willful lying while on oath
abjure: to renounce on oath
adjure: to beg or command

LECT/LEG: to select, to choose
collect: to gather together or assemble
elect: to choose; to decide
select: to choose with care
eclectic: selecting ideas, etcetera from various sources
predilection: preference, liking

LEV: lift, light, rise
relieve: to mitigate; to free from a burden
alleviate: to make easier to endure, lessen
relevant: bearing on or pertinent to information at hand
levee: embankment against river flooding
levitate: to rise in the air or cause to rise
levity: humor, frivolity, gaiety

LOC/LOG/LOQU: word, speech
dialogue: conversation, esp. in a literary work
elocution: art of clear and expressive speaking
prologue: introduction to poem, play, etc.
eulogy: speech or writing in praise of someone
colloquial: of ordinary or familiar conversation
grandiloquent: pompous or inflated in language
loquacious: talkative

LUC/LUM/LUS: light
illustrate: to make intelligible with examples or analogies
illuminate: to supply or brighten with light
illustrious: highly distinguished
translucent: permitting light to pass through
lackluster: lacking brilliance or radiance
lucid: easily understood, intelligible
luminous: bright, brilliant, glowing

LUD/LUS: to play
allude: to refer casually or indirectly
illusion: something that deceives by producing a false impression of reality
ludicrous: ridiculous, laughable
delude: to mislead the mind or judgment of, deceive
elude: to avoid capture or escape defection by
prelude: a preliminary to an action, event, etc.

LAV/LUT/LUV: to wash

lavatory: a room with equipment for washing hands and face

dilute: to make thinner or weaker by the addition of water

pollute: to make foul or unclean

deluge: a great flood of water

antediluvian: before the biblical flood; extremely old

ablution: act of cleansing

MAG/MAJ/MAX: big

magnify: to increase the apparent size of

magnitude: greatness of size, extent, or dimensions

maximum: the highest amount, value, or degree attained

magnate: a powerful or influential person

magnanimous: generous in forgiving an insult or injury

maxim: an expression of general truth or principle

MAL/MALE: bad, ill, evil, wrong

malfunction: failure to function properly

malicious: full of or showing malice

malign: to speak harmful untruths about, to slander

malady: a disorder or disease of the body

maladroit: clumsy, tactless

malapropism: humorous misuse of a word

malfeasance: misconduct or wrongdoing often committed by a public official

malediction: a curse

MAN: hand

manual: operated by hand

manufacture: to make by hand or machinery

emancipate: to free from bondage

manifest: readily perceived by the eye or the understanding

mandate: an authoritative order or command

MIN: small

minute: a unit of time equal to one-sixtieth of an hour, or sixty seconds

minutiae: small or trivial details

miniature: a copy or model that represents something in greatly reduced size

diminish: to lessen

diminution: the act or process of diminishing

MIN: to project, to hang over

eminent: towering above others; projecting

imminent: about to occur; impending

prominent: projecting outward

preeminent: superior to or notable above all others

minatory: menacing, threatening

MIS/MIT: to send

transmit: to send from one person, thing, or place to another

emissary: a messenger or agent sent to represent the interests of another

intermittent: stopping and starting at intervals

remit: to send money

remission: a lessening of intensity or degree

MISC: mixed

miscellaneous: made up of a variety of parts or ingredients

miscegenation: the interbreeding of races, esp. marriage between white and nonwhite persons

promiscuous: consisting of diverse and unrelated parts or individuals

MON/MONIT: to remind; to warn

monument: a structure, such as a building, tower, or sculpture, erected as a memorial

monitor: one that admonishes, cautions, or reminds

summon: to call together; convene

admonish: to counsel against something; caution

remonstrate: to say or plead in protect, objection, or reproof

premonition: forewarning, presentiment

MORPH: shape
amorphous: without definite form; lacking a specific shape

metamorphosis: a transformation, as by magic or sorcery

anthropomorphism: attribution of human characteristics to inanimate objects, animals, or natural phenomena

MORT: death
immortal: not subject to death

morbid: susceptible to preoccupation with unwholesome matters

moribund: dying, decaying

MUT: change
commute: to substitute; exchange; interchange

mutation: the process of being changed

transmutation: the act of changing from one form into another

permutation: a complete change; transformation

immutable: unchangeable, invariable

NAT/NAS/NAI: to be born
natural: present due to nature, not to artificial or man-made means

native: belonging to one by nature; inborn; innate

naive: lacking worldliness and sophistication; artless

cognate: related by blood; having a common ancestor

renaissance: rebirth, esp. referring to culture

nascent: starting to develop

NIC/NOC/NOX: harm
innocent: uncorrupted by evil, malice, or wrongdoing

noxious: injurious or harmful to health or morals

obnoxious: highly disagreeable or offensive

innocuous: having no adverse effect; harmless

NOM: rule, order
astronomy: the scientific study of the universe beyond the earth

economy: the careful or thrifty use of resources, as of income, materials, or labor

gastronomy: the art or science of good eating

taxonomy: the science, laws, or principles of classification

autonomy: independence, self-governance

NOM/NYM/NOUN/NOWN: name
synonym: a word having a meaning similar to that of another word of the same language

anonymous: having an unknown or unacknowledged name

nominal: existing in name only; negligible

nominate: to propose by name as a candidate

nomenclature: a system of names; systematic naming

acronym: a word formed from the initial letters of a name

NOV/NEO/NOU: new
novice: a person new to any field or activity

renovate: to restore to an earlier condition

innovate: to begin or introduce something new

neologism: a newly coined word, phrase, or expression

neophyte: a recent convert

nouveau riche: one who has lately become rich

NOUNC/NUNC: to announce
announce: to proclaim

pronounce: to articulate

renounce: to give up, especially by formal announcement

OB/OC/OF/OP: toward, to, against, over
obese: extremely fat, corpulent

obstinate: stubbornly adhering to an idea, inflexible

obstruct: to block or fill with obstacles

oblique: having a slanting or sloping direction

obstreperous: noisily defiant, unruly

obtuse: not sharp, pointed, or acute in any form

obfuscate: to render indistinct or dim; darken

obsequious: overly submissive

OMNI: all
omnibus: an anthology of the works of one author or of writings on related subjects
omnipresent: everywhere at one time
omnipotent: all powerful
omniscient: having infinite knowledge

PAC/PEAC: peace
appease: to bring peace to
pacify: to ease the anger or agitation of
pacifier: something or someone that eases the anger or agitation of
pact: a formal agreement, as between nations

PAN: all, everyone
panorama: an unobstructed and wide view of an extensive area
panegyric: formal or elaborate praise at an assembly
panoply: a wide-ranging and impressive array or display
pantheon: a public building containing tombs or memorials of the illustrious dead of a nation
pandemic: widespread, general, universal

PAR: equal
par: an equality in value or standing
parity: equally, as in amount, status, or character
apartheid: any system or caste that separates people according to race, etc.
disparage: to belittle, speak disrespectfully about
disparate: essentially different

PARA: next to, beside
parallel: extending in the same direction
parasite: an organism that lives on or within a plant or animal of another species, from which it obtains nutrients
parody: to imitate for purposes of satire
parable: a short, allegorical story designed to illustrate a moral lesson or religious principle
paragon: a model of excellence
paranoid: suffering from a baseless distrust of others

PAS/PAT/ PATH: feeling, suffering, disease
sympathy: harmony or of agreement in feeling
empathy: the identification with the feelings or thoughts of others
compassion: a feeling of deep sympathy for someone struck by misfortune, accompanied by a desire to alleviate suffering
dispassionate: devoid of personal feeling or bias
impassive: showing or feeling no emotion
sociopath: a person whose behavior is antisocial and who lacks a sense of moral responsibility
pathogenic: causing disease

PAU/PO/POV/PU: few, little, poor
poverty: the condition of being poor
paucity: smallness of quantity; scarcity; scantiness
pauper: a person without any personal means of support
impoverish: to deplete
pusillanimous: lacking courage or resolution
puerile: childish, immature

PED: child, education
pedagogue: a teacher
pediatrician: a doctor who primarily has children as patients
pedant: one who displays learning ostentatiously
encyclopedia: book or set of books containing articles on various topics, covering all branches of knowledge or of one particular subject

PED/POD: foot
pedal: a foot-operated lever or part used to control
pedestrian: a person who travels on foot
expedite: to speed up the progress of
impede: to retard progress by means of obstacles or hindrances
podium: a small platform for an orchestra conductor, speaker, etcetera
antipodes: places diametrically opposite each other on the globe

PEN/PUN: to pay; to compensate

penal: of or pertaining to punishment, as for crimes

penalty: a punishment imposed for a violation of law or rule

punitive: serving for, concerned with, or inflicting punishment

penance: a punishment undergone to express regret for a sin

penitent: contrite

PEND/PENS: to hang; to weight; to pay

depend: to rely; to place trust in

stipend: a periodic payment; fixed or regular pay

compensate: to counterbalance, offset

indispensable: absolutely necessary, essential, or requisite

appendix: supplementary material at the end of a text

appendage: a limb or other subsidiary part that diverges from the central structure

PER: completely

persistent: lasting or enduring tenaciously

perforate: to make a way through or into something

perplex: to cause to be puzzled or bewildered over what is not understood

peruse: to read with thoroughness or care

perfunctory: performed merely as routine duty

pertinacious: resolute

perspicacious: shrewd, astute

PERI: around

perimeter: the border or outer boundary of a two-dimensional figure

periscope: an optical instrument for seeing objects in an obstructed field of vision

peripatetic: walking or traveling about; itinerant

PET/PIT: to go; to seek; to strive

appetite: a desire for food or drink

compete: to strive to outdo another for acknowledgment

petition: a formally drawn request soliciting some benefit

centripetal: moving toward the center

impetuous: characterized by sudden or rash action or emotion

petulant: showing sudden irritation, esp. over some annoyance

PHIL: love

philosophy: the rational investigation of the truths and principles of being, knowledge, or conduct

philatelist: one who loves or collects postage stamps

philology: the study of literary texts to establish their authenticity and determine their meaning

bibliophile: one who loves or collects books

PLAC: to please

placid: pleasantly calm or peaceful

placebo: a substance with no pharmacological effect which acts to placate a patient who believes it to be a medicine

implacable: unable to be pleased

complacent: self-satisfied, unconcerned

complaisant: inclined or disposed to please

PLE: to fill

complete: having all parts or elements

deplete: to decrease seriously or exhaust the supply of

supplement: something added to supply a deficiency

implement: an instrument, tool, or utensil for accomplishing work

replete: abundantly supplied

plethora: excess, overabundance

PLEX/PLIC/PLY: to fold, twist, tangle, or bend
  complex: composed of many interconnected
    parts
  replica: any close copy or reproduction
  implicit: not expressly stated, implied
  implicate: to show to be involved, usually in an
    incriminating manner
  duplicity: deceitfulness in speech or conduct,
    double-dealing
  supplicate: to make humble and earnest entreaty

PON/POS/POUND: to put; to place
  component: a constituent part, elemental ingre-
    dient
  expose: to lay open to danger, attack, or harm
  expound: to set forth in detail
  juxtapose: to place close together or side by side,
    esp. for contract
  repository: a receptacle or place where things are
    deposited

PORT: to carry
  import: to bring in from a foreign country
  export: to transmit abroad
  portable: easily carried
  deportment: conduct, behavior
  disport: to divert or amuse oneself
  importune: to urge or press with excessive persis-
    tence

POST: after
  posthumous: after death
  posterior: situated at the rear
  posterity: succeeding in future generations collec-
    tively
  post facto: after the fact

PRE: before
  precarious: dependent on circumstances beyond
    one's control
  precocious: unusually advanced or mature in
    mental development or talent
  premonition: a feeling of anticipation over a
    future event
  presentiment: foreboding
  precedent: an act that serves as an example for
    subsequent situations
  precept: a commandment given as a rule of
    action or conduct

PREHEND/PRISE: to take; to get; to seize
  surprise: to strike with an unexpected feeling of
    wonder or astonishment
  enterprise: a project undertaken
  reprehensible: deserving rebuke or censure
  comprise: to include or contain
  reprisals: retaliation against an enemy
  apprehend: to take into custody

PRO: much, for, a lot
  prolific: highly fruitful
  profuse: spending or giving freely
  prodigal: wastefully or recklessly extravagant
  prodigious: extraordinary in size, amount, or
    extent
  proselytize: to convert or attempt to recruit
  propound: to set forth for consideration
  provident: having or showing foresight

PROB: to prove; to test
  probe: to search or examine thoroughly
  approbation: praise, consideration
  opprobrium: the disgrace incurred by shameful
    conduct
  reprobate: a depraved or wicked person
  problematic: questionable
  probity: honesty, high-mindedness

PUG: to fight
  pugnacious: to quarrel or fight readily
  impugn: to challenge as false
  repugnant: objectionable or offensive
  pugilist: a fighter or boxer

PUNC/PUNG/POIGN: to point; to prick
  point: a sharp or tapering end
  puncture: the act of piercing
  pungent: caustic or sharply expressive
  compunction: a feeling of uneasiness for doing
    wrong
  punctilious: strict or exact in the observance of
    formalities
  expunge: to erase, eliminate completely

QUE/QUIS: to seek
acquire: to come into possession of
exquisite: of special beauty or charm
conquest: vanquishment
inquisitive: given to research, eager for knowledge
query: a question, inquiry
querulous: full of complaints
perquisite: a gratuity, tip

QUI: quiet
quiet: making little or no sound
disquiet: lack of calm or peace
tranquil: free from commotion or tumult
acquiesce: to comply, give in
quiescence: the condition of being at rest, still, inactive

RID/RIS: to laugh
riddle: a conundrum
derision: the act of mockery
risible: causing laughter

ROG: to ask
interrogate: to ask questions of, esp. formally
arrogant: making claims to superior importance or rights
abrogate: to abolish by formal means
surrogate: a person appointed to act for another
derogatory: belittling, disparaging
arrogate: to claim unwarrantably or presumptuously

SAL/SIL/SAULT/SULT: to leap, to jump
insult: to treat with contemptuous rudeness
assault: a sudden or violent attack
somersault: to roll the body end over end, making a complete revolution
salient: prominent or conspicuous
resilient: able to spring back to an original form after compression
insolent: boldly rude or disrespectful
exult: to show or feel triumphant joy
desultory: at random, unmethodical

SACR/SANCT/SECR: sacred
sacred: devoted or dedicated to a deity or religious purpose
sacrifice: the offering of some living or inanimate thing to a deity in homage
sanctify: to make holy
sanction: authoritative permission or approval
execrable: abominable
sacrament: something regarded as possessing sacred character
sacrilege: the violation of anything sacred

SCI: to know
conscious: aware of one's own existence
conscience: the inner sense of what is right or wrong, impelling one toward right action
unconscionable: unscrupulous
omniscient: knowing everything
prescient: having knowledge of things before they happen

SCRIBE/SCRIP: to write
scribble: to write hastily or carelessly
describe: to tell or depict in words
script: handwriting
postscript: any addition or supplement
proscribe: to condemn as harmful or odious
ascribe: to credit or assign, as to a cause or course
conscription: draft
transcript: a written or typed copy
circumscribe: to draw a line around

SE: apart
select: to choose in preference to another
separate: to keep apart, divide
seduce: to lead astray
segregate: to separate or set apart from others
secede: to withdraw formally from an association
sequester: to remove or withdraw into solitude or retirement
sedition: incitement of discontent or rebellion against a government

SEC/SEQU: to follow

second: next after the first
prosecute: to seek to enforce by legal process
sequence: the following of one thing after another
obsequious: fawning
non sequitur: an inference or a conclusion that does not follow from the premises

SED/SESS/SID: to sit; to be still; to plan; to plot

preside: to exercise management or control
resident: a person who lives in a place
sediment: the matter that settles to the bottom of a liquid
dissident: disagreeing, as in opinion or attitude
residual: remaining, leftover
subsidiary: serving to assist or supplement
insidious: intended to entrap or beguile
assiduous: diligent, persistent, hardworking

SENS/SENT: to feel; to be aware

sense: any of the faculties by which humans and animals perceive stimuli originating outside the body
sensory: of or pertaining to the senses or sensation
sentiment: an attitude or feeling toward something
presentiment: a feeling that something is about to happen
dissent: to differ in opinion, esp. from the majority
resent: to feel or show displeasure
sentinel: a person or thing that stands watch
insensate: without feeling or sensitivity

SOL: to loosen; to free

dissolve: to make a solution of, as by mixing in a liquid
soluble: capable of being dissolved or liquefied
resolution: a formal expression of opinion or intention made
dissolution: the act or process of dissolving into parts or elements
dissolute: indifferent to moral restraints
absolution: forgiveness for wrongdoing

SPEC/SPIC/SPIT: to look; to see

perspective: one's mental view of facts, ideas, and their interrelationships
speculation: the contemplation or consideration of some subject
suspicious: inclined to suspect
spectrum: a broad range of related things that form a continuous series
retrospective: contemplative of past situations
circumspect: watchful and discreet, cautious
perspicacious: having keen mental perception and understanding
conspicuous: easily seen or noticed; readily observable
specious: deceptively attractive

STA/STI: to stand; to be in place

static: of bodies or forces at rest or in equilibrium
destitute: without means of subsistence
obstinate: stubbornly adhering to a purpose, opinion, or course of action
constitute: to make up
stasis: the state of equilibrium or inactivity caused by opposing equal forces
apostasy: renunciation of an object of one's previous loyalty

SUA: smooth

suave: smoothly agreeable or polite
persuade: to encourage; to convince
dissuade: to deter
assuage: to make less severe, ease, relieve

SUB/SUP: below

submissive: inclined or ready to submit
subsidiary: serving to assist or supplement
subliminal: existing or operating below the threshold of confidence
subtle: thin, tenuous, or rarefied
subterfuge: an artifice or expedient used to evade a rule
supposition: the act of assuming

SUPER/SUR: above
surpass: to go beyond in amount, extent, or
  degree
superlative: the highest kind or order
supersede: to replace in power, as by another person or thing
supercilious: arrogant, haughty, condescending
superfluous: extra, more than necessary
surmount: to get over or across, to prevail
surveillance: a watch kept over someone or something

TAC/TIC: to be silent
reticent: disposed to be silent or not to speak
  freely
tacit: unspoken understanding
taciturn: uncommunicative

TAIN/TEN/TENT/TIN: to hold
detain: to keep from proceeding
pertain: to have reference or relation
tenacious: holding fast
abstention: the act of refraining voluntarily
tenure: the holding or possessing of anything
tenable: capable of being held, maintained, or
  defended
sustenance: nourishment, means of livelihood
pertinacious: persistent, stubborn

TEND/TENS/TENT/TENU: to stretch; to thin
tension: the act of stretching or straining
tentative: of the nature of, or done as a trial,
  attempt
tendentious: having a predisposition towards a
  point of view
distend: to expand by stretching
attenuate: to weaken or reduce in force
extenuating: making less serious by offering
  excuses
contentious: quarrelsome, disagreeable, belligerent

THEO: god
atheist: one who does not believe in a deity or
  divine system
theocracy: a form of government in which a deity
  is recognized as the supreme ruler
theology: the study of divine things and the
  divine faith
apotheosis: glorification, glorified ideal

TRACT: to drag; to pull; to draw
tractor: a powerful vehicle used to pull farm
  machinery
attract: to draw either by physical force or by an
  appeal to emotions or senses
contract: a legally binding document
detract: to take away from, esp. a positive thing
abstract: to draw or pull away, remove
tractable: easily managed or controlled
protract: to prolong, draw out, extend

TRANS: across
transaction: the act of carrying on or conduct to
  a conclusion or settlement
transparent: easily seen through, recognized, or
  detected
transition: a change from one way of being to
  another
transgress: to violate a law, command, or moral
  code
transcendent: going beyond ordinary limits
intransigent: refusing to agree or compromise

US/UT: to use
abuse: to use wrongly or improperly
usage: a customary way of doing something
usurp: to seize and hold
utilitarian: efficient, functional, useful

VEN/VENT: to come or to move toward
convene: to assemble for some public purpose
venturesome: showing a disposition to undertake
  risks
intervene: to come between disputing factions,
  mediate
contravene: to come into conflict with
adventitious: accidental

VER: truth
verdict: any judgment or decision
veracious: habitually truthful
verity: truthfulness
verisimilitude: the appearance or semblance of
  truth
aver: to affirm, to declare to be true

VERD: green
   verdant: green with vegetation; inexperienced
   verdure: fresh, rich vegetation

VERS/VERT: to turn
   controversy: a public dispute involving a matter
     of opinion
   revert: to return to a former habit
   diverse: of a different kind, form, character
   aversion: dislike
   introvert: a person concerned primarily with
     inner thoughts and feelings
   extrovert: an outgoing person
   inadvertent: unintentional
   covert: hidden, clandestine
   avert: to turn away from

VI: life
   vivid: strikingly bright or intense
   vicarious: performed, exercised, received, or suf-
     fered in place of another
   viable: capable of living
   vivacity: the quality of being lively, animated,
     spirited
   joie de vivre: joy of life (French expression)
   convivial: sociable

VID/VIS: to see
   evident: plain or clear to the sight or understand-
     ing
   video: the elements of television pertaining to the
     transmission or reception of the image
   adviser: one who gives counsel
   survey: to view in a general or comprehensive
     way
   vista: a view or prospect

VIL: base, mean
   vilify: to slander, to defame
   revile: to criticize with harsh language
   vile: loathsome, unpleasant

VOC/VOK: to call
   vocabulary: the stock of words used by or known
     to a particular person or group
   advocate: to support or urge by argument
   equivocate: to use ambiguous or unclear expres-
     sions
   vocation: a particular occupation
   avocation: something one does in addition to a
     principle occupation
   vociferous: crying out noisily
   convoke: to call together
   invoke: to call on a deity

VOL: to wish
   voluntary: undertaken of one's own accord or by
     free choice
   malevolent: characterized by or expressing bad
     will
   benevolent: characterized by or expressing good-
     will
   volition: free choice, free will; act of choosing

VOR: to eat
   voracious: having a great appetite
   carnivorous: meat-eating
   omnivorous: eating or absorbing everything

APPENDIX B

Top GRE Words in Context

The GRE tests the same kinds of words over and over again. (Remember, for ETS, consistency is key.) In this appendix, we've not only listed the most popular GRE words with their definitions, but we've also used all of these words in context to help you to remember them. If you see a word that's unfamiliar to you, take a moment to study the definition and, most importantly, reread the sentence with the word's definition in mind.

Remember: Learning vocabulary words in context is one of the best ways for your brain to retain the words' meanings. A broader vocabulary will serve you well on all four GRE Verbal question types and will also be extremely helpful in the Analytical Writing section.

ABATE: to reduce in amount, degree, or severity
As the hurricane's force ABATED, the winds dropped and the sea became calm.

ABSCOND: to leave secretly
The patron ABSCONDED from the restaurant without paying his bill by sneaking out the back door.

ABSTAIN: to choose not to do something:
During Lent, practicing Catholics ABSTAIN from eating meat.

ABYSS: an extremely deep hole
The submarine dove into the ABYSS to chart the previously unseen depths.

ADULTERATE: to make impure
The restaurateur made his ketchup last longer by ADULTERATING it with water.

ADVOCATE: to speak in favor of
The vegetarian ADVOCATED a diet containing no meat.

AESTHETIC: concerning the appreciation of beauty
Followers of the AESTHETIC Movement regarded the pursuit of beauty as the only true purpose of art.

AGGRANDIZE: to increase in power, influence, and reputation
The supervisor sought to AGGRANDIZE himself by claiming that the achievements of his staff were actually his own.

ALLEVIATE: to make more bearable
Taking aspirin helps to ALLEVIATE a headache.

AMALGAMATE: to combine; to mix together
Giant Industries AMALGAMATED with Mega Products to form Giant-Mega Products Incorporated.

AMBIGUOUS: doubtful or uncertain; able to be interpreted several ways
The directions he gave were so AMBIGUOUS that we disagreed on which way to turn.

AMELIORATE: to make better; to improve
The doctor was able to AMELIORATE the patient's suffering using painkillers.

ANACHRONISM: something out of place in time
The aged hippie used ANACHRONISTIC phrases like *groovy* and *far out* that had not been popular for years.

ANALOGOUS: similar or alike in some way; equivalent to
In a famous argument for the existence of God, the universe is ANALOGOUS to a mechanical timepiece, the creation of a divinely intelligent "clockmaker."

ANOMALY: deviation from what is normal
Albino animals may display too great an ANOMALY in their coloring to attract normally colored mates.

ANTAGONIZE: to annoy or provoke to anger
The child discovered that he could ANTAGONIZE the cat by pulling its tail.

ANTIPATHY: extreme dislike
The ANTIPATHY between the French and the English regularly erupted into open warfare.

APATHY: lack of interest or emotion
The APATHY of voters is so great that less than half the people who are eligible to vote actually bother to do so.

ARBITRATE: to judge a dispute between two opposing parties
Since the couple could not come to agreement, a judge was forced to ARBITRATE their divorce proceedings.

ARCHAIC: ancient, old-fashioned
Her ARCHAIC Commodore computer could not run the latest software.

ARDOR: intense and passionate feeling
Bishop's ARDOR for landscape was evident when he passionately described the beauty of the scenic Hudson Valley.

ARTICULATE: able to speak clearly and expressively
She is such an ARTICULATE defender of labor that unions are among her strongest supporters.

ASSUAGE: to make something unpleasant less severe
Serena used aspirin to ASSUAGE her pounding headache.

ATTENUATE: to reduce in force or degree; to weaken
The Bill of Rights ATTENUATED the traditional power of government to change laws at will.

AUDACIOUS: fearless and daring
Her AUDACIOUS nature allowed her to fulfill her dream of skydiving.

AUSTERE: severe or stern in appearance; undecorated
The lack of decoration makes Zen temples seem AUSTERE to the untrained eye.

BANAL: predictable, clichéd, boring
He used BANAL phrases like *Have a nice day*, or *Another day, another dollar.*

BOLSTER: to support; to prop up
The presence of giant footprints BOLSTERED the argument that Sasquatch was in the area.

BOMBASTIC: pompous in speech and manner
The dictator's speeches were mostly BOMBASTIC; his boasting and outrageous claims had no basis in fact.

CACOPHONY: harsh, jarring noise
The junior high orchestra created an almost unbearable CACOPHONY as they tried to tune their instruments.

CANDID: impartial and honest in speech
The observations of a child can be charming since they are CANDID and unpretentious.

CAPRICIOUS: changing one's mind quickly and often
Queen Elizabeth I was quite CAPRICIOUS; her courtiers could never be sure which of their number would catch her fancy.

CASTIGATE: to punish or criticize harshly
Americans are amazed at how harshly the authorities in Singapore CASTIGATE perpetrators of what would be considered minor crimes in the United States.

CATALYST: something that brings about a change in something else
The imposition of harsh taxes was the CATALYST that finally brought on the revolution.

CAUSTIC: biting in wit
Dorothy Parker gained her reputation for CAUSTIC wit from her cutting, yet clever, insults.

CHAOS: great disorder or confusion
In most religious traditions, God created an ordered universe from CHAOS.

CHAUVINIST: someone prejudiced in favor of a group to which he or she belongs
The attitude that men are inherently superior to women and therefore must be obeyed is common among male CHAUVINISTS.

CHICANERY: deception by means of craft or guile
Dishonest used car salesmen often use CHICANERY to sell their beat-up old cars.

COGENT: convincing and well reasoned
Swayed by the COGENT argument of the defense, the jury had no choice but to acquit the defendant.

CONDONE: to overlook, pardon, or disregard
Some theorists believe that failing to prosecute minor crimes is the same as CONDONING an air of lawlessness.

CONVOLUTED: intricate and complicated
Although many people bought *A Brief History of Time*, few could follow its CONVOLUTED ideas and theories.

CORROBORATE: to provide supporting evidence
Fingerprints CORROBORATED the witness's testimony that he saw the defendant in the victim's apartment.

CREDULOUS: too trusting; gullible
Although some 4-year-olds believe in the Easter Bunny, only the most CREDULOUS 9-year-olds also believe in him.

CRESCENDO: steadily increasing volume or force
The CRESCENDO of tension became unbearable as Evel Knievel prepared to jump his motorcycle over the school buses.

DECORUM: appropriateness of behavior or conduct; propriety
The countess complained that the vulgar peasants lacked the DECORUM appropriate for a visit to the palace.

DEFERENCE: respect, courtesy
The respectful young law clerk treated the Supreme Court justice with the utmost DEFERENCE.

DERIDE: to speak of or treat with contempt; to mock
The awkward child was often DERIDED by his "cooler" peers.

DESICCATE: to dry out thoroughly
After a few weeks of lying on the desert's baking sands, the cow's carcass became completely DESICCATED.

DESULTORY: jumping from one thing to another; disconnected
Diane had a DESULTORY academic record; she had changed majors 12 times in 3 years.

DIATRIBE: an abusive, condemnatory speech
The trucker bellowed a DIATRIBE at the driver who had cut him off.

DIFFIDENT: lacking self-confidence
Steve's DIFFIDENT manner during the job interview stemmed from his nervous nature and lack of experience in the field.

DILATE: to make larger; to expand
When you enter a darkened room, the pupils of your eyes DILATE to let in more light.

DILATORY: intended to delay
The congressman used DILATORY measures to delay the passage of the bill.

DILETTANTE: someone with an amateurish and superficial interest in a topic
Jerry's friends were such DILETTANTES that they seemed to have new jobs and hobbies every week.

DIRGE: a funeral hymn or mournful speech
Melville wrote the poem "A DIRGE for James McPherson" for the funeral of a Union general who was killed in 1864.

DISABUSE: to set right; to free from error
Galileo's observations DISABUSED scholars of the notion that the Sun revolved around the Earth.

DISCERN: to perceive; to recognize
It is easy to DISCERN the difference between butter and butter-flavored topping.

DISPARATE: fundamentally different; entirely unlike
Although the twins appear to be identical physically, their personalities are DISPARATE.

DISSEMBLE: to present a false appearance; to disguise one's real intentions or character
The villain could DISSEMBLE to the police no longer—he admitted the deed and tore up the floor to reveal the body of the old man.

DISSONANCE: a harsh and disagreeable combination, often of sounds
Cognitive DISSONANCE is the inner conflict produced when long-standing beliefs are contradicted by new evidence.

DOGMA: a firmly held opinion, often a religious belief
Linus' central DOGMA was that children who believed in the Great Pumpkin would be rewarded.

DOGMATIC: dictatorial in one's opinions
The dictator was DOGMATIC—he, and only he, was right.

DUPE: to deceive; a person who is easily deceived
Bugs Bunny was able to DUPE Elmer Fudd by dressing up as a lady rabbit.

ECLECTIC: selecting from or made up from a variety of sources
Budapest's architecture is an ECLECTIC mix of eastern and western styles.

EFFICACY: effectiveness
The EFFICACY of penicillin was unsurpassed when it was first introduced; the drug completely eliminated almost all bacterial infections for which it was administered.

ELEGY: a sorrowful poem or speech
Although Thomas Gray's "ELEGY Written in a Country Churchyard" is about death and loss, it urges its readers to endure this life, and to trust in spirituality.

ELOQUENT: persuasive and moving, especially in speech
The Gettysburg Address is moving not only because of its lofty sentiments but also because of its ELOQUENT words.

EMULATE: to copy; to try to equal or excel
The graduate student sought to EMULATE his professor in every way, copying not only how she taught, but also how she conducted herself outside of class.

ENERVATE: to reduce in strength
The guerrillas hoped that a series of surprise attacks would ENERVATE the regular army.

ENGENDER: to produce, cause, or bring about
His fear and hatred of clowns was ENGENDERED when he witnessed the death of his father at the hands of a clown.

ENIGMA: a puzzle; a mystery
Speaking in riddles and dressed in old robes, the artist gained a reputation as something of an ENIGMA.

ENUMERATE: to count, list, or itemize
Moses returned from the mountain with tablets on which the commandments were ENUMERATED.

EPHEMERAL: lasting a short time
The lives of mayflies seem EPHEMERAL to us, since the flies' average life span is a matter of hours.

EQUIVOCATE: to use expressions of double meaning in order to mislead
When faced with criticism of his policies, the politician EQUIVOCATED and left all parties thinking he agreed with them.

ERRATIC: wandering and unpredictable
The plot seemed predictable until it suddenly took a series of ERRATIC turns that surprised the audience.

ERUDITE: learned, scholarly, bookish
The annual meeting of philosophy professors was a gathering of the most ERUDITE, well-published individuals in the field.

ESOTERIC: known or understood by only a few
Only a handful of experts are knowledgeable about the ESOTERIC world of particle physics.

ESTIMABLE: admirable
Most people consider it ESTIMABLE that Mother Teresa spent her life helping the poor of India.

EULOGY: speech in praise of someone
His best friend gave the EULOGY, outlining his many achievements and talents.

EUPHEMISM: use of an inoffensive word or phrase in place of a more distasteful one
The funeral director preferred to use the EUPHEMISM "sleeping" instead of the word "dead."

EXACERBATE: to make worse
It is unwise to take aspirin to try to relieve heartburn; instead of providing relief, the drug will only EXACERBATE the problem.

EXCULPATE: to clear from blame; prove innocent
The adversarial legal system is intended to convict those who are guilty and to EXCULPATE those who are innocent.

EXIGENT: urgent; requiring immediate action
The patient was losing blood so rapidly that it was EXIGENT to stop the source of the bleeding.

EXONERATE: to clear of blame
The fugitive was EXONERATED when another criminal confessed to committing the crime.

EXPLICIT: clearly stated or shown; forthright in expression
The owners of the house left a list of EXPLICIT instructions detailing their house-sitters' duties, including a schedule for watering the house plants.

FANATICAL: acting excessively enthusiastic; filled with extreme, unquestioned devotion

The stormtroopers were FANATICAL in their devotion to the Emperor, readily sacrificing their lives for him.

FAWN: to grovel

The understudy FAWNED over the director in hopes of being cast in the part on a permanent basis.

FERVID: intensely emotional; feverish

The fans of Maria Callas were unusually FERVID, doing anything to catch a glimpse of the great opera singer.

FLORID: excessively decorated or embellished

The palace had been decorated in an excessively FLORID style; every surface had been carved and gilded.

FOMENT: to arouse or incite

The protesters tried to FOMENT feeling against the war through their speeches and demonstrations.

FRUGALITY: a tendency to be thrifty or cheap

Scrooge McDuck's FRUGALITY was so great that he accumulated enough wealth to fill a giant storehouse with money.

GARRULOUS: tending to talk a lot

The GARRULOUS parakeet distracted its owner with its continuous talking.

GREGARIOUS: outgoing, sociable

She was so GREGARIOUS that when she found herself alone she felt quite sad.

GUILE: deceit or trickery

Since he was not fast enough to catch the roadrunner on foot, the coyote resorted to GUILE in an effort to trap his enemy.

GULLIBLE: easily deceived

The con man pretended to be a bank officer so as to fool GULLIBLE bank customers into giving him their account information.

HOMOGENOUS: of a similar kind

The class was fairly HOMOGENOUS, since almost all of the students were senior journalism majors.

ICONOCLAST: one who opposes established beliefs, customs, and institutions

His lack of regard for traditional beliefs soon established him as an ICONOCLAST.

IMPERTURBABLE: not capable of being disturbed

The counselor had so much experience dealing with distraught children that she seemed IMPERTURBABLE, even when faced with the wildest tantrums.

IMPERVIOUS: impossible to penetrate; incapable of being affected

A good raincoat will be IMPERVIOUS to moisture.

IMPETUOUS: quick to act without thinking

It is not good for an investment broker to be IMPETUOUS, since much thought should be given to all the possible options.

IMPLACABLE: unable to be calmed down or made peaceful

His rage at the betrayal was so great that he remained IMPLACABLE for weeks.

INCHOATE: not fully formed; disorganized

The ideas expressed in Nietzsche's mature work also appear in an INCHOATE form in his earliest writing.

INGENUOUS: showing innocence or childlike simplicity

She was so INGENUOUS that her friends feared that her innocence and trustfulness would be exploited when she visited the big city.

INIMICAL: hostile, unfriendly

Even though the children had grown up together they were INIMICAL to each other at school.

INNOCUOUS: harmless

Some snakes are poisonous, but most species are INNOCUOUS and pose no danger to humans.

INSIPID: lacking interest or flavor

The critic claimed that the painting was INSIPID, containing no interesting qualities at all.

INTRANSIGENT: uncompromising; refusing to be reconciled

The professor was INTRANSIGENT on the deadline, insisting that everyone turn the assignment in at the same time.

INUNDATE: to overwhelm; to cover with water

The tidal wave INUNDATED Atlantis, which was lost beneath the water.

IRASCIBLE: easily made angry

Attila the Hun's IRASCIBLE and violent nature made all who dealt with him fear for their lives.

LACONIC: using few words

She was a LACONIC poet who built her reputation on using words as sparingly as possible.

LAMENT: to express sorrow; to grieve

The children continued to LAMENT the death of the goldfish weeks after its demise.

LAUD: to give praise; to glorify

Parades and fireworks were staged to LAUD the success of the rebels.

LAVISH: to give unsparingly (v.); extremely generous or extravagant (adj.)

She LAVISHED the puppy with so many treats that it soon become overweight and spoiled.

LETHARGIC: acting in an indifferent or slow, sluggish manner

The clerk was so LETHARGIC that, even when the store was slow, he always had a long line in front of him.

LOQUACIOUS: talkative

She was naturally LOQUACIOUS, which was a problem in situations in which listening was more important than talking.

LUCID: clear and easily understood

The explanations were written in a simple and LUCID manner so that students were immediately able to apply what they learned.

LUMINOUS: bright, brilliant, glowing

The park was bathed in LUMINOUS sunshine which warmed the bodies and the souls of the visitors.

MALINGER: to evade responsibility by pretending to be ill

A common way to avoid the draft was by MALINGERING—pretending to be mentally or physically ill so as to avoid being taken by the Army.

MALLEABLE: capable of being shaped

Gold is the most MALLEABLE of precious metals; it can easily be formed into almost any shape.

METAPHOR: a figure of speech comparing two different things; a symbol

The METAPHOR "a sea of troubles" suggests a lot of troubles by comparing their number to the vastness of the sea.

METICULOUS: extremely careful about details

To find all the clues at the crime scene, the investigators METICULOUSLY examined every inch of the area.

MISANTHROPE: a person who dislikes others

The character Scrooge in *A Christmas Carol* is such a MISANTHROPE that even the sight of children singing makes him angry.

MITIGATE: to soften; to lessen

A judge may MITIGATE a sentence if she decides that a person committed a crime out of need.

MOLLIFY: to calm or make less severe

Their argument was so intense that is was difficult to believe any compromise would MOLLIFY them.

MONOTONY: lack of variation

The MONOTONY of the sound of the dripping faucet almost drove the research assistant crazy.

NAIVE: lacking sophistication or experience

Having never traveled before, the hillbillies were more NAIVE than the people they met in Beverly Hills.

OBDURATE: hardened in feeling; resistant to persuasion

The President was completely OBDURATE on the issue, and no amount of persuasion would change his mind.

OBSEQUIOUS: overly submissive and eager to please

The OBSEQUIOUS new associate made sure to compliment her supervisor's tie and agree with him on every issue.

OBSTINATE: stubborn, unyielding

The OBSTINATE child could not be made to eat any food that he disliked.

OBVIATE: to prevent; to make unnecessary

The river was shallow enough to wade across at many points, which OBVIATED the need for a bridge.

OCCLUDE: to stop up; to prevent the passage of

A shadow is thrown across the Earth's surface during a solar eclipse, when the light from the sun is OCCLUDED by the moon.

ONEROUS: troublesome and oppressive; burdensome

The assignment was so extensive and difficult to manage that it proved ONEROUS to the team in charge of it.

OPAQUE: impossible to see through; preventing the passage of light

The heavy buildup of dirt and grime on the windows almost made them OPAQUE.

OPPROBRIUM: public disgrace

After the scheme to embezzle the elderly was made public, the treasurer resigned in utter OPPROBRIUM.

OSTENTATION: excessive showiness

The OSTENTATION of the Sun King's court is evident in the lavish decoration and luxuriousness of his palace at Versailles.

PARADOX: a contradiction or dilemma

It is a PARADOX that those most in need of medical attention are often those least able to obtain it.

PARAGON: model of excellence or perfection
She is the PARAGON of what a judge should be: honest, intelligent, hardworking, and just.

PEDANT: someone who shows off learning
The graduate instructor's tedious and excessive commentary on the subject soon gained her a reputation as a PEDANT.

PERFIDIOUS: willing to betray one's trust
The actress's PERFIDIOUS companion revealed all of her intimate secrets to the gossip columnist.

PERFUNCTORY: done in a routine way; indifferent
The machinelike bank teller processed the transaction and gave the waiting customer a PERFUNCTORY smile.

PERMEATE: to penetrate
This miraculous new cleaning fluid is able to PERMEATE stains and dissolve them in minutes!

PHILANTHROPY: charity; a desire or effort to promote goodness
New York's Metropolitan Museum of Art owes much of its collection to the PHILANTHROPY of private collectors who willed their estates to the museum.

PLACATE: to soothe or pacify
The burglar tried to PLACATE the snarling dog by saying, "Nice doggy," and offering it a treat.

PLASTIC: able to be molded, altered, or bent
The new material was very PLASTIC and could be formed into products of vastly different shape.

PLETHORA: excess
Assuming that more was better, the defendant offered the judge a PLETHORA of excuses.

PRAGMATIC: practical as opposed to idealistic
While daydreaming gamblers think they can get rich by frequenting casinos, PRAGMATIC gamblers realize that the odds are heavily stacked against them.

PRECIPITATE: to throw violently or bring about abruptly; lacking deliberation
Upon learning that the couple married after knowing each other only two months, friends and family members expected such a PRECIPITATE marriage to end in divorce.

PREVARICATE: to lie or deviate from the truth
Rather than admit that he had overslept again, the employee PREVARICATED and claimed that heavy traffic had prevented him from arriving at work on time.

PRISTINE: fresh and clean; uncorrupted
Since concerted measures had been taken to prevent looting, the archeological site was still PRISTINE when researchers arrived.

PRODIGAL: lavish, wasteful
The PRODIGAL Son quickly wasted all of his inheritance on a lavish lifestyle devoted to pleasure.

PROLIFERATE: to increase in number quickly
Although he only kept two guinea pigs initially, they PROLIFERATED to such an extent that he soon had dozens.

PROPITIATE: to conciliate; to appease
The management PROPITIATED the irate union by agreeing to raise wages for its members.

PROPRIETY: correct behavior; obedience to rules and customs
The aristocracy maintained a high level of PROPRIETY, adhering to even the most minor social rules.

PRUDENCE: wisdom, caution, or restraint
The college student exhibited PRUDENCE by obtaining practical experience along with her studies, which greatly strengthened her résumé.

PUNGENT: sharp and irritating to the senses
The smoke from the burning tires was extremely PUNGENT.

QUIESCENT: motionless
Many animals are QUIESCENT over the winter months, minimizing activity in order to conserve energy.

RAREFY: to make thinner or sparser
Since the atmosphere RAREFIES as altitudes increase, the air at the top of very tall mountains is too thin to breathe.

REPUDIATE: to reject the validity of
The old woman's claim that she was Russian royalty was REPUDIATED when DNA tests showed she was of no relation to them.

RETICENT: silent, reserved
Physically small and RETICENT in her speech, Joan Didion often went unnoticed by those upon whom she was reporting.

RHETORIC: effective writing or speaking
Lincoln's talent for RHETORIC was evident in his beautifully expressed Gettysburg Address.

SATIATE: to satisfy fully or overindulge
His desire for power was so great that nothing less than complete control of the country could SATIATE it.

SOPORIFIC: causing sleep or lethargy
The movie proved to be so SOPORIFIC that soon loud snores were heard throughout the theater.

SPECIOUS: deceptively attractive; seemingly plausible but fallacious
The student's SPECIOUS excuse for being late sounded legitimate, but was proved otherwise when his teacher called his home.

STIGMA: a mark of shame or discredit
In *The Scarlet Letter*, Hester Prynne was required to wear the letter "A" on her clothes as a public STIGMA for her adultery.

STOLID: unemotional; lacking sensitivity
The prisoner appeared STOLID and unaffected by the judge's harsh sentence.

SUBLIME: lofty or grand
The music was so SUBLIME that it transformed the rude surroundings into a special place.

TACIT: done without using words
Although not a word had been said, everyone in the room knew that a TACIT agreement had been made about which course of action to take.

TACITURN: silent, not talkative
The clerk's TACITURN nature earned him the nickname "Silent Bob."

TIRADE: long, harsh speech or verbal attack
Observers were shocked at the manager's TIRADE over such a minor mistake.

TORPOR: extreme mental and physical sluggishness
After surgery, the patient experienced TORPOR until the anesthesia wore off.

TRANSITORY: temporary, lasting a brief time
The reporter lived a TRANSITORY life, staying in one place only long enough to cover the current story.

VACILLATE: to sway physically; to be indecisive
The customer held up the line as he VACILLATED between ordering chocolate chip or rocky road ice cream.

VENERATE: to respect deeply
In a traditional Confucian society, the young VENERATE their elders, deferring to the elders' wisdom and experience.

VERACITY: filled with truth and accuracy
She had a reputation for VERACITY, so everyone trusted her description of events.

VERBOSE: wordy
The professor's answer was so VERBOSE that his student forgot what the original question had been.

VEX: to annoy
The old man who loved his peace and quiet was VEXED by his neighbor's loud music.

VOLATILE: easily aroused or changeable; lively or explosive
His VOLATILE personality made it difficult to predict his reaction to anything.

WAVER: to fluctuate between choices
If you WAVER too long before making a decision about which testing site to register for, you may not get your first choice.

WHIMSICAL: acting in a fanciful or capricious manner; unpredictable
The ballet was WHIMSICAL, delighting the children with its imaginative characters and unpredictable sets.

ZEAL: passion, excitement
She brought her typical ZEAL to the project, sparking enthusiasm in the other team members.

APPENDIX C

Math Reference

The math on the GRE covers a lot of ground—from basic algebra to symbol problems to geometry.

Don't let yourself be intimidated. We've highlighted the 100 most important concepts that you need and listed them in this appendix. Although you probably learned most of this stuff in high school, this list is a great way to refresh your memory.

The GRE math tests your understanding of a relatively limited number of mathematical concepts. It is possible to learn all the math you need to know for the GRE in a short time. In fact, you've seen it all before. Listed on the following pages are 100 things you need to know for the GRE, divided into three levels.

Level 1 is the most basic. You couldn't answer any GRE math questions if you didn't know Level 1 math. Most people preparing to take the GRE are already pretty good at Level 1 math. Look over the Level 1 list below just to make sure you're comfortable with the basics.

Level 2 is the place for most people to start their review of math. These skills and formulas come into play quite frequently on the GRE, especially in the medium and hard questions. If you're like a lot of students, your Level 2 math is probably rusty.

Level 3 is the hardest math you'll find on the GRE. These are skills and formulas that you might find difficult. Don't spend a lot of time on Level 3 if you still have gaps in Level 2. But once you've about mastered Level 2, then tackling Level 3 can put you over the top.

Level 1
(Math You Probably Already Know)

1. How to add, subtract, multiply, and divide WHOLE NUMBERS

2. How to add, subtract, multiply, and divide FRACTIONS

3. How to add, subtract, multiply, and divide DECIMALS

4. How to convert FRACTIONS TO DECIMALS and DECIMALS TO FRACTIONS

5. How to add, subtract, multiply, and divide POSITIVE AND NEGATIVE NUMBERS

6. How to plot points on the NUMBER LINE

7. How to plug a number into an ALGEBRAIC EXPRESSION

8. How to SOLVE a simple EQUATION

9. How to add and subtract LINE SEGMENTS

10. How to find the THIRD ANGLE of a TRIANGLE, given the other two angles

Level 2
(Math You Might Need to Review)

11. How to use PEMDAS

When you're given an ugly arithmetic equation, it's important to know the order of operations. Just remember PEMDAS (as in "Please excuse my dear Aunt Sally"). What PEMDAS means is this:

Clean up **Parentheses** first; then deal with **Exponents**; then do the **Multiplication** and **Division** together, going from left to right; and finally do the **Addition** and **Subtraction** together, again going from left to right.

Example:

$9 - 2 \times (5 - 3)^2 + 6 \div 3 =$

Begin with the parentheses: $9 - 2 \times (2)^2 + 6 \div 3$.

Then do the exponent: $9 - 2 \times 4 + 6 \div 3$.

Now do multiplication and division from left to right: $9 - 8 + 2$.

Finally, do addition and subtraction from left to right:

$9 - 8 + 2 = 1 + 2 = 3$

12. How to use the PERCENT FORMULA

Identify the part, the percent, and the whole.

$$Part = percent \times whole$$

> **HINT: You'll usually find the part near the word *is* and the whole near the word *of*.**

Example: (Find the part)

What is 12 percent of 25?

Setup:

$Part = \frac{12}{100} \times 25 = 3$

Example: (Find the percent)

45 is what percent of 9?

Setup:

$45 = Percent \times 9 = 5 \times 9$

$Percent = 5 \times 100\% = 500\%$

Example: (Find the whole)

15 is $\frac{3}{5}$ percent of what number?

Setup:

$\frac{3}{5}$ percent $= \frac{3}{500}$

$15 = \frac{3}{500} \times$ whole

Whole = 2,500

13. How to use the PERCENT INCREASE/DECREASE FORMULAS

Identify the original whole and the amount of increase/decrease.

$$Percent\ increase = \frac{amount\ of\ increase}{original\ whole} \times 100\%$$

$$Percent\ decrease = \frac{amount\ of\ decrease}{original\ whole} \times 100\%$$

Example:

The price goes up from \$80 to \$100. What is the percent increase?

Setup:

Percent increase = $\frac{20}{80} \times 100\% = 25\%$

> **HINT: Be sure to use the original whole—not the new whole—for the base.**

14. How to predict whether a sum, difference, or product will be ODD or EVEN

Don't bother memorizing the rules. Just take simple numbers like 1 and 2 and see what happens.

Example:

If m is even and n is odd, is the product mn odd or even?

Setup:

Say $m = 2$ and $n = 1$.
2×1 is even, so mn is even.

15. How to recognize MULTIPLES OF 2, 3, 4, 5, 6, 9, and 10

2: Last digit is even.
3: Sum of digits is a multiple of 3.
4: Last two digits are a multiple of 4.
5: Last digit is 5 or 0.
6: Sum of digits is a multiple of 3 and last digit is even.
9: Sum of digits is a multiple of 9.
10: Last digit is 0.

16. How to find a COMMON FACTOR

Break both numbers down to their prime factors to see what they have in common. Then multiply the shared prime factors to find all common factors.

Example:

What factors greater than 1 do 135 and 225 have in common?

Setup:

First find the prime factors of 135 and 225. $135 = 3 \times 3 \times 3 \times 5$, and $225 = 3 \times 3 \times 5 \times 5$. The numbers share $3 \times 3 \times 5$ in common. Thus, aside from 3 and 5, the remaining common factors can be found by multiplying 3, 3, and 5 in every possible combination: $3 \times 3 = 9$, $3 \times 5 = 15$, and $3 \times 3 \times 5 = 45$.

17. How to find a COMMON MULTIPLE

The product is the easiest common multiple to find. If the two numbers have any factors in common, you can divide them out of the product to get a lower common multiple.

Example:

What is the least common multiple of 28 and 42?

Setup:

The product $28 \times 42 = 1,176$ is a common multiple, but not the least. $28 = 2 \times 2 \times 7$, and $42 = 2 \times 3 \times 7$. They share a 2 and a 7, so divide the product by 2 and then by 7. $1,176 \div 2 = 588$. $588 \div 7 = 84$. The least common multiple is 84.

18. How to find the AVERAGE

$$Average = \frac{sum\ of\ terms}{number\ of\ terms}$$

Example:

What is the average of 3, 4, and 8 ?

Setup:

Average $= \frac{3 + 4 + 8}{3} = \frac{15}{3} = 5$.

19. How to use the AVERAGE to find the SUM

$$Sum = (average) \times (number\ of\ terms)$$

Example:

17.5 is the average (arithmetic mean) of 24 numbers. What is the sum?

Setup:

Sum $= 17.5 \times 24 = 420$

20. How to find the AVERAGE of CONSECUTIVE NUMBERS

The average of evenly spaced numbers is simply the average of the smallest number and the largest number. The average of all the integers from 13 to 77, for example, is the same as the average of 13 and 77:

$$\frac{13 + 77}{2} = \frac{90}{2} = 45$$

21. How to COUNT CONSECUTIVE NUMBERS

The number of integers from A to B inclusive is $B - A + 1$.

Example:

How many integers are there from 73 through 419, inclusive?

Setup:

$419 - 73 + 1 = 347$

HINT: Don't forget to add 1.

---

22. How to find the SUM OF CONSECUTIVE NUMBERS

$$Sum = (average) \times (number\ of\ terms)$$

Example:

What is the sum of the integers from 10 through 50, inclusive?

Setup:

Average $= (10 + 50) \div 2 = 30$

Number of terms $= 50 - 10 + 1 = 41$

Sum $= 30 \times 41 = 1,230$

23. How to find the MEDIAN

Put the numbers in numerical order and take the middle number. (If there's an even number of numbers, the average of the two numbers in the middle is the median.)

Example:
What is the median of 88, 86, 57, 94, and 73?

Setup:
Put the numbers in numerical order and take the middle number:

$$57, 73, 86, 88, 94$$

The median is 86. (If there's an even number of numbers, take the average of the two in the middle.)

24. How to find the MODE

Take the number that appears most often. For example, if your test scores were 88, 57, 68, 85, 98, 93, 93, 84, and 81, the mode of the scores is 93 because it appears more often than any other score. (If there's a tie for most often, then there's more than one mode.)

25. How to find the RANGE

Simply take the difference between the highest and lowest values. Using the previous example, if your test scores were 88, 57, 68, 85, 98, 93, 93, 84, and 81, the range of the scores is 41, the difference between the highest and lowest values (98 − 57 = 41).

26. How to use actual numbers to determine a RATIO

To find a ratio, put the number associated with *of* on the top and the word associated with *to* on the bottom.

$$Ratio = \frac{of}{to}$$

The ratio of 20 oranges to 12 apples is $\frac{20}{12}$, or $\frac{5}{3}$.

27. How to use a ratio to determine an ACTUAL NUMBER

Set up a proportion.

Example:
The ratio of boys to girls is 3 to 4. If there are 135 boys, how many girls are there?

Setup:
$$\frac{3}{4} = \frac{135}{x}$$
$$3 \times x = 4 \times 135$$
$$x = 180$$

28. How to use actual numbers to determine a RATE

Identify the quantities and the units to be compared. Keep the units straight.

Example:
Anders typed 9,450 words in $3\frac{1}{2}$ hours. What was his rate in words per minute?

Setup:
First convert $3\frac{1}{2}$ hours to 210 minutes. Then set up the rate with words on top and minutes on bottom:

$$\frac{9,450 \text{ words}}{210 \text{ minutes}} = 45 \text{ words per minute}$$

HINT: The unit before *per* goes on top, and the unit after *per* goes on the bottom.

29. How to deal with TABLES, GRAPHS, AND CHARTS

Read the question and all labels extra carefully. Ignore extraneous information and zero in on what the question asks for. Take advantage of the spread in the answer choices by approximating the answer wherever possible.

30. How to count the NUMBER OF POSSIBILITIES

In most cases, you won't need to apply the combination and permutation formulas on the GRE. The number of possibilities is generally so small that the best approach is just to write them out systematically and count them.

Example:

How many three-digit numbers can be formed with the digits 1, 3, and 5?

Setup:

Write them out. Be systematic so you don't miss any: 135, 153, 315, 351, 513, 531. Count them: six possibilities.

31. How to calculate a simple PROBABILITY

$$Probability = \frac{number\ of\ favorable\ outcomes}{total\ number\ of\ possible\ outcomes}$$

Example:

What is the probability of throwing a 5 on a fair six-sided die?

Setup:

There is one favorable outcome—throwing a 5. There are 6 possible outcomes—one for each side of the die.

$$Probability = \frac{1}{6}$$

32. How to work with new SYMBOLS

If you see a symbol you've never seen before, don't freak out: it's a made-up symbol. Everything you need to know is in the question stem. Just follow the instructions.

33. How to MULTIPLY POLYNOMIALS

First multiply to eliminate all parentheses. Each term inside one parentheses is multiplied by each term inside the other parentheses. All like terms are then combined.

Example:

$$(3x^2 + 5x)(x - 1) =$$
$$3x^2(x - 1) + 5x(x - 1) =$$
$$3x^3 - 3x^2 + 5x^2 - 5x =$$
$$3x^3 + 2x^2 - 5x$$

34. How to FACTOR certain POLYNOMIALS

Learn to spot these classic factorables:

$$ab + ac = a(b + c)$$
$$a^2 + 2ab + b^2 = (a + b)^2$$
$$a^2 - 2ab + b^2 = (a - b)^2$$
$$a^2 - b^2 = (a - b)(a + b)$$

35. How to solve for one variable IN TERMS OF ANOTHER

To find x "in terms of" y: isolate x on one side, leaving y as the only variable on the other.

36. How to solve an INEQUALITY

Treat it much like an equation—adding, subtracting, multiplying, and dividing both sides by the same thing. Just remember to reverse the inequality sign if you multiply or divide by a negative number.

Example:
Rewrite $7 - 3x > 2$ in its simplest form:

Setup:
$7 - 3x > 2$. Subtract 7 from both sides:
$7 - 3x - 7 > 2 - 7$.
So $-3x > -5$. Now divide both sides by -3, and remember to reverse the inequality sign:
$$x < \frac{5}{3}$$

37. How to handle ABSOLUTE VALUES

The *absolute value* of a number n, denoted by $|n|$, is defined as n if $n \geq 0$ and $-n$ if $n < 0$. It's also referred to as the distance from zero to the number on the number line:

$$|-5| = 5$$

If $|x| = 3$, then x could be 3 or -3.

Example:
If $|x - 3| < 2$, what is the range of possible values for x?

Setup:
$|x - 3| < 2$, so $(x - 3) < 2$ and $-(x - 3) < 2$.
So $x - 3 < 2$ and $x - 3 > -2$.
So $x < 2 + 3$ and $x > -2 + 3$.
So $x < 5$ and $x > 1$.
So $1 < x < 5$.

38. How to TRANSLATE ENGLISH INTO ALGEBRA

Look for the key words and systematically turn phrases into algebraic expressions and sentences into equations.

Here's a table of key words that you may have to translate into mathematical operations:

Operation	Key Words
Addition	sum, plus, and, added to, more than, increased by, combined with, exceeds, total, greater than
Subtraction	difference between, minus, subtracted from, decreased by, diminished by, less than, reduced by
Multiplication	of, product, times, multiplied by, twice, double, triple, half
Division	quotient, divided by, per, out of, ratio of __ to __
Equals	equals, is, was, will be, the result is, adds up to, costs, is the same as

HINT: Be extra careful of the order you place numbers in when subtraction is called for.

39. How to find an ANGLE formed by INTERSECTING LINES

Vertical angles are equal. Adjacent angles add up to 180°.

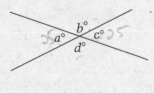

$$a = c$$
$$b = d$$
$$a + b = 180°$$
$$a + b + c + d = 360°$$

40. How to find an angle formed by a TRANSVERSAL across PARALLEL LINES

All the acute angles are equal. All the obtuse angles are equal. An acute plus an obtuse equals 180°.

Example:

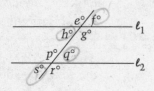

ℓ_1 is parallel to ℓ_2
$$e = g = p = r$$
$$f = h = q = s$$
$$e + q = g + s = 180°$$

41. How to find the AREA of a TRIANGLE

$$Area = \frac{1}{2}(base)(height)$$

Example:

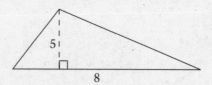

Setup:

$Area = \frac{1}{2}(5)(8) = 20$

> **HINT: You might have to construct an altitude, as we did in the triangle above.**

42. How to work with ISOSCELES TRIANGLES

Isosceles triangles have two equal sides and two equal angles. If a GRE question tells you that a triangle is isoceles, you can bet that you'll need to use that information to find the length of a side or a measure of an angle.

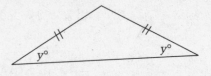

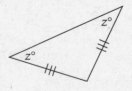

43. How to work with EQUILATERAL TRIANGLES

Equilateral triangles have three equal sides and three 60° angles. If a GRE question tells you that a triangle is equilateral, you can bet that you'll need to use that information to find the length of a side or a measure of an angle.

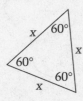

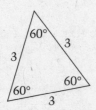

44. How to work with SIMILAR TRIANGLES

In similar triangles, corresponding angles are equal and corresponding sides are proportional. If a GRE question tells you that triangles are similar, you'll probably need that information to find the length of a side or the measure of an angle.

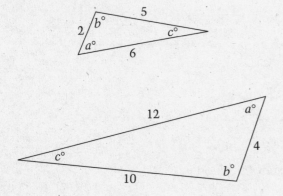

45. How to find the HYPOTENUSE or a LEG of a RIGHT TRIANGLE

Pythagorean theorem: $a^2 + b^2 = c^2$

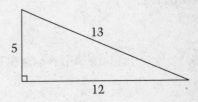

HINT: Most right triangles on the GRE are "special" right triangles (see below), so you can often bypass the Pythagorean theorem.

46. How to spot "SPECIAL" RIGHT TRIANGLES

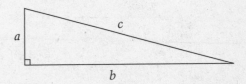

3-4-5
5-12-13
30-60-90
45-45-90

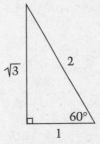

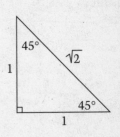

HINT: Learn to spot "special" right triangles—the less you have to calculate the Pythagorean theorem, the more time you save.

47. How to find the PERIMETER of a RECTANGLE

$$Perimeter = 2(length + width)$$

Example:

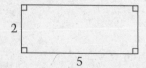

Setup:

Perimeter = 2(2 + 5) = 14

48. How to find the AREA of a RECTANGLE

$$Area = (length)(width)$$

Example:

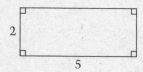

Setup:
Area = 2 × 5 = 10

49. How to find the AREA of a SQUARE

$$Area = (side)^2$$

Example:

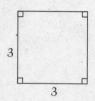

Setup:

Area = 3^2 = 9

50. How to find the AREA of a PARALLELOGRAM

$$Area = (base)(height)$$

Example:

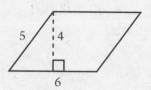

Setup:
Area = 6 × 4 = 24

51. How to find the AREA of a TRAPEZOID

A trapezoid is a quadrilateral having only two parallel sides. You can always drop a line or two to break the figure into a rectangle and a triangle or two triangles. Use the area formulas for those familiar shapes. You could also apply the general formula for the area of a trapezoid:

$$Area = (Average\ of\ parallel\ sides) \times (height)$$

Example:

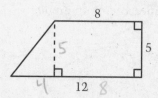

Setup:

Area of rectangle = 8 × 5 = 40

Area of triangle = $\frac{1}{2}$(4 × 5) = 10

Area of trapeziod = 10 × 5 = 50

HINT: Any time you're asked to find the area of an unfamiliar shape, try dropping lines to break it into familiar shapes that you can work with.

---

52. How to find the CIRCUMFERENCE of a CIRCLE

$$Circumference = 2\pi r$$

Example:

Setup:

Circumference $= 2\pi(5) = 10\pi$

53. How to find the AREA of a CIRCLE

$$Area = \pi r^2$$

Example:

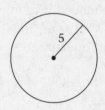

Setup:

Area $= \pi \times 5^2 = 25\pi$

54. How to find the DISTANCE BETWEEN POINTS on the coordinate plane

If two points have the same x's or the same y's—that is, they make a line segment that is parallel to an axis—all you have to do is subtract the numbers that are different.

Example:

What is the distance from $(2, 3)$ to $(-7, 3)$?

Setup:

The y's are the same, so just subtract the x's.

$$2 - (-7) = 9$$

If the points have different x's and different y's, make a right triangle and use the Pythagorean theorem.

Example:

What is the distance from $(2, 3)$ to $(-1, -1)$?

Setup:

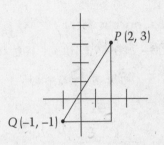

It's a 3-4-5 triangle!

$PQ = 5$

HINT: Look for "special" right triangles.

---

55. How to find the SLOPE of a LINE

$$Slope = \frac{rise}{run} = \frac{change\ in\ y}{change\ in\ x} \quad \left(\frac{y_1 - y_2}{x_1 - x_2} \right)$$

Example:

What is the slope of the line that contains the points $(1, 2)$ and $(4, -5)$?

Setup:

Slope $= \frac{2 - (-5)}{1 - 4} = -\frac{7}{3}$

Level 3 (Math You Might Find Difficult)

56. How to determine COMBINED PERCENT INCREASE/DECREASE

Start with 100 and see what happens.

Example:

A price rises by 10 percent one year and by 20 percent the next. What's the combined percent increase?

Setup:

Say the original price is $100.

Year one: $100 + (10% of 100) = 100 + 10 = 110.

Year two: 110 + (20% of 110) = 110 + 22 = 132.

From 100 to 132—That's a 32 percent increase.

57. How to find the ORIGINAL WHOLE before percent increase/decrease

Think of a 15 percent increase over x as $1.15x$ and set up an equation.

Example:

After decreasing by 5 percent, the population is now 57,000. What was the original population?

Setup:

.95 × (Original Population) = 57,000

Original Population = 57,000 ÷ .95 = 60,000

58. How to solve a SIMPLE INTEREST problem

With simple interest, the interest is computed on the principal only and is given by:

interest = (principal) × (interest rate*) × (time**)

*   expressed as a decimal
**   expressed in years

Example:

If $12,000 is invested at 6 percent simple annual interest, how much interest is earned after 9 months?

Setup:

$(12,000) \times (.06) \times \left(\frac{9}{12}\right) = \$540$

59. How to solve a COMPOUND INTEREST problem

If interest is compounded, the interest is computed on the principal as well as on any interest earned. To compute compound interest:

$(final\ balance) = (principal) \times (1 + \frac{interest\ rate}{C})^{(time)(C)}$

where C = the number of times compounded annually

Example:

If $10,000 is invested at 8 percent annual interest, compounded semiannually, what is the balance after 1 year?

Setup:

Final balance

$= (10,000) \times \left(1 + \frac{.08}{2}\right)^{(1)(2)}$

$= (10,000) \times (1.04)^2$

$= \$10,816$

HINT: Often on the GRE, you don't have to do the work of calculating compound interest. Try calculating the simple interest and looking for the answer that's just a little bit larger.

60. How to solve a REMAINDERS problem

Pick a number that fits the given conditions and see what happens.

Example:

When n is divided by 7, the remainder is 5. What is the remainder when $2n$ is divided by 7 ?

Setup:

Find a number that leaves a remainder of 5 when divided by 7. A good choice would be 12. If $n = 12$, then $2n = 24$, which, when divided by 7, leaves a remainder of 3.

61. How to solve a DIGITS problem

Use a little logic—and some trial and error.

Example:

If A, B, C, and D represent distinct digits in the addition problem below, what is the value of D ?

$$\begin{array}{r} AB \\ + BA \\ \hline CDC \end{array}$$

Setup:

Two 2-digit numbers will add up to at most something in the 100s, so $C = 1$. B plus A in the units' column gives a 1, and since it can't simply be that $B + A = 1$, it must be that $B + A = 11$, and a 1 gets carried. In fact, A and B can be just about any pair of digits that add up to 11 (3 and 8, 4 and 7, etcetera), but it doesn't matter what they are, they always give you the same thing for D :

$$\begin{array}{r} 47 \\ +74 \\ \hline 121 \end{array} \qquad \begin{array}{r} 83 \\ +38 \\ \hline 121 \end{array}$$

62. How to find a WEIGHTED AVERAGE

Give each term the appropriate "weight."

Example:

The girls' average score is 30. The boys' average score is 24. If there are twice as many boys as girls, what is the overall average?

Setup:

$$\text{Weighted Avg.} = \frac{1 \times 30 + 2 \times 24}{3} = \frac{78}{3} = 26$$

HINT: Don't just average the averages.

---

63. How to find the NEW AVERAGE when a number is added or deleted

Use the sum of the terms of the old average to help you find the new average.

Example:

Michael's average score after four tests is 80. If he scores 100 on the fifth test, what's his new average?

Setup:

Find the original sum from the original average:
$$\text{Original sum} = 4 \times 80 = 320$$
Add the fifth score to make the new sum:
$$\text{New sum} = 320 + 100 = 420$$
Find the new average from the new sum:
$$\text{New average} = \frac{420}{5} = 84$$

64. How to use the ORIGINAL AVERAGE and NEW AVERAGE to figure out WHAT WAS ADDED OR DELETED

Use the sums.

Number added = (new sum) − (original sum)

Number deleted = (original sum) − (new sum)

Example:

The average of five numbers is 2. After one number is deleted, the new average is −3. What number was deleted?

Setup:

Find the original sum from the original average:

Original sum = 5 × 2 = 10

Find the new sum from the new average:

New sum = 4 × (−3) = −12

The difference between the original sum and the new sum is the answer.

Number deleted = 10 − (−12) = 22

65. How to find an AVERAGE RATE

Convert to totals.

$$Average\ A\ per\ B = \frac{Total\ A}{Total\ B}$$

Example:

If the first 500 pages have an average of 150 words per page, and the remaining 100 pages have an average of 450 words per page, what is the average number of words per page for the entire 600 pages?

Setup:

Total pages = 500 + 100 = 600

Total words = 500 × 150 + 100 × 450 = 120,000

$$Average\ words\ per\ page = \frac{120,000}{600} = 200$$

To find an average speed, you also convert to totals.

$$Average\ speed = \frac{total\ distance}{time}$$

Example:

Rosa drove 120 miles one way at an average speed of 40 miles per hour and returned by the same 120-mile route at an average speed of 60 miles per hour. What was Rosa's average speed for the entire 240-mile round trip?

Setup:

To drive 120 miles at 40 mph takes 3 hours. To return at 60 mph takes 2 hours. The total time, then, is 5 hours.

$$Average\ speed = \frac{240\ miles}{5\ hours} = 48\ mph$$

HINT: Don't just average the rates.

66. How to solve a WORK PROBLEM

In a work problem, you are given the rate at which people or machines perform work individually, and asked to compute the rate at which they work together (or vice versa). The work formula states: The inverse of the time it would take everyone working together equals the sum of the inverses of the times it would take each working individually. In other words:

$$\frac{1}{r} + \frac{1}{s} = \frac{1}{t}$$

where r and s are, for example, the number of hours it would take Rebecca and Sam, respectively to complete a job working by themselves, and t is the number of hours it would take the two of them working together.

Example:

If it takes Joe 4 hours to paint a room and Pete twice as long to paint the same room, how long would it take the two of them, working together, to paint the same room, if each of them works at his respective individual rate?

Setup:

Joe takes 4 hours, so Pete takes 8 hours; thus:

$$\frac{1}{4} + \frac{1}{8} = \frac{1}{t}$$

$$\frac{1}{4} + \frac{1}{8} = \frac{3}{8} = \frac{1}{\frac{8}{3}}$$

So it would take them $\frac{8}{3}$ hours, or 2 hours 40 minutes, to paint the room together.

67. How to determine a COMBINED RATIO

Multiply one or both ratios by whatever you need to in order to get the terms they have in common to match.

Example:

The ratio of a to b is 7:3. The ratio of b to c is 2:5. What is the ratio of a to c?

Setup:

Multiply each member of a:b by 2 and multiply each member of b:c by 3 and you get a:b = 14:6 and b:c = 6:15. Now that the b's match, you can just take a and c and say a:c = 14:15.

68. How to solve a DILUTION or MIXTURE problem

In dilution or mixture problems, you have to determine the characteristics of the resulting mixture when substances with different characteristics are combined. Or, alternatively, you have to determine how to combine substances with different characteristics to produce a desired mixture. There are two approaches to such problems—the straightforward setup and the balancing method.

Example:

If 5 pounds of raisins that cost $1.00 per pound are mixed with 2 pounds of almonds that cost $2.40 per pound, what is the cost per pound of the resulting mixture?

Setup:

The straightforward setup:

$5(1.00) + 2(2.40) = 9.80$

The cost per pound is $\frac{9.80}{7} = \$1.40$

Example:

How many liters of a solution that is 10 percent alcohol by volume must be added to 2 liters of a solution that is 50 percent alcohol by volume to create a solution that is 15 percent alcohol by volume?

Setup:

The balancing method:

Make the weaker and stronger (or cheaper and more expensive, etc.) substances balance. That is: (percent/price difference between the weaker solution and the desired solution) × (amount of weaker solution) = (percent/price difference between the stronger solution and the desired solution) × (amount of stronger solution).

In this case:

$n(15 - 10) = 2(50 - 15)$

$n \times 5 = 2(35)$

$n = \frac{70}{5} = 14$

So 14 liters of the 10 percent solution must be added.

HINT: The balancing method is also effective on weighted average questions.

---

69. How to solve a GROUP problem involving BOTH/NEITHER

Some GRE word problems involve two groups with overlapping members, and possibly elements that belong to neither group. It's easy to identify this type of question because the words "both" and/or "neither" appear in the question. These problems are quite easy if you just memorize the following formula:

$$Group_1 + Group_2 + Neither - Both = Total$$

Example:

Of the 120 students at a certain language school, 65 are studying French, 51 are studying Spanish, and 53 are studying neither language. How many are studying both French and Spanish?

Setup:

$65 + 51 + 53 - Both = 120$

$169 - Both = 120$

$Both = 49$

70. How to solve a GROUP problem involving EITHER/OR CATEGORIES

Other GRE word problems involve groups with distinct "either/or" categories (male/female, blue collar/white collar, etc.). The key to solving this type of problem is to organize the information in a grid.

Example:

At a certain professional conference with 130 attendees, 94 of the attendees are doctors and the rest are dentists. If 48 of the attendees are women, and $\frac{1}{4}$ of the dentists in attendance are women, how many of the attendees are male doctors?

Setup:

To complete the grid, each row and column adds up to the corresponding total:

	Doctors	Dentists	Total
Male	55	27	82
Female		9	48
Total	94	36	130

After you've filled in the information from the question, simply fill in the remaining boxes until you get the number you are looking for—in this case, that 55 of the attendees are male doctors.

71. How to work with FACTORIALS

You may see a problem involving factorial notation. If n is an integer greater than 1, then n factorial, denoted by $n!$, is defined as the product of all the integers from 1 to n. In other words:

$2! = 2 \times 1 = 2$

$3! = 3 \times 2 \times 1 = 6$

$4! = 4 \times 3 \times 2 \times 1 = 24$, etc.

By definition, $0! = 1! = 1$.

Also note: $6! = 6 \times 5!= 6 \times 5 \times 4!$, etc. Most GRE factorial problems test your ability to factor and/or cancel.

Example:

$$\frac{8!}{6! \times 5!} = \frac{8 \times 7 \times 6!}{6! \times 5 \times 4 \times 3 \times 2 \times 1} = \frac{7}{15}$$

KAPLAN

72. How to solve a PERMUTATION problem

Factorials are useful for solving questions about permutations, i.e., the number of ways to arrange elements sequentially. For instance, to figure out how many ways there are to arrange 7 items along a shelf, you would multiply the number of possibilities for the first position times the number of possibilities remaining for the second position, and so on—in other words: $7 \times 6 \times 5 \times 4 \times 3 \times 2 \times 1$, or $7!$.

If you're asked to find the number of ways to arrange a smaller group that's being drawn from a larger group, you can either apply logic or you can use the permutation formula:

$$P = \frac{n!}{(n-k)!}$$

where n = (# in the larger group) and k = (# you're arranging).

Example:

Five runners run in a race. The runners who come in first, second, and third place will win gold, silver, and bronze medals respectively. How many possible outcomes for gold, silver, and bronze medal winners are there?

Setup:

Any of the 5 runners could come in first place, leaving 4 runners who could come in second place, leaving 3 runners who could come in third place, for a total of $5 \times 4 \times 3 = 60$ possible outcomes for gold, silver, and bronze medal winners. Or, using the formula:

$$P = \frac{5!}{(5-3)!} = \frac{5!}{2!} = 5 \times 4 \times 3 = 60$$

73. How to solve a COMBINATION problem

If the order or arrangement of the smaller group that's being drawn from the larger group does NOT matter, you are looking for the numbers of combinations, and a different formula is called for:

$$C = \frac{n!}{k!(n-k)!}$$

Where n = (# in the larger group) and k = (# you're choosing)

Example:

How many different ways are there to choose 3 delegates from 8 possible candidates?

Setup:

$$C = \frac{8!}{3! \times 5!} = \frac{8 \times 7 \times 6 \times 5!}{3 \times 2 \times 1 \times 5!} = 56$$

So there are 56 different possible combinations.

74. How to solve a MULTIPLE-EVENT PROBABILITY problem

Many hard probability questions involve finding the probability of a certain outcome after multiple events (a coin being tossed several times, etc.). These questions come in two forms: those in which each individual event must occur a certain way, and those in which individual events can have different outcomes.

To determine multiple-event probability where each individual event must occur a certain way:

• Figure out the probability for each individual event.

• Multiply the individual probabilities together.

Example:

If 2 students are chosen at random from a class with 5 girls and 5 boys, what's the probability that both students chosen will be girls?

Setup:

The probability that the first student chosen will be a girl is $\frac{5}{10} = \frac{1}{2}$, and since there would be 4 girls left out of 9 students, the probability that the second student chosen will be a girl is $\frac{4}{9}$. Thus the probability that both students chosen will be girls is $\frac{1}{2} \times \frac{4}{9} = \frac{2}{9}$.

To determine multiple-event probability where individual events can have different outcomes:

- Find the *total number of possible outcomes* by determining the number of possible outcomes for each individual event and multiplying these numbers together.

- Find the *number of desired outcomes* by listing out the possibilities.

Example:

If a fair coin is tossed 4 times, what's the probability that at least 3 of the 4 tosses will come up heads?

Setup:

There are 2 possible outcomes for each toss, so after 4 tosses there are a total of $2 \times 2 \times 2 \times 2 = 16$ possible outcomes.

List out all the possibilities where "at least 3 of the 4 tosses" come up heads:

H, H, H, T

H, H, T, H

H, T, H, H

T, H, H, H

H, H, H, H

So there's a total of 5 possible desired outcomes. Thus, the probability that at least 3 of the 4 tosses will come up heads is $\frac{\text{number of desired outcomes}}{\text{number of possible outcomes}} = \frac{5}{16}$.

75. How to deal with STANDARD DEVIATION

Like mean, mode, median, and range, standard deviation is a term used to describe sets of numbers. Standard deviation is a measure of how spread out a set of numbers is (how much the numbers deviate from the mean). The greater the spread, the higher the standard deviation. You'll never actually have to calculate the standard deviation on test day, but here's how it's calculated:

- Find the average (arithmetic mean) of the set.

- Find the differences between the mean and each value in the set.

- Square each of the differences.

- Find the average of the squared differences.

- Take the positive square root of the average.

Although you won't have to calculate standard deviation on the GRE, you may be asked to compare standard deviations between sets of data, or otherwise demonstrate that you understand what standard deviation means.

Example:

High temperatures, in degrees Fahrenheit, in 2 cities over 5 days:

September	1	2	3	4	5
City *A*	54	61	70	49	56
City *B*	62	56	60	67	65

For the 5-day period listed, which city had the greater standard deviation in high temperatures?

Setup:

Even without trying to calculate them out, one can see that City A has the greater spread in temperatures, and therefore the greater standard deviation in high temperatures. If you were to go ahead and calculate the standard deviations following the steps described above, you would find that the standard deviation in high temperatures for City $A = \sqrt{\frac{254}{5}} \approx 7.1$, while the same for City $B = \sqrt{\frac{74}{5}} \approx 3.8$.

76. How to MULTIPLY/DIVIDE POWERS

Add/subtract the exponents.

Example:

$x^a \times x^b = x^{(a+b)}$
$2^3 \times 2^4 = 2^7$

Example:

$\frac{x^c}{x^d} = x^{(c-d)}$

$\frac{5^6}{5^2} = 5^4$

77. How to RAISE A POWER TO A POWER

Multiply the exponents.

Example:

$(x^a)^b = x^{ab}$
$(3^4)^5 = 3^{20}$

78. How to handle ZERO POWERS

Zero raised to any power equals zero.

Example:

$0^4 = 0^{12} = 0^1 = 0$

Any number raised to the 0 power equals 1.

Example:

$3^0 = 15^0 = (0.34)^0 = 345^0 = \pi^0 = 1$

The lone exception is 0 raised to the 0 power, which is *undefined*.

79. How to handle NEGATIVE POWERS

A number raised to the exponent $-x$ is the reciprocal of that number raised to the exponent x.

Example:

$5^{-3} = \frac{1}{5^3} = \frac{1}{5 \times 5 \times 5} = \frac{1}{125}$
$n^{-1} = \frac{1}{n}$, $n^{-2} = \frac{1}{n^2}$, and so on.

80. How to handle FRACTIONAL POWERS

Fractional exponents relate to roots. For instance, $x^{\frac{1}{2}} = \sqrt{x}$.

Likewise, $x^{\frac{1}{3}} = \sqrt[3]{x}$, $x^{\frac{2}{3}} = \sqrt[3]{x^2}$, and so on.

HINT: The rules for multiplying powers, dividing powers, and raising powers to powers also apply nicely to negative, zero, and fractional exponents.

Example:

$4^{\frac{1}{2}} = \sqrt{4} = 2$
$(x^{-2})^{\frac{1}{2}} = x^{(-2)(\frac{1}{2})} = x^{-1} = \frac{1}{x}$

81. How to handle CUBE ROOTS

The cube root of x is just the number that multiplied by itself 3 times (i.e., cubed) gives you x. Both positive and negative numbers have one and only one cube root, denoted by the symbol $\sqrt[3]{}$, and the cube root of a number is always the same sign as the number itself.

Example:

$(-5) \times (-5) \times (-5) = -125$, so $\sqrt[3]{-125} = -5$

$\frac{1}{2} \times \frac{1}{2} \times \frac{1}{2} = \frac{1}{8}$, so $\sqrt[3]{\frac{1}{8}} = \frac{1}{2}$

82. How to ADD, SUBTRACT, MULTIPLY, and DIVIDE ROOTS

You can add/subtract roots only when the parts inside the $\sqrt{}$ are identical.

Example:

$$\sqrt{2} + 3\sqrt{2} = 4\sqrt{2}$$
$$\sqrt{2} - 3\sqrt{2} = -2\sqrt{2}$$

$\sqrt{2} + \sqrt{3}$—cannot be combined.

To multiply/divide roots, deal with what's inside the $\sqrt{}$ and outside the $\sqrt{}$ separately.

Example:

$(2\sqrt{3})(7\sqrt{5}) = (2 \times 7) \, (\sqrt{3 \times 5}) = 14\sqrt{15}$

$\frac{10\sqrt{21}}{5\sqrt{3}} = \frac{10}{5}\sqrt{\frac{21}{3}} = 2\sqrt{7}$

83. How to SIMPLIFY A SQUARE ROOT

Look for perfect squares (4, 9, 16, 25, 36...) inside the $\sqrt{}$. Factor them out and "unsquare" them.

Example:

$$\sqrt{48} = \sqrt{16} \times \sqrt{3} = 4\sqrt{3}$$
$$\sqrt{180} = \sqrt{36} \times \sqrt{5} = 6\sqrt{5}$$

84. How to solve certain QUADRATIC EQUATIONS

Forget the quadratic formula. Manipulate the equation (if necessary) into the "_____ = 0" form, factor the left side, and break the quadratic into two simple equations.

Example:

$$x^2 + 6 = 5x$$
$$x^2 - 5x + 6 = 0$$
$$(x - 2)(x - 3) = 0$$
$$x - 2 = 0 \text{ or } x - 3 = 0$$
$$x = 2 \text{ or } 3$$

Example:

$$x^2 = 9$$
$$x = 3 \text{ or } -3$$

HINT: Watch out for x^2.
There can be two solutions.

---

85. How to solve MULTIPLE EQUATIONS

When you see two equations with two variables on the GRE, they're probably easy to combine in such a way that you get something closer to what you're looking for.

Example:

If $5x - 2y = -9$ and $3y - 4x = 6$, what is the value of $x + y$?

Setup:

The question doesn't ask for x and y separately, so don't solve for them separately if you don't have to. Look what happens if you just rearrange a little and "add" the equations:

$$
\begin{array}{r}
5x - 2y = -9 \\
-4x + 3y = 6 \\
\hline
x + y = -3
\end{array}
$$

HINT: Don't do more work than you have to. Look for the shortcut.

---

86. How to solve a SEQUENCE problem

The notation used in sequence problems scares many test takers, but these problems aren't as bad as they look. In a sequence problem, the nth term in the sequence is generated by performing an operation, which will be defined for you, on either n or on the previous term in the sequence. Familiarize yourself with sequence notation and you should have no problem.

Example:

What is the difference between the fifth and fourth terms in the sequence 0, 4, 18, . . . whose nth term is $n^2(n - 1)$?

Setup:

Use the operation given to come up with the values for your terms:

$n_5 = 5^2(5 - 1) = 25(4) = 100$

$n_4 = 4^2(4 - 1) = 16(3) = 48$

So the difference between the fifth and fourth terms is $100 - 48 = 52$.

HINT: Many GRE sequence problems invite you to backsolve.

---

87. How to solve a FUNCTION problem

You may see classic function notation on the GRE. An algebraic expression of only one variable may be defined as a function, f or g, of that variable.

Example:

What is the minimum value of the function $f(x) = x^2 - 1$?

Setup:

In the function $f(x) = x^2 - 1$, if x is 1, then $f(1) = 1^2 - 1 = 0$. In other words, by inputting 1 into the function, the output $f(x) = 0$. Every number inputted has one and only one output (although the reverse is not necessarily true). You're asked to find the minimum value, so how would you minimize the expression $f(x) = x^2 - 1$? Since x^2 cannot be negative, in this case $f(x)$ is minimized by making $x = 0$: $f(0) = 0^2 - 1 = -1$, so the minimum value of the function is -1.

88. How to handle GRAPHS of FUNCTIONS

You may see problem that involves a function graphed onto the xy-coordinate plane, often called a "rectangular coordinate system" on the GRE. When graphing a function, the output, $f(x)$, becomes the y-coordinate. For example, in the previous example, $f(x) = x^2 - 1$, you've already determined 2 points, $(1, 0)$ and $(0, -1)$. If you were to keep plugging in numbers to determine more points and then plotted those points on the xy-coordinate plane, you would come up with something like this:

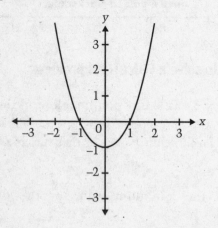

This curved line is called a *parabola*. In the event that you should see a parabola on the GRE (it could be upside down or squatter or more elongated than the one shown), you will most likely be asked to choose which equation the parabola is describing. These questions can be surprisingly easy to answer. Pick out obvious points on the graph, such as $(1, 0)$ and $(0, -1)$ above, plug these values into the answer choices, and eliminate choices that don't jibe with those values until only one answer is left.

89. How to handle LINEAR EQUATIONS

You may also encounter linear equations on the GRE. A linear equation is often expressed in the form

$$y = mx + b, \text{ where:}$$

- m = the slope of the line = $\frac{rise}{run}$.

  For instance, a slope of 3 means that the line rises 3 steps for every 1 step it makes to the right. A positive slope slopes up from left to right. A negative slope slopes down from left to right. A slope of zero (e.g., $y = 5$) is a flat line.

- b = the y-intercept (where the line passes the y-axis).

Example:

The graph of the linear equation $y = -\frac{3}{4}x + 3$ is:

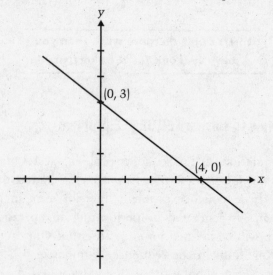

Note: The equation above could also be written in the form $3x + 4y = 12$.

To get a better handle on an equation written in this form, you can solve for y to write it in its more familiar form. Or, if you're asked to choose which equation the line is describing, you can pick obvious points such as $(0, 3)$ and $(4, 0)$ above, and use these values to eliminate answer choices until only one answer is left.

90. How to find the *x*- and *y*-INTERCEPTS of a line

The *x*-intercept of a line is the value of *x* where the line crosses the *x*-axis. In other words, it's the value of *x* when $y = 0$. Likewise, the *y*-intercept is the value of *y* where the line crosses the *y*-axis, i.e., the value of *y* when $x = 0$, also the value *b* when the equation is in the form: $y = mx + b$. For instance, in the line shown in the previous example, the *x*-intercept is 4 and the *y*-intercept is 3.

91. How to find the MAXIMUM and MINIMUM lengths for a SIDE of a TRIANGLE

If you know two sides of a triangle, you know that the third side is between the difference and the sum.

Example:

The length of one side of a triangle is 7. The length of another side is 3. What is the range of possible lengths for the third side?

Setup:
The third side is greater than the difference $(7 - 3 = 4)$ and less than the sum $(7 + 3 = 10)$.

92. How to find one angle or the sum of all the ANGLES of a REGULAR POLYGON

Sum of the interior angles in a polygon with n sides =
$(n - 2) \times 180$

Degree measure of one angle in a regular polygon with
n sides = $\frac{(n - 2) \times 180}{n}$

Example:

What is the measure of one angle of a regular pentagon?

Setup:

Plug $n = 5$ into the formula:

Degree measure of one angle =

$$\frac{(5 - 2) \times 180}{5} = \frac{540}{5} = 108$$

93. How to find the LENGTH of an ARC

Think of an arc as a fraction of the circle's circumference.

$$Length\ of\ arc = \frac{n}{360} \times 2\pi r$$

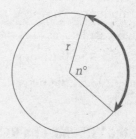

94. How to find the AREA of a SECTOR

Think of a sector as a fraction of the circle's area.

$$Area\ of\ sector = \frac{n}{360} \times \pi r^2$$

95. How to find the dimensions or area of an INSCRIBED or CIRCUMSCRIBED FIGURE

Look for the connection. Is the diameter the same as a side or a diagonal?

Example:

If the area of the square is 36, what is the circumference of the circle?

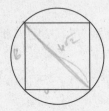

Setup:

To get the circumference, you need the diameter or radius. The circle's diameter is also the square's diagonal, which (it's a 45-45-90 triangle!) is $6\sqrt{2}$.

$$\text{Circumference} = \pi(\text{diameter}) = 6\pi\sqrt{2}$$

96. How to find the VOLUME of a RECTANGULAR SOLID

$$Volume = length \times width \times height$$

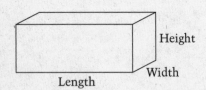

97. How to find the SURFACE AREA of a RECTANGULAR SOLID

To find the surface area of a rectangular solid, you have to find the area of each face and add them together. Here's the formula.

Surface area =
2(length × width + length × height + width × height)

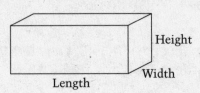

98. How to find the DIAGONAL of a RECTANGULAR SOLID

Use the Pythagorean theorem twice, unless you spot "special" triangles.

Example: What is the length of *AG* ?

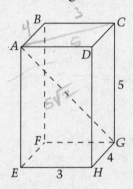

Setup: Draw diagonal *AC*.

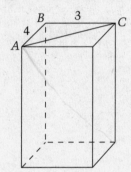

ABC is a 3-4-5 triangle, so *AC* = 5. Now look at triangle *ACG:*

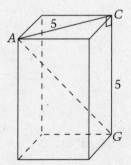

ACG is another special triangle, so you don't need to use the Pythagorean theorem. *ACG* is a 45-45-90, so $AG = 5\sqrt{2}$.

99. How to find the VOLUME of a CYLINDER

$$Volume = \pi r^2 h$$

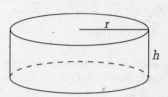

100. How to find the VOLUME of a SPHERE

$$Volume = \frac{4}{3}\pi r^3$$

APPENDIX D

Paper and Pencil Strategies

The Paper and Pencil GRE test is comprised of five sections: Analytical Writing (which has one issue task and one argument task), two Verbal Sections, and two Quantitative sections.

Sometimes the test-makers include a Pretest—a section containing questions that are being considered for use on future tests. It can appear in any position after the Analytical Writing Section. The Pretest is unscored and will not count toward your final GRE score. You most likely won't be able to tell which section is the Pretest, so don't waste valuable time trying to guess.

You have a total of 3 hours and 45 minutes to complete the entire test. The Analytical Writing Section will always be first. The Verbal (38 questions per section) and Quantitative (30 questions per section) Sections may appear after the Analytical Writing Section in any order.

In general, we recommend that you look for answer choices that jump out. When you're dealing with the easy questions, generally the most obvious answer is the right one. Looking for obvious answer choices also helps with hard questions because then the obvious answer choice is usually a trap.

Another strategy we recommend is that you keep track of your answers—particularly ones you've eliminated—by crossing out wrong answer choices. This will also help you grid your answers more accurately. You can also say the question number and answer choice (silently, of course) to yourself as you grid, to help make sure you're gridding carefully.

Verbal Section

Before you start a Verbal Section, glance over it completely, but quickly, to familiarize yourself with it. With Reading Comprehension, you can preview question stems but don't try to memorize them or answer the questions without reading the passages. We recommend that you do the questions you're most comfortable with first. Make sure you set aside about 15 minutes in each Verbal Section for Reading Comprehension.

Remember, the short verbal questions are in ascending order of difficulty, so always try to be aware of where you are in a set. If you find yourself running into trouble with a particular group of questions, move on and come back to them if you have time. Don't get hung up on hard questions. On the GRE, quantity counts. The easy questions are worth as many points as the hard questions, so rack up as many points as you can.

Quantitative Section

Like short Verbal questions, Quantitative questions are arranged in ascending order of difficulty, so try to be aware of the level of each question. This will help you determine how much time you should be spending on the question, and whether or not it's a question that should have an obvious answer.

In addition, calculators are not permitted on the GRE, so don't forget to utilize that scrap paper. Feel free to skip around within this section as well, and do all the problems you can do; then come back to the harder ones.

Analytical Writing

For the Analytical Writing Section, you will have to handwrite your essay so we suggest you write clearly and legibly.

Remember, for the Issue task two essay topics will be presented and you will be able to choose one on which to write. The Argument task, however, does not present a choice of topics. Instead, one topic will be presented and you will write a response to the given topic. For more tips and strategies for conquering the Analytical Writing Section, refer to Chapter Four.